£16.008.

K

D0302941

The Chartist Experience

The Chartist Experience: Studies in Working-Class Radicalism and Culture, 1830 – 60

EDITED BY
JAMES EPSTEIN
AND
DOROTHY THOMPSON

M

First published 1982 by

THE MACMILLAN PRESS LTD
London and Basingstoke
Companies and representatives throughout the world

ISBN 0 333 32971 6 (hc)
ISBN 0 333 32972 4 (pbk)

Typeset in 10/12 Press Roman by
MULTIPLEX techniques ltd

Printed in Hong Kong

Contents

CONTENTS

Acknowledgements

THE papers in this volume evolved out of a seminar on Chartism held in the summer of 1977. Members were originally invited on an informal basis, numbers were kept small, and after the first meeting papers were circulated for discussion and comment by all members. A grant from the Social Science Research Council (SSRC) enabled the seminar to be reconvened the following summer, and also paid for the duplication and distribution of some of the papers. The editors and contributors wish to express their gratitude to the SSRC for their help, and also to those members of the seminar who did not in the end contribute a chapter to this volume but whose comments have been extremely useful. In particular we wish to thank Owen Ashton, John Baxter, John Sanders, Nicholas Cotton, Beryl Ruehl, John Ryan and Edward Thompson. Iorwerth Prothero and John Harrison did not manage to attend the meetings of the seminar, but did read and comment upon papers, and for this we would like to express our gratitude.

Nearly every chapter contains material from the Public Records Office, and quotations from this material appear by permission of the Controller of HM Stationery Office.

The staff of many libraries throughout the country have helped with the collection of the material: we particularly wish to thank the staffs of the Bradford Public Library, the Birmingham City Reference Library, the Nottinghamshire County Library, and the Reading Room and Newspaper Departments of the British Library.

Introduction

JAMES EPSTEIN and
DOROTHY THOMPSON

IT is twenty-two years since the publication of the volume of *Chartist Studies* edited by Asa Briggs. That volume set a pattern for local studies of Chartism, and in the years since its publication very many such studies have appeared. It is clear to historians of popular movements that Chartism has to be studied in the localities in which most of the activity occurred. Nevertheless many people now feel that the focus has become rather too local, and that the pattern set twenty-two years ago has in some ways limited the areas to be studied.

The present volume is based largely on local research. The studies are not, however, intended to illustrate the same problems as they occurred in different districts during the period, but rather to look at a series of different problems which can be studied particularly well in certain districts, using local material to illuminate them. The concentration here is on questions of belief, of ideology and what may perhaps be called cultural experience, rather than on straightforward political organisation. Thus the important question of the relationship between Chartism and the trade societies is examined in a south Lancashire context; the Chartist 'riot' is described from the Staffordshire experience; the later developments of Chartism in the post-1848 years are looked at in Halifax; the attempts to build alternative cultural and educational institutions are seen from the perspective of Nottingham; and the breakdown of working-class and middle-class co-operation are examined in Birmingham, a town in which such co-operation is often thought to have been particularly long-lived and fruitful. It is important to point out that these studies are not intended to be studies of the typical. In fact the districts chosen are in all cases ones in which the problems studied were strongly highlighted for various reasons. They can, however, help to illuminate the same or similar questions in districts where the outlines were not always so clear. Two chapters are concerned with London, one of which, the profile of the London Democratic Association, is of local and national interest as an illustration of the continuities between Chartism and earlier radical movements, and the other, the study of 1848 and the collapse of the mass platform, describes the dramatic metropolitan manifestation of a national phenomenon.

The chapters which examine problems on a national scale attempt to take account of local evidence, but are of necessity less rich in illustrative material than the local studies. The opening chapter looks at some of the political beliefs and formulations of the early Chartist period, and the limits which such beliefs placed upon action. The chapter on the legal restraints on Chartist actions and that on the place of Irish people and Irish problems in the movement also attempt a national coverage of problems which affected every branch and every district.

We hope that from these studies, and from some of the work which is being done by the contributors to this volume and by other scholars, a newer more flexible picture of Chartism will emerge. Chartism was not simply a political challenge, it was a challenge to authority and to doctrinaire ideology in a whole number of areas. Industrial action, cultural confrontation, resistance to domination from the pulpit as well as from employers and local and national government, were offered by the working people in the Chartist period at a whole number of different levels. Resistance may have been in the name of traditional and customary beliefs and behaviour, or it may have been in the name of a more radical enquiry and challenging set of beliefs. In all cases it was informed by a strong sense of class identity, a strong defence of working-class institutions and customs, and a pervasive belief in the importance and the strength of democratic process, both at the level of local and national politics, and in the work-place and in the community. We hope that the papers which make up this volume will illustrate at least some of these challenges which were offered by the Chartists to the hegemonic ideology of the ruling classes of the period, and in particular to the increasingly pervasive ideology of *laissez-faire* political economy. Finally we should note that while this volume was conceived as a product of co-operative scholarship, that there has been no attempt to impose a uniform view of the Chartist Movement. We offer this volume rather as part of an ongoing discussion of the character of popular social and political protest during the Chartist years.

1. The Language of Chartism

GARETH STEDMAN JONES

WHO were the Chartists? The Chartists' own view was stated by Thomas Duncombe, introducing the 1842 Petition: 'those who were originally called radicals and afterwards reformers, are called Chartists'.[1] But this was never accepted by the great bulk of contemporary opinion. From the moment that Chartism first emerged as a public movement, what seized the imagination of contemporaries were not the formally radical aims and rhetoric of its spokesmen, but the novel and threatening social character of the movement. A nation-wide independent movement of the 'working classes' brandishing pikes in torchlight meetings in pursuit of its 'rights' was an unprecedented event, and whatever Chartism's official self-identity, contemporary observers could not refrain from projecting onto it deeper unavowed motives and sentiments. Thomas Carlyle's distinction between the 'distracted incoherent embodiment of Chartism' and its 'living essence'. . . 'the bitter discontent grown fierce and mad, the wrong condition therefore or the wrong disposition, of the Working Classes of England', with its implied gulf between the real and formal definition of Chartism, set the terms of the predominant response, whatever the precise definition given to these terms.[2] Chartists in vain protested their respect for property.[3] Macaulay, debating the 1842 Petition, deduced the Chartist position on property from the social composition of its constituency. To accept the petition would be to commit government to a class which would be induced 'to commit great and systematic inroads against the security of property'. 'How is it possible that according to the principles of human nature, if you give them this power, it would not be used to its fullest extent?'[4] Even the more sympathetic middle-class observers virtually ignored the political case of the Chartists. Mrs Gaskell's novel *Mary Barton*, for instance, analysed Chartism solely in terms of anger, distress and the breakdown of social relationships. Thus, from the beginning, there was virtual unanimity among outside observers that Chartism was to be understood, not as a political movement, but as a social phenomenon.

From the continental Communist left, the young Engels, also deeply impressed by Carlyle's depiction of the condition of England problem, made a similar assumption. 'The middle class and property are dominant; the poor man has no rights, is oppressed and fleeced, the constitution repudiates him and the law mistreats him'. Thus, in Engels's view, the form of democracy represented by Chartism was not that 'of the French Revolution whose antithesis was monarchy and feudalism, but *the* democracy whose antithesis is the middle class and property'... 'The struggle of democracy against aristocracy in England is the struggle of the poor against the rich. The democracy towards which England is moving is a *social* democracy'.[5] Engels's picture of Chartism, developed in *The Condition of the English Working Class in 1844*, was seen retrospectively as a major empirical confirmation of the later Marxist conception of 'class consciousness', elaborated in such works as the *German Ideology*, the *Poverty of Philosophy* and the *Communist Manifesto*. The premiss of this position was, in Marx's words, that 'the struggle' against capital in its developed modern form, in its decisive aspect is 'the struggle of the industrial wage worker against the industrial bourgeois'.[6] Thus, applied to Chartism, whatever its formal professions, its living essence was that of a class movement of the proletariat born of the new relations of production engendered by modern industry. Its real enemy was the bourgeoisie and the revolution it would have to effect would amount to the overthrow of this class. As Chartism disencumbered itself from its middle-class allies – a process which Engels considered to have culminated in 1842[7] – the proletarian character of the struggle would assume an ever more conscious form.

While Engels's optimistic conclusions have, for obvious reasons, not been accepted, many of his basic ways of seeing this period have been incorporated into the subsequent historiography of Chartism. The relationship between Chartism, modern industry and class consciousness has remained a prominent theme of labour and socialist historians. His contrast between Manchester and Birmingham, between the class relations of the factory town and that of a city of small workshops, has been amply developed by social historians and sociologists. But it is important to insist that Engels's emphasis upon the social character of Chartism, however brilliantly argued, was – as the testimony of Carlyle and Macaulay suggests – in no sense the peculiar property of a proto-Marxist position. The social interpretation represented the predominant approach of contemporaries. The analysis of the young Engels represented one particular variant of it – that which interpreted Chartism as the political expression of the new industrial proletariat. Another variant, elements of which could also be traced back to liberal commentators at the time, has been equally, if not more influential in the subsequent historiography of Chartism: that which locates Chartism, not as the expression of modern factory workers, but of handloom weavers and other declining 'pre-industrial' groups. The period since the Second World War has yielded further and equally distinct variants of the social approach – the correlation between Chartism and the trade cycle, associated with Rostow, and the identification of Chartism with atavistic responses to modernisation, associated with Smelser.[8] Indeed in nearly all writings on Chartism, except that of Chartists themselves, it has been the movement's class character, social composition or more simply the hunger and distress of which it was thought to be the manifestation, rather than its platform or programme which have formed the focal point of enquiry.

It is not surprising that historians have placed these themes at the centre of their studies of Chartism. But it is surprising that there has not been more recognition of the interpretative costs of such an approach. Generally doubts that have been expressed about particular versions of a social approach have not extended to the limitations of the social approach as such. The prevalent mode of criticism has been as resolutely social in its assumptions as that of the interpretation to be opposed. Critical discussion has mainly clustered around such questions as the exploitative character of industrialisation itself, the reality of the threat to living standards and the real extent or depth of class hostilities. The difficulty of this form of criticism is that pressed to its conclusions, it makes the very existence of a combative mass movement difficult to explain, irrespective of its precise character. Far more problematic, yet barely touched upon by the critics of the various social interpretations of Chartism, is the general neglect of the specific political and ideological form within which this mass discontent was expressed and the consequent tendency to elide the Chartist language of class with a range of Marxist or sociological notions of class consciousness. What has not been sufficiently questioned is whether this language can simply be analysed in terms of its expression of, or correspondence to, the putative consciousness of a particular class or social or occupational group. If an analysis of this language does not confirm such a relation of direct manifestation or correspondence, what implication does this have for the interpretation of Chartism as a whole? The language itself has seldom been subjected to detailed examination.[9] But even in cases where it has, the gravitational pull exercised by the social interpretation has generally been powerful enough to inhibit any major revision of the conventional picture of the movement.

The intention of this essay is to suggest the rudiments of such a reinterpretation. In contrast to the prevalent social-historical approach to Chartism, whose starting-point is some conception of class or occupational consciousness, it argues that the ideology of Chartism cannot be constructed in abstraction from its linguistic form. An analysis of Chartist ideology must start from what Chartists actually said or wrote, the terms in which they addressed each other or their opponents. It cannot simply be inferred – with the aid of decontextualised quotation – from the supposed exigencies, however plausible, of the material situation of a particular class or social group. Nor is it adequate, as an alternative, to adopt a more subjective approach and to treat Chartist language as a more or less immediate rendition of experience into words. This way of interpreting Chartism possesses the virtue of paying more serious attention to what Chartists said. But it too ultimately resolves problems posed by the form of Chartism into problems of its supposed content. Against this approach, it is suggested that the analysis of the language itself precludes such a directly referential theory of meaning. What is proposed instead is an approach which attempts to identify and situate the place of language and form, and which resists the temptation to collapse questions posed by the form of Chartism into questions of its assumed substance. It is argued that if the interpretation of the language and politics is freed from *a priori* social inferences, it then becomes possible to establish a far closer and more precise relationship between ideology and activity than is conveyed in the standard picture of the movement.

In adopting this approach, however, it is not intended to imply that the analysis of language can provide an exhaustive account of Chartism, or that the social conditions of existence of this language were arbitrary.[10] It is not a question of replacing a social interpretation by a linguistic interpretation, it is how the two relate, that must be rethought. Abstractly the matter determines the possibility of the form, but the form conditions the development of the matter. Historically there are good reasons for thinking that Chartism could not have been a movement except of the working class, for the discontents which the movement addressed were overwhelmingly, if not exclusively, those of wage-earners, and the solidarities upon which the movement counted were in fact also those between wage-earners. But the form in which these discontents were addressed cannot be understood in terms of the consciousness of a particular social class, since the form pre-existed any independent action by such a class and did not significantly change in response to it. Moreover, the form was not, as is sometimes implied in the social interpretation, a mere shell within which a class movement developed. For it was what informed the political activity of the movement, it defined the terms in which oppression was understood and it was what provided the vision of an alternative. It was further what defined the *political* crisis from which Chartism emerged and it fashioned the political means by which that crisis was resolved. The type of explanation which ascribes the movement to distress or the social changes accompanying the industrial revolution, never confronts the fact that the growth and decline of Chartism was a function of its capacity to persuade its constituency to interpret their distress or discontent within the terms of its political language. Chartism was a political movement and political movements cannot satisfactorily be defined in terms of the anger and disgruntlement of disaffected social groups or even the consciousness of a particular class. A political movement is not simply a manifestation of distress and pain, its existence is distinguished by a shared conviction articulating a political solution to distress and a political diagnosis of its causes. To be successful, that is to embed itself in the assumptions of masses of people, a particular political vocabulary must convey a practicable hope of a general alternative and a believable means of realising it, such that potential recruits can think within its terms. It must be sufficiently broad and appropriate to enable its adherents to inhabit its language in confronting day-to-day problems of political and social experience, to elaborate tactics and slogans upon its basis, and to resist the attempts of opposing movements to encroach upon, reinterpret or replace it. Thus the history of Chartism cannot satisfactorily be written in terms of the social and economic grievances of which it is argued to be the expression. Such an approach does not explain why these discontents should have taken a Chartist form, nor why Chartism should not have continued to express the changing fears and aspirations of its social constituency in new circumstances. It is with these questions that this essay is concerned. But before embarking upon such a discussion, we must first attempt to demonstrate more concretely what the interpretative costs of the social approach have been.

One major consequence of the social interpretation of Chartism is that when the actual demands of the movement have been discussed, they have been treated more as a legacy from its prehistory than as a real focal point of activity. Given the assumption that Chartism represented the first manifestation of a modern working-class movement, there has appeared something paradoxical in the fact that such a movement could have come together behind a series of radical constitutional demands first put forward over half a century before. But even in works in which no strong assumptions are made about the modernity or class character of Chartism, little effort is made to explain why distress and unemployment should find expression in a movement for universal suffrage rather than more immediate pressure for relief from the state. Instead, ever since 1913 when Edouard Dolléans first suggested that the cause of Chartism was to be discovered in the working-class reaction against the industrial revolution,[11] historians have tended to downplay the political programme of the Chartists as merely expressive of discontents whose true sources and remedies lay elsewhere.

Such an approach has been compounded by another emphasis in Chartist historiography, originally unconnected to the social interpretation, but which in the course of the twentieth century has increasingly coalesced with it. From the time when Chartism first began to be written about, attention was focused on the divided nature of the movement. The first generation of Chartist historians, embittered ex-Chartists like Gammage, Lovett and Cooper, concentrated disproportionately upon rifts in organisation and the angry and divisive battles between leading personalities.[12] In subsequent historiography, concentration upon the social character of the movement lent itself easily to the analysis of these divisions in social and economic terms. Divergencies of personality and cultural formation were now made to correspond to divergencies of economic situation and locality. The antagonism between Lovett and O'Connor was given a sociological coloration. It became a symbol of the supposed incompatibility between the non-industrialised constitutionally minded artisans of London and Birmingham – followers of Lovett, Attwood and Sturge, inclined to class alliance and moral force – and northern factory workers or declining handloom weavers, followers of O'Connor, hostile to the middle class, ill-educated and quasi-insurrectionary.[13] Later and more sophisticated versions of this approach, freed from some of the Fabian assumptions which had originally structured it, shifted arguments about Chartism even further from the battles and ideas of the leaders to the differing social textures of protest in different regions, and these regions themselves were arranged along a scale of progressive class polarisation determined by the extent of industrialisation.[14] Such polarities, however, have been weakened by more recent research. Despite Birmingham's well-publicised reputation for harmonious inter-class radicalism in the nineteenth century, its Chartists rejected the Birmingham Political Union leadership and for four years after 1838 looked mainly to O'Connor and stressed class independence.[15] It has similarly been shown that London Chartism in the 1840s was neither particularly weak, nor particularly moderate, as the old interpretation supposed. By 1848 it had become one of Chartism's most militant centres.[16] Conversely factory and heavy industrial areas like south Lancashire and the north east, distinctly militant centres in the early years of Chartism were far less prominent in 1848.[17] Moreover recent occupational analysis of Chartist adherence in its early years appears to suggest that the extent to which certain trades were disproportionately represented – shoemakers or handloom weavers, for instance – has been exaggerated and that Chartism attracted a more representative cross-section of the main trades in each locality than has usually been assumed.[18] If this is the case, it implies that too much attention to local or occupational peculiarities can obscure the extent to which Chartism was *not* a local or sectional movement. Chartism was a national movement. Yet this more surprising phenomenon – the extent of unity in the early Chartist Movement and the enduring loyalty of a sizeable minority over more than a decade to the remedies of the Charter, despite all disagreement and difference – has been left in the realm of commonsense assumption.

Thus the stress upon division and local differences has tended to accentuate the weak points in the social interpretation of Chartism: its tendency to neglect the political form of the movement and thus to render obscure and inconsequential the reasoning that underlay the demand for the Charter. Mark Hovell, still perhaps the most influential historian of Chartism, set the terms of the predominant approach when he argued that 'by 1838 the Radical Programme was recognised no longer as an end in itself, but as the means to an end, and the end was the social and economic regeneration of society'. This was a seemingly unexceptionable statement and something like it had been said on occasion by Chartists themselves. But Hovell's amplification of it betrayed a basic misunderstanding, which rendered the Charter an oddity and the 'end' incoherent. 'The most optimistic of Chartist enthusiasts', he wrote, 'could hardly have believed that a new heaven and a new earth would be brought about by mere improvements of political machinery'. But, he continued, 'social Chartism was a protest against what existed, not a reasoned policy to set up anything in its place. Apart from machinery, Chartism was largely a passionate negation'.[19] Subsequent landmarks in the historiography of Chartism have, if anything, only strengthened the impression of incoherence at the core of the movement. For G. D. H. Cole, 'the Chartist movement was essentially an economic movement with a purely political programme'. 'A common idea might have held them together; the Charter, a mere common programme, was not enough to prevent them from giving their mutual dislikes free rein'.[20] For Asa Briggs, writing in *Chartist Studies* in 1959, the Charter was not so much a focus as 'a symbol of unity'. But 'it concealed as much as it proclaimed – the diversity of local social pressures, the variety of local leaderships, the relative sense of urgency among different people and different groups.[21]

In the face of this interpretative consensus, it is worth citing the position of the first historian of Chartism, R. G. Gammage, writing in 1854. Gammage certainly did not deny the social origins of political discontent in the sense that 'in times of prosperity there is scarce a ripple to be observed on the ocean of politics'. Nor did he deny that the people, once victorious, would adopt 'social measures' to improve their condition. But significantly, he does not talk of 'political machinery', 'a mere common programme' or 'a symbol'. He states, on the contrary, that it is the existence of great social wrongs which principally teaches the masses the value of political rights; and his explanation of the thinking behind the Charter places the emphasis quite differently from Hovell and the historians who have followed him. In a 'period of adversity', he wrote,

> The masses look on the enfranchised classes, whom they behold reposing on their couch of opulence, and contrast that opulence with the misery of their own condition. Reasoning from effect to cause there is no marvel that they arrive at the conclusion – that their exclusion from political power is the cause of our social anomalies.[22]

Political Power is the cause. *Opulence* is the effect. But to subsequent historians whether liberal, social democratic or Marxist, it has been axiomatic that economic power is the cause, political power the effect. If this axiom is read back into the political programme of the Chartists, there is no marvel that that programme should have appeared incoherent.

Not all historians have assumed that Chartists must have meant the economic and social, when they spoke about the political. The under-estimation of the political character and context of the popular struggles in the pre-Chartist period has been magnificently remedied by Edward Thompson's *Making of the English Working Class*. As he demonstrates, the experience of the plebeian movement between 1780 and 1830 was not simply that of intensified economic exploitation, but also of sharp and semi-permanent political repression. Moreover, the attitude of the government and the unreformed Parliament to customary trade practices often seemed yet more cavalier than that to be found in the localities. Thus he can argue with some force that 'the line from 1832 to Chartism is not a haphazard pendulum alternation of "political" and "economic" agitation, but a direct progression, in which simultaneous and related movements converge towards a single point. This point was the vote'.[23]

The great achievement of Thompson's book is to have freed the concept of class consciousness from any simple reduction to the develop-ment of productive forces measured by the progress of large-scale industry and to have linked it to the development of a political move-ment which cannot be reduced to the terminology of incoherent protest. To have established this connection is a vital advance. But we must go further. Thompson's concept of class consciousness still assumes a relatively direct relationship between 'social being' and 'social conscious-ness' which leaves little independent space for the ideological context within which the coherence of a particular language of class can be re-constituted. A simple dialectic between consciousness and experience cannot explain the precise form assumed by Chartist ideology. A high-lighting of the experience of exploitation and political oppression, would not in itself account for Gammage's statement. It was not simply experience, but rather a particular linguistic ordering of experience which could lead the masses to believe that 'their exclusion from political power is the cause of our social anomalies' and that 'political power' was the cause of 'opulence'. Consciousness cannot be related to experience except through the interposition of a particular language which organises the understanding of experience, and it is important to stress that more than one language is capable of articulating the same set of experiences. The language of class was not simply a verbalisation of perception or the rising to consciousness of an existential fact, as

Marxist and sociological traditions have assumed. But neither was it
simply the articulation of a cumulative experience of a particular form
of class relations. It was constructed and inscribed within a complex
rhetoric of metaphorical association, causal inference and imaginative
construction. Class consciousness – 'a consciousness of identity of
interests between working men of the most diverse occupations and
levels of attainment' and 'consciousness of the identity of interests of
the working class or productive classes as against those of other classes',
as Thompson defines it[24] – formed part of a language whose systematic
linkages were supplied by the assumptions of radicalism: a vision and
analysis of social and political evils which certainly long predated the
advent of class consciousness, however defined.

In England radicalism first surfaced as a coherent programme in the
1770s, and first became a vehicle of plebeian political aspirations from
the 1790s. Its strength, indeed its definition, was a critique of the
corrupting effects of the concentration of political power and its corrosive influence upon a society deprived of proper means of political
representation. As such, in variant forms, it could provide the vocabulary
of grievance to a succession of political and social groups.[25] Elements
of this vocabulary went back to the seventeenth-century revolutions
and were reforged by those who felt excluded by the settlements of
1688 or 1714 or by the so-called 'country party' during the years of
Walpolean or Pelhamite dominance. The particular resonance, still
alive in the Chartist period, of words like 'patriot' or 'independent' and
the demonological associations of fundholding and stock-jobbing dated
back to this time. From the 1760s the tenancy of this language tended
to pass from right to left. Country Toryism receded – though it never
disappeared – in the face of radical Whiggery. New components of the
vocabulary were added by the Americans and their English supporters,
and echoes of a less decorous seventeenth-century radicalism could
again be detected. With the Wilkesite controversy, a radical movement
in a full sense began. The focus was no longer simply upon court and
city coteries and the corruption of patronage and place, but more
consistently and determinedly upon the constitution and the means of
representation. The unbalanced and disordered constitution could
only be restored to health by drawing upon the 'people', and at the same
time the definition of the people was widened, with a shift of emphasis
from property to person. In the 1790s radicalism became plebeian and
democratic, and successes in America, Ireland and above all, France,
lent it a revolutionary edge. It was accordingly repressed, a condition

which, given its survival, bestowed upon it a yet more intransigent sense of its righteousness and the accuracy of its diagnosis. In the post-war situation radicalism found itself forced to stretch its vocabulary to encompass new sources of distress and discontent within its terms. For not only did it find itself confronted by a new economic situation but also it found its nostrums challenged, though in quite different ways, by the novel emphases of political economy and Owenism, both of which cut across its premises. In response, radicalism attributed a growing number of economic evils to a political source and in the following thirty years managed to withstand these rival analyses with some success. It accommodated many of the preoccupations of the Owenites, while rejecting with less and less equivocation any compromise with political economy. The cost of this process was an increasing distance from the bulk of its former middle-class constituency. But however much radicalism extended its scope during this period, it could never be the ideology of a specific class. It was first and foremost a vocabulary of political exclusion; whatever the social character of those excluded. Thus, if it *de facto* became the more and more exclusive property of the 'working classes' in the 1830s and 40s, this did not lead to a basic restructuring of the ideology itself. The self-identity of radicalism was not that of any specific group, but of the 'People' or the 'nation' against the monopolisers of political representation and power *and hence* financial or economic power.

It is in this sense that the growing political hostility between the middle and working classes after 1832 must be understood. In radical terms, in 1832 the 'people' became the 'working classes'. Explaining the emergence of Chartism in 1838, for instance, the *Northern Star* considered:

The attention of the labouring classes – the real 'people' – has been successively (and yet to a certain degree simultaneously) aroused by the injuries they have sustained by the operation of a corrupt system of patronage hanging around their necks a host of locusts, in the shape of idle and useless pensioners and a swarm of hornets, in the form of mischievous placemen and commissioners to support whom they are weighed to the earth by the pressures of taxation; by the operation of the Corn Laws which made rents high and bread dear; by the iniquitous protection of the fundholders which made money dear and labour cheap; by the horrors of the factory system which immolates their progeny and coins the blood of their children into gold, for merciless grasping ruffians and by the abominations of the poor law act which virtually and practically denies them the right to live. All these and one hundred minor grievances, subservient to the same grand end (of making the working classes beasts of burden – hewers of wood and drawers of water – to the aristocracy, Jewocracy, Millocracy, Shopocracy, and every other Ocracy which feeds on human vitals) have roused the feelings of the people and prompted the respective parties to seek a remedy for the smarting of their wounds.[26]

By the same token, as a group, the middle classes had ceased to be part of the 'people'. For they had joined the system of oppressors and were henceforth answerable for the actions of the legislature. Indeed rigorously speaking, government now became that of the 'middle classes'. Speaking of the Reform Bill, the *Poor Man's Guardian* wrote a year later:

By that Bill, the government of the country is essentially lodged in the hands of the middle classes; we say the middle classes – for though the aristocracy have their share of authority, it is virtually absorbed in that of the middlemen who form the great majority of the constituency.[27]

Now, if it is true that the language of class – at least in its usage by the popular movement – was the language of radicalism, then a number of consequences follow. The most obvious one is that the political demands of the popular movement should be placed at the centre of the story of Chartism, rather than treated as symbolic or anachronistic; and not only the demands, but also the presuppositions which underlay them. For these were neither the superficial encasement of proletarian class consciousness, nor a simple medium of translation between experience and programme. If the history of Chartism is re-analysed in this manner, then the chronology of its rise and decline can be made more precise. The central tenet of radicalism – the attribution of evil and misery to a political source – clearly differentiated it both from a Malthusian-based popular political economy which placed the source of dissonance in nature itself[28] and from Owenite socialism which located evil in false ideas which dominated State and civil society alike.[29] But it also suggested that the success of radicalism as the ideology of a mass movement would depend upon specific conditions, those in which the State and the propertied classes in their *political and legal capacity* could be perceived as the source of all oppression. The programme of Chartism remained believable so long as unemployment, low wages, economic insecurity and other material afflictions could convincingly be assigned political causes. If, for instance, lack of political representation and a corrupt system of power rather than economic phenomena were responsible for the misery of the working classes, then it followed from this that partial reforms like the ten hours bill or the repeal of the Corn Law, could not bring real improvement, indeed were more likely to hasten deterioration, since they left the system intact. Nor could trade unionism be thought a realistic alternative since, if the labour market was politically determined, then differences of bargaining power between different groups within the working classes were largely illusory. So long as the empirical forecasts which followed from radical premises appeared to be borne out, Chartists had little reason to expect widespread defections from their ranks. Once, however, the evidence suggested that real reform was possible within the unreformed system, that the State did not wholly correspond to the radical picture and conditions changed in such a way that differences in the fortunes of various trades became clearly visible, despite the identity of their political situation, then radical ideology could be expected to lose purchase over large parts of its mass following. Such an approach suggests a different way of looking at the period of mid-Victorian stabilisation, from that prevalent among social historians.[30] In radical ideology the dividing line between classes was not that between employer and employed, but that between the represented and the unrepresented. Thus hostility to the middle classes was not ascribed to their role in production, but to their participation in a corrupt and unrepresentative political system, and it was through this political system that the producers of wealth were conceived to be deprived of the fruits of their labour. Once therefore the conviction of the totally evil character of the political system itself began to fade and distress became less pervasive, there was no independent rationale within radical ideology for antagonism towards the middle class as such. If this is the case, there is then little need to introduce ambitious sociological explanations, such as the emergence of a labour aristocracy, co-option by the middle class or the invention of new and subtle means of social control in order to explain the disappearance of Chartism. Such approaches ignore the more elementary point that as a system of beliefs, Chartism began to fail, when a gulf opened up between its premises and the perception of its constituency. Local and everyday awareness of difference of social position, of course, remained but it was no longer linked across the country through the language of radicalism to a shared conviction of a realisable institutional and political alternative. Thus if expressed hostility to the middle classes declined, despite the continuation of capitalist relations of production, this should be no occasion for surprise. For it was the product of the decline of a political movement whose expressed reasons for hostility to the middle class had had little to do with the character of the productive system in itself.

We have so far argued for an analysis of Chartism which assigns some autonomous weight to the language within which it was conceived. If the language of Chartism is interpreted, not as a passive medium through which new class aspirations could find expression, but rather as a complex rhetoric binding together in a systematic way, shared premisses, analytical routines, strategic options and programmatic demands, we can then introduce some notion of a limit beyond which radical analysis could not be stretched without abandoning its basic tenets and thus losing coherence as an inter-related set of assumptions. But before attempting to suggest some of the points at which these limits were reached, we must first explore what were the inter-related assumptions of post-1830 radicalism and Chartism and show how the language of class was tied to radical premises.

It is best to begin with the simple question, why the Charter was considered desirable. According to Lovett who framed the Charter, 'the end and object of all despotism being to uphold monopolies, there can be no escape from it, so long as the exclusive power of law making shall be suffered to abide with the monopolists'.[31] From the ultra-left of the movement, although the vocabulary certainly differs, the mode of reasoning is similar. According to the Manifesto of the London Democratic Association, which aspired to emulate the Jacobins in the coming revolution, 'because the institutions of the country are in the hands of the oppressors, because the oppressed have no voice in the formation of the laws that rule their destiny – the masses are socially – because they are politically slaves. To put an end to the present cannibal system – we must! We will!! have universal suffrage.' Hetherington similarly attributed the major cause of poverty to the 'monopoly of the power of legislation in the hands of the few'. The monopoly of land and the monopoly of machinery as an instrument of production were basically attributable to 'the still more glaring injustice of the monopoly of law making as an instrument of distribution'. For law-making, as O'Brien put it, was a 'monopoly by virtue of which property owners are enabled to keep continually augmenting their property out of the labourer's plundered wages'.[32] The case for universal suffrage was not generally argued on an abstract plane as a universal right inhering in every citizen. The case was more usually put in practical and corporate terms and closely tied to the Chartist analysis of the cause of the condition of the working classes. While outside observers often regarded Chartism as an assault on the propertied by the property-less, Chartists did not regard the working classes as property-less. For since the only legitimate source of property was labour, labourers were therefore in possession of the most fundamental form of all property. As Cobbett had stated in his *Address to the Journeymen and Labourers of England* in 1817, 'whatever the pride of rank, or riches or of scholarship may have induced some men to believe, or affect to believe, the real strength and all the resources of the country, have ever sprung and ever must spring from the labour of its people'.[33] The aim therefore was not an expropriation of the rich by the poor, but the ending of a monopoly situation in which all other forms of property were afforded political and legal support, while that of labour was left at the mercy of those who monopolised the State and the law. As Joseph Crabtree of Barnsley observed:

> It had once been observed that without the Suffrage their property could not be protected; but the working class were told they had no need of the suffrage as they had no property to protect. They had indeed none save that which was in the strength of their arms; and from that property, every description of property arose, and therefore, theirs was the only property of real value and ought to be the first in the world to have legislative protection. If they would not endeavour to attain such laws as would procure the protection of their only property, they could not wonder at seeing mansions spring up at the corners of every field they passed and the aristocracy feeding on their labour more than ever.[34]

Or as O'Brien put it,

> Knaves will tell you that it is because you have no property, you are unrepresented. I tell you on the contrary, it is because you are unrepresented that you have no property... your poverty is the result not the cause of your being unrepresented.[35]

In the absence of any legislative protection for labour, those who possessed political power could simply engross property by legislative fiat. Not only could they impose taxes at will, but also they could manipulate the money supply to enrich themselves. Thus, just as the 1815 Corn Law was defined as a 'starvation law' for the benefit of the landed interest, so the resumption of cash payments in 1819 was a law made for the benefit of the fundholders, through which millions were thought to have been transferred from debtors into the pockets of creditors.[36] The property amassed by these measures was 'artificial'. It was not the product of labour, but literally the creation of law. The growing polarity between the poverty of the working classes and this 'artificial wealth' could therefore be seen as the result of a process of legal robbery, made possible by the monopoly of law-making. It was in this sense that O'Connor argued that, all such laws were a fiction, 'because they have been made for the protection of fictitious money, which represents nothing but the produce of your wealth while in a state of transition from one pack of moneymongers to another pack of speculators'. It is certainly possible to discover differences of tone and emphasis between Chartist spokesmen in the discussions of these issues, but what emerges most clearly in the late 1830s was the remarkable unanimity of reasoning that lay behind the demand for the Charter. There was no dissension on this score between O'Connor, Lovett, Harney and the countless speakers up and down the country reported in the *Northern Star*. Poverty and oppression could be removed only with the abolition of the monopoly of law-making, or as O'Connor put it 'there was no vice in the people for which he could not assign a legal reason'.[37] The spectrum of positions between moderate and extreme lay *within* radicalism, not *between* radicalism and something else.

If this was the general sense in which Chartists could concur in attributing the oppression of the working classes to their exclusion from political representation, it suggests a far greater continuity between Chartism and preceding forms of radicalism than most historians have admitted. The tendency of most recent accounts has been to highlight the differences between the radicalism of the 1815-19 period and that which developed after 1829. In this scenario, the period between 1815 and 1832 is often viewed as one in which the popular movement became a working-class movement with distinctively working-class ways of looking at politics and society. Trade unionism, co-operation, Owenism, so-called 'Ricardian socialism', the unstamped press, the GNCTU (Grand National Consolidated Trades Union) and Tolpuddle are then seen as stepping stones in a learning process through which class consciousness was formed. Confirmation at an ideological level is provided by the argument that Paineite or Cobbettite radicalism which placed its emphasis upon the State and taxation as the sole source of oppression gave way to a more class-based conception of exploitation of workers in their role as producers rather than consumers, and thereby to an emphasis upon the class character of the popular movement and a class hostility to the middle class. Thus radicalism in its initial form is conceived as receding as class consciousness advances and the political division between middle and working class established in 1832 is seen as ratifying a process that had already been long in maturation.

There is unfortunately not space to engage with these arguments here.[38] Instead it is only possible summarily to state that, at least at the level of utterance, this picture is not confirmed by evidence of ideological change of an appropriate kind. Certainly changes took place in radicalism between 1815 and 1840 and Chartism incorporated many of the new themes which became prominent in the 1820s, but not in such a way as to breach its basic presuppositions, nor necessarily in directions which drew it closer towards a later class-based language of socialism. While the trade union movement grew in strength and articulacy in the 1820s, the diagnosis which it produced of its situation was generally stated in familiar radical terms. Composed largely of workers from threatened trades, its critique was aimed at 'unfair' masters and foreign competition and was underpinned by notions of 'fair' (that is, customary) wages and 'fair' competition. Clearly Owenism, with its more elaborated notion of competition as a system, enriched radical conceptions of the *malaise* of the working classes. But even among those of its working-class supporters, most wedded to co-operative aims, Owenism did not dislodge the primacy of the demand for universal suffrage within the popular movement, nor the radical premises upon which that demand was based. Even among those Owenite-inspired journals like the *Crisis* and the *Pioneer* which emerged from the general unionism of 1833-4, the conception of a 'general strike' did not mark such an important breach with older radical traditions, as it has often been assumed. It is certainly true that these journals developed a strikingly non-constitutional definition of universal suffrage, centering upon the formation of a house of trades to supplant the House of Commons. But despite this substantial difference in strategy, the analysis of the divide between the 'working classes' and their oppressors was not very different from that to be found elsewhere in the working-class radical press. The initial hope, analogous in this respect to the 'general holiday' scheme of William Benbow, was that both masters and men would join in a movement which might isolate and finally dislodge the parasitic state of landlords and 'capitalists' and as in the establishment of the National Union of the Working Classes, the juxtaposition was not between working class and employing class, but between the working classes and the idle classes. Lastly, while considerable attention has been paid to the shift away from a Paineite or Cobbettite conception of taxation, as the principal means by which the working class were oppressed, it would be mistaken to suppose that this represented a movement out of radicalism in the direction of a class-based theory of exploitation of a social democratic or Marxist kind. The critiques to be found in Hodgskin and Gray, and in a more popular form in the *Poor Man's Guardian* were not of employers, whose antagonistic relation to workers was inscribed within the economic system, but of 'capitalists' as parasitic middlemen whose privileged and tyrannical position was an aberration resulting from the monopoly of political and legal power possessed by the propertied governing classes. Whether the critique was directed at tax-eaters, as in the older vision, or more generally at 'capitalists' in the newer, the political source and origins of oppression remained equally clear. The evidence of the 1820s and early 1830s suggests that radicalism in a strict sense remained the predominant ideology of the popular movement, defining both the understanding of oppression and the popular vocabulary of class, and further, that rival perspectives, notably Owenism, offered, if anything a less class-oriented mode of viewing society and politics than the radicalism to which they were counterposed.

This bare summary of developments in the 1820s and early 1830s must suffice to explain why, for theorists of 'unequal exchange', spokesmen of the new form of radicalism in the unstamped press and later Chartists, the fundamental conflict was not between employers and employed, but between the working classes and the idle classes. As the *Poor Man's Guardian* stated in 1833:

There are two great parties in the state – two great moving principles. . . These parties are, 1 – those that are willing to work; and 2 – those that are not. The principles are labour and capital.[39]

The employer, like the shopkeeper, was subsumed under the category of the middleman. He literally occupied a middle or intermediate position between the labouring producer and the idle consumer and was subject to the conflicting pressures of both. As a middleman, whose interest was to buy cheap and sell dear, he certainly took up a position alongside other oppressors, but more as lackey than controller of the system. He was thus attacked, not as the ultimate beneficiary but rather as the willing complier in the tyrannical rule of property. The 'Political Corrector' provided a characteristic picture of his role in the newer form of radicalism:

When the farmer sells his corn; instead of paying money to his work-men for doing the work, as he ought to do, he gives it to the idlers in the name of rent, tithe, usury, toll or retains it himself in the name of profit. The master in every useful branch of manufacture acts upon the same principle with the money he obtains for the produce of his workmen.

And the point was made more explicitly by the *Poor Man's Guardian* in 1835:

The grand point to understand is this – that the tendency of the present system is to give the proprietors of *land* and *money* – of money especially – unlimited control over the productive power of the country. Under this system the producer receives not what he earns – not the equivalent of his services – not the value of his pro-duce in money or other produce – but what these parties choose to give him. If he produces a pound's worth of goods, he does not receive a pound, or a pound's worth of other goods in exchange, as he ought to do, but only what his employer can induce him to take in preference to starving. . . . Not that his employer pockets the rest. We know that in the majority of cases he does not – nay, that he often gets less than the producer himself. But, then, in such cases the wealth is received by other parties, who claim it as rent, tithe, pension, annuity, or some such form. . . As the employer, and the other parties alluded to, make the institutions by which this distri-bution is made, it is manifest that, inasmuch as they profit by them, they can have no interest in changing them.[40]

This conception of the employer as the middleman between the two principal contending classes is well-illustrated by the discussion of the strategy of a general strike in 1834. Historians have rightly noted the novelty of the suggestion of a general strike mounted by trade unions – rather than simply, the industrious classes, as in Benbow's original formulation. But it is also important to note the continuity of the radical conception that underlay it.[41] 'The capitalist will never increase wages except through fear of the physical force of the labourers', wrote a correspondent to the *Poor Man's Guardian*, 'let there be a universal strike for some minimum of wages in every trade'. The rationale of this position, beyond the improvement of the position of the producer himself, was not the destruction of the class power of employers, but rather to strike a blow against the propertied idlers and their state. Either it was thought that the result would be a rise in prices that would hit the idle consumer rather than the working classes, or, it could be argued:

> High wages involves low rents, low rates, low profits, low usury, low taxes, low everything that is levied on industry. Take for instance the agricultural labourer. You cannot raise *his* wages without reducing the farmer's profits. Do this and you compel the farmer to mulct the landlord and parson of a part of their rent and tithe; and these being reduced, it is plain the tax gatherer must go without a portion of his taxes. Thus to raise wages is to lower rents, tithes, taxes and every other impost on labour.

Like the labour note scheme of 1833, this proposal clearly represented an alternative to the orthodox radical strategy, but like that scheme it operated within the same set of assumptions about the nature of power and class relations. It was therefore not difficult for radicals to reject the argument. 'How can we overthrow the present system?' wrote the *Poor Man's Guardian* immediately after the trade union demonstration against the Tolpuddle verdict. 'We say by employing the organisation of the Unions to carry universal suffrage', and it went on:

> With the present system, the masters *could* not if they would, and *would* not if they could increase the wages of the men, for so un-natural is the position in which competition has placed them, that they cannot as a body do justice to the men, without doing injury to themselves. Thousands of employers can barely exist at the present rate of profits. Affect these profits by ever so slight an increase of wages, and they are ruined.

On the other hand, it concluded, the master had no comparable reason to refuse universal suffrage. 'He can have no objection to urge against the labourer's enfranchisement, that is not founded upon ignorance and fraud'.[42]

The employer, like other middlemen, was criticised in this newer form of radicalism, not on account of his economic role, but his political beliefs and social attitudes. As Hetherington wrote,

> No individual is blameable for accumulating all he can earn as employer, shopkeeper, pawnbroker, or otherwise, so long as the present system endures. That system leaves an individual no choice but to *live by it* or die.
>
> At all events, it leaves him, no alternative but that of enslaving others or being a slave himself. The guilt, then, is not in living *by* the system or *according to it* — it is in supporting it.

It was therefore quite consistent that the attitude of the radicals to employers, middlemen and the middle classes in general should fluctuate according to the attitude of the middle classes to the demands of the people. Now that the middle classes were enfranchised, their attitudes could reasonably be inferred from the actions of the legislature. The question therefore, for post-1832 radicals and later for the Chartists, was not how to overturn the middle classes, but rather why in the prevailing conditions, the middle classes did not support the demands of the people and how they could be persuaded or forced to do so. If the middle classes were not to be trusted, it was because their political actions demonstrated their base selfishness. As the *Poor Man's Guardian* noted in April 1833:

> Since their accession to the franchises conferred by the Reform Bill, the middle classes thought only of themselves. . . the experience of the last three months convinces us that the spirit in which they desire to exercise the franchise is as exclusively selfish as the aristo-cratic spirit which gave them a monopoly of it was arbitrary and unjust.[43]

And this had been demonstrated by their narrow interest in house and window taxes, triennial Parliaments and the ballot in contrast to their silence about taxes on bread, malt, hops, tobacco, sugar, glass, spirits and the newspaper stamp.

The reason for their debility and baseness related to the artificial position of the middleman in the property-dominated political system. Writing in the aftermath of the passing of measures for Irish coercion by the middle-class legislature, the *Poor Man's Guardian* gave the following characterisation of their position:

Even the shopkeepers and master manufacturers, amounting (with their dependents) to more than six millions of the population, are more or less interested in the system – their business being to buy labour *cheap* from the poor, and sell it *dear* to the aristocracy, they are immediately dependent on the latter for support. Besides, taken as a body they are the basis of society, occupying an intermediate position between the workman and the aristocrat – employing the one and being employed by the other, they insensibly contract the vices of both tyrant and slave; tyrants to those below them – sycophants to those above them – and usurers from necessity and habit – they prey on the weakness of the workman, while they extort all they can from the vanity of the aristocrat. Indeed, the middle classes are the destroyers of liberty and happiness in all countries. It is their interest (under the present form of society) that the poor should be weak and the rich extravagant and vain; and this being the case, the man who expects from them any real opposition to despotism, from inclination, must be a fool or a madman.

It was for the same sorts of reasons that 'PC' considered that 'the master of every useful working man is the greatest tyrant that man has to contend with':

He readily accedes to, and gives it to the idlers without a murmur, at the same time he calls in the aid of the constable, the police, the military and the law, to suppress the just demands of his workmen. . . Why does he not resist the idlers instead of his workmen? Why the reason is this – because in giving the money to those idlers who have no right to it, he thereby obtains their sanction and protection in keeping in the name of *profit* much more than he has a right to himself, and of accumulating that profit into what he calls *property,* which soon enables him to become an *idler,* and live on rent and usury.

But such attacks, based as they were upon inferences from middle-class political behaviour, could always in the light of changing evidence, be contested within the radical framework. Allen Davenport, objecting to the *Guardian*'s attack upon middlemen, pointed to their support of the people, in the case of the Calthorp Street jury:

> Had you launched your thunder against the great capitalist, and monopolisers of every description, whether shopholders, fund-holders, landholders, or church-holders, I should have liked the article better; but your indiscriminate attack on the whole body of shopkeepers is badly timed, to say the least of it. . . It appears to me that men act nearly alike under the same circumstances; therefore, as we cannot create a new race of men, we had better direct our efforts towards creating new circumstances.[44]

The radical position in relation to the middle classes was less inconsequential than is sometimes thought. There was general agreement, that given their contradictory position involving both servility and tyranny, the middle classes as a whole, would only support the claims of the people when pressured by necessity. This was not a new discovery of the post-1832 period. As Cobbett recalled, 'hundreds of times did I tell Major Cartwright that there never would be Reform to any extent as long as the paper money system remained unshaken', and he attributed the reform agitation of the Birmingham middle class to the pressure upon prices and credit resulting from Peel's resumption of cash payments in 1819.[45] The attempt to create such pressure remained a consistent radical strategy in the post-1832 and Chartist period. The predominant image of the middle classes was of a timid and fearful as well as petty-tyrannical group, who would only ally with the people out of necessity or expediency. Their natural sympathies within the prevailing artificial system lay with property and they themselves were thought to aspire to become idlers. To combat this situation, therefore, the *Poor Man's Guardian* thought that 'the democratic spirit' must be pushed 'upwards', as the 'aristocratic principle' was now pushed 'downwards'. Moreover, the middle class, as the radicals conceived it, was not only amenable to pressure, it was already a split class:

> The force of society is in their hands. They have the press – the House of Commons – the capital of the country – the weight of opinion – unlimited means of combination – in short the whole artillery of society. So irresistible is their power, that were they to

act unitedly, destruction would be inevitable for any individual who would wag a jaw against them. Fortunately, however, they are not united; for, independently of their mutually conflicting interests, a large portion of them depend entirely on the custom or patronage of the poor, and another considerable portion are governed by humane feelings in despite of their selfish interests. These two portions, acting with the intelligent part of the working classes, offer a considerable counterpoise to the rest of their body, which is nevertheless a decided majority of the whole.

This in turn was why radicals and Chartists, while supporting exclusive dealing, tended to oppose combined trade union action to secure higher wages, rather than political change. Reflecting on trade union activity in 1834, the *Guardian* wrote:

You could easily, for instance, convince the clerk in a counting house with only £30 or £40 a year, that he might have a much better reward for his time and labour under institutions which did not bestow the rewards of industry upon aristocratic idlers or accumulating usurers; but you could never show him any advantage was to be gained by having the price of shoes and clothes, and bread, raised upon him by combinations to raise wages while no similar raise was to take place in his own. The trades began at the wrong end. They began by arousing against themselves the class that immediately pressed upon them, instead of involving the aid of that class against those laws and institutions which made both poor for the benefit of the aristocracy – landed and commercial. Almost all the small shopkeepers and small masters could be easily taught that they have a decided, an exalted and enduring interest in the changes, which we of the *Guardian* seek![46]

This attempt to draw in the middle classes through threat or persuasion did not basically change during the Chartist period. In the light of the experience of the 1830s and as the depression deepened from 1837, the suspicion and indignation against the middle classes increased. All their basest characteristics within the existing system had been amply confirmed. But since the fundamental assumptions remained unchanged, the proneness to courting, threatening or ignoring the middle classes, fluctuated according to the political situation, rather than moving in a unilinear direction.

Thus, after the withdrawal of the Birmingham middle-class leaders from the Convention in 1839, ostensibly in the face of the prospect of 'ulterior measures', O'Connor noted 'the first note of the retreat of the timid middle classes, who, believe me, never intended joining you upon the question of universal suffrage without the understanding that they should say "thus far shalt thou go and no further"'. Anger was expressed at the middle-class desertion, all their basest qualities were paraded and the intrinsic difficulties of an alliance between 'the men who buy cheap and sell dear' and 'the men who sell cheap and buy dear' were emphasised. Already at the end of 1838, O'Connor had stated his determination not to moderate the agitation at the behest of the 'money mongers' who considered the movement was going too far: 'Guard yourselves my friends, against all men who would attempt to throw dissension among you. I commence this battle with the fustian coats, unshorn chins and blistered hands. . .' But this should not be regarded as an abandonment of the radical strategy, it was rather an attempt to pressurise the legislature by 'a strong portrayal of your moral power' on the part of the unrepresented working classes. As he told O'Connell in June 1839:

> We do *not* exclude the middle classes from our ranks, but on the contrary we court them. The middle classes have *not* the same interests in good and cheap government that the operatives have; because the middle classes, many of them, live by bad, and prosper by dear government. The middle classes are the authors of all those sufferings which *they* experience at the hands of the aristocracy, while they are also the authors of all the miseries which the working classes experience from the middle classes, from the aristocracy and dear and bad government; because the government emanates from a majority of the middle classes, and therefore we must look upon them as the authors of their own misery.

The problem, as he told Chartists, was 'that they have no inheritance save in your labour, and they are not sufficiently sagacious to discover that upon your independence depends their prosperity'. After the failure of the Convention and the ultra-radical plans of the summer and autumn of 1839, different tactics were tried. McDouall came out of prison in 1840, stating that 'nothing had been gained by attacking the middle classes'; O'Brien similarly moved to a more conciliatory strategy, after having stated in 1839 that 'the middle classes are not your friends. They never will be your friends as long as the present commercial system endures.'[47] O'Connor and most of the Chartist leadership backed the Conservatives in 1841 as another means of bringing pressure upon the middle classes by helping to throw out the Whigs.[48] Similarly the difficulties surrounding the possibilities of allying with Sturge and the Complete Suffrage Union in 1842 concerned, not the desirability of attracting middle-class support, but agreeing the terms upon which it could be based. True middle-class friends of universal suffrage would declare for the Charter, and in the light of the political record of political organisations like the Birmingham Political Union and the Anti-Corn Law League, any proposal to merge Chartism behind a middle-class organisation was bound to meet with resistance. But ambition to recruit the middle classes to the standard of the Charter when times were propitious, was not abandoned and in 1847–8, O'Connor, McDouall and Ernest Jones once again attempted to mobilise the middle classes against the moneycrats.[49]

Undoubtedly there was a shift of emphasis and imagery in the Chartist period. The campaign over factory slavery, the introduction of the new Poor Law into the north, the fate of the handloom weavers and the growth of cyclical and technological unemployment all raised factory owners to a prominence which they had not possessed in 1832. According to the *Northern Star* in 1839:

The progress of machinery has been so rapid, so unchecked and so self-protecting in its course, that those who have been engaged in the pursuit, have, as if by magic, become the monied aristocracy of the country; and, as our rulers declare for, and our system sanctions a monied franchise as a proof of legislative fitness, it is not to be wondered at if the social rank of the money mongers becomes equal to their possessions; and if ere long we find that general, which has been progressive, namely a complete change of situation between the steam and landed aristocracy of the country.[50]

Similarly McDouall considered:

The factory system originated in robbery and was established in injustice. . . The factory masters have destroyed a race of the best and most intelligent class – the handloom weavers. . . English society has been so completely undermined and public confidence has been so destroyed by the accursed factory system that a despotic government can introduce any measure, whether poor law or centralisation among them.[51]

Such a position was greatly reinforced by the campaign of radicals of Tory provenance.[52] Summarising Rayner Stephens' position, Mr Tong of Bury explained why he had been arrested:

> It was because Mr Stephens had denounced the present system of government which made virtue a crime and rewarded vice (applause), because he had declared openly and candidly, that the children of the poor ought not to be called out to work long before the sun had risen above the horizon, and ground to dust long after he had set; because he had declared that women ought not to labour at all, but their duties ought to be confined to the household; that little boys ought to play about the country at 'hop, skip and jump' and girls ought to be brought up under the immediate control and instruction of their parents, to be taught to sew, knit, bake and brew, because he said that every Englishman ought to be in possession of as much wages as would make his family comfortable – (hear, hear) because he told the tyrants to their teeth that their money was blood money and that God almighty had sworn an oath that he would draw his sword of vengeance and slay the oppressors of the poor (great applause).[53]

The movement of the Chartist period incorporated a much broader cross-section of the working population than that of the early 1830s. It is not surprising that in the light of the experiences and agitations of the 30s, the factory owners at the end of the 1830s should – in the north – be identified as the main tyrants. The degree of hostility towards this group was evident in the Chartist antagonism towards the Anti-Corn Law League, which they saw as a diversionary ploy of the manufacturers or a means of intensifying their tyranny – although in fact the League was more characteristically a movement of the lower-middle classes.[54] Similarly, the new Poor Law was unilaterally associated with the new industrial middle class, although in fact landowners had been more responsible than employers for getting the bill through Parliament. And even more sinister schemes were attributed to their inspiration. Referring to the probably satirical ultra-Malthusian pamphlet of 'Marcus' in 1839, Harney told a Derby crowd:

> The want of universal suffrage has allowed the horrors of the factory system so long to continue – that bloody system deforming the

bodies and debauching the minds of our children. Oh! Ye millowners and factory lords! How will ye answer for the wholesale murders ye have committed – how will ye answer at God's judgement seat for your crimes against humanity... With the bloody law of Marcus in force only one step more will be wanting to complete the system, and that will be a law to authorise the millowners, the Factory Lords and the shopocracy generally to put you to death when worn out.

As the *Northern Star* put it, writing on factory legislation in April 1839: 'If they (the people), as they easily may, compel the tottering imbeciles who now hold the reins of government to restore their rights of universal suffrage – a parliament so chosen will soon teach these mill devils to dance a very different tune'. There can be no doubt about the intensity of the hostility towards factory owners in 1839, and it spilled over into rage against the middle classes in general, as William Benbow found when he addressed a meeting at Abbey Leigh near Gorton around the same time:

Mr Benbow said – I address myself to the working men, and also the middle class men of Gorton. I do it on the principle that there are good men as working men, and also good men as middle class men (here some in the meeting misunderstood the gentleman, which caused a few interruptions). Gentlemen – allow me, and I will set you right. I do not pretend to say that there are no middle class men who do not seek on all occasions to dock your wages.[55]

But, while the depth and extent of antagonism is not to be questioned, it should not therefore be assumed that the radical analysis that lay behind the Charter was in the course of displacement by a different and more class-conscious mode of thought. James Leach, a factory worker, a future leader of the National Charter Association and one of the Chartists most concerned with the factory question, addressing the same meeting as Benbow, stated: 'Not a working man in this vast assembly receives more than 5*s* to the pound of real value – (shame, shame) – the other fifteen are taken from him to support the aristocracy'. The terminology – 'millocrat', 'cotton lord', 'steam aristocracy' – is indicative of some radical uncertainty about how to define factory owners in relation to landlords, money lords and the middle classes. But the belief that they had now displaced the old aristocracy did not weaken the conviction of the political origin and determination of oppression; and if anything it strengthened the idea that the politically enforced expropriation from the land remained the ultimate source of the condition of the working classes and the growing tyranny of the money and factory lords. Not only, as we have seen, were such assertions already being made in the 1820s, but since oppression was to be derived from the usurpation and monopolisation of property, rather than a particular form of production, it was quite logical to continue to see the monopolisation of land as the prime cause of the misery of the worker, with the monopolisation of money and machinery as secondary derivatives. Unlike profit, which could be justified in moderation as the wages of supervision, rent and interest were the product of no labour, and there was therefore no natural right which could justify them. According to John Gray, for example,

> The earth is the habitation, the natural inheritance of all mankind of ages present and to come; a habitation belonging to no man in particular, but to every man; and one in which all have an equal right to dwell ... There are but three ways in which it is possible to become rightly possessed of property. The first is by making it; the second by purchasing it; the third is by donation from another, whose property it was. Now it is clear that neither our present land-owners, nor their ancestors ... can be the proprietors of an inch of it.[56]

The chain of reasoning was equally clear to Bray, 'individual possession of the soil has been one cause of inequality of wealth – that inequality of wealth necessarily gives rise to inequality of labour – and that inequality of wealth and labour and enjoyments, constitute the wrong as a whole.'[57] Moreover, although in the newer form of radicalism, the capitalist ownership of machinery was often stressed as the reason for competition between labourers, low wages and the existence of 'a reserve corps of labour', it remained true that the usurpation of their natural rights to cultivate the soil, had made them 'landless' wage slaves in the first place and that the resumption of rights to the land would be the most effective answer to the tyranny of the millowner. As O'Connor observed,

> The besetting sin – the great grievance under which the working classes labour, namely the living from hand to mouth, and being in a

complete state of dependency upon their employers and hence the difference between English and Irish agitation. If every man had his months provisions in the storehouse (which, with the blessing of God, universal suffrage will give him), there would be an end to your sophistry.

Such a position was reinforced in the 1830s by the older critique of landed property made by the Spenceans. The *Northern Star* noted that 'the Spencean doctrine is not only preached, but details for its practical workings are brought prominently to public view'. It connected the resurgence of interest in Spence with what was regarded as a further usurpation of the rights of the poor to a portion of the income from land enacted by the new Poor Law.

> The people who never before that Reform Bill seriously canvassed the landlord's title to his share in the land, but who merely complained of his legislatorial interference with that proportion of its produce which belongs to the nation, now discover that so long as the title exists, so long will the prejudicial interference continue.[58]

Spenceans argued against all private property in land, basing their arguments not only upon natural right and biblical foundation, but also upon the insistence that the land had historically belonged to the poor and that it had been stolen from them.[59] During the 1840s the end to the monopolisation of the land was in fact the main Chartist solution to the existence of industrial capitalism. According to James Leach, 'If they would take away all chance of a working man being enabled to live by his labour as a mechanic, they ought, at least, to give him the means of falling back on the land as a security for liberty and life'.[60] There was no disagreement between O'Connor and more socialistic Chartists about the identification of the land as the centre point of a Chartist social programme. The argument, so far as it was political, was about whether land schemes should be inaugurated before the winning of the Charter and about whether it should be divided between peasant proprietors or whether as Harney advocated, following the Spenceans, the land was to be the 'people's farm'. Similarly, after 1848, in the period of 'charter socialism', when Chartists were demanding 'the Charter and something more', nothing is more striking than the basic continuity of their analysis, despite the change of nomenclature. 'The feudal lords are doomed', wrote Harney,

But the money-lords are full of life and energy, and resolutely re-solved to establish their ascendancy on the ruins of the rule of their once masters, but now perishing rivals. . . The feudal lords have scourged the proletarians with whips, but the money lords (if they prosper in their designs) will scourge them with scorpions. . . The feudal aristocracy being doomed to expire, care should be taken that no new aristocracy be allowed to take their place. With that view THE LAND MUST BE MADE NATIONAL PROPERTY. . . THE LAND BELONGS TO ALL, and the natural right of all is superior to the falsely asserted rights of conquest or purchase.[61]

It will be noticed that even in this last phase of Chartism, and even in a passage where the influence of Marx and Engels is directly detect-able, a language of natural right still predominated. It was this language, and its residual but ineradicable individualist presuppositions, which lay at the centre of the English radical conception of classes, providing it with all the force of its militant convictions, but also firmly demar-cating its analytical boundaries. Outside Owenism, the labour theory of property was inextricably tied to a theory of natural rights – the natural rights of the producer to his *property*, the fruits of his labour. After the rejection of the second Chartist petition in May 1842, the *Northern Star* replied to Macaulay's attack in the House of Commons, 'the wretchedness, starvation and fearful despair of the operative classes loudly proclaim that *their property* – their labour and its fruits, are not secured to them, but on the other hand are the common prey of all the legal plunderers of society'.[62] The force and limits of the analysis appear similarly in O'Brien's argument about the land:

It is assumed that land, mines, rivers &c., are fit and proper subjects of private property, like bales of cloth, pottery wares, or any other product of man's skill and industry, and that accordingly, the works of God's creation may be bought and sold in the market, the same as if they were the works of human hands. This is a principle so utterly abhorrent to common sense and reason – it is on the face of it so great a perversion of natural justice, that the rights of property cannot possibly be reconciled with it, nor coexist for a moment in the presence of it. . . and for this simple reason, because the rights of labour and the rights of property, which ought to be really one and the same, are utterly irreconcilable under such a system.[63]

A thought not so dissimilar from that expressed by Thomas Spence over seventy years before:

> All Men, to Land, may lay an equal Claim;
> But Goods, and Gold, unequal Portions frame;
> The first, because, All Men on Land, must Live;
> The Second's the Reward Industry ought to give.[64]

If the land could be socialised, the national debt liquidated, and the bankers' monopoly control over the supply of money abolished, it was because all these forms of property shared the common characteristic of not being the product of labour. It was for this reason that the feature most strongly picked out in the ruling class was its idleness and parasitism. It was for this reason that Hodgskin and those who followed him, excluded from condemnation all those features which distinguished the millocrat from the shopocrat. It is striking that despite the intensity of hostility to the 'steam-producing class' in the Chartist period, no proposal was ever made to take over the mills and expropriate their owners.[65] The most that was proposed was that fixed capital should be purchased by the producers and paid in the form of labour bonds, and even this proposal – by Bray – remained strictly within the terms of the labour theory:

> If a working man pay gold to a capitalist, or one capitalist pay gold to another, he merely gives a representative of the things which labour *has produced* – if he give a bond to pay at a future time, he merely promises to pay what Labour *will produce*. The past, the present and the future transactions of Capital all depend on Labour for their fulfilment. Such being the case, why should not Labour itself make a purchase?[66]

Compulsory purchase or even expropriation was the deserved fate of the rentier, the necessity to labour was to be the just deserts of the idler, henceforth the 'drones' would have to work as hard as the 'bees'; but high wages, short hours, a tax on machinery and renewed access to land enforced by a democratic government was generally the most that was specifically advocated against the tyranny of the millocrat. Before anything further could be conceived, the whole labour theory based on natural right would have to be jettisoned.

We have attempted to demonstrate the interrelatedness of the presuppositions upon which the Charter could appear to be the remedy for the plight of the working classes in particular and the people in general. The hope that the Charter represented, as we have tried to show, was only comprehensible within the language of radicalism. Chartists could incorporate a discussion about competition and the power of 'capitalists', while still maintaining with Paine that the origins and basis of the system rested on the forces of force and fraud. As the *Poor Man's Guardian* stated, there was no objection to 'Paine's principles, only 'to his remedial measures as a practical reformer'.[67] We are also now in a better position to appreciate the strength of the Chartist position in the second half of the 1830s and to understand why the mounting discontent took a Chartist form. For radicalism was premised upon the active and oppressive role of monopoly political power and the State. The aggressive and interventionist activity of government and Parliament in the 1830s in restructuring institutions and forwarding the competitive system at the expense of the working classes therefore strongly vindicated the radical position. The measures for Irish coercion in 1833 could be seen as a dry run for an assault upon the producers in England. The treatment of the handloom weavers – in which radical and conservative proposals of a minimum wage enforced by trade boards was rejected in favour of leaving the workers to the forces of competition – confirmed the worst fears about a government of middlemen.[68] As the *Northern Star* wrote:

> Let the poor handloom weaver bear in mind that the unrestricted use of machinery has thrown him completely out of the market and let those who are yet fortunate enough to be at work recollect that the said handloom weavers at all times serve as a corps of reserve to be cheaply purchased by the masters and hold those at work in submission.

For, speaking of manufacturers, it went on:

> The effect of the Reform Bill has been to throw power into the hands of the possessors of this description of property, and their support of the government is conditional upon the government's support of their claim to the unrestricted use of the labour of the country.[69]

It was for this reason that trade union alternatives to universal suffrage and Owenite schemes of 'regeneration' had foundered. Speaking of 1834, the *Poor Man's Guardian* stated:

> The trade unions made an attempt last year to make a very partial change; and what was the consequence? Why they got transported and dispersed for their pains; and that, not satisfied with crushing them for the moment, the middlemen's government has taken ef- fectual measures to prevent their revival again by passing a law to drive all applicants for parish relief into the workhouse or the grave. . . We have here at a glance the history of the Dorsetshire convicts and of the murderous Poor Law Amendment Bill. They were both the work of the middle classes, through their tool the reformed Parlia- ment.[70]

The completeness of the failure of the trade unions was also clear to John Bray, writing in 1837:

> The capitalist and the employer have ultimately been too strong for them; and the trade unions have become, amongst the enemies of the working class, a bye word of caution or contempt – a record of the weakness of Labour when opposed to Capital – an indestructible memento of the evil working of the present system in regard to the two great classes which now compose society.[71]

The trial of the Glasgow cotton-spinners in 1838 drove home the same lesson. It was pointless to expect effective reform, when political power remained a monopoly of the propertied. The history of the 1833 Factory Act demonstrated that, and as O'Connor added:

> If they were to work six hours a day with their present machinery they would even then have their markets overstocked with goods. It was impossible, therefore, even with a ten hours bill, unless they had the same control over their labour which the agriculturalist had over his produce, namely to send it into the markets when the supply was required. In all other instances, people could do this, and the capitalists knowing such was the case, endeavoured to throw their factory labourers out of their position by breaking down trade combinations.

And the same was *a fortiori* true of the Repeal of the Corn Laws. Even if the common suspicion that it was designed to lower wages, was discounted, the *Northern Star* could still state:

> We must repeat that we do not believe the oligarchy would permit
> even the repeal of the Corn Laws to work well for the community.
> If heaven were to rain down 'manna' – corn, wine and oil – the
> privileged class would still find a way to appropriate the bounty
> to themselves. While the aristocracy hold a monopoly of power,
> be sure they will never give up, unless nominally and collusively,
> any monopoly of profit.[72]

Above all, the sequence of legislation and government activity in the
1830s could convincingly be portrayed as forming a system. A tyranny
was in process of construction, whose aim was to complete the enslavement of the producer. The advance of machinery and the enactment of
the new Poor Law were intimately connected. 'We have repeatedly
avowed our conviction', wrote the *Northern Star,*

> that the spirit and tendency of this law was to enhance and make
> permanent the thraldom of the industrious classes by compelling
> them to give their labour on whatever terms the middle class money-
> mongers might choose to offer. . . Its object and intention is to pro-
> vide the means of at once sweeping from the face of the earth the
> shoals of population, which having been made redundant by a mono-
> poly of the productive powers of machinery on the part of the rich,
> come to be regarded as a pecuniary burden by the villains who have
> robbed them of the means of independence.

And answering the scepticism of southern radical journals about the
vehemence of the Anti-Poor Law campaign in the north, the *Northern
Star* stated that it was not merely opposed to the measure, but saw it
as 'the basis of a new constitution':

> The auxiliaries of this infernal law are the factory scheme, the rural
> police, and the complete destruction of trade associations, which is
> the last remnant of power in the hands of the working classes and by
> which supply and demand could be wholesomely regulated. If the
> masters saw their own interests in a true light, they would encourage
> and not assist in suppressing trade associations.[73]

The great strength of the Charter in 1838-9, therefore, lay in its identification of political power as the source of social oppression, and thus, its ability to concentrate the discontent of the unrepresented working classes upon one common aim. As O'Connor put it, 'the Chartists of the present day, have what the radicals of 1819 had not, unity and a directing energy'.[74] But the great difficulty of radicalism, particularly in its Chartist form, was that the viability of its strategy depended, not merely upon the mobilising of the working classes, but of the vast majority of the people. The petition and the 'General Convention of the Industrious Classes' were not premised upon proletarian politics. They depended for their coherence upon the juxtaposition between the State and its parasitic supporters, landlords, money lords and capitalists on the one hand, and the industrious part of the nation, including a substantial portion of the middle classes on the other. In other words, something like a repeat of 1832. Most of the 'ulterior measures' proposed in 1839 – withdrawal from savings banks, abstention from excisable goods, tax refusal and even 'the sacred month' equally assumed the pressure of the industrious upon the idle. The problem was, however, that even in the radicals' own terms, such a scenario was highly problematic. For not only was there a general radical conviction that the middle class would only join the people when pressured by necessity, but also from 1832 onwards, the middle classes formed part of the legislative classes and had thus become the authors of the miseries of which the working classes complained. While a portion of middle-class opinion was prepared to support the Chartist petition, there was no corresponding support for the Convention as a rival legislative body threatening Parliament. Thus, while many Chartist spokesmen remained sanguine in the first half of 1839 that, despite the withdrawal of the Birmingham leaders, 'as sure as the sun had set today, so surely must the middle classes join the ranks of the people',[75] the mounting evidence of lack of conclusive support from the people for the powers and measures of the Convention, first shook the determination of the working classes in the localities and finally led to an ignominious dissolution of the Convention itself. As Parssinen has observed, the idea of an anti-parliamentary convention was conspicuously absent during the general strike of 1842, and was only half-heartedly believed in even by the delegates themselves in 1848.[76]

With the discrediting of the Convention idea by the events of 1839 however, one important rampart had been removed from the radical defence. It was a commonly cited radical assumption that 'for a nation to be free, it was sufficient that she wills it'. It had also been widely assumed that in countering this will, violence would be initiated by the State, even before the coming together of the nation's representatives. As the *Poor Man's Guardian* had stated in 1834, 'The time will come (and it will come soon) when the usurers will drive you to resist the law, but not before they have first violated it themselves. By a rigid obedience of the law, you will drive them to that course'.[77] A middle class, pressured by material necessity and alienated by State violence, would then join the people in their justified resistance. However the events of 1839 demonstrated that the radical picture of the State – based as it was on the period of the Napoleonic Wars and the Six Acts – was already ceasing to be a reliable guide to action. For the government allowed the Convention to go ahead. It did not arrest the delegates *en bloc* and was confident enough of middle-class opinion to allow the Convention debates to proceed unimpeded. This placed the initiative unwelcomely in the hands of the delegates, producing demoralising divisions over the issues of moral v. physical force. Attempts to provoke violence from the authorities only widened the splits between left and right and frightened off most of what middle-class support there was. The Monmouth rising completed the process of middle-class withdrawal and Chartist disarray, and the prudent decision to commute the sentence on Frost removed the last potential focal point of unity.[78] Thus 1839 destroyed any simple notion of the unity of the people and the malignant predictability of the State.

If 1839 demonstrated the inadequacy of an inherited radical conception of political change, 1842 demonstrated radicalism's inability to gain any advantage from a new type of struggle. The difficulty of a radical strategy pursued – this time, exclusively – by one class in society, was even more strikingly exemplified, and confusion was the result. In one sense, the 1842 strike represented a high point of radical success. In 1839 trade societies had not officially endorsed Chartism, they had played only a passive role in the agitation, and they had not even been consulted about the organisation of the 'sacred month'. By 1842 on the other hand in certain areas, trade societies not only had been convinced of the validity of the Chartist diagnosis, but also were prepared to take the lead in the movement for the Charter.[79] It represented a triumph for the strategy which the *Poor Man's Guardian* had advocated in 1834 and for which Chartists like McDouall and Leach had been pressing in the preceding two years. The declared aims of the strike in much of the Manchester area and many other regions were in strict

accordance with Chartist analysis. As William Muirhouse told the
7 August Mottram Moor meeting, which initiated the turn-outs in
Lancashire, it was 'not a wage question', but 'a national question'. The
enemy was not employers as such, but 'class legislation'. As the Delegate
Conference of Trades in Manchester resolved on 12 August:

> We, the delegates representing the various trades of Manchester and
> its vicinities with delegates from various parts of Lancashire and
> Yorkshire, do most emphatically declare that it is our solemn and
> conscientious conviction that all the evils that afflict society, and
> which have prostrated the energies of the great body of the pro-
> ducing classes, arise solely from class legislation; and that the only
> remedy for the present alarming distress and widespread destitution
> is the immediate and unmutilated adoption and carrying into law,
> the document known as the Peoples' Charter.

Nor was the radical aim of carrying the whole of the people behind the
movement dropped. The Manchester Delegates' Conference of 15 August
declared:

> The meeting proposes appointing delegates to wait upon and confer
> with shopkeepers, dissenting clergymen and the middle classes
> generally for the purpose of ascertaining how far they are prepared
> to assist and support the people in the struggle for the attainment
> of their political rights.[80]

Nor was there any simple division between those who wanted the
Charter and those who wanted 'a fair day's wage for a fair day's work'.
In many areas the attainment of the one had come to be seen as the precondition for the attainment of the other. As the unemployed colliers
of Hanley declared, 'it is the opinion of this meeting that nothing but
the People's Charter can give us the power to have "a fair day's wage
for a fair day's work"'.[81]

But in other respects, the strike hastened the involution of Chartism.
Without preparation or organisation and without the prior mobilisation
of public opinion, it is difficult to conceive how the strike leaders
thought the government might be induced to cave in. Nor, unlike 1839,
was there any question of the government facing an armed people – an
essential component of Benbow's original plan. The Chartist leadership
was mainly taken by surprise and disunited. Well-grounded fears of

government repression and the consequent absence of any proposal for a convention or political organisation capable of focusing the demands of the strike, the inability of the trades delegates to give leadership to the movement after the middle of August, and the effective refusal of the National Charter Association to provide more than a passive endorsement of the demands of the turn-out destroyed whatever slight chances of success the movement might have had.[82] The rationale of the strike was never made clear. Even Richard Pilling, generally recognised to have been one of the principal instigators of the movement, remained equivocal about the relation between the wage question and the Charter. On the one hand, he stated at his trial, 'It is not *me* that is the father of this movement; but that house. Our addresses have been laid before that house, and they have not redressed our grievances; and from there and there alone the cause comes.' But in his conclusion, he stated, 'Whatever it may have been with others it has been a wage question with me. And I do say that if Mr O'Connor has made it a chartist question, he has done wonders to make it extend through England, Ireland and Scotland. But it was always a wage question, and ten hours bill with me'. So confused was the National Charter Association (NCA)'s attitudes to the strike, that its declaration of support could without embarrassment be treated by a prominent Chartist like Harney as an injunction to prevent the extension of the strike. The NCA in its declaration of 16 August pledged itself to disperse to the localities 'to give a proper direction to the people's efforts':

Well, gentlemen, what was my conduct on my return to Sheffield? What was the direction I gave to the people's efforts. Why, I opposed the extension of the strike to that town, and prevented any strike or turnout taking place.[83]

The strike remained confined to operatives; middle-class opinion in those areas where the political aim of the strike was most clear-cut, was generally sharply divided from Chartism by the antagonism which had developed over the issue of the repeal of the Corn Laws. The effort by O'Connor and the bulk of the Chartist leadership to blame the strike upon the Anti-Corn Law League or to claim the strike was simply a wage struggle contradicted the radical premises of the operatives' demands. The year 1842 even more than 1839 dramatised the dissonance between the attempt to pursue a radical strategy and a movement almost exclusively working-class in composition and increasingly debarred from exercising anything other than forceful pressure on middle-class opinion.

How far the strike produced a reorientation of government policy rather than confirming it on a course of action it already intended to pursue, is uncertain.[84] What is certain, however, is that government policy became less and less vulnerable to radical critique as the 1840s wore on, while the coherence of radicalism became increasingly blurred. After the failure of the strike, the continued concentration of energy on the Charter proved impossible to sustain. The depression lifted and the Chartist solution – discredited by the experiment of 1842 – no longer attracted many trade societies, now more confident of exercising bargaining power within the system. Elements of the alternative language of popular political economy, held at bay for most of the decade between 1832 and 1842, crept into popular usage. There was certainly no simple capitulation to the liberal ideology of self-help and the identity of interest between employer and employed, as some historians have claimed.[85] But there was greater acceptance of determination by market forces and increasing usage of the terms, 'labour' and 'capital' without reference to the political system, in which in the radicalism of the 1830s, these terms were inextricably inscribed. For committed Chartists, 1843 'was the year of slumber' and 1844 'scarce gave us breath to fill our sails'.[86] In the factory districts, even Chartist stalwarts found their interest deflected towards the campaign for the ten hours bill. As James Leach put it, 'he would stand second to no man in the advocacy of the Charter', but 'he did not think this a proper time for its introduction'.[87] The near success of the ten hours measure in 1844 and the triumph of 1847 considerably strengthened the impetus towards reformism and single issue campaigns – 'crotchets', as O'Connor had called them – at the end of the 1830s, which deflected the people from the real cause of their miseries. The fact that a factory act could not only pass, but also within a few years be generally recognised as effective[88] proved another blow to the radical conception of the corrupt, unrepresentative and self-interested State.

More immediately serious, however, for the coherence of the radical platform was O'Connor's adoption of the land plan. It not only divided Chartists in their attitudes towards a policy for the land but also represented a far more fundamental breach in the radicalism of the 1830s, since it implied that improvement was possible within the existing political system. As O'Brien remarked:

The strangest thing of all [is] that the philanthropic Feargus should have dragged millions of people after him to torchlight meetings, demonstrations, etc., all attended with great sacrifice of time and money, and caused the actual ruin of thousands through imprisonment, loss of employment and expatriation, when all the while he had only to establish a 'National Chartist Cooperative Land Society' to ensure social happiness for us all, and when, to use his own words. . . he had discerned that 'political equality can only spring from social happiness'. Formerly, he taught us that social happiness was to proceed from political equality.[89]

Moreover, what O'Brien pinpointed as the disintegrative effect of the land plan upon the assumptions of radicalism, was borne out by O'Connor's volte-face on the Corn Laws. Seen from the new perspectives of the land plan, the same disastrous consequences which Chartists had predicted from a repeal at the behest of the moneymongers, were now seen as a benefit. As Gammage put it: 'When the League was in bad odour, nothing but ruin was predicted by O'Connor in case of its success. Now it would make the Land Plan triumphant, by bringing down the price of land and thus enable the people more freely to purchase'.[90] All the old conviction and vehemence of the radical castigation of the state had gone. The interrelatedness of radical premises and the consequentiality of its arguments was now intersected with special cases and qualifying clauses. Commenting on Peel's Repeal of the Corn Laws, the *Northern Star* wrote:

> Now had free trade been proposed in the Whig style – had it been granted as a boon to the increasing power of the League and a sop to the monied interest, unaccompanied with those wise, salutary and statesmanlike adjustments proposed by SIR ROBERT PEEL, not all the power at the disposal of the government could have averted the horrors of a revolution.[91]

There could be no more fitting testimony to Peel's achievement.

Interpretations of Chartism, as was noted at the beginning of this essay, have focussed overwhelmingly upon its working-class character. This emphasis has obscured some crucial dimensions of the character and timing of the movement. Historians in search of evidence of class consciousness are apt to miss the real preconditions of Chartist success and failure. For if Chartism became a movement of workers, it became so not out of choice, but from necessity – a result of its diminishing ability to convince any significant proportion of the middle classes of the feasibility of its position and the attractiveness of its social vision: and finally, of course, it ceased to hold the loyalty of any substantial portion of the working classes themselves. Viewed from this angle – as a form of radicalism and not simply as the movement of a class – Chartism can be situated in two different perspectives, the first long-term and secular, the second short-term and conjunctural.

As a secular phenomenon, Chartism was the last, most prominent, and most desperate – though not perhaps the most revolutionary – version of a radical critique of society, which had enjoyed an almost continuous existence since the 1760s and 1770s. The vision which lay behind this critique was of a more or less egalitarian society, populated exclusively by the industrious and needing minimal government. Political power, as Chartists conceived it, in line with eighteenth-century radicals, was essentially a negative phenomenon, the freedom from present oppression and the legal or legislative prevention of its recurrence. As Harney summarised even the ostensibly most Jacobin variant of this picture:

> The Charter was a means to an end – the means was their political rights, and the end was social equality. Did he mean that they all should have their food dressed alike, their houses built in parallelograms, their coats having one uniform cut? God bless you. No such thing. He only meant that all men should have what they earned, and that the man 'who did not work, neither should he eat' (Cheers).[92]

In such a society reward would be proportional to labour, dependence and clientage would be eliminated, there would be equal access to the land and the restoration of balance between town and country.[93] Corruption, tyranny and the polarity between wealth and poverty within existing society was ascribed to the political depradation of a parasitic class – landlords, tithe-holders, fund-holders, bankers, and in the Chartist version, the aristocracy of wealth, middlemen and factory lords. From first to last, the contrast between the real and the artificial creation of wealth remained a constant feature of radical rhetoric, whatever the changes in the personnel catalogued or given salience under these respective headings. The distinction was not primarily between ruling and exploited classes in an economic sense, but rather between the beneficiaries and the victims of corruption and monopoly political power. The juxtaposition was in the first instance moral and political and dividing lines could be drawn as much within classes as between them. In the eighteenth century, radicals like Wyvill, Price and Cartwright made a strong distinction between those dependent upon patronage and place and those who maintained their independence. Suspicion was directed not only at highly placed pensioners, but also at the dependent poor.[94] At least into the 1870s radical rhetoric of a republican kind referred contemptuously to the inequality of treatment meted out to royal paupers at the top of society and workhouse paupers at the bottom.[95] A similar moral disdain for those who unwittingly or uncritically benefited from the present artificial system characterised the Chartist distrust of the enfranchised middle classes. Hence the admiration for those true 'patriots' who maintained their independence of judgement, irrespective of their economic roles. In this context it is not surprising that John Fielden, one of the largest cotton manufacturers in the north, should have occupied such a revered placed in the radical movement. His political stance was living proof that there was no inherent necessity in the association between employers and Malthusian political economy, the Anti-Corn Law League or the Whiggery of a Brougham, Baines or Macaulay. His defence of the handloom weavers, his unwearying support of the factory movement and his advocacy of universal suffrage exemplified the type of support Chartists expected, but increasingly failed to obtain from the uncorrupted portion of the middle classes. Moreover, his picture of a more balanced relationship between land and industry closely resembled the alternative vision of the economy held by many Chartists. 'There is no natural cause for our distress', wrote Fielden,

> We have fertile land, the finest herds and flocks in the world, and the most skilled herdsmen. We have rivers and ports, and shipping unequalled; and our ingenuity and industry have given us manufactures which ought to complete these blessings. I am a manufacturer; but I am not one of those who think it time we had dispensed with the land. I think that these interests are conducive to the prosperity of the nation, that all must go together and that the ruin of either will leave others comparatively insecure.[96]

There was always a minority of employers like Fielden, gentlemen like Duncombe, or local notables like Frost, even in this last phase of eighteenth-century radicalism, to make its view of the polity and its class system credible. Even during the strike of 1842, there were evidently some employers who sympathised with the Chartist case. In Dundee, for instance, it was recorded:

> Easson (first shop) - 33 men - went to master and asked rise - Mr E. stated he would give none, the trade could not afford it - He considered class legislation at the bottom of all their evils - 18 out of the 33 agreed to come out if the strike be national, the rest not to move.[97]

Conversely it is noteworthy that in the 1842 strikes, those singled out for aggressive attack were those noted for their obnoxious political views. In Manchester it was the Birley mills, the owner of which being held primarily responsible for the Peterloo massacre. In the Potteries riots, as the researches of Robert Fyson shows, it was unpopular magistrates and Poor Law commissioners, not employers who were the objects of violence - in particular the Rector of Longton, a man noted for the excellence of his wine cellar, who had advised the poor to use dock leaves as a substitute for coffee.

Chartism has often been seen as a response to the industrial revolution and the changes in social relations that it engendered. But such an approach presupposes the observation of a social fact whose definition was common to contemporaries and later historians. The social aspects of the process which later historians were to call industrialisation were envisaged by radicals and Chartists in terms quite distinct from those of twentieth-century social and economic historians, terms which reproduced the emphases of eighteenth-century radicalism. Thus, radical and Chartist politics make no sense if they are interpreted as a response to the emergence of an industrial capitalism conceived as an objective, inevitable and irreversible economic process. The radical picture was of a far more arbitrary and artificial development whose source was to be found not in the real workings of the economy, but in the acceleration and accentuation of a process of financial plunder made possible by the political developments of the preceding fifty years. The remote stepping stones in this sequence could be traced back to the Norman Yoke, the loss of suffrage rights in medieval England or the dissolution of the monasteries, all of which had consolidated the monopoly of the landholders.[98] But the more immediate prehistory of the present began with the establishment of the national debt and the growth of new financial practices around the end of the seventeenth century, grew worse with the enclosures of the eighteenth century and culminated in the enormous spoils reaped from speculation during the French wars. According to O'Brien, writing about the French Revolutionary wars:

It was to open to the monied class of England, and the Continent, a new and inexhaustible field of investment for masses of fictitious or fraudulent capital which without such investment [i.e. war] would become a drug in the market and soon be of no more value than the same nominal amount of French assignats, or the Continental money of America in the last stage of depreciation. . .

The extension of trade, manufactures and machinery had engendered fresh swarms of capitalists who must also be enabled to convert their stagnant pools of rotten wealth into perennial streams of sound wealth. In plain English, after appropriating and consuming most of the produce of the then existing generation of labourers they must be enabled to appropriate also the produce of generations unborn to the use of their heirs, assigns and representatives, in all times to come. To accomplish this they lent upwards of £500 millions to our government to carry on the French revolutionary wars – thereby swelling our national debt from £280 millions to upwards of £800 millions, and thus, as it were killing two birds with one stone, that is to say, helping to destroy French Democrats and the Rights of Man on the one hand, and securing for themselves and their posterity the privilege of being everlasting pensioners on the nation on the other hand.[99]

But the infamy of the process did not stop with the French wars. It was compounded during the peace. According to John Fielden:

But when the war terminated, England returned to a gold currency, and restored the dealings of those within this country to an exchange in a metallic currency, subject to a debt contracted in paper; and out of this had arisen all those changes they had seen from that day to this. And we were now on the high road to tyranny at a quicker pace than we ever were before. The long and short of it was that this debt contracted in paper, could never be paid in gold.[100]

It was the French wars which had produced the vast expansion of foreign at the expense of home trade, the growth of machinery at the expense of operatives, the growth of paper speculation at the expense of real industry. The post-war situation had consolidated the position of these jumped-up speculators and gamblers at the expense of all other classes of society. As the *Northern Star* stated:

> Thus as the gambler who sits down at the gambling table with a bank of a million, is sure to gather unto himself at the long run all the small banks at the table, so is the present system sure to sacrifice both labourer, small capitalist and shopkeeper – to those who can command most money and the largest credit until at length the whole commercial speculations of the country will be vested in the hands of the most successful gambler.[101]

It was not least for these reasons that plebeian radicals and after them Chartists lived in hope of making an alliance with those disadvantaged classes to reverse the process.

What was peculiar to the Chartist phase of radicalism, therefore, was neither the abandonment of an inherited radical ambition to construct a broad popular alliance, nor a novel and class-specific way of looking at recent history in terms of what later historians were to describe as industrialisation. In both these areas there existed a strong continuity between Chartism and preceding versions of radicalism. What was specific to Chartism was firstly the equation of the people with the working classes as a result of 1832 and secondly a corresponding shift of emphasis upon the relationship between the state and the working classes, dramatised by the Whig legislation which followed 1832. As a result of this shift, less emphasis was placed upon the State as a nest of self-interest and corruption – 'old corruption' in Cobbett's phrase; instead it increasingly came to be viewed as the tyrannical harbinger of a dictatorship over the producers. As the 1830s progressed, the pre-dominant image was no longer merely of placemen, sinecurists and fund-holders principally interested in revenues derived from taxes on consumption to secure their unearned comforts – but something more sinister and dynamic, a powerful and malevolent machine of repression, at the behest of capitalists and factory lords, essentially and actively dedicated to the lowering of the wages of the working classes through the removal of all residual protection at their command, whether trade societies, legal redress, poor relief or what survived of the representation of the interests of the working classes in local government.[102] As a conjunctural phenomenon, Chartism represented the rapid upsurge and gradual ebbing away of this specific vision of the state.

The full dimensions of the activist and innovative character of the

State in the 1830s has been somewhat obscured in recent years by the form of the debate about 'the nineteenth-century revolution in government'.[103] Discussions of innovations in policy and administration have implied that the phenomenon can be summarised either in terms of the impact of Benthamite doctrines of efficiency and expertise, or as a series of pragmatic responses to new social problems. What is obscured is the importance of the political and ideological context, in which such changes were made. To many contemporaries the reforms which followed 1832 appeared to be of an alarming revolutionary character, and from a radical and Chartist perspective, as we have seen, the ominous political significance of the new policies is hard to underestimate. The new Poor Law, and the assisted migration of southern paupers to northern towns, both of which were considered part of a plot to lower wages by means of centralised non-representative State bodies, the Municipal Corporations Act and the extension of the police system, which effectively excluded the working classes from participation in local government, the refusal of factory legislation, the denial of protection to the handloom weavers and the attack upon trade unions, could all be seen in Fielden's words as a part of 'the highroad to tyranny'; or, as Peter Bussey thought, speaking of the rural police, 'in effect another standing army – to make the people submit to all the insults and oppressions which government contemplates forcing upon them'.[104] The legislative record from Peel's introduction of the Metropolitan Police to the petering out of the Whig reform programme in the late 1830s, did indeed signify the most consequential attempt to dismantle or transform the decentralised treatment of problems of crime, poverty and social order characteristic of the eighteenth-century State.[105] This apparently single-minded effort of the Whig government to create the coercive and administrative framework of a society wholly to be based on free competition proceeded at the expense of all those forces given voice by Chartism, 'Tory Radicalism' and other still strong and diffuse forms of 'country' sentiment surviving from the previous century. The activity of the State could thus be seen as the brutal culmination of the ambitions of artificial wealth and monopoly power, which had been at work ever since 1688. The centralisation of the powers of the State at the expense of local representation combined with the apparent scheme to establish a tyranny over the producers in the context of the structural changes and cyclical difficulties experienced in the economy created a potentially formidable opposition in the localities – both working and middle class, radical and Tory. The premises of radicalism were ideally suited to concentrate and focus this novel activity of the State. This is one reason why social discontent took a Chartist form. Chartism could not simply be said to have begun in 1832; it was the combined effect of 1832 and the gathering reaction to the legislative measures of the Whig government. The tendency of historians of the State to conceive 'the revolution in government' too narrowly as an administrative phenomenon, and of labour and socialist historians to treat Chartism as a social phenomenon has obscured the closeness of interconnection between the two processes. The Chartist sentiment of 1837–9 was in large part a response to 'the revolution in government'.

But the very vehemence of opposition which these policies had provoked, forced a change of course. At the end of the 1830s the State was already beginning to withdraw from this exposed position. A policy of straightforward repression, such as that which had been mounted by Sidmouth, was not repeated by Russell.[106] The apparently blatant 'class legislation' of the early 1830s was now beginning to be nuanced by moves of a less unmediatedly sinister character – towards state-provided education, for instance and the discussion of measures to improve the health of towns.[107] In such circumstances Chartist agitation never had more than an outside chance of success, since the enfranchisement of the middle class in 1832 placed a major obstacle in the way of Chartist/middle-class alliance. There was no necessity for middle-class discontent to take a Chartist form. Some portion of middle-class opinion expressed its dissent from the doctrinaire policy of the Whigs in the 1830s by voting Conservative in the 1841 election. But fear and dislike of government extremism was counter-balanced by anxiety about the threatening and potentially insurrectionary character of Chartist discontent. The electorate therefore voted for a strong government promising to maintain and protect existing institutions. Peel made no political concessions to Chartism, but his avowed aim was to remove the material sources of popular discontent and to avoid identifying the State with any particular fraction or economic interest of the propertied class.[108] He followed the Scottish theologian, Thomas Chalmers, in believing that the competitive system was a theologically sanctioned system, in which the industrious would be rewarded and the profligate punished through the autonomous operation of its laws.[109] In order for such a moralised capitalism to exist, however, the legislature would have to ensure that unnecessary State interference in the operation of the economy was halted, that burdens upon industry and enterprise be removed and that clear lines be drawn between the quick profits from speculation and the real gains of industry. A consistent object of his administration was to reduce taxes on consumption, even if this meant re-introducing the income tax, and in his banking and company legislation, to regularise the operation of credit, whose mal-adjustment he considered responsible for the commercial crises which had periodically afflicted the country since the 'fatal' resort to paper money in 1797.[110] There were therefore significant areas of convergence between the priorities of the Peel government and the issues raised by the Chartist platform, but the intended effects of such reforms was precisely to remove the social disorder and disrespect for established institutions, of which Chartism and the Anti-Corn Law League were thought to be the manifestations.

If Chartist rhetoric was ideally suited to concert the opposition to the Whig measures of the 1830s, by the same token it was ill-equipped to modify its position in response to the changed character of State activity in the 1840s. The Chartist critique of the State and the class oppression it had engendered was a totalising critique. It was not suited to the discrimination between one legislative measure and another, since this would be to concede that not all measures pursued by the State were for obviously malign class purposes and that beneficial reforms might be carried by a selfish legislature in an unreformed system. Peel's reduction of taxes on consumption, continued with crusading zeal by Gladstone in the mid-Victorian period, his care however un-realistic to distinguish between moral and immoral economic activity, the high moral tone of the proceedings of the government and the effective raising of the State above the dictates of particular economic interests – whether landlords, financiers or manufacturers – was high-lighted by the Mines Act of 1842, the 1842 Budget, the Joint Stock Company Act, the Bank Charter Act and above all by the manner of the passing of the Repeal of the Corn Laws. All this proved fatal to the conviction and self-certainty of the language of Chartism, especially in the period after 1842, when some real measure of prosperity returned to the economy. The unrepresentative House of Commons, the aristo-cratic character of the Constitution, the privileged position of the Church and the exclusion of the working classes from the legislature still remained evils about which all radicals could agree. Political power remained as concentrated as it had been before; Bishops, Lords and placemen were scarcely less entrenched.[111] But the tight link forged be-tween the oppression of the working classes and the monopoly of political power exercised through the medium of 'class legislation' – the essence of Chartist rhetoric – began to loosen. The Chartist capitulation on the issue of Repeal and Free Trade wholly undercut the emphasis upon the home market and underconsumption. The labour market and the fate of the producer could no longer be presented simply as politically determined phenomena. Economics and politics were increasingly sundered and the embryonic features of mid-Victorian liberalism began to emerge. Chartism was again to revive in 1847–8, but the staleness and anachronistic flavour of its rhetoric became apparent even to its strongest supporters. That the stabilisation of the economy and the mid-century boom finally killed off all but a few beleaguered Chartist outposts is a fact acknowledged by all historians of Chartism. But as a coherent political language and a believable political vision, Chartism disintegrated in the early 1840s, not the early 1850s. Chartist decline was not initially the result of prosperity and economic stabilisation. For it effectively preceded them. Attention to the language of Chartism suggests that its rise and fall is to be related in the first instance not to movements in the economy, divisions in the movement or an immature class consciousness, but to the changing character and policies of the State – the principal enemy upon whose actions radicals had always found that their credibility depended.

NOTES

This is an abridged version of a larger essay entitled 'Rethinking Chartism' (to appear shortly). I should like especially to thank Sally Alexander, Istvan Hont and Raphael Samuel for the critical help and encouragement they have given me in the development of this essay. I would also like to thank Dorothy Thompson for generously putting at my disposal her own work and knowledge about Chartist history.

   1.   *Hansard*, 3rd series, vol. LXIII, 13–91; cf. O'Connor's observation:
The movement party was known, had become strong and united under the political term radical, when, lo! – and to shew there is much in a name, our political opponents rebaptised us, giving us the name of Chartists. Now although there was no earthly difference between the principles of a Radical and of a Chartist, yet did the press of both parties. . . contrive to alarm the prejudices of the weak, the timid and the unsuspecting, until at length they accomplished their desired object – a split between parties seeking one and the same end.
               (*The Trial of Feargus O'Connor* (1843) p. ix.)
The left wing of the movement tended to describe itself as 'democrat' rather than 'radical', see Bennett's ch. 3 below.
   2.   T. Carlyle, *Chartism* (1839) ch. I.

3. 'MR. DOUBTFUL: But where is the clause for the redistribution of property? Have you forgotten that?

RADICAL: That is a base and slanderous calumny which those who profit by things as they are have forged to damage our cause. There never was the slightest foundation for such a charge, although judges on the benches and parsons in the pulpit have not scrupled to give currency to the falsehood.'

'The Question "What is a Chartist?" Answered' (Finsbury Tract Society, 1839) reprinted in D. Thompson (ed.), *The Early Chartists* (1971) p. 92. Given the Chartist definition of property, however, it is not surprising that the propertied classes should feel threatened.

4. *Hansard*, 3rd series, vol. LXIII, 13–91.

5. F. Engels, 'The Condition of England, the English Constitution', Karl Marx, Frederick Engels, *Collected Works* (1973) vol. 3, p. 513.

6. K. Marx, 'The Class Struggles in France, 1848 to 1850', *Collected Works*, vol. 10, p. 57.

7. F. Engels, 'The Condition of the Working-Class in England', *Collected Works*, vol. 4, p. 523.

8. W. W. Rostow, *The British Economy of the 19th Century* (Oxford, 1948); N. J. Smelser, *Social Change in the Industrial Revolution* (London, 1959).

9. For two analyses which do illuminatingly focus upon the language and politics of radicalism during this period, see T. M. Parssinen, 'Association, Convention and Anti-Parliament in British Radical Politics, 1771–1848', *English Historical Review*, LXXXVII (1973); I. Prothero, 'William Benbow and the Concept of the "General Strike"', *Past & Present*, 63 (1974).

10. Nor is it intended to suggest that what is being offered here is an exhaustive analysis of the language of Chartism. The language analysed here is largely taken from radical literature and speeches reported in the radical press. Quite apart from the fact that such reported speech took no account of accent or dialect, it is not suggested that this is the only language Chartists employed. What is examined here is only the public political language of the movement. Much further research would be required before a full account of the language of Chartism could be produced.

11. E. Dolléans, *Le Chartisme, 1831–1848* (rev. edn, Paris, 1949) p. 319 and ch. 1.

12. R. G. Gammage, *The History of the Chartist Movement* (London, 1855); W. Lovett, *Life and Struggles of William Lovett, in his pursuit of Bread, Knowledge and Freedom* (London, 1876), T. Cooper, *Life of Thomas Cooper, Written by Himself* (London, 1872).

13. See in particular M. Hovell, *The Chartist Movement* (Manchester, 1918).

14. See for instance A. Briggs, 'The Local Background of Chartism', in Briggs (ed.), *Chartist Studies* (London, 1959).

15. See Behagg's ch. 2 below; see also T. Tholfson, 'The Chartist Crisis in Birmingham', *International Review of Social History*, vol. III (1958).

16. See I. Prothero, 'Chartism in London', *Past & Present*, 44 (1969); D. Goodway, 'Chartism in London', *Bulletin for the Society for the Study of Labour History*, 20 (1970).

17. On the north-east, see W. H. Maehl, 'Chartist Disturbances in Northeastern England, 1839', *International Review of Social History*, VIII (1963); on south

Lancashire, see Sykes's ch. 5 below; see also J. Foster, *Class Struggle and the Industrial Revolution. Early Industrial Capitalism in three English Towns* (London, 1974); P. Joyce, *Work, Society and Politics* (Brighton, 1980).

18.   D. Thompson, 'The Geography of Chartism' (unpublished MS); see also her remarks on this in the Introduction to Thompson (ed.), *The Early Chartists*.

19.   Hovell, *The Chartist Movement* (1970 edn) p. 7; ibid. p. 303.

20.   G. D. H. Cole, *A Short History of the British Working Class Movement, 1789–1947* (London, 1948), p. 94; ibid., p. 120.

21.   Briggs, *Chartist Studies*, p. 26.

22.   Gammage, *History of the Chartist Movement* (facsimile reprint of 1894 edn., London, 1976) p. 9.

23.   E. P. Thompson, *The Making of the English Working Class* (London, 1963) p. 826.

24.   Ibid., p. 807.

25.   For sources on country party ideology in the eighteenth century and its connections with radicalism, see the following: C. Hill, 'James Harrington and the People', in *Puritanism and Revolution* (London, 1958); P. Zagorin, *The Court and the Country. The Beginning of the English Revolution* (London, 1969); D. Rubini, *Court and Country 1688–1702* (London, 1967); C. Robbins, *The Eighteenth-Century Commonwealthman* (New York, 1968); I. Kramnick, *Bolingbroke and his Circle: The Politics of Nostalgia in the Age of Walpole* (Cambridge, Mass., 1968); J. G. A. Pocock, *The Machiavellian Moment* (Princeton, 1975); Pocock, 'Virtue and Commerce in the 18th Century' *Journal of Interdisciplinary History*, 3 (1972); M. Peters, 'The "Monitor" on the Constitution, 1755–1765: new light on the ideological origins of English Radicalism', *English Historical Review*, LXXXVI (1971); J. Brewer, *Party Ideology and Popular Politics at the Accession of George III* (Cambridge, 1976); Brewer, 'English Radicalism in the age of George III' in Pocock (ed.), *Three British Revolutions* (Princeton, 1980); Kramnick, 'Religion and Radicalism. English Political Theory in the Age of Revolution', *Political Theory*, 5 (1977); C. H. Hay, 'The Making of a Radical: The Case of James Burgh', *Journal of British Studies*, 18 (1979); M. Canovan, 'Two Concepts of Liberty – Eighteenth Century Style', *Price-Priestley Newsletter*, 2 (1978); I. Hampshire-Monk, 'Civic Humanism and Parliamentary Reform: the Case of the Society of the Friends of the People', *Journal of British Studies*, 18 (1979); J. M. Murrin, 'The Great Inversion, or Court versus Country: A Comparison of the Revolution Settlements in England (1688–1721) and America (1776–1813)' in Pocock (ed.), *Three British Revolutions;* D. O. Thomas, 'Richard Price and the Tradition of Civic Humanism' (unpublished paper given to the 'Political Economy and Society', Seminar, Research Centre, King's College, Cambridge, 1980).

26.   *Northern Star (NS)*, 4 August 1838.

27.   *Poor Man's Guardian (PMG)* 17 August 1833.

28.   Malthus's *Essay on the Principle of Population* was originally written as a polemic against radical egalitarianism, in the first instance, William Godwin's *Enquiry Concerning Political Justice*. The directness and pointedness of Malthus's attack was strongly reinforced by his intimacy with the radical Dissenting and 'country' tradition, from which Godwin's work in large part sprang. It was a tradition in which he himself had been brought up, and the Essay of 1798 represented the moment at which he decisively rejected it. The bitter hostility of

radicals against Malthus and the isolated position of those like Francis Place who attempted to combine Malthusianism and radicalism, is scarcely surprising. On this, see B. Fontana, I. Hont and M. Ignatieff, 'The Politics of Malthus' First Essay and the Scottish Tradition' (paper given to the Malthus Colloque, Paris, May 1980). The incorporation of Malthusian propositions into the emerging discipline of political economy, at least by some of its best-known practitioners, also explains, more than any other single factor, the anathema in which political economy was held by the great majority of the radical movement. By the late 1830s those who combined radicalism and Malthus were generally referred to as 'sham radicals'. Adam Smith was not included in this hostility. For the use of Smith to buttress Chartist arguments, see the remarks of Peter Bussey, *NS* 16 February 1839 and William Lovett, *NS* 31 March 1838.

29. For an analysis of the defining features of a 'socialist' position in the period up to 1848, see G. Stedman Jones, 'Utopian Socialism Reconsidered', *History Workshop Journal* (forthcoming).

30. See for example H. J. Perkin, *The Origins of Modern English Society, 1780–1880* (London, 1969), N. J. Smelser, *Social Change in the Industrial Revolution* (London, 1959); Tholfson, *Working Class Radicalism in Mid-Victorian England* (London, 1976); Foster, *Class Struggle.*

31. *London Mercury* 4 March 1837, reprinted in D. Thompson (ed.), *The Early Chartists*, p. 58.

32. *NS* 13 October 1838; 20 April 1839; 6 October 1838.

33. *Cobbett's Weekly Political Register,* 2 (November 1816), pp. 545–6; see also on this, E. Thompson, *Making of the English Working Class*, p. 772; Prothero, 'Benbow', 158.

34. *NS* 19 June 1839.

35. Cited in A. Plummer, *Bronterre, A Political Biography of Bronterre O'Brien* (London, 1971) pp. 177–8.

36. See for instance O'Connor's speech in Glasgow, *NS* 28 July 1838.

37. *NS* 22 June 1839; 15 September 1838.

38. For reasons of space, it has been necessary to drop the section developing the arguments stated in the following paragraph. The full version of this essay will be published in a collection of essays of mine dealing with problems of radicalism, class consciousness and culture in nineteenth-century England, to appear shortly.

39. *PMG* 3 August 1833; cf. Hodgskin's remark, 'The contest now appears to be between masters and journeymen, or between one species of labour and another, but it will soon be displayed in its proper characters; and will stand confessed a war of honest industry against idle profligacy which has so long ruled the affairs of the political world with undisputed authority...' *Labour Defended*, pp. 103–4.

40. *PMG* 22 February 1834; 25 July 1834.

41. See for example Prothero, 'Benbow', 166–71.

42. *PMG* 30 August 1834; 22 February 1834; 26 April 1834; ibid.

43. *PMG* 14 February 1835; 6 April 1833.

44. *PMG* 23 March 1833; 1 March 1834; 24 August 1833.

45. From Cobbett's *Register* cited in *PMG* 29 October 1831.

46. *PMG* 25 October 1834; 11 July 1835; 30 May 1835.

47. *NS* 30 March 1839; 29 December 1838, 8 June 1839; 30 March 1839; 22 August 1840; 22 September 1838.

48. Chartists were only to back Conservative candidates, however, in the last resort, in the absence of any candidate supporting the extension of the suffrage.

49. See Belchem's ch. 8 below.

50. *NS* 16 March 1839; for the range of policies suggested to regulate the advance of machinery, see M. Berg, *The Machinery Question and the Making of Political Economy 1815–1848* (Cambridge, 1980) esp. pt 5.

51. *NS* 23 March 1839.

52. When the interconnections are traced between radicalism and eighteenth-century country ideology, points of affinity between Tories like Oastler and leading radicals, become easier to understand.

53. *NS* 16 March 1839.

54. See V. A. C. Gattrell, 'The Commercial Middle Classes in Manchester 1820–57' (Univ. of Cambridge Ph. D. thesis, 1972).

55. *NS* 9 February 1839; 27 April 1839; 20 April 1839.

56. J. Gray, *A Lecture on Human Happiness* (London, 1825) p. 35.

57. J. F. Bray, *Labour's Wrongs and Labour's Remedies: or the Age of Might and the Age of Right* (Leeds, 1839) p. 34.

58. *NS* 8 June 1839; 16 June 1838.

59. On Spence and his doctrine see T. R. Knox, 'Thomas Spence: the Trumpet of Jubilee', *Past & Present*, 76 (1977).

60. Cited in D. Jones, *Chartism and the Chartists* (London, 1975) p. 130.

61. (G. J. Harney), 'The Charter and Something More', *Democratic Review* (February 1850) 351.

62. In A. R. Schoyen, *The Chartist Challenge* (1958) p. 117.

63. J. B. O'Brien, *The Rise, Progress and Phases of Human Slavery* (London, 1885) pp. 127–8.

64. Cited in Knox, 'Thomas Spence', 87.

65. For a characterisation of the conflict within modern industry during this period, see Stedman Jones, 'England's First Proletariat', *New Left Review*, 90 (1975).

66. Bray, *Labour's Wrongs*, p. 173.

67. *PMG* 14 February 1835.

68. See P. Richards, 'The State and early Capitalism: the Case of the Hand-loom Weavers', *Past & Present*, 83 (1979).

69. *NS* 23 June 1838.

70. *PMG* 21 March 1835.

71. Bray, *Labour's Wrongs*, p. 100.

72. *NS* 23 June 1838; 9 February 1839.

73. *NS* 3 March 1838; 23 June 1838.

74. *NS* 3 August 1839.

75. Speech of R. J. Richardson, *NS* 27 April 1839.

76. Parssinen, 'British Radical Politics', 530–1.

77. *PMG* 12 April 1834.

78. The importance of the commutation of Frost's sentence is emphasised in D. Thompson (ed.), *The Early Chartists*, pp. 21–2. The commutation was not the result of Whig government policy, however, but occurred because of the strong insistence of the Lord Chief Justice.

79. See Sykes's ch. 5 below.

80. Cited in M. Jenkins, *The General Strike of 1842* (London, 1980) p. 68; p. 264; p. 266.

81. *NS* 20 August 1842.

82. Many aspects of the thinking behind the 1842 strike movement remain mysterious. For accounts of the strike, see A. G. Rose, 'The Plug Riots of 1842 in Lancashire and Cheshire', *Transactions of the Lancashire and Cheshire Antiquarian Society*, LXVII (1958); F. C. Mather, 'The General Strike of 1842; A Study in Leadership, Organisation and the Threat of Revolution during the Plug Plot Disturbances' in J. Stephenson and R. Quinault, *Popular Protest and Public Order* (London, 1974); Jenkins, *General Strike of 1842*.

83. *The Trial of Fergus O'Connor*, p. 249; pp. 254-5; p. 235.

84. The suggestion that the strike did cause a re-orientation in government policy is put forward by John Foster in Jenkins, *General Strike of 1842*, pp. 3-4. While a good case has been made out for the change of government tactics during the trial which followed the strike, (see Jenkins, ch. 10) the larger claim remains doubtful. It is argued below that the State had already begun to retreat from the ideologically exposed position of the 1830s before the strike began, see also G. Kitson Clark, 'Hunger and Politics in 1842', *Journal of Modern History* (1953).

85. See for instance Perkin, *Modern English Society;* B. Harrison and P. Hollis, 'Chartism, Liberalism and the Life of Robert Lowery', *English Historical Review,* LXXXII (1967).

86. Cited in J. T. Ward, *Chartism* (London, 1973) p. 176.

87. Ibid., p. 175; for Leach's thinking on the factory question, see James Leach, *Stubborn Facts from the Factories by a Manchester Operative* (London, 1844).

88. See Joyce, *Work, Society and Politics*, pp. 69-70.

89. *National Reformer* 15 and 22 May 1847, cited in Gammage, *History of the Chartist Movement*, p. 269.

90. Ibid., p. 270.

91. *NS* 17 January 1846

92. *NS* 15 June 1839.

93. For the way in which the predominantly urban 'middling sort' of the 1760s and 1770s adapted country ideology to their own purposes, see Brewer, 'English Radicalism'.

94. See Prothero, *Artisans and Politics in Early Nineteenth-Century London* (Folkestone, 1979) pp. 26-7.

95. On mid-Victorian republicanism, see R. Harrison, *Before the Socialists* (London, 1965) ch. V.

96. J. Fielden, *The Curse of the Factory System* (London, 1836) p. iii.

97. *Dundee Warder* August 1842, cited in C. Bebb, 'The Chartist Movement in Dundee' (Univ. of St. Andrews B. Phil. thesis, 1977).

98. On the changing character of the argument about the Norman Yoke from the seventeenth to the nineteenth century, see C. Hill, 'The Norman Yoke', *Puritanism and Revolution* (London, 1958).

99. J. B. O'Brien, *The Life and Character of Maximilian Robespierre proving by facts and arguments that that much calumniated person was one of the greatest men and one of the purest and most enlightened reformers that ever existed in the world* (London, 1838) vol. 1, pp. 254-5.

100. *NS* 9 June 1838.

101. *NS* 12 May 1838.

102. The tension was exacerbated by the extent to which employers took over the magistracy in industrial regions in the 1830s; see D. Philips, 'The Black Country Magistracy 1835–60: a changing local élite and the exercise of its power', *Midland History* (1976).

103. The debate is summarised in A. J. Taylor, *Laissez-faire and State Intervention in Nineteenth Century Britain* (Economic History Society, 1972); for a critique and suggested reinterpretation, see P. Richards, 'State Formation and Class Struggle, 1832–48', in P. Corrigan (ed.), *Capitalism, State Formation and Marxist Theory* (London, 1980).

104. *NS* 9 March 1839.

105. On the role and function of law in the eighteenth-century State, see Hay, 'Property, Authority and the Criminal Law' in D. Hay, P. Lineburgh, J. Rule, E. P. Thompson and C. Winslow, *Albion's Fatal Tree* (London, 1975); Thompson, *Whigs and Hunters* (London, 1975).

106. See F. C. Mather, *Public Order in the Age of the Chartists* (Manchester, 1959).

107. See in connection with this, the shift in statistical societies from preoccupation with wages and employment to that of housing, health and education, Eileen Yeo, 'Social Science and Social Change: A Social History of some aspects of Social Science and Social Investigation in Britain, 1830–1890' (Sussex University, unpublished Ph. D. thesis, 1972) ch. 3; see also on education P. Hollis, *The Pauper Press, a study in working-class radicalism of the 1830s* (OUP, 1970), chs 1, 111; R. Johnson 'Educational Policy and Social Control in early Victorian England', *Past & Present*, 49 (1970).

108. See N. Gash, 'Peel and the Party System', *Transactions of the Royal Historical Society* (1951); N. Gash, *Reaction and Reconstruction in English Politics 1832–1852* (Oxford, 1964) ch. V.

109. See B. Hilton, *Corn, Cash, Commerce* (Oxford, 1977), pp. 308–13; B. Hilton, 'Peel: a Reappraisal', *Historical Journal* (1979).

110. See Peel's speech introducing the Bank Charter Act, 6 May 1844, *Speeches of the late Rt. Hon. Sir Robert Peel delivered in the House of Commons*, 4 vols (London, 1853) vol. IV, p. 349 *et seq*.

111. For the changed character of radicalism in the post-Chartist period, see F. Gillespie, *Labour and Politics in England 1850–1867* (Durham, N. C., 1927); F. M. Leventhal, *Respectable Radical, the Life of George Howell* (London, 1971) Harrison, *Before the Socialists*.

2. An Alliance with the Middle Class: the Birmingham Political Union and Early Chartism

CLIVE BEHAGG

THE question of the feasibility and the desirability of an alliance between working-class and middle-class radicals was one which permeated Chartist debate. The locality where such an alliance seemed most likely to succeed was Birmingham. The Birmingham Political Union (BPU) under the leadership of the banker Thomas Attwood had played a leading role in the agitation surrounding the passing of the Reform Bill in 1832. Within the BPU working-class and middle-class radicals had worked closely throughout the campaign. Historians have chosen to see this closeness, within the radical movement, as a reflection of the town's economic structure. Professor Briggs has maintained that Birmingham's multiplicity of small workshops, producing mostly small metalware, was conducive to a closeness between masters and men not to be found in towns where the factory dominated production.[1] This analysis of the economic structure sits easily alongside the conventional picture of Birmingham's role in the Chartist Movement over which there has been broad agreement amongst historians for the last century or so. Chartism, it has been argued, grew directly from the revival of the BPU in 1837. This time, however, its middle-class leadership was frightened off by the violent rhetoric of the national leadership, notably in the form of Stephens and O'Connor. There followed a brief, and for Birmingham rather uncharacteristic, period of class conflict culminating in the Bull

Ring riots of July 1839. Nevertheless, the analysis concludes, such conflict subsided allowing O'Neill's Chartist Church and Joseph Sturge's initiative within the Complete Suffrage Union of 1842, to restate in organisational form the essential unity of interests between masters and men within the town.[2]

Despite its long and distinguished pedigree this construction has little to recommend it. The standard analysis of the town as a centre of class harmony tells us much about its traditional workship norms and especially of the closely structured relationship within the artisan class between the skilled workman and the small master. But the remarkable feature of the BPU in both its phases (1829–34 and 1837–9) was the leading part played by a group of large-scale industrialists, merchants and bankers in its activities. No amount of concentration on the workshop sector of the economy can explain their participation. At the same time the predicament of Birmingham's middle-class radicals, who were present at the birth of Chartism and who subsequently denied paternity, deserves to be placed in a far broader context than that provided by the suggestion that the period was but a temporary lull in the town's endemic class harmony. The inability of the middle-class elements of the Political Union to remain within Chartism after March 1839, and the strength of their subsequent reaction against the Chartists themselves, highlights a number of general problems created by the participation of an urban middle class in a radical working-class movement. Throughout the Chartist period the urban middle class generally, with 1832 very much in mind, acknowledged the utility of a mass base for achieving those ends that remained unsatisfied by the Reform Act. The Chartists for their part, whilst committed to the mass platform, were fully aware of the weight that might be added to their case by the whole-hearted lobby of men of property. For a brief period a section of middle-class and working-class agitators came together in one organisation and a single radical programme embraced by the BPU. This chapter seeks to explore, through an examination of the break-up of the alliance that the BPU represented, the different ideological perspectives the classes brought to bear within the political programme of early Chartism.

Above all, the acrimonious breakdown of the alliance emphasised the impoverishment of the middle-class concept of a unity of interests within production in the face of structural economic change and the emergence of ideologies of conflict. The concept of a unity of interests between masters and men was by no means confined to Birmingham.

Rather, it was a basic tenet that underpinned individualism and ultimately removed from the shoulders of the manufacturer the responsibility for the worst excesses of political economy. In Birmingham Attwood developed this theme through his currency theories, constructing in the process a social philosophy which attempted to harness the inherent conflicts of capitalist production and redirect them to reinforce manufacturing interests. However, by the late 1830s the town's middle-class radicals found themselves in an uncomfortable duality of roles. On the one hand they espoused the unity of class interests in the work-place via the concept of the 'productive classes', as a separate interest group including both masters and men. On the other hand they fulfilled the role of employers at a time of reduced wages and structural economic change. At the same time middle-class leadership of any mass-based radical movement necessarily depended upon presenting itself as part of an excluded class in political terms. This, after all, had been the basis of its credibility in 1832. After the Reform Bill the case for the *de facto* separation of middle-class manufacturing interests from the intrinsic nature of the State was obviously a more difficult one to make. In Birmingham the claim of the middle-class radicals, that they were still effectively excluded from the process of political decision-making, was at odds with their success when the town's first municipal election was held in December 1838. The granting of a Charter of Incorporation had in fact transposed a number of the middle-class radicals from anti-establishment to establishment figures. In the one role they invoked the right of physical resistance to unconstitutional government, in the other they became responsible, locally, for suppressing any such resistance. In this way the Municipal Corporations Act of 1835 went some considerable distance towards completing the process of the assimilation of middle-class energies that had been embodied in the Reform Act itself.[3]

The stress in the past upon the class harmony of the BPU and the picture of its destruction by outside forces particularly in the form of Feargus O'Connor and his supposed brand of physical-force Chartism, has served to mask some of the more important lessons to be learned from its breakup. The BPU was an alliance of very different social groups with their own political perspectives and aspirations relating not only to the nature of the radical movement but also to the democratic form that might result from its endeavours. These groups were held together by a number of factors not explicable simply by an analysis of the social relations of production which were in fact, by the late 1830s,

operating as a force for disunity. The crucial and ultimately irreconcilable differences of political perspective between middle-class and
working-class radicals only became apparent because the programme of
early Chartism developed within the context of structural economic
change and the reform of local government.

The BPU's middle-class leadership often claimed to have actually
created any sense of political awareness that might have been evinced
by the working class in Birmingham in the 1830s. However, by the time
of the founding of the Union in 1830 the working-class element within
the town's radical movement had already undergone various formative
stages.[4] Many of the artisans who became active in the BPU were
veteran reformers of the post-war period when there had been little
support from the town's upper-middle class. Radical organisation had
centred on a local Hampden Club in 1816–17, under the chairmanship
of George Edmonds, a button-burnisher turned schoolmaster. The Club
began a tradition of open-air meetings and radical publications attacking
Old Corruption and calling for economic retrenchment and representative government via universal suffrage. In 1819 mass meetings were
resumed, the most celebrated being the attempt in July to elect Sir
Charles Wolesley as an unofficial Parliamentary representative or 'Legislatorial Attorney' for the town.[5] In the following month the Union
Society was formed from a corpus of Hampden Club members.

As was the case in most artisan centres after the war this movement
was crucial in terms of politicising grievances. Inevitably it trod a
delicate path between constitutionalism and conspiracy. Hampden Club
members were involved in disturbances directed against a local Tory in
November 1816, which resulted in the town being placed under military
control for two days.[6] Charles Whitworth, later to be Chairman of the
Union Society, was involved in the plans of Oliver the Spy in 1817.
There is some evidence to suggest that the Union Society began to arm
in 1819, following Peterloo.

A full analysis of the post-war campaign must fall outside the scope
of this chapter, but two points must be stressed. Firstly that by the
1820s artisan radicalism had evolved a political programme centred on
universal suffrage. Secondly this period of agitation took place without
the support of that sector of the upper-middle class which was to be so
active later in the BPU. This had the effect of rendering the movement
vulnerable to attack from local Tories, organised in 1819 as the Loyal
Association for the Suppression and Refutation of Blasphemy and
Sedition.[7] Acting in concert with Liverpool's government the Associ-

ation was involved in the prosecution of leading radicals. By 1821 eleven of the local leaders were in prison for seditious offences.

The vulnerability of a radical movement without 'respectable' support had been the great lesson of the post-war agitation as far as Birmingham's artisans were concerned. Hence there was a willingness, during the Reform Bill agitation, for the working-class leadership to subsume its wider programme and identity within a reform movement of a broader complexion. Bronterre O'Brien, editor of the *Midland Representative*, announced that the working class were 'willing to receive [the Bill] as an installment, or part payment of the debt right due to us'.[8] After all, piecemeal reform was yet to be discredited. Attwood for his part, though he was consistent in his condemnation of universal suffrage shrewdly kept the dialogue on further reform open at BPU meetings. Nevertheless the absence of the BPU's middle-class radicals from earlier campaigns had to be accounted for. George Edmonds introduced Attwood to one of the Union's first open-air meetings in the following way:

> Gentlemen I beg to assure you that Mr. Attwood has long been the sincere friend of reform, and that although ten or a dozen years ago he did not think it the right time to push the question of Parliamentary reform, yet in his heart he has always been a reformer.[9]

In the wake of the Reform Bill campaign working-class energies were contained within three distinct organisations, the Committee of the Non Electors, the United Trades, and the Committee of the Unemployed Artisans. These were under the respective chairmanships of James Larkin, Henry Watson and Thomas Baker, all of whom had been active members of the Union Society.[10]

As the full impact of the failure of the Reform Bill campaign to achieve a comprehensive measure of reform became apparent the working class fell back on the programme of the earlier period of radicalism. A meeting of the Unemployed Artisans in September 1832 declared for Universal Suffrage, the ballot, annual Parliaments and the abolition of the property qualification for MPs. This was part of a broad programme which also called for repeal of the Corn Laws and a restriction of the size of the army.[11] This programme was endorsed fully in November at a meeting to form a Midland Union of the Working Class (MUWC). This was designed to be a branch of the National Union of the Working Classes and the meeting was addressed by Hunt,

Hetherington and Cleave. It also aimed to unite the three working-class organisations in the town, all of whom took part. In moving the adoption of universal suffrage Baker stated:

> It must be remembered that the working classes only consented to receive the Bill as part of their rights and as a step to further and more efficient reforms, which should not leave out any classes but embrace the whole population.[12]

The significance of the establishment of the MUWC at this point has often been underestimated.[13] This is understandable since it was short-lived and the 5000 or so that attended its founding meeting compares unfavourably with the BPU's monster demonstrations. Nevertheless its establishment followed the rejection by the BPU's leadership in July 1832 of a petition from members of the Union for the adoption of universal suffrage as part of its programme. The MUWC is a reminder of potential areas of tension within the BPU and an indication that the town's working class entered the 1830s with both a leadership and a programme.

The new union existed alongside the BPU and its organisers were at pains to point out that there was no intention to supplant it. Nevertheless its formation is indicative of the aspirations of some working-class radicals to a share of the leadership so scrupulously denied them within the BPU. Attwood, who was more sensitive than most to the delicacy of the alliance of classes within the BPU even at this stage, chose to see the development as a breach of faith. 'If the working classes cannot trust the middle classes', he asked, 'how could the middle classes trust them?'[14] Most of the wrath of the BPU's Political Council was directed at the Revd Arthur Wade, the clergyman from Warwick who had chaired the meeting to form the MUWC. Wade, himself a member of the BPU's Political Council, insisted that a separate working-class union was essential, 'because the leaders in the Unions, being men of property, living upon the rental of land, the interest of money, or the profit of trade, have separate and distinct interests from the working man. . .'[15]

It would have been foolish in the extreme for working-class radicals to challenge at this point the leadership of the popular movement, within the town, by Attwood's group. The middle-class leadership of the BPU had come through the campaign with their credibility intact. They had led the Union into open defiance of the government. The possibility of revolution, however it might look to historians a century and a half later, had seemed real enough in Birmingham in May 1832. Whatever his personal reservations might have been there was little doubt in the popular mind that Attwood would have led it. Hence working-class admiration for Attwood, for his stand in 1832, was genuine and, whatever his future transgressions might be, the working-class movement was always eager to draw him into any reform agitation.[16]

There are indications that in the wake of the Reform Act Attwood's popularity was increasing. By September 1833 membership of the BPU stood at 20,000.[17] This was partly because Attwood made public his disappointment with the Bill and remained active in radical politics. The BPU called a mass meeting in May 1833 to object to the 'Polandisation' of Ireland through the Coercion Bill. Attwood's declaration to this meeting: 'My friends, I have been grievously deceived. . .', accurately reflected popular feeling on the effects of the Reform Act.[18] Lord George Hervey, who attended the meeting found the rather more explicit sentiment, 'Damn Earl Grey's bloody head off', chalked on the walls of the town.[19]

At this stage fundamental differences, in terms of political programmes, existed between middle- and working-class radicals in the town. Crucially most of the Attwood group remained vociferous opponents of universal suffrage. But such areas of potential tension were offset, for the moment, by the total impression given by the standpoint of the middle-class radicals. Over the next few years Attwood's reports to public meetings served to confirm exactly the image of Old Corruption that the post-war reformers had drawn. For example he told a meeting in 1834 that: 'It [the Reform Act] has given us a House of Commons but little better, I am sorry to acknowledge, than the old concern . . . the House of Commons is not what it ought to be; one half consists of Lawyers, Jews of Change Alley and monks of Oxford – the other half consists of country gentlemen.'[20]

Two further factors which helped to unify the BPU in the early 1830s should be examined. Firstly many of the viewpoints of the Attwood group were defined against those of other influential middle-class groups in the locality. This inevitably increased their credibility to a working-class audience, particularly where they related to important areas like local government reform or attitudes to poverty. Secondly through a variety of ideological refinements in which his currency theories figured strongly, Attwood was able to steer his political views so close to the democratic ideal of the early radical movement that it was not until the severe testing of the Chartist period that their crucial dissimilarities became fully apparent.

There was always a reciprocal dynamism between the role of the BPU's middle-class element within the wider reform movement and its activities as an oppositional group in the locality. Hovell's suggestion that the Attwood group were interested only in currency reform whilst the working class were interested only in the vote is too simplistic to stand close scrutiny.[21] By shifting the question of currency reform to one of political reform in the late 1820s, Attwood was attempting to take over the form of the post-war radical movement in the town, whilst rejecting a large part of its content. This alienated him from substantial sectors of Birmingham's middle class who remained outside the BPU. Though sympathetic generally to the representation of the urban interest in Parliament, they drew back from a popular campaign. Throughout the early 1830s the BPU attacked the oligarchal control, by Whig and Tory groups, of the organs of local government. These were always represented as local manifestations of the innate corruptness of the system of parliamentary representation. Alongside this, a vigorous campaign against church rates gave ample opportunity to restate the 'no taxation without representation' principle. After 1835 these energies were channelled into the agitation for a Charter of Incorporation. Such charters, predicted Attwood, by giving towns locally elected councils, 'would establish real and legal Political Unions in every borough which would succeed the necessity of such formidable political bodies as he had the honour to be head of.'[22]

The move locally for a Charter of Incorporation after 1835 should be seen as part of what Derek Fraser has called the 'struggle for supremacy within the urban middle class itself'.[23] In Birmingham it took the form of an attempt to break through the dominance of local administrative bodies by family-oriented factions and to move towards cheap, efficient local government that answered the needs of the ratepayers. Above all, for Birmingham, it was an attempt, by an assertive urban middle class, to sever the County nexus. A constant theme for example, throughout the move for incorporation, was the need to 'purify the magistracy'.[24] The campaign ran in the town from late 1837 to December 1838 when the first municipal elections were held. These resulted in a victory for the radicals in an alliance with certain Whig groups. Of the thirty-four members of the BPU Political Council in 1837, fourteen were elected to the first Town Council. Many of these were to become aldermen whilst one, William Scholefield, became first mayor of the borough. Other radicals, like George Edmonds, and R. K. Douglas (editor of the *Birmingham Journal*), received posts within the new Corporation.

But perhaps the central unifying feature of the BPU, at least in the early 1830s, was the social philosophy derived from Attwood's economic thought. His belief, that through the medium of a flexible paper currency industrial production could increase to meet potential demand to the full, removed the responsibility for economic ills from the shoulders of the manufacturer and placed it squarely with the government. Attwood frequently stated his opinion that: 'The doctrine of over-production and over-population was preposterous'.[25] Thus it was not the over-production of manufactured goods that lay at the heart of the periodic economic recessions but rather a continuing crisis of under-consumption caused by an inflexible money supply. This was a comforting philosophy for an expanding urban middle class. It also had an obvious appeal for a working class for whom the fact of under-consumption seemed all too apparent. But whatever the working-class element of the BPU felt about the relative merits of a paper or a metal currency the presence of such a rigorous economic analysis of trade depressions provided, in the early 1830s at least, a force for unity with radical middle-class elements.[26]

This can be seen particularly with regard to the attitudes to the problem of poverty in this period. Since the currency theories represented a formula for prosperity the most pressing recommendation for their application lay in a recognition of the existence of poverty. At the same time they proposed economic first causes and so implicitly rejected a moral analysis of poverty. The BPU radicals were very ready to acknowledge the extent of poverty, as this simply reflected their own condition of reduced profits. Both nationally and within the locality this represented a heterodox middle-class stance which became a vital tie with the working-class leadership during the 1830s. In 1832 the Unemployed Artisans had taken to parading the streets every Monday behind a band of music in order to convince the broader middle class who appeared to doubt the existence of the problem. As Baker explained to the September meeting:

It was no novel thing to be treated in this sort of way. The middle and higher classes had long been trying to persuade them, the working classes, that their bellies were full when they were alarmingly and feelingly convinced that they were empty. Or if they allowed that distress did exist they were always very ready to attribute it to idleness and profligacy. It had long been the custom of those who were fattening on the products of their labour and absolutely wallowing in wealth, not a particle of which they created, to turn round upon the workman who was in want and tell him it was because he was drunken, vicious and immoral; forgetting their own vice and immorality in procuring luxuries at the workman's expense and leaving him without necessaries.[27]

The shared attitudes towards poverty, between working class and middle class within the BPU, was of great importance since, as will be shown later, the initial coming together of the classes in the late 1830s, prior to the emergence of Chartism, was in the formation of a committee to investigate the problem of poverty in the town. From its inception the BPU's ultimate test of the government's unrepresentative nature lay in its unwillingness to acknowledge the true state of the country. G. F. Muntz, a merchant-manufacturer and a member of the BPU's political council, claimed during the Reform Bill campaign that, 'It appeared, indeed, to him that His Majesty's ministers knew no more about the state of the country than the Hottentots.' On the cause of distress he endorsed the working classes' own rejection of a moral analysis:

> If the people were a set of idle, drunken vagabonds it was not to be wondered at; but when he knew honest and skilful men to have been out of employ for 6, 9, 12 or even 24 months who formerly had a high sense of honour and would have scorned to apply to a work-house for assistance; this was proof sufficient that the country had been, and still was, grossly misgoverned.[28]

In economic terms Attwood drew a very firm line between productive and non-productive capital. In political terms he drew attention to the unrepresented nature of the interests of the 'productive classes', which he saw as including 'masters and men in every branch of Agriculture, Manufacture, Commerce and Trade'.[29] Within this concept masters and men were drawn together by a joint interest in the prosperity of industry and the excluded nature of their class.

> The rich man's hand has been heavy upon the poor. The industrious manufacturer and mechanic have laboured early and late but the honest fruits of their labour have been too often twisted out of their

hands. The foul birds have descended, as it were, from the heavens to snatch the bread from the working man's mouth and the capital and income from the hands of his industrious employer.[30]

The concept of the 'productive' or 'industrious' classes united labour and capital, and defined their common interests against a landed and moneyed aristocracy invested with political power through an unrepresentative Parliament. The term, of course, was not coined by Attwood. Rather it was a standard part of the radical vocabulary which he appropriated and infused with a particular class meaning. Its strength was that it neatly sidestepped the knotty problems of the social relations of production and the distributions of rewards within the productive classes. However, by the late 1830s economic change had revealed this construction to be a fairly hackneyed formula which had to be constantly reiterated by Attwood precisely because the class unity it implied was increasingly at odds with work-place reality.

In the context of Sheffield, for this period, Baxter and Donnelly have rejected the term 'artisans' in favour of Soboul's 'dependent artisanry'.[31] This term, they have argued, is more evocative of the changing experience of the skilled worker. This was also the direction of economic change in Birmingham in the first half of the nineteenth century. Whilst the typical unit of production remained the small workshop held in master-artisan hands, the relationship between large- and small-scale units of production was changing. Factories emerged in most industries, increasing the degree of competition within trades generally. The 1830s saw an increase in the application of steam-power. In 1815 there had been 42 steam-engines at work in the town; by 1830 this had risen to 120 and by 1838 to 240. At the same time the small master found himself increasingly dependent upon the market and credit facilities of either the merchant, the factor or the large-scale manufacturer, a relationship which continually eroded his traditional independence. There is considerable evidence to suggest that this was a period of downward spiralling prices, whilst the 1830s themselves were punctuated by periods of either under-employment or unemployment. In these periods the artisan often became a 'garret-master' a move which invariably exacerbated the problem of falling prices and which, in itself, casts some doubt upon the simple equation between independent production and upward social mobility.[32]

The artisan answered this process of economic change in two ways both of which ultimately emphasised class divisions. These were Owenism and the development of trade society activity. Owenism maintained a constant presence within the town from the late 1820s to the mid-1840s. On one level it appealed to the tradition of free thought; on another the economic analysis behind Owenism was one calculated to appeal to the artisan. In attempting to put the consumer directly in contact with the producer, the middleman, who had been insinuating himself increasingly in the local economy, was circumvented. Whilst the co-operative ven tures and the Labour Exchange failed in themselves the ideological per spectives gained added a new stridency to the approach of the working-class leadership. Henry Watson reminded one of the first meetings of the received BPU in 1838 that:

> Labour was not only the mine of real wealth, but that mine was the sole property of those who toiled. No man had a right to another man's labour without an equivalent; not even a king upon his throne, any more than that more useful man who delves in the mine, ploughs the field or throws the shuttle.[33]

The upper-middle-class radicals of the BPU opted out of Owenism from the start. Both Attwood and the Scholefields refused to have any-thing to do with the scheme to start a Labour Exchange. G. F. Muntz after displaying initial enthusiasm withdrew swiftly as the movement entered its trade union phase. As he told the BPU in June 1837:

> He was said by his enemies to be on the side of the people right or wrong. That was false. Did he not oppose the Trades Union? Did he not tell them it was neither right nor equitable to endeavour to ob tain those prices by resistance, which masters could not afford to give.[34]

As these sentiments suggest, the 1830s was a decade of work-place confrontation over the structural changes taking place in most trades. As I have tried to demonstrate elsewhere the 1830s was an important period for the expansion of trade society activities.[35] The early years saw a degree of organisational co-ordination with the establishment for a brief period of the United Trades, whilst union activists like James Morrison, Henry Watson and T. H. Etherington (of the United Building Trades) played important parts in the establishment of the MUWC. The decade also experienced at least thirty strikes and the prosecution of over fifty-three individuals for trade society activities. This activity was mostly clustered in the better economic years of the middle of the decade. But as early as September 1832 Thomas Baker suggested at the meeting of the Unemployed Artisans, that Attwood's currency panacea would not necessarily raise wages. 'Before the rate of wages could be raised they must wait till all the hands were brought into full work, and then they had in most cases to turn out and get into serious quarrels with their employers before they obtained an advance.'[36]

The accelerating process of economic change meant that the structural constraints on the emergence of further radical movements were also changing. This acted to weaken many of the elements which had previously helped to unify differing social groups within the BPU. This, in turn, effectively highlighted the crucial differences in political perspective between middle- and working-class radicals. It was these differences which ultimately destroyed the alliance within the revived Political Union. These areas of tension related far more to the basic perception of the democratic form than to the question of physical or moral force tactics within the radical movement. A brief analysis of the formation and destruction of the alliance will demonstrate this point.

In April 1837 the Reform Association, an organisation formed in the mid-1830s to maintain the radical momentum of the original BPU, called a public meeting to consider the declining state of trade. It proposed the revival of the Political Union. In the main the speeches, mostly from the old leaders like Salt, Douglas, Hadley and Edmonds, emphasised the failure of the Reform Act to shift the nature of representation significantly towards the 'productive classes'. Currency solutions were discussed and, even at this early stage, Salt reminded his audience that 'if ever the Government violated the law, physical resistance would become a duty'.[37] It was agreed that when 4000 individuals had subscribed to the Union it would be formally reconstituted. In the next six weeks just over 5000 individuals enrolled.

Independent of this development, in the middle of May 1837 a meeting of the unemployed, held at the Public Office, drew up a memorial to be submitted to the principal masters and merchants. It requested a joint meeting to discuss the nature of the prevailing distress and was drawn up by the Working Men's Memorial Committee which included both Watson and Baker in its ranks. It contained over 13,000 signatures. The requested meeting took place on 30 May, at which the Memorial Committee made it quite clear that they were not in pursuit of charity. Baker informed the meeting that: 'They did not want the miseries of the soup shop, nor did they wish to live upon the miserable pittance of the Workhouse. What they wanted was labour . . . '[38] A joint committee of working men and masters was appointed to investigate the extent of poverty in the town. Although Political Union radicals were active both at the meeting and later on the committee itself, at this stage the two movements remained effectively separate.

Towards the end of June 1837 the BPU, with a newly constituted council, called a meeting on Newhall Hill to declare its policy. Attwood, supported by Muntz and Edmonds pointed to the inflexibility of the currency as the root cause of the distress and, with perhaps one eye on the Working Men's Memorial Committee, guaranteed that, were his measures implemented, they would restore £60,000 per week to the town within a month. Despite a certain amount of discussion in council over the preceding weeks, concerning a truly massive extension of the franchise, the Union declared for household suffrage along with triennial Parliaments and the Ballot.[39]

In October 1837 the Working Men's Memorial Committee called a town's meeting to petition Parliament over the distress in the town. At this John Collins, a tool-maker and fitter in Joseph Gillot's pen factory, warned of 'a point beyond which it was not right for the government to force the people'.[40] Baker spoke bluntly of the process of estrangement between masters and men that had resulted from the periodic recessions of the previous decade:

> When the masters found by these fluctuations in trade, their interests were being sacrificed and they could not maintain their prices they turned upon the men and reduced their wages in the hope of being able, by that means, to meet the competition and carry on. Had they, in place of doing so, taken their workmen by the hand and gone to the government and represented their mutual distresses; and insisted upon relief . . . they would, ere that time, have obtained effectual redress, but in place of doing so the masters carried on the murderous system of competition; wages were reduced to the lowest scale of endurance; and general poverty, distrusts, dislikes and combinations were the consequences.[41]

The middle-class leadership of the revived BPU actively supported the petition though they felt such a move would prove ultimately ineffective. Attwood's tactics were clear: in his own words, 'if the Ministry would turn a deaf ear to their memorial, . . . their conduct would force the people into the arms of the Political Union'[42] After a frustrating interview with Lord Melbourne the petitioners reported back their lack of success at a town's meeting. It was here that Union radicals first floated the idea of a massive agitation, lobbying other towns on the basis of a national petition for political reform rather than the currency question.[43]

Four weeks later after extensive discussions the BPU's political council declared, officially, its support of the principle of universal suffrage with Attwood claiming that his conversion stemmed from shock at the Queen's recent speech, containing as it did no reference to distress at home.[44] This policy decision was endorsed at a meeting of the Political Union at the Town Hall on 15 January 1838.[45] The next week, on 23 January, the Working Men's Memorial Committee sent a deputation to the political council's meeting. They now formally declared themselves within the orbit of the BPU. Baker explained to Attwood that the reason for the move was the Council's shift in policy.

> The Council [of the BPU] had been agitating for sometime past with no great success, and why? Because the great mass of people felt no great interest in their measures; but now they had come forward to advocate the real liberties and inalienable rights and only security for the people, and hence it was that the working men thought it their duty and interest to come forward . . . and stand by . . . the men who were endeavouring to obtain for them substantial relief.[46]

So, nine months after the revival of the BPU the political council's adoption of universal suffrage gave the movement the mass base that it required. Throughout the spring and summer of 1838 the work of agitation went on, culminating in the election of delegates to the Convention in August. But Attwood's approach to the question of universal suffrage was always openly pragmatic. As he said, 'the masses of the people constituted the only engine through which it was possible to obtain reform, and that mighty engine could not be roused into efficient action without the agency of Universal Suffrage.'[47] The sentiments permeated the approach of most of the political council. R. K. Douglas, for example, in January 1838 echoed Attwood's words when he claimed that universal suffrage was, 'not only right and safe but it was the only proposal by which they could lay hold of the hearts of the masses'.[48] Certainly the shift in policy on the part of the council, whether occasioned by the Queen's speech, Russell's finality declaration or the need for a mass base, involved much heart-searching for BPU leaders. Attwood announced in January 1838 that he was 'a thorough convert to Universal Suffrage and if ever I uttered a word against it I now altogether retract it.' G. F. Muntz was a little more guarded in his statements, 'although not originally a friend to Universal Suffrage he did not regret to find they had adopted the principle'.[49]

The slowness of the move to universal suffrage and the pragmatism of the political council when forced, by prevailing circumstances, to adopt it, throws an important light upon their idea of the nature of representation. Attwood and his group had developed the concept of the 'productive classes' such that it could potentially draw middle-class and working-class discontent into the same movement. But at the same time it had been deliberately evolved as a concept which very forcefully legitimised middle-class leadership. For the 'productive classes' to be represented in Parliament universal suffrage was by no means essential, and this is why the council arrived at it so late. All that was necessary was an adjustment that shifted the centre of political gravity towards a representation of productive capital. By definition its representation in Parliament would benefit both masters and men. G. F. Muntz announced in May 1837, that is prior to his rather circumspect conversion to universal suffrage, that the BPU in its second agitation should aim at 'extending the franchise so as to enable them to return to the House of Commons a majority of *men of business who understood the true interests of the people*, instead of lordlings and scions of nobility'[50] (my italics). His brother, P. H. Muntz, a member of the political council and a Chartist delegate, was more frankly utilitarian, when he spoke in February 1839:

> He would acknowledge no abstract right of suffrage in either rich or poor. Prove to him that the good of the community at large could be promoted by the destruction of the right he possessed and most cheerfully he would resign it tomorrow. The suffrage that would produce the greatest happiness for the greatest number of his fellow men was the suffrage he would look for.[51]

The BPU radicals were steered, by their underlying philosophy, dangerously close to a theory of 'virtual representation' of working-class interests by the middle class. This was always presented within the ethos of social mobility by which master-manufacturers could be seen simply as successful working men. In 1841 P. H. Muntz in his capacity as borough mayor deplored the divisions that had grown within the work-place, for which he largely blamed a class-conscious Chartist agitation.

> With respect to the masters and workmen, he must say there never was a graver delusion than to try to persuade the latter that the interest of the former was quite separate and distinct from theirs. How such a deceit could have succeeded in Birmingham he knew not. Half the masters in Birmingham had been working men.[52]

But by the late 1830s the appeal to the 'productive classes' was being made through the medium of a tradition of social mobility which was, in fact, being rendered irrelevant, and apparently so, by the increasing capital demands of a changing industrial structure. Muntz himself was a second-generation industrialist.

In Attwood's own nomenclature the working class were generally referred to as the 'masses', but with the addition of the productive element of the middle class they became the 'people'. This was an approach embodied in the structure of the Political Union itself. Attwood informed his wife in a letter of June 1837: 'Salt writes me word that 8,000 men have now re-enrolled their names and paid up their subscriptions to the Union and that the Council is better and stronger than ever'.[53] The political council that he referred to contained no working men, its thirty-five members being composed of one banker, five merchants, three factors, sixteen manufacturers (generally large-scale), five professionals, two shopkeepers and one gentleman of some means. The emphasis on property was quite deliberate. Looking back on the period from 1841 Attwood claimed: 'There is no instance in history in which political movements have been successful without leaders and in almost every instance those leaders have been men of wealth and influence.'[54] Given its social composition the political council was to be invested with absolute control of the movement. As Attwood again remembered:

> The very essence of the Birmingham Union, under the law, was un-limited obedience to their leaders who formed the Political Council . . . . Who would ever think of building a railroad without a committee or of sending even a disciplined army into the field without officers.[55]

However the working-class leadership within the Union refused to accept the alliance on these terms. At the mass meeting at Holloway Head in August 1838, designated by Mark Hovell as 'the official beginning of the Chartist movement',[56] the working-class membership demanded the election of seven working men to the BPU's political council, and also the adoption of John Collins as one of the Chartist delegates.[57] By November tensions became clear as some of the working-class councillors began to complain of the way the council worked. Henry Watson pointed to 'a tendency to an aristocratic feeling amongst them that when a wealthy man moved they generally carried those resolutions.'[58]

Thus, the tensions and final rift between the middle-class radicals and the broader movement which culminated in the resignation from the Convention of Hadley, Muntz, Salt and Douglas in March 1839, cannot be adequately explained as the clash between physical and moral force that it has been portrayed as in the past. In the wake of the resignations, Feargus O'Connor asked rhetorically, 'Had none of the Birmingham leaders ever used strong words?'[59] Arguably the whole tenor of the BPU's approach was one of physical force. One member of the political council said of the government at the start of the campaign that 'the terrors of a few Newhall Hill meetings would induce them to relax the screw . . .'[60] Although the political council liked to draw a distinction between this approach, which it referred to as 'wholesome terror', and actually advocating the use of force, in the first half of 1838 they went much further. At the main meeting of August Attwood revived memories of May 1832 by claiming that 'if our enemies shed blood – if they attack the people – they must take the consequences upon their own heads'.[61]

Nor can the tensions be contained adequately within an explanation reliant upon the clash of personalities between O'Connor and the BPU leadership. Certainly the question of the control of the movement was central, but it actually revolved around the level of participation allowed to the working-class element. This was the crucial issue. Edward Brown's comment on middle-class participation, made after the resignations of March 1839, was characteristic of working-class feeling. 'Did they think they were going to lead the working men by the nose any longer?'[62] Above all this related not only to participation within Chartism, the movement, but also to the question of working-class participation in any democratic form that might emerge in the event of its exertions being successful. This was surely in O'Connor's mind when he claimed

of the BPU radicals that 'it was always their intention to stop universal
suffrage morally, if they could'.[63] The middle-class and working-class
elements within the BPU had arrived at Chartism via two different
routes. Though they shared the same political programme their concept
of the emergent democratic form was essentially different. Working-
class aspirations within Chartism lay not only in obtaining political
rights, but also in using them effectively. Any social programme, implicit
in the six points, was dependent upon the full exercise of those rights at
all levels of political life. Thus the pragmatism of the middle-class radicals
of the BPU robbed the working man of his first demand for *'égalité*:
equality of citizenship.'[64] The alliance in fact fell at the first hurdle.

Tension built up within the BPU in the second half of 1838. The differences between Salt and O'Connor over violence of language were
settled amicably at a public meeting in November, but they seemed to
point to a more fundamental division. The political council met every
Tuesday evening, the Working Men's Committee met on Thursdays (as
did working-class sectional groups throughout the town). By January
1839 there was obviously disagreement between the two since Edward
Brown of the Working Men's Committee felt constrained to explain: 'It
had been said of them they wished to dictate to the council. That was
not the case.' In the same month some of the political council, Edmonds
in particular, were barracked by the Chartists at a public meeting designed to initiate a local movement for Corn Law Repeal. At the same
meeting Thomas Weston a member of both the political council and the
Town Council, betrayed a crucial doubt on the possible immediacy of
universal suffrage. 'I don't think we shall get it this week', he told a
hostile audience, 'It may take years'.[65]

Nevertheless the stand taken by most of the Political Union against
the move to start a separate Anti-Corn Law campaign, enabled it to
weather this particular storm with its credibility intact. But the full
attendance of middle-class radicals at the dinner at the end of February
1839 to celebrate the anniversary of incorporation contrasted noticeably with the dwindling attendance of political councillors at the
Tuesday sessions. These sometimes had to be abandoned as they were
inquorate. In March Watson complained that: 'It appeared some of
them must be forced on, that the people must take the lead.' A week
later the council attempted to disband the National Rent Committee
alleging misappropriation of funds by the working-class leadership.
The committee had been established to raise funds for the Convention
and had emerged as the focus of the working-class element within the

Union. The abortive attempt to disband it represents a last-ditch attempt by the middle-class radicals of the BPU to snatch back the leadership of the movement. On March 19 the Working Men's Committee submitted a resolution deprecating the non-attendance of councillors and censuring Hadley, Salt, Muntz and Douglas for not agitating the locality in accordance with a Convention direction. Salt, Hadley, Douglas and Pierce resigned as delegates to the Convention at the end of March. A week later the BPU, now with a membership of less than 300, was disbanded.[66]

It has often been suggested that it was the flagging interest of the Union's middle-class radicals that created a local working-class leadership in the early months of 1839. But this is to confuse cause and effect. For it was the strength and articulacy of the working-class leadership in both its local and national forms that convinced the middle-class radicals that Chartism would not provide the platform for the kind of democratic form they envisaged. Locally the working-class leadership drew on its own tradition of political radicalism particularly that of the post-war period. The sectional meeting of the Cross Guns, Lancaster Street, declared in February 'that with nothing short of Liberty and Prosperity will we be content! or we will die in the attempt!' It also published the following verse:

> Britons arise and yet be free
> Demand your rights and liberty,
> Tyrants long have shared the spoil,
> The Working Class share all the toil,
> Now! or never! strike the blow!
> Exert yourselves and crush the foe![67]

It was a verse, for the publication of which Charles Whitworth as Chairman of the Union Society, had been imprisoned for six months in 1819. In the same vein John Fussell told a meeting at Holloway Head in April 1839 after the delegates had resigned that, 'First they must petition; secondly demand; and while they demanded they must adopt and act upon the advice of Major Cartwright and Wooller and demand with arms in their hands and then they should have some attention paid to them'.[68] Cartwright and Wooller had been present at the 'Legislatorial Attorney' meeting of July 1819. With the failure of the alliance the rhetoric of the working-class radicals sought strength from an earlier period of agitation when the movement had been purer.

However by the end of 1838, through the reform of local government, the middle-class leadership of the BPU had achieved locally the
kind of democratic form that they had hoped the Chartist Movement
might produce nationally. A painfully small municipal electorate (a
mere 3 per cent of the population[69], less even than the 1832 roll of
voters) returned a radical middle-class council in December 1838,
charged with the task of defending the interests of the ratepayer against
a range of non-elected bodies representing local vested interest, which
had hitherto dominated local government. The middle-class leadership
of the BPU had hoped that parliamentary reform would produce a similar effect upon the State, with the interests of the Church, the aristocracy and all non-producing capital subordinated to those of the 'productive classes' whom they hoped to represent. Admittedly the new
corporation was the middle-class radical dream writ small. Nevertheless
most were prepared to settle for this given the alternative which Chartism
by now so obviously offered, that is, a full-scale democracy with the
working class as the dominant element. The timing is crucial since the
agitations for the People's Charter and for Birmingham's Charter of
Incorporation ran concurrently. To the Chartists there was an inescap-
able correlation between the success of the middle-class radicals at the
municipal elections of 1838 and their gradual withdrawal from the
Chartist Movement. Speaking to the Convention in April 1839, Dr Taylor
claimed that as far as Birmingham was concerned incorporation had
proved to be 'the grave of Radicalism'.[70]

At the same time success in the local elections for key figures on the
BPU political council, transformed a mass-based agitation in which they
were participants into a problem of law and order. In no issue was this
metamorphosis exemplified more completely than in the question of
the meetings in the Bull Ring. During the Reform Bill agitation the BPU's
middle-class leadership had fostered these meetings to maintain momentum within the movement. Their revival in January 1839 under working-
class direction, however, was a manifestation of the tension between
the working-class and middle-class leadership within the BPU. In April
after the resignations of the delegates these meetings grew in attendance.
By the first week in May, just prior to the Convention's move from
London to Birmingham, they were being held twice a day. On 10 May
they were declared illegal by the magistrates who, since incorporation
included three ex-political councillors. One of these, P. H. Muntz, had
himself been elected as a delegate to the Convention. On 16 May three
days after the arrival of the Convention, Fussell and Brown were arrested

for holding meetings and using violent language. On 17 and 26 June Henry Wilkes, Joseph Nisbett, a gunmaker, and William Smallwood were prosecuted, before a bench of magistrates which included P. H. Muntz. They were charged with obstruction whilst holding Bull Ring meetings. Nisbett and Smallwood were unable to pay a fine and were imprisoned.[71] The irony of Muntz's position as a poacher turned gamekeeper was not lost on the Chartists.

The story of the attack on the crowd in the Bull Ring on the evening of 4 July by a body of London police drafted in by the mayor, William Scholefield, an ex-political council member, is familiar enough. It was followed by a fortnight of tension and further disturbances on 15 July. These involved an attack on the police billeted at the Public Office and the destruction of some shops in the Bull Ring.[72] This followed a long campaign by Bull Ring shopkeepers for the suppression of the meetings held there on the grounds that they were damaging trade. During this period twenty-eight local men were arrested and later prosecuted. Of these thirteen were imprisoned for periods ranging from one month to eighteen months and three, sentenced to death, were subsequently transported for life.[73] But the first casualty of the fortnight was the concept of a unity of interests within the productive classes: any residual ambiguity surrounding the nature of local class relationships evaporated. During the extensive post-mortem that followed the incidents, it became apparent that the middle-class radicals regretted the decision to draft in sixty London policemen (augmented by a further forty on 5 July). It is a decision that is particularly difficult to understand given that the town contained some four troops of Dragoons (about one hundred men) and two additional troops of infantry assigned to it when the Convention decided to move to Birmingham. In addition over 2000 special constables had been sworn in.[74] Nevertheless the decision stands as a demonstration of the extent to which the middle class feared a radical working-class movement that was not directly under its own control. Certainly Scholefield had little faith in Colonel Thorn, the area's military commander. In addition he had been under considerable pressure from local property owners to act positively to suppress the meetings. This pressure on the town's newly appointed officials increased after the arrival of the Convention. At this point Scholefield had suggested that the Home Secretary authorise the arrest of the leaders of the Convention while they were in the town.[75] Throughout June he attempted to procure the use of the Town Hall as an alternative venue for the Bull Ring meetings. This might have gone some distance towards avoiding confrontation but the Street Commissioners, who still controlled the use of the hall, were slow to accede to the request. As a self-elected body the Commissioners had been a prime target of the BPU's middle-class leadership during the campaign for local government reform. The Commissioners now rather relished the difficulties which a duality of roles had created for men like Muntz and Scholefield. As Francis Lloyd put it: 'The Political Union had taught them [the Chartists] lessons, and they were too apt scholars to forget them at any man's command. Let the commissioners attend to their own duty and not be dragged through the dirt to save other people from the consequences of their folly and wickedness.'[76]

The history of Chartism in the town in the wake of the disturbances of July 1839 has hardly had justice done to it in the past. This is not the place for a comprehensive overview, but certain key areas should be drawn out to indicate that there was at least some continuity of organisation within the local movement. There is a wealth of material available in the Home Office papers where the reports of the numerous spies who infiltrated the movement in the wake of the riots are to be found. As elsewhere the movement was deeply split and disorientated. Groups continued to meet through the second half of 1839 in the Lawrence Street Chapel and in a room in Allison Street. According to the spies' reports at least one group were preparing themselves for armed resistance.[77] A further group established themselves in a coffee-house in Ladywell Walk in March 1840.[78] The movement was still able to draw upon mass support as was shown in August 1840 when Collins was released and greeted by 70,000 people on entering Birmingham.[79] In November 1840 a branch of the National Charter Association was established. A year later there were six branches of the Association and also a Chartist Co-operative Society in the town. In addition Arthur O'Neill's Chartist Church, the New Jerusalem Chapel in Newhall Street, opened in December 1840 and maintained an important presence through the next few years.[80] In August 1842 there were further clashes with the authorities which resulted in George White's imprisonment. John Mason the shoemaker, now an important local figure, was arrested in June for agitation in the Black Country, and Arthur O'Neill arrested for similar activities in August.[81]

Chartists in Birmingham in the 1840s were undoubtedly divided among themselves as to the way forward. But the presence of internecine quarrels should not be allowed to obscure the shared perspective of class. In Birmingham subsequent responses to middle-class radical initiatives were shaped by the early Chartist experience. This is evident even in the attitudes of those members of the movement most anxious to keep the dialogue with the middle classes open. John Collins can probably be safely placed in this group. As a Birmingham delegate to the Leeds Reform Association Conference of 1841, and the Complete Suffrage Conferences of 1842, a pastor of the Christian Chartist Church and co-author of the founding text for Lovett's 'new move', he had a finger in more 'moderate' pies than probably anyone. Yet, as he was to emphasise in March 1841, 'If ever the middle classes united with them again it must be upon the principle of equality.'[82] This was the heritage of the BPU experience. John Mason, replying to early Complete Suffrage initiatives a year later, emphasised that the lesson had been learned: 'If there were to be a union between the middle and working classes', he said, 'he hoped the working men would take care to have their share of representation.'[83]

However, when Thomas Attwood decided to move again politically and form a 'National Union' in 1843 he was approached by local Chartists. John Follows, deputed as spokeman by a public meeting presented its sentiments:

> that if it is your design again to stand forth as an advocate of those great and inviolable principles of political justice embodied in the Peoples Charter, with a clear recognition of that *Sacred Document* as the only basis of just and legitimate government we shall hail your return to public life with enthusiasm .... But if you have excluded that measure from your plans, you have excluded us ....[84]

The determination of most Chartists after 1839 to stand by the Charter 'name and all' is often presented as an almost sentimental approach born of the movement's martyred past. Hovell's history, for example, suggests that it was a 'point of honour' to retain the name at the Complete Suffrage Conference of December 1842. But an examination of the breaking of the BPU would suggest that it was something much more than this. The social philosophy behind the BPU enabled it to offer only a virtual representation of working-class interests, by men of wealth, to a movement that claimed the inclusion of that class into the political system on a basis of equality. To accept the name, the 'People's Charter', was to accept the totality of this claim. As such, because it represented not only a political programme but also an approach within a programme, the name itself became the acid test of any middle-class initiative.

NOTES

1. A. Briggs, 'Thomas Attwood and the Economic Background of the Birmingham Political Union', *Cambridge Historical Journal*, IX, 2 (1948); 'The Background of the Parliamentary Reform Movement in Three English Cities (1830-2)', *Cambridge Historical Journal*, X, 3 (1952); 'Social Structure and Politics in Birmingham and Lyons 1825-1848', *British Journal of Sociology*, 1 (1950); *Victorian Cities* (London: Pelican, 1968) pp. 184-8; *Chartist Studies* (London: Macmillan, 1968) pp. 7-28. See also T. R. Tholfsen, 'The Artisan and the Culture of Early Victorian Birmingham', *University of Birmingham Historical Journal*, IV (1953-4). J. Hamburger, *James Mill and the Art of Revolution*, 2nd edn (Connecticut: Greenwood, 1977) pp. 74-139.

2. The clearest exposition of this analysis is to be found in T. R. Tholfsen, 'The Chartist Crisis in Birmingham', *International Review of Social History*, 3 (1958). The groundwork for this approach, with its emphasis on O'Connor and 'physical force' as the major disruptive influence on an otherwise unified BPU was undoubtably laid by R. G. Gammage with the publication in 1854 of his *History of the Chartist Movement* (London, Merlin: 1969, reprint of 1894 edn) pp. 83-4, 107-35. Mark Hovell developed this analysis as part of a polemic against O'Connor in *The Chartist Movement* (2nd edn, Manchester: Manchester University Press, 1925) pp. 99-135. See also Julius West, *A History of the Chartist Movement* (London: Butler and Tanner, 1925) pp. 53-5, 101-3, 135-8; F. F. Rosenblatt, *The Chartist Movement in its Social and Economic Aspects* (Haarlem, 1967, reprint of 1916 edn) pp. 153-9; J. T. Ward, *Chartism* (London: Batsford, 1973) pp. 79-82, 109-42. D. Read, *The English Provinces, c. 1760-1960* (London: Edward Arnold, 1964) pp. 113-22. The most recent history of the BPU is C. Flick, *The Birmingham Political Union and the Movements for Reform in Britain 1830-1839* (Connecticut: Archon, 1978). This analysis of the organisation (in which its working-class members make only the most fleeting of appearances) accepts the idea of O'Connor's responsibility for the breaking up of the Union and largely ignores the problems of the alternative roles assumed by the BPU's middle-class radicals at this time (as employers, ratepayers, magistrates, etc.). As a result the importance of a separate working-class consciousness, developed through trade unionism, Owenism and earlier political movements, is overlooked as is the vital reciprocal relationship between parliamentary and municipal reform. For an analysis that is more sensitive to the importance of the working-class presence see D. J. Moss, 'A Study in Failure: Thomas Attwood, M.P. for Birmingham 1832-1839', *Historical Journal*, 21, 3 (1978).

3. On this point see M. Brock, *The Great Reform Act* (London: Hutchinson, 1973) pp. 316-17. Joseph Parkes, a vital figure in Birmingham during the passing of the act saw the 1835 Municipal Corporations Act as 'the Postscript to the Reform Bills of 1832'. Quoted in G. B. A. M. Finlayson 'The Politics of Municipal Reform, 1835', *English Historical Review (EHR)* CCCXXI (October 1966) 690.

4. R. B. Rose, 'The Origins of Working Class Radicalism in Birmingham', *Labour History*, IX (November 1965); W. B. Stephens (ed.), *A History of the County of Warwick: Victoria Country History, Vol VII The City of Birmingham*, pp. 270-306.

5. *Edmonds Weekly Recorder*, 17 July 1819. Wolesley, who was to be the

incarnation of the right to petition, was not able to fulfil his role. The meeting was declared illegal and its organisers prosecuted and imprisoned. The implications of the meeting are discussed in T. M. Parssinen, 'Association, Convention and Anti-Parliament in British Radical Politics 1771–1848', *EHR*, LXXXVII (July (1973) 516–17.

6. *Aris's Birmingham Gazette* (*A G*) 17 November 1816.

7. *A G* 8 November 1819.

8. *Midland Representative* 18 February 1832.

9. *A G* 1 February 1830.

10. *Poor Man's Guardian* (*P M G*) 20 October, 3 November 1832.

11. *Birmingham Journal* (*B J*) 22 September 1832.

12. *P M G* 3 November 1832.

13. For example Tholfsen, 'Chartist Crisis', 478; Flick, *Birmingham Political Union*, p. 128.

14. *B J* 3 November 1832.

15. *P M G* 17 November 1832. For Wade, see T. H. Lloyd, 'Dr Wade and the Working Class', *Midland History*, II, 2 (Autumn 1973).

16. O'Connor, for example, gave Attwood an ecstatic welcome when he declared for universal suffrage in 1838. For an examination of this aspect see J. Epstein, 'Feargus O'Connor and the English Working Class Radical Movement 1832–1841; A Study in National Chartist Leadership' (unpub. Univ. of Birmingham, Ph. D. thesis, 1977) pp. 201–4. As Epstein shows, O'Brien, who had been present in Birmingham during the Reform Bill agitation and knew Attwood's brand of radicalism, was a little more circumspect.

17. *B J* 21 September 1833.

18. Ibid., 25 May 1833.

19. Hervey to General Charles Grey, May 1833 (n.d.)(Grey Papers, Dept of Paleography and Diplomatic, University of Durham).

20. *A G* 22 September 1834.

21. Hovell, *The Chartist Movement*, pp. 101–2.

22. *B J* 4 November 1837. On this point see N. Edsall, 'Varieties of Radicalism: Attwood, Cobden and the Local Politics of Municipal Incorporation', *Historical Journal*, XVI, I (1973) 95–9.

23. D. Fraser, *Urban Politics in Victorian England* (Leicester: Leicester University Press, 1976) p. 115.

24. *B J* 10 November 1838.

25. Ibid., 7 October 1837.

26. Many of the early historians of Chartism followed Place's assessment of Attwood's economic theories and dubbed him a currency crank, e.g. BM Add. MSS 27, 798, 137; Hovell, *The Chartist Movement*, pp, 109–15; West, *A History of the Chartist Movement*, p. 54. The move to restore him as a serious economic theorist was begun by G. D. H. Cole in *Chartist Portraits*, 2nd edn (London: Macmillan, 1965) pp. 111–16. This was developed later by S. G. Checkland, 'The Birmingham Economists 1815–1850', *Economic History Review*, 2nd series, I (1948). The task has been completed convincingly by D. J. Moss, 'Thomas Attwood. The Biography of a radical' (Univ. of Oxford, D. Phil. thesis, 1973) see esp. pp. 46–249 and 434.

27. *BJ* 22 September 1832.

28. Ibid., 2 March 1832.

29. C. M. Wakefield, *Life of Thomas Attwood* (London: privately published, 1885) p. 389.

30. *B J* 7 November 1837.

31. F. K. Donnelly and J. L. Baxter, 'Sheffield and the English Revolutionary Tradition 1791–1820', in S. Pollard and C. Holmes (eds), *Essays in the Economic and Social History of South Yorkshire* (South Yorks County Council, 1976) pp. 90–2.

32. For a more detailed account of the growing economic dependence of the artisan upon large-scale capital, see C. Behagg, 'Custom, Class and Change: the Trade Societies of Nineteenth Century Birmingham', *Social History*, 4, no.3 (October 1979).

33. *B J* 20 January 1838.

34. Ibid., 24 June 1837.

35. Behagg, 'Custom, Class and Change'.

36. *B J* 22 September 1832.

37. Ibid., 22 April 1837.

38. Ibid., 3 June 1837.

39. Ibid., 24 June 1837.

40. There has been a certain amount of confusion over Collins's occupation. He is generally claimed to be either a journeyman penmaker or a shoemaker. However, on the flyleaf of *Chartism: a New Organisation of the People* which he wrote with William Lovett whilst in Warwick Gaol for his part in the Bull Ring disturbances, he clearly describes himself as a Tool-maker. This is confirmed by his obituary, *Birmingham Mercury* 28 August 1852.

41. *BJ* 7 October 1837.

42. Ibid., 11 November 1837.

43. Ibid.

44. Ibid., 23 December 1837.

45. Ibid., 20 January 1838.

46. Ibid., 27 January 1838.

47. Ibid., 23 December 1837.

48. Ibid., 20 January 1838.

49. Ibid.

50. Ibid., 27 May 1837.

51. Ibid., 23 February 1839. For a similar sentiment levelled against the Chartists by the *Manchester Guardian* which in November 1837 claimed that the suffrage was not a right 'it is merely an expedient for obtaining good government; that and not the franchise it is to which the public have a right.' Quoted in D. Read, 'Chartism in Manchester, in Briggs, *Chartist Studies*, p. 38.

52. *BJ* 10 July 1841.

53. Attwood to his wife 9 June 1837 (Attwood papers: in the possession of Mrs Priscilla Williams, Earls Court, London).

54. *BJ* 17 July 1841.

55. Ibid.; for a similar attitude towards a popular agitation adopted by the Anti-Corn Law League, see D. Thompson, *The Early Chartists* (London: Macmillan, 1971) p. 15.

56. Hovell, *The Chartist Movement*, p. 107.

57. *BJ* 11 August 1838.
58. Ibid., 17 November 1838.
59. Ibid., 6 April 1839.
60. Ibid., 24 April 1837.
61. Ibid., 11 August 1838.
62. Ibid., 6 April 1839.
63. *Northern Star* (*NS*) 6 April 1839.
64. See E. P. Thompson, *The Making of the English Working Class*, 2nd end (Harmondsworth: Pelican, 1968) p. 910.
65. *BJ* 1 December 1838; 26 January 1839.
66. Ibid., 23 February, 9 March, 23 March, 25 May 1839.
67. BM Add. MSS 34, 245.
68. *BJ* 6 April 1839.
69. E. P. Hennock, *Fit and Proper Persons* (London: Edward Arnold, 1973) pp. 10–14.
70. *NS* 13 April 1839.
71. *BJ* 11 May, 22 June, 29 June, 1839.
72. *Report of the Committee appointed by the Town Council, 3 September 1839, to Investigate the Causes of the Late Riots* (Birmingham 1840). See also correspondence HO 40/50.
73. For a full list of prisoners and sentences see Calendar of Warwickshire Summer Assizes, Warwick Record Office, QS 26/1.
74. HO 40/50.
75. William Scholefield to Russell 13 May 1839, HO 40/50.
76. *BJ* 29 June 1839.
77. HO 40/50.
78. *NS* 28 March 1840.
79. Ibid., 1 August 1840.
80. Ibid., 21 November 1840, 23 October, 6 November, 27 November 1841.
81. Ibid., 27 August, 3 September 1842; *BJ* 30 July, 13 August 1842.
82. *BJ* 13 March 1841. A common front was presented to the early initiatives of the Anti-Corn Law League. Cobden wrote to George Wilson in October 1841 of a visit to Birmingham: 'I called along with Jos. Sturge upon Collins and two other leaders of the *new move*, but they are not a whit more reasonable upon our question than the O'Connorites.' Quoted in N. McCord, *The Anti-Corn Law League* (London: Unwin, 1968) p. 116.
83. *BJ* 5 March 1842.
84. *Address of the People of Birmingham, 8 August 1843* (Attwood Papers).

3. The London Democratic Association 1837 – 41: a Study in London Radicalism

JENNIFER BENNETT

THE East London Democratic Association was founded in 1837, on 29 January the birthday of Thomas Paine,[1] and became in 1838 the London Democratic Association, on 10 August, a date memorable for the overthrow of the French Monarchy. As such it played a brief but stormy part in the Chartist Movement before being absorbed in 1841 into the wider movement it had helped to create.

Its character and significance have been matters of dispute among historians, depending to some extent upon what was known about the organisation when they wrote, but also upon their points of view.

The Democratic Association has been regarded by many as little more than an extension of the personality of George Julian Harney, a figure regarded as the firebrand of the Chartist Movement, 'who dreamed of pikes and saw himself as the English Marat', and whose 'views scarcely went beyond the need for a terror';[2] and by others as the proto-type for future Marxist and Communist leaders who, however, failed subsequently to match up to Marx's requirements for the role.[3]

The Democratic Association has been seen as founded by Feargus O'Connor or, at least, as a thoroughgoing O'Connorite body; as 'a violent and reckless body';[4] and as the party of 'the most extreme advocates of insurrection'; as 'a rival to Lovett's London Working Men's Association';[5] and as 'the mass party of the Metropolis', 'the most militant of the radical political associations'.[6] It has been seen also as 'the only organisation at the time which succeeded, to a certain extent, in properly connecting the ultimate aims of the economic emancipation of the proletariat with its political class action, thus creating the supreme synthesis, which was subsequently to be embodied in the modern labour movement'.[7]

Though the Democratic Association may have been some of these things, it could not have been all of them, and the differences to be found among historians demands a closer look at the composition, activities and role of the Association if its part in the Chartist Movement can be accurately assessed.

The East London Democratic Association (ELDA) when formed in January 1837 had its headquarters in the Minories, in a room adjoining an umbrella shop.[8] There is no evidence to suggest that O'Connor had anything to do with its formation nor, indeed, much contact with the body until the Palace Yard meeting of September 1838.[9] O'Connor was in London seeking support for a new radical organisation in the metropolis and campaigning against the new Poor Law. The Democratic Association, like the London Working Men's Association (LWMA), stemmed from the National Union of the Working Classes, and both association had similar political aims, namely the five points later to be incorporated into the Charter. But the Democratic Association was already expressing, in its opposition to the new Poor Law, opinions which, while welcomed by O'Connor, were not shared by all the members and patrons of the LWMA. The differences which were to divide the Democratic Association from the latter body could thus be discerned from the time of its foundation; and such differences were to be the cause of much of the dissension in the later Chartist Movement. The emphasis with leaders of the Democratic Association was always to be on the social and class issues that were constantly to divide middle-class from working-class radicals. The Association was not without competent leaders of its own. It was led by a group composed of veteran radicals of the metropolitan working-class movement, and a number of younger militants. Indeed its roots ran deeply in the soil of a traditional London radicalism concerned as much with social as with political matters. The Democratic Association is linked with the Spencean Philanthropists and Owenites through Allen Davenport; with the Cato Street plot through Samuel Waddington; with the London Corresponding Society, the Spenceans and Thistlewood through Thomas Preston; with a variety of reform movements of nearly fifty years through William George; with the stormy episodes of the early 1830s through John Harper; with the National Union of the Working Classes through Charles Neesom;[10] and with the unstamped press agitation through younger men such as George Julian Harney, Richard Luckins, Thomas Ireland and J. H. B. Lorymer,[11] William Burton had taken part in O'Connor's Universal Suffrage Club, and several other leading ELDA members joined the Central National Association, which was set up by James Bernard, John Bell and O'Connor, and which Francis Place described as 'a wild project'. These included Edward Harvey, Joseph Fisher, Thomas Ireland, Henry Ross, Allen Davenport and George Julian Harney.[12] It is this episode which has led some historians to ignore all but a few months in the lives of radicals connected with reform movements for decades and to pass them over merely as O'Connor's men. It was with the collapse of the Central National Association that the ELDA became the single metropolitan alternative to the LWMA, although it should be stressed that neither association had the kind of mass support among the working community enjoyed by some radical associations in the manufacturing districts.[13]

But at first the ELDA did not necessarily consider itself a rival body organisationally to the LWMA, and this is suggested by its local character, its indifference at the beginning to recruiting members in parts of London other than the east, and by the decision of some of its leading members to join the LWMA. Those who applied were Harney, Davenport, Ireland and Neesom, and all of them except Neesom, whose application was the subject of some argument, were admitted at once.[14] As early as March 1837 the ELDA had argued that certain common aims existed between the Associations and has published an address to the LWMA, in which the first objects of the Democratic Association were given as the political and social education of the people and the advocacy of the rights of the oppressed.[15] There is little evidence to support Lovett's claim that the deliberate intention of the ELDA members in going into the LWMA was to gain control of it.[16] It seems more likely that, despite the LWMA's exclusive character, they were prepared to accept it as representative of an influential group in the metropolis. The new recruits may have hoped, however, that with their adhesion, the influence of the Malthusian and Benthamite middle-class radicals would have been weakened, and that they could have added their support to the left-wing LWMA members – men like James Cane Coombe and James Chapman, both of whom later left to join the Democratic Association when it had been transformed into an all-London body, and Major Beniowski, who found it possible to belong to both organisations at the same time.[17]

Events, however, forced latent differences into the open and revealed the substantial gulf between the two groups. It was the case of the

Glasgow cotton-spinners that brought matters to a head. At the end of 1837 Daniel O'Connell, an honorary member of the LWMA, attacked trade unionism in the House of Commons, during a debate on the cotton-spinners. There was widespread protest. Harney and other left-wing members commenced an agitation for the LWMA to break with O'Connell. Harney himself, at a meeting in January 1838, brought forward five resolutions denouncing O'Connell, and he also wrote a public letter to O'Connell, which was published in *The Times* in February. O'Connell sent his reply to LWMA giving the members leave to publish it or not. They chose not to and, more than this, they brought a motion of censure against Harney for the action he had taken. On 6 March, together with Tom Ireland and Charles Neesom, he resigned from the LWMA.[18]

The reasons for this breakaway were given in an 'Address to the Working Millions of Great Britain and Ireland', published in March 1838.[19] The LWMA, it said, believed that 'sham patriots' like Grote, Warburton and O'Connell would help attain the objects of the people; what they failed to realise was that, while education, on which many middle-class men placed their hopes, was of great importance, any system of education would merely perpetuate the peoples' slavery, as long as political rights were withheld. The passive obedience and non-resistance preached by the LWMA were of no use, since the interests of the middle class were directly opposed to those of the working class, and no collaboration with the latter could be of benefit.

Not long after this, Harney and his friends began to organise the ELDA, which appears to have been dormant for some months, into a society which offered a definite alternative to the LWMA. The Democratic Association began to expand and to make a deliberate appeal to wider sections of working-class London. In May 1838 Harney wrote, 'A new organisation of the proletarian classes of the metropolis is in progress'.[20] By August what had been the East London Democratic Association was transformed into the London Democratic Association (LDA).

In the constitution of the new body, it was stated that no efficient organisation of the masses had existed in London since the National Union of the Working Classes and that the LDA would fill the gap left by the exclusion of all but 'respectables' from the other radical clubs. 'No man is too poor to unite with us; on the contrary, the poorer, the more oppressed, the more welcome'.[21] The objects of the Association included five of the points of the Charter, on which working-class radicals had been united for many years, but added the establishment of social, political and universal equality, a free press, an eight-hour day, the repeal of the new Poor Law, support for working men when in conflict with the capitalist class, a programme of public instruction, the destruction of inequality and the establishment of general happiness.

The Association was to be organised into seven divisions, corresponding to the electoral divisions of London, and these were to be subdivided into sections of twenty-five members, each section having one leader.[22] From each division, two 'tribunes' were to attend a central council, but this council was open to all members, who had equal powers of voting with the tribunes. There were to be no restrictions on who could hold office; and arrangements for elections and for regular meetings were laid down. No fixed subscription was stipulated for each section, but the amount collected was to be divided equally to cover the general expenses of the Association, the expenses of the section which had collected the money, and a fund for the relief of members in distress.

During the latter part of 1838 and the beginning of 1839, the council met at the Green Dragon in Fore Street – in a first-floor room above the beershop kept by Mr Crouch. By March 1839 the Association had taken rooms at Ship Yard, Temple Bar, perhaps because the accommodation itself was more satisfactory, but probably because the LDA's growing reputation for extremism made publicans more wary of letting rooms to it. In February a crowd of LDA supporters had been denied access to their usual meeting place at the Hall of Science, City Road;[23] indeed problems in finding suitable meeting rooms were fairly common in the Chartist Movement throughout the country.

There is no doubt that the council meetings of the LDA aroused suspicion; some hostile reports of them survive in Home Office papers. One informant's report of a meeting held in April 1839 highlights the financial problems of the group. The treasurer, Thomas Ireland, received 10s. 8½d. in subscriptions. When 7s. had been paid out for the weekly rent of the room, and 7d. for the cost of candles, a mere 3s. 1½d. remained, while 14s. was still owing to cover the cost of printing membership cards.[24]

But, despite the difficulties which beset the council, the Association seems to have expanded to cover a wide area of London. By early 1839 'sections' had been set up in Bermondsey, the Old Kent Road, Deptford, Lambeth, Westminster, Marylebone, St Pancras, Islington,

Shoreditch and Hammersmith, Chiswick and Kensington. The Tower Hamlets 'Division' had been established at the Barley Mow in Upper Thames Street in September 1838.[25]

By October 1838 O'Connor, addressing members at the Green Dragon, was impressed by the LDA's strength. He wrote, 'the Democratic Association was extensive and organised beyond our expectations. We never saw a finer set of men, nor yet a set more determined to be free'.[26]

In January 1839 the Shoreditch section was formed at the Albion, Church Street; about the same time, the *Operative* published a letter from W. B. Norcott, who had this to say:

A few of us, who have been led to serious thought on our oppressions and the origin of them, and, from an ardent desire (not only for ourselves but for all the class to which we belong) that we may and they may be delivered from the state of abject slavery and despotism, of which we are the subjects; professing ourselves democrats, we have endeavoured in emulation of our brothers in London and the country to establish an auxiliary in the Old Kent Road.[27]

These men succeeded in getting 'something like a meeting' when eleven members were enrolled. Soon after a room was found at the Spotted Cow, a beershop in the Old Kent Road run by a sailor.[28] Here gatherings were held every Monday night.

Meeting at Chesney's Rooms, the Marylebone Democratic Association, which came into existence at the beginning of 1839, was soon expanded into the West London Democratic Association. This body, drawing on the strong radical tradition in Marylebone, was at first separate from the main LDA organisation, although agreeing with its principles. In April 1839 the two bodies decided to amalgamate by forming a joint committee and consolidating finances. In the same month a London Female Democratic Association was formed, among the leading members of which were relatives of the male democrats: Mary Ireland, Elizabeth Turner, Martha Dymmock, and the secretary, Elizabeth Neesom.[29]

By this time spokesmen of the LDA were claiming a membership of three thousand in comparison with a few hundred LWMA members, making the Association more representative of the London workers.[30]

The Democratic Association had an important part to play in London and national Chartism, in its doctrines, in the lines of action it put forward for the whole movement and in its independent activities. It was prominent from 1837 to 1841, when it became part of the newly founded National Charter Association. Its members continued to be active in Chartist ranks for many years.

The creed of the Association drew to a large extent upon the early Socialist writers of the 1820s, and upon the work of Spence and the Spenceans. In an address to the Polish Democratical Society in 1837, the Democrats wrote, 'We agree with you that without equality there is no liberty; for while a class or classes live on the labour of others, such men must of necessity be tyrants, and all who labour must be slaves'.[31] In 1838 Harney was writing, 'We are generally branded as levellers', when expounding some of the doctrines especially emphasised by the Democrats, and spoke of the abolition of the profit system as essential to social equality. In 1839 J. C. Coombe was stressing the need for political and social equality, 'the mountains of wealth must be pulled down and the valleys of want filled up'.[32] The picture drawn was one of a distinct 'class' of oppressed men, not one particular social group of working men, but ALL working men upon whom the other classes weighed. The enemy was not only the property owner whom Spence so vehemently attacked, but also the employing class who usurped the right of the workers to the full rewards of their labour. Sometimes this took the form of merely protesting about the injustice and tyranny of the governing classes. The poem, 'A London Democrat', about the arrest of Joseph Rayner Stephens and published in the *Operative*, perhaps demonstrates this:

> Justice we call, to thee we bend the knee;
> Redress our wrongs, and set our Champion free;
> Save from the tyrant's power our ardent friend,
> Truth's sacred cause sure Justice will defend.
> Envy and malice may join hand in hand;
> Power may arm the mean and servile band:
> Hell may unite with Aristrocratic spawn,
> E'er they shall harm him, swords shall be withdrawn,
> Nor sheath'd till buried in a tyrant's life –
> Save! Justice save us! from a civil strife.[33]

The Democratic Association, however, did advocate more than this. It is true to say that the notion of 'the Charter and something more', upheld by Harney and others during the late 1840s and early 1850s, was evident in the earlier movement. The objects of the LDA published in July 1838, which demanded more than political reforms, have been noted above. The decisive difference between the LDA and the LWMA over the Charter, which the LDA saw as merely one demand in a whole programme of change, was emphasised by J. C. Coombe:

> I have a great objection to its [the Charter] being considered as a panacea for all the evils under which you labour . . . . The disease which is now preying on your vitals is much too deeply seated to be effected by remedies of this kind. Your whole social system requires 'revolution', your commercial system requires 'revolution', and nothing short of actual convulsion will effect a cure . . . . Establish the 'People's Charter' tomorrow, and the working man would have not one difficulty the less to contend with.[34]

In an acceptance of urgent class issues, combined with the ultimate aim of the overthrow of an unjust society, the Democratic Association advanced policies that were to be the mainspring of Harney's subsequent activities. Speaking at a dinner held in 1845 to commemorate the foundation of the LDA, Harney described the members of that Association as Democrats of extreme principles of political and social equality – Chartists and something more; they spoke a direct language understood by working men, and 'called things by their right names'.[35] The stand of the LDA was a strong one: they refused to compromise on any issues, particularly that of collaboration with the middle class. Even as late as April 1841 at the end of the Democratic Association's active existence, the members were opposing the 'new move' – the educational scheme proposed by Lovett and Collins as an alternative to the National Charter Association. A resolution was passed stating 'that we the members of the ELDA consider the attempt of the new move gentry to turn the minds of the Chartists from their present organisation as impolitic, unwise and unjust'.[36]

The Democratic Association has always been seen as linked with the physical-force Chartists of the north. Clearly the aim of the members was to arouse London to the same state of militancy and 'preparedness' as existed in other areas, particularly districts like Newcastle, with which Harney was closely associated. Resolutions of support were frequently passed in favour of Oastler, Stephens and O'Connor, and full support was given by the Democratic Association to the campaign against the new Poor Law. In their extremist stand within the Convention, Harney,

Rider and Marsden received the approbation of the Democratic Association. And when Marsden, who was a Preston weaver, was imprisoned in 1840, £2 5s. 6d. was collected for him by the ELDA – the proceeds from a ball held in his honour.[37]

Francis Place summed up his view on the character of the Democratic Association by saying, 'Its members were the most outrageous of those who preached violence in almost every form'.[38] How far, it must be asked, did the Association incorporate an acceptance of physical-force methods into their plans for the making of a new society? It is clear that a large number of Democrats came to adhere to a plan of campaign of which some kind of armed uprising was an integral part. They saw the need for a convention, as the elected parliament of the people, which, by a series of mass demonstrations and strikes, would take over the government from the unrepresentative Parliament at Westminster. Because the 'oppressors' were arming the middle classes, as well as making extensive military preparations to crush the movement, it was necessary for the people to train themselves in the use of arms to protect the Convention, and to reply to force with force, should it be necessary. Insurrection in this setting became the final act in a series of activities by the people themselves. Much of this was drawn from French Revolutionary experiences, and particularly the study made of Marat and the 'Mountain'.[39] Some Democrats saw the Babeuf Insurrection of 1796, which was intended to stimulate a mass uprising of the people, as a model, but a majority based their strategy on power passing to the Convention. It is possible, however, that some of the old Spenceans of Cato Street days may have hoped for a *coup* and these hopes may have been fostered by the Polish influences as represented by Beniowski.

The violent measures that were advocated by the Democrats were, therefore, seen at first as defensive actions against government aggression and later as demonstrations of Chartist strength to gain concessions and to stimulate the people to further activity. On the membership cards of the LDA were printed the mottoes:

'Our rights – peaceably if we may, forcibly if we must',
and
'He that hath no sword let him sell his garment and buy one'.
The Democrats saw the need to be prepared for the government's refusal to concede demands and their banners bore mottoes used by Stephens in the north. One showed a hand holding a dagger, beneath which was inscribed:

> For children and wife
> We war to the knife!
> So help us God![40]

In February 1839 Coombe was urging the use of physical force if the government refused to make the Charter law, and arguing that 'this is the time for action and action only.' His newspaper the *London Democrat* included articles by Major Beniowski on military tactics, and leading articles warned that the times for a stand against tyranny was coming and that the men of London should show themselves worthy of the confidence of the northern militants.[41]

It is possible that in the spring of 1839 such threats were more than mere words, and that some kind of armed demonstration was being planned. In April a man was present at one of the LDA meetings to sell pikes to members. Harney, Coombe and Ireland met him the following week at the Hole-in-the-Wall public house in Fleet Street.[42] At a meeting at Ship Yard following a Clerkenwell Green demonstration, one man, a schoolmaster, vowed that because of the government's treatment of Stephens and Vincent he would hang a pike on the wall of his schoolroom.[43] When in May 1839 the police arrested thirteen people at Ship Yard, several pikes were found in the room, but this discovery did not give the authorities sufficient grounds for prosecution as no proof could be found that they were intended for use.[44]

After these arrests, and after the failure on 6 May of what was hoped would be an armed demonstration and an indication of the militancy of London, a feeling of disillusion clouded the Democratic Association. The *London Democrat* accused the men of London of being too well fed and clothed to join heartily in the cause.[45] It will be seen later that the extremists in the LDA did not cease to be active, but mass support for violent measures did not exist in London. The failure to rouse the men of London to militancy had a profound effect on Harney's attitude to physical-force measures. In a letter to Engels several years later, he expressed doubt as to the possibility of revolution in England. On the people's attitude to violent measures, he wrote,

> They applaud it at public meetings, but that is all. Notwithstanding all the talk in 1839 about 'arming', the people did not arm and they will not arm . . . . I do not suppose that the great changes that will come in this country will come altogether without violence, but

combats such as we may look for in France, Germany, Italy and Spain, cannot take place in this Country.[46]

Throughout 1838 and 1839 the LDA stood firm for its ideas and plans on working-class strategy. Two definite areas of action can be distinguished in which it had a particular role to play in London Chartism: first as a pressure group, working to stimulate the leaders within the Convention to more decisive measures; and secondly as the spokesmen of active insurrectionary Chartism.

A number of more moderate Chartists felt that the behaviour of the Democratic Association was detrimental to the Chartist Movement as a whole, and such feeling increased when the Chartist Convention opened in London, and the critical role of the LDA became more evident. During the months immediately prior to the opening of the Convention, the Democrats confidently gave it their support. In January Thomas Ireland was pledging confidence in it, and the different sections of the Association were passing votes of support.[47]

The Democrats played their part in organising and agitating London and in collecting the National Rent. But when the Convention met only three delegates could be called LDA men – William Cardo, shoemaker, elected for the borough of Marylebone, Harney, for Derby, Newcastle and Norwich, and Neesom for Bristol. London's major representation, quite unreasonably, was in the hands of the LWMA, gained through their unscrupulous management of the Palace Yard meeting.

As the Convention appeared to be indecisive and relatively ineffectual, the Democrats began attacking it without reserve. William Lovett wrote later,

The delay, too, in presenting the petition gave great offence to the physical-force party, and more especially to the Democratic Association of London, at the head of which was Mr George Julian Harney, one of the most indiscreet, if not the most violent among them.[48]

At a Democratic meeting at the Hall of Science, three provocative resolutions were passed: firstly that if the Convention did its duty, the Charter would be the law of the land in less than a month; secondly that no delay should take place in the presentation of the National Petition; and thirdly that every act of injustice and oppression should be immediately met by resistance. These resolutions were submitted to the Convention in March 1839 and represent the essence of the aggressive policy being pressed on the Convention and the Chartist Movement generally. The Democrats received no support. On the contrary Harney, Rider and Marsden, who had been present at the meeting, were asked to apologise for their behaviour, although it was not for several days, and after expulsion had been threatened, that a half-hearted apology was accepted.[49]

After this, it was clear that the Democrats had little influence in the Convention as it was constituted, and they realised that, if they were to affect its actions in any way, they would have to see to the election of more of their own men. A meeting was called for the purpose of electing a delegate for East Surrey, and although Charles Westerton, a moderate, was proposed, the Democrats' candidate, Joseph Williams, was elected by a great majority. But his attempt to take his seat was met with much opposition. The LDA was accused of trying to swamp the Convention, and it was only after much discussion, and the support of O'Connor, that Williams was allowed to sit. The Democratic Association then set up a committee for the purpose of organising the election of further delegates and another LDA man, William Drake, was elected for Tower Hamlets; this time the Convention refused to admit him.[50]

Although it is clear that the LDA had support in London, and was often able to muster numbers large enough to defeat the more moderate Chartists, there was also much antagonism to its manoeuvres. Several meetings were held to consider the necessity of taking a stand against its actions as, for instance, at the meeting in Waterloo Town, Bethnal Green, at which confidence in the Convention was asserted and the LDA attacked. Six men, who joined the Democratic Association because they agreed with its leaders that it was necessary to prepare for the worst, promptly left again when they learnt that Harney and others were creating dissension within the Convention.[51]

For the LDA was losing what faith it had once had in the Convention. After the Petition had been presented, J. H. B. Lorymer, the West London Democratic Association leader, contended that the Convention served no useful purpose. The LDA, he said, should act as a Jacobin Club and scrutinise the proceedings of the national body.[52] The Democrats did not go as far as this, but they certainly continued to criticise the Convention's vacillations, particularly on the issue of the sacred month. Uproar was caused at a Clerkenwell Green meeting in August 1839 when Coombe violently attacked the Convention for failing to take suitable action when Birmingham Chartists were sentenced to death. Coombe who, according to the reporter, 'has been for some time at variance with the Convention and who is looked upon with suspicion by the Chartists generally' was opposed by others at the meetings and in the confusion a fight ensued in the speakers' waggon between 'Little' Waddington and Joseph Williams, the baker.[53]

Clearly there were some, even among the Democrats, who disliked open attack on the Convention, or who were still not prepared to abandon hope in it. But by now some Chartists were considering more desperate measures.

In September the Convention was dissolved on the instigation of Dr Taylor and Harney, both of whom were associated with insurrectionary Chartism, and both of whom had been criticising the cowardly and vacillating conduct of the Convention for some time. Already some Chartists had begun to look to more conspiratorial and revolutionary ways of achieving the Charter. Forced to abandon hope of the Convention's assuming power and rallying the people to the struggle, some now began to think in terms of a series of military demonstrations or insurrections in different areas which would reinvigorate the disillusioned Chartist Movement. During the summer and autumn insurrectionary plans were almost certainly discussed and military preparations of some kind undertaken in London.

In August the police spy, Edward Hancock, informed the Home Office that a conspiracy involving Joseph Goulding, Major Beniowski and Joseph Williams (all LDA men), was being organised, and Beniowski's involvement in a conspiracy at this time is borne out by the story of a certain Polish refugee, Joseph Bobiowski, whose efforts to obtain a passport in order to leave England brought him in contact with a group of Chartists and Polish exiles. These men, it appears, sought Bobiowski's services because he had been a military man in his own country, and he was taken to a private house, given beer and asked to join the cause. Twenty-two men were present, including Dr Taylor and Beniowski, and mention was made of secret preparations in hand, and of the arming of vast numbers of men, who would be ready to rise at a given signal.[54] Nothing apparently came of these plans, but preparations of some kind appear to have continued for several months.

Any plans made for a rising in early November were abandoned on news of the defeat of the Welsh action. Preparations were resumed again for new risings planned to save Frost. In mid-November the Home Office received communications from an agent, which outlined 'a deep and dangerous conspiracy' to be carried through, probably immediately before the execution of Frost. According to this man, a council of three was sitting in London, and a meeting of delegates from the London associations had been held at the Trades Hall, Abbey Street, Bethnal Green, at which Neesom, Beniowski, Williams and Henry Ross were present, and at which it was stated that O'Connor would donate £500 towards arms. From then on, the Democratic Association met nightly at the house of Williams the baker; communications were received directly from Wales; and fireballs were secretly manufactured at the instigation of the Shoreditch Association. The plan, it was said, was to fire the shipping in the docks and to bring the sailors into the insurrection. It is interesting that, during the Cato Street plot too, the sailors were to be rallied, as were the Tower Hamlets' militia under 'General' Thomas Preston.[55]

Exactly how much of this story was based on fact must remain a mystery, but it appears to be a prelude to what followed in January. The areas which had failed to rise with the Welsh in November now planned a rising on or around 14 January 1840 to save Frost from the expected death sentence; and in this the London Chartists had a special role to play. This was to stage a mock rebellion which would occupy the police and large forces of troops stationed in the metropolis, and prevent their use in areas where the risings were to take place. When Joseph Williams died in 1849, his part in the Chartist activity of 1839 and 1840 was summed up by a fellow Chartist, Edmund Stallwood, at the graveside, as follows:

> The Convention dispersed, various movements occurred in diverse places, amongst others, at Abbey Street, Bethnal Green, at which the shrewdness of the democrats defeated the wily crafty dealing of the Whig spies and saved the people from the arms of the police and soldiery. In this affair our departed friend was deeply engaged.[56]

The exact number concerned in the January plot is unknown, but certainly many of those involved were LDA men. The plan, it appears, was to spread rumours which would reach the Home Office and the newspapers that a rising was to occur in the metropolis on the night of 14 January; intelligence of this, it was hoped, would occupy the forces in London and prevent their being used in the provinces, where risings were planned.[57] To spread such rumours would not have been difficult; there were several spies and informers within the LDA organisation. Apart from Michael Conway, who was known by the Chartists to be a policeman, there was W. P. Stuart, who claimed to be the secretary of the East London Democrats and who offered to show the minute

book to the Home Office; and there was J. Towler, a member of the
Old Kent Road Democratic Association, who gave information about
Chartist meetings and a 'Cato Street' conspiracy, probably in the hope
of receiving some remuneration for his services. (Apparently he made
very little money as a shoemaker, and his wife had to supplement their
income by taking in washing.)[58]

The Democrats were obviously aware of the presence of informers
among them and deliberately fed them with exaggerated stories drawn
in some cases from the recollections of the old Cato Street men. The
Home Office received reports of a dangerous plot, and on 14 January
the Home Secretary was writing to the Lord Mayor: 'I have received
information that some evil disposed persons contemplate disturbing
the Metropolis in the course of this night'.[59] Accordingly great preparations were made. The police, fire stations and military were alerted,
extra troops were stationed at the Tower, the soldiers at the Hounslow
barracks were ordered to march to the metropolis and floating fire-
engines were manned on the Thames. The conspirators could not have
asked for a better result. The citizens of London were shocked and
surprised the following morning, when they read in their newspapers
articles praising the government for having nipped an insurrectionary
plot in the bud by their speedy action. 'Of the admirable arrangements
of Commissioner of Police, it is difficult to speak too highly', wrote a
reporter on the *Post*. The *Southern Star* naturally ridiculed the
government's preparations as a scheme to equate the Chartists with
incendiarism and spoliation.[60]

Apparently all that actually occurred on the Tuesday evening in
question was a weekly meeting of 700 Chartists at the Trades Hall.
When the Chartists met there again on the Thursday, the police entered
the room and arrested several men, including Charles Neesom, Richard
Spurr, Joseph Williams and Joseph Goulding; some of them were
charged with having been present at an illegal meeting, others with
possessing arms. The case for the prosecution was far from strong,
resting as it did upon the contradictory testimonials of several policemen present at the meeting. The trials were carried over until the next
session and even as late as November, the cases of Neesom and Boggis
(arrested shortly afterwards) were not settled.[61]

The insurrections in the country had failed, London had played its
part and could do no more. Interest in the 'plot' dwindled with the
passing of the emergency, the trials dragged on, but no information
was subsequently revealed about the actual plans. Nevertheless, during

the months that followed, an issue arose which could easily have brought
the whole plot into the open: this was the case of Joseph Goulding,
who betrayed the Chartists by giving information to the police. A
shoemaker by trade, Goulding had been an active member of the
LWMA and of the 'Charter' subscribers' committee. He became connected with the Democratic Association, speaking at their meetings
and often advocating militant views. When arrested with the other
Chartists at Trades Hall, it seems that he agreed to give information to
the police and was exempted from appearing with the rest at Bow
Street; he had been a policeman himself some years earlier.[62] Later he
helped to identify and secure the arrest of George Boggis, a Chartist
who had been a good friend of his, and at whose table he had eaten
many a Sunday dinner. Before the hearing of the arrested Chartist,
Goulding was instrumental in a plan to secure for Mr Hobler, the
counsel for the prosecution, certain depositions of the Chartist witnesses.
A Mr Harris was sent to obtain these, but was apprehended in doing
so, and the whole scheme was revealed with fatal results for Goulding
and Hobler. Goulding's treachery now became known to his fellows and
several meetings were held at the Trades Hall to prove the validity of
the accusations against him.[63]

The apprehension of Harris caused much anxiety to the authorities.
They found it necessary to pay his bail themselves and to ship him and
his family to Australia. Mr Hobler wrote to the Home Office asking
for remuneration for this expensive case, but was refused. Goulding,
too, wrote in March and again in July, stating the services he had
rendered to the government and complaining that the Chartists were
depriving him of his livelihood by boycott and that he was reduced to
great distress. Once again the Home Office did not respond to the plea.[64]

These dramatic incidents marked a high point of the Democrats'
activities in London. From then on, they shared in the general disillusionment which weakened the Chartist associations, and when
revival came it was to different organisations that the metropolitan
Chartists rallied. In the spring of 1839 the Convention proposed that
London should be organised into trade and district Charter Associations
under one General Metropolitan Charter Association. One or two
Democratic divisions, including Tower Hamlets, unwilling perhaps to
accept their fellows' criticism of the Convention and anxious to become,
as it were, a part of the national movement, took up this idea and
formed themselves into Charter Associations.[65] But it was not until late
in the year 1840 after the foundation of the National Charter Associ-

ation, that a general change occurred and more branches took on the new name. In November, for example, the West London Democratic Association became the Marylebone Charter Association and its entire assets – £1 – were transferred by the treasurer, Charles Rennie.[66] Probably many Democrats were disheartened by the failure of militant Chartism during and after the Newport rising and O'Connor's adoption of the idea of a National Charter Association certainly would have dispelled any apprehension about discarding the old name of 'Democratic Association'. In January 1841 the last remnant of the old Association, based on the Bethnal Green branch and now using the early name of East London Democratic Association again, became in effect a Charter Association, although notices of its meetings still bore the old name for some time after.[67] By April 1842 there were thirty National Charter Associations in the London area and these constituted the main body of political Chartism in the metropolis.[68] The Democrats had always worked for a representative Chartist body in London, and besides helping to form the National Charter Associations, many of them had begun to support movements for unity and to form bodies such as the London Association of United Chartists and the Metropolitan Charter Union.[69]

Other Democrats joined in the growing movement for temperance. Many no doubt had adhered to the principle for some time; George Boggis, a temperance man, for example, used to preach every Sunday at Weymouth Terrace, Hackney, spreading the word of 'Jesus Christ, the Great Reformer of Nazareth'. Richard Spurr, an active Chartist leader, was arrested and brought before the magistrates, charged with being drunk at a teetotal meeting! The whole affair was a mistake, it appears, Spurr having been an abstainer for three years, and the real reason for his arrest being the fact that he raised political questions at a non-political meeting.[70]

The temperance and teetotal meetings were part of the movement to persuade working men to put their time and money into the establishment of institutes and lecture halls, and a number of prominent Chartists, such as Vincent and Lovett, gave it their support. In London Lovett helped to form the National Association or 'New Move' and this initially attracted a number of the more intellectual Democrats, including Charles Neesom, Thomas Ireland, William Burton, George Boggis and Allen Davenport, although these men did not necessarily share Lovett's views on the need for alliance with middle-class radicals.[71]

In some ways, then, the movement of the Democratic members

after the decline of their Association reflected the national movement of the Chartists. As the trade unions became more active with the passing of the depression, LDA members became more prominent in their own trades: William Drake, for instance, in the East of London Shoemakers' Mutual Protection Society, and J. W. Parker in the United Tailors.[72] Joseph Williams took a leading part in the activities of the Journeymen Bakers, pressing for shorter hours and the abolition of night work; he was involved, too, in London Chartism in 1848, and died of cholera in prison,[73] where he was serving a two-year sentence for sedition.

As far as can be judged the active Democrats continued to press, in the wider Chartist Movement, for both political and social changes; and some doubtless gave more attention, in the later period, to the social and economic questions, than to the continued agitation for the six points. A number, among them Charles Keen, Henry Ross, John Goodwin and Thomas Ireland followed Harney into the Fraternal Democratic Society in which many of the ideas of international socialism were to find early expression.[74]

At the time of its greatest influence, the Democratic Association spread widely over the London of that time and even beyond. Divisions and sections were in existence as far to the west as Hammersmith, Chiswick and Kensington, northwards at Marylebone, St Pancras and Islington, on the north-eastern fringes of the City at Shoreditch and Finsbury, and further east in various of the Tower Hamlets. South of the river there were branches at Lambeth, Southwark, Bermondsey and the Old Kent Road, and as far out as Deptford, not then regarded as part of London.

Meeting places, such as taverns, coffee-houses and members' homes, for semi-private meetings, give some indication of the main areas of the Association's support. Of a score or more places at which the Democrats met, a large proportion were situated on the outer fringes of the City and West End – at, for instance, Islington and the City Road, Holborn, Finsbury, Shoreditch and also eastwards through Bethnal Green and Whitechapel, and along the south side of the Thames from Lambeth to Bermondsey. Among the meeting places used by the Democratic Association could be found the Albion Coffee House, Church Street, Shoreditch, the Standard of Liberty, Brick Lane, (a beershop kept by William Drake),[75] the Endeavour Coffee House, Oxford Street, the Spotted Cow, a beerhouse in the Old Kent Road, the Barley Mow, Upper Thames Street, the Hand and Marigold, Southwark, the Market Coffee Rooms,

Smithfield, the Canterbury Arms, Lambeth, and various trades halls, lecture rooms and private houses.

It is difficult to place in the precise districts the homes of many of the Democratic Association's members, but a survey of a sample of the Democrats' home addresses confirms that the Association's greatest strength was to be found in that area of London stretching from the fringes of Islington, along the City Road, encompassing parts of Hackney, Shoreditch, Bethnal Green and Spitalfields, and running through Brick Lane to Whitechapel. In this large area, directly north and east of the City no less than 34 per cent of the identified members lived. Closer in, on the perimeters of the City was to be found a further 16 per cent and across the river, in Lambeth, Southwark and Bermondsey, 20 per cent. In the East End beyond Whitechapel there was another 12 per cent; some 6 per cent were scattered around the Holborn area and 6 per cent in Marylebone, while approximately 5 per cent resided in the northern area from Somers Town to Hampstead.

The Democrats' choice of public meeting places, in which to hold open-air meetings is sometimes, though not always an accurate guide to areas of support. It might indicate where support already existed, but could just as easily indicate an attempted expansion of support. In the case of the meeting at Smithfield in April 1839 which 'carried the Charter into the City'[76] the LDA appears to have been engaged in proving that it and not the LWMA was actively proselytising for the Charter in London. Regular meetings do suggest a fair amount of stable support and these were held, for instance, at Stepney Green and at the open space in Weymouth Terrace, Hackney, as well as at the better-known radical meeting places, Clerkenwell Green and Kennington Common. The actual numbers which the Democratic Association could muster are difficult to assess, not only because the sources of information were usually biased, but also because much Chartist support was undoubtedly general, consisting of people who would not necessarily have belonged to any particular association. What can be said is that where the LDA called a purely local meeting, the numbers would be an indication of local members and supporters. For example, the 300 persons who assembled at Weymouth Terrace on 12 August 1839 and then marched, with a band in front, to Kennington Common to support a general demonstration on behalf of the sentenced Birmingham Chartists, would have been mainly Democrats from the Shoreditch district; and for a weekday turn-out from one area, this suggests a fairly reliable group of active supporters. At Kennington Common itself about 100 Democrats, probably from the Lambeth branch, were addressed by Joseph Williams, before the arrival of the other contingents. The final assembly totalled around 4000 and, very likely, a large number of these were drawn from the ranks of the Democrats or were democratic sympathisers, although the issue on which the meeting was called would have attracted others too. The choice of speakers – O'Connor, Dr Taylor and O'Brien appears to confirm the militant character of the demonstration.[77]

Figures for regular or special meetings called by the LDA are bound to show comparatively small attendances, and should not be compared with the much larger figures for meetings summoned or supported by the entire radical movement in the metropolis. But in the predominantly working-class areas of London, the Democratic Association were considerably more influential and commanded a great deal more support than the LWMA, whose activities in the metropolis have been over-estimated, almost certainly due to too much reliance upon information provided by Francis Place.

Divisions and branches, members' houses, private and public meetings all combine to show that, although the Democrats had support in many districts of London, their heaviest concentration was in a wide area skirting the City to the north-east, east and south-east. It can hardly escape attention that these were areas in which certain trades predominated, most notably shoemaking, tailoring, furniture-making and weaving. The link between the Democrats and the weavers was noted by Gammage, who wrote, 'the main strength of the Democratic Association lay among the distressed and starving Spitalfields Weavers'; and other historians, including Schoyen, have endorsed this opinion. G. D. H. Cole adds 'dockers . . . and Irish labourers' to the Spitalfields weavers as LDA supporters.[78] Some historians have clearly been influenced by the Democrats' own predilection for regarding themselves as champions of the lowest sections of society and by their frequent repudiation of what they dubbed the 'respectables' in the London population. Such expressions need to be understood in the light of the political situation in London and particularly of the relations between the embittered artisans of the 'dishonourable' trades and the élite of the LWMA.

D. J. Rowe has challenged the support for Chartism among the Spitalfields weavers asserting that, 'there is no evidence that the silk handloom weavers of the Spitalfields and Bethnal Green area of London, a few individuals apart, played any part in Chartist activity.' The only weavers to be found, he continues, were in the LWMA and 'none of the leading members of the ELDA, where their occupations are ascertainable, were silk-weavers.'[79] It is hard to understand how this conclusion was reached, for a close examination of the active members of the Democratic Association between 1837 and 1841 shows that weavers constitute the second-largest occupational group in the organisation.[80] Out of the identified members whose occupations are ascertainable, no less than 12.5 per cent were silk-weavers; of those who were very probably Democrats, but whose actual card membership cannot be verified, some 10 per cent were weavers.

Just as the weaving industry in the area gave considerable support to the Democratic Association, so, too, did the other predominant trades. Tailors, carpenters, cabinet-makers and other furniture-makers, printers, bricklayers and brassfounders were all fairly numerous in the Association, but by far the largest ascertainable group of identifiable members was the shoemakers, who made up no less than 22.5 per cent of the certain members and 20 per cent of the probable members. Of the men arrested when the police raided the Ship Yard headquarters, four out of thirteen members or supporters – William Cornish, William Burton, Thomas Ward and Samuel Waddington, were in the shoemaking trade.[81]

The radical temper of the shoemakers is well-known; in the history of working-class movements they were always prominent. Engaged in a long struggle to preserve their status as artisans and their standards of living, they were also very busy in political movements and tended to extremism. They were active in the London Corresponding Society; in 1803 the London Society of Journeymen Boot and Shoemakers voted money to help Colonel Despard and his fellow members of the 'United Englishmen', tried for treason; they were active in the dissemination of Spence's ideas and in the Spencean Philanthropist's Society; the Cato Street conspiracy was hatched in shoemakers' workshops; they were among the supporters of Owenite trade unions. When the Charter Associations were formed in 1839, the shoemakers were one of the first to form a Trades Charter Association.[82]

Shoemakers, therefore, were to be expected in the forefront of the Democratic Association, and they certainly do not fit into the suggested divisions sometimes made between LWMA and LDA supporters – that of skilled and unskilled. The distinction is much more likely to have been the difference between the 'honourable' and 'dishonourable' sections of trades, and particularly between trades in which the journeymen craftsmen worked fairly closely with the master and kept his skills and standards, and the trades where the work, increasingly subdivided, was done in small workshops under the control of middlemen.[83] Most of the Democrats appear to have possessed traditional skills and many were journeymen, though often in trades suffering by the poverty of their customers, and from overcrowding and excessive competition. Joseph Williams, 'a short stout man', was a journeyman baker in Brick Lane, earning sometimes as little as five shillings a week, on which he had to keep a wife and six children.[84] Very few of the members were substantial enough to figure in the Trade Directories of the time.[85] Most of the evidence uncovered points to the fact that the supporters were from those groups whose independence and conditions were being destroyed and who were often very poor. Reports of LDA meetings describes the crowds as 'mechanics and labourers', or as 'destitute-looking individuals', or 'of miserable appearance'.[86] But such accounts depend upon the social criteria adopted by the reporter, rather than on an accurate knowledge of working-class life and its gradations at the time.·

Indeed it has proved impossible to find more than one 'labourer' among the Democrats, and Cole's statement that the membership included a number of Irish labourers appears unfounded. Not only were there few labourers, but also many of the Irish workers in the capital were divided from the London workers by nationality, religion and politics, for large numbers of them were under the influence of O'Connell, the *bête noire* of the LDA. At this time the Irish were most likely to be in the O'Connellite Precursor Societies.[87]

The Democratic Association does seem to have attracted a fair proportion of the intelligent and thinking working men, some of whom were clearly held down by their environment and found in Chartism an expression of their ideas and aspirations. There were many such people among the leaders of the Democratic Association; younger men like Julian Harney, son of a sailor, active with Hetherington in the unstamped press fight, described as 'one of the most interesting and articulate of the London Jacobins'.[88] Lack of knowledge about Harney's childhood has tended to affect the way in which historians have viewed his actions. Most have followed Gammage's belief that he was an orphan, and that this was the main cause of his bitterness and 'extremism'. In fact examination of the Census material of 1841 shows that Harney's mother – Sarah – was alive at this time and that she lived with several children at 2 Heralds Place, Horsleydown, Bermondsey. This information is borne out by documents pertaining to Harney in the records of the Royal Naval School, Greenwich, which he attended. Harney was eligible for this school as the son of a seaman and as an 'object of charity', and not because he was an orphan, as has been thought. Both his parents were living when he was sent to the school at the age of nine; his brother, John, also became a pupil five years later in 1831, by which time the family had moved from Deptford to Bermondsey. Harney's father was described as a 'Rigger'. He did not die until 1850.[89]

The Democratic Association also attracted to its ranks James Coombe, the chemist, editor of the *London Democrat*; the fluent and literate warehouseman, Thomas Ireland; men like Thomas Sherman, who ran ale rooms and a library in Queenhithe; J. H. B. Lorymer, described as 'a well-known democratic writer of the French republican school', who wrote for the *London Democrat*, and appealed to medical students, clerks and shopmen to join the Chartist cause;[90] and veterans like Charles Neesom, the tailor, active in politics all his life, who set up at this time a small library and bookshop at William Drake's premises in Brick Lane;[91] and Allen Davenport, the poet–politician. The international strain, which was to be so prominent in the later activities of Harney and other Democrats, attracted at least two Polish members to the Association – Major Beniowski and Martha Schellvietinghoff.[92]

In the ranks of the Democratic Association, then, were to be found a representative group of London artisans, ranging from printers to the exploited coalwhippers,[93] leavened by the occasional intellectual and led by a combination of veteran radicals and younger radicals. These men were able to exercise a not inconsiderable influence on the movement to which they belonged and, in many cases, pioneered ideas, doctrines and strategies that were to have a substantial influence on the labour movements of the nineteenth century.

From the evidence now available it is possible to say that much in earlier assessments of the Democratic Association needs substantial revision. Though some features of its policy and activities remain necessarily obscure, it is now possible to be certain on a number of important points.

The Democratic Association was not founded by O'Connor, nor in any important aspect dominated by him. It had its own leaders and its own distinctive policy. Some of its leading members associated with O'Connor during his attempts, through the Universal Suffrage Club and the Central National Association, to create a united metropolitan organisation of the radical working class; during his London campaign against the new Poor Law; and because of a mutual hostility to the middle-class Benthamite radicals, and a distrust of the leaders of the LWMA.

Nevertheless the Democratic Association was not merely a factious rival to the LWMA, though it was in opposition to it and did deny its right to speak for the majority of the London working class. The Association developed out of contemporary political and social conditions in the metropolis. It was indigenous to London, its people and its history. It reflected majority working-class needs and aspirations in a way that the more exclusive LWMA failed to do. It mirrored the deep-rooted divisions between middle-class radicalism and the immediate and long-term interests of the working people. Trade regulations, maintenance of skills and independence, protection from cheap labour at home and abroad, and social justice for all were incompatible with *laissez-faire*, free trade, harsh factory discipline and an open labour market. No compromise was possible between these policies in the view of the Democrats, and in the view of many thousands in the north of England, who were engaged in bitter struggle against the epitome of middle-class reform, the new Poor Law. The majority of the LWMA probably shared hostility to many of the aims of middle-class radicalism, but with them, caution and absolute faith in reasoned argument, education and the ultimate benefits of the franchise tended to blinker their view of the contemporary scene and blur the basic differences. The Democratic Association believed it spoke for the true interests of the London trades and the London poor, and in performing this function, it was clearly doing much more than merely opposing the LWMA, or merely conniving at pressurising it and the Convention.

The Democratic Association was not an organisation of wretched, ragged, often demoralised, depressed rabble – though its propagandists tended at times to give this impression. Nor was it necessarily representative of the unskilled worker as opposed to the craftsmen of the LWMA. The Democrats were drawn from and supported by the lower trades in London – the shoemakers, tailors, building-workers and others, but the support the workers gave to the Democrats was more a reflection of their resolute radicalism than a matter of their trade classification; and, though many might be classified as 'dishonourable' and were often in depressed conditions, they had been engaged in a continuous struggle over decades to maintain crafts and status, and still thought of themselves as skilled and independent men. They were the same type of craftsmen who had been active in London radical movements for over half a century.

The quality of the membership affirms clearly enough that the Democratic Association was not, as some have suggested, a group extension of the personality of Harney, the best-known of its leaders. His major role in the wider Chartist Movement and his later associations tend to encourage this idea, especially as it was largely through his activities that the Democratic Association featured so prominently in the Convention and in Chartism in the years 1838 to 1840. The Association, as has been shown, had from the beginning leaders well-known to the radicals in the metropolis, most of them holding distinct opinions and many of them representatives of the old Spencean tradition.

Nor was the Democratic Association made up of 'extremists', if that word is used to mean irresponsible, assertive champions of force for the sake for force. There was, of course, a long history of popular outbreaks in London; some of the older men would have had memories of the United Englishmen, Spa Fields and Cato Street, and there was constant reference to the French Revolution, especially to the 'Conspiracy of the Equals'. But the most energetic Democratic leaders saw arming and insurrection as a piece, not the whole, of Chartist strategy, and based their expectations on the creation of an alternative government, in the form of the Convention, around which the might of an uprisen people was to be assembled. Arms and insurrection were but complementary to this, not a substitute for mass action and support. That, in the period which followed the Convention, some of the more resolute Democrats became involved in revolutionary plots, in no way invalidates this; and it should be noted that the Democrats in London did in fact replace conspiracy by small numbers with an organised diversionary exercise that partially achieved its purpose – to throw the authorities into a state of alarm, and slow down the dispatch of reinforcements elsewhere.

The word 'Democrat' was chosen, quite obviously, to distinguish the group from the other working- and middle-class radical movements, and had a special significance. Democratic Associations were set up quite often in areas where there were already Working Men's Associations – Tower Hamlets, for example. That the adoption of the name 'Democrat' marked a break in the policy and activity, with the other types of suffrage groups can be seen by the fact that Democratic Associations sprang up in areas outside London – Leeds, Norwich, Nottingham and some parts of Scotland – and were in direct contact with the London Democrats. The Norwich Association, formed as early as December 1838, was almost certainly the main instrument in securing the choice of Harney as Norwich delegate to the Convention. The Leeds Democratic Association was founded in June 1839 out of the 'East End

Union', and modelled itself on the London body, making Harney, Coombe and Beniowski honorary members.[94] When Thomas Ireland replied to a suggestion that the 'distinction of names' within the London Chartist organisations should be dropped, and that unity was all-important, he upheld the belief in the word 'Democracy' in its social and political sense and insisted that, 'A true union of purpose can only be based upon principle'.[95]

A clue to the special meaning attached to the title 'Democrat' can be found in the dates chosen for the foundation of the ELDA and the LDA, the first on the birthday of Thomas Paine (which was celebrated by numerous local branches on subsequent anniversaries),[96] and the second, in the month of anniversaries of the overthrow of the French monarchy in 1792 and the proclamation of the Constitution of 1793. These two strands of English working-class radicalism were a constant feature of the Democrats' activity and propaganda. Use was made of French Revolutionary examples and symbols within the Association. For example, one of the banners carried on demonstrations bore a cap of liberty encircled by the words 'Free we live and free we die'.[97] When J. C. Coombe began to publish the *London Democrat*, its views reflected the opinions of the republican thinkers within the LDA – strongly internationalist, and constantly referring back to the French Revolution. Harney wrote articles on the history of France during the Revolutionary years and extracts from O'Brien's life of Robespierre were published. In the second number the LDA was compared to the Jacobin Clubs: 'In the Democratic Association the Jacobin club again lives and flourishes, and the villainous tyrants shall find to their cost, that England too has her Marats, St. Justs and Robespierres'.[98]

The native tradition – the other dominant theme in the LDA – has already been referred to. E. P. Thompson has said:

> By 1797 it is clear that some of the extreme Jacobins had come to despair of constitutional agitation. From this time forward for more than twenty years, there was a small group of London Democrats (Spencean or republican) who saw no hope but in a *coup d'etat*, perhaps aided by French arms, in which some violent action would encourage the London 'mob' to rise in their support.[99]

If this is correct, then this tradition found its expression in the Democratic Association, led as it was by a group of radicals whose connections stretched back through several decades; and supported as it was by those trades which had been prominent in London agitations from the days of Wilkes. It was from these trades that there came support for all the more militant radical movements.

What does seem most distinctive of all about the Democratic Association membership is that it was drawn, largely though not entirely, from the men of the small workshops and home workshops, often clinging fiercely to their independence.

The bitter radicalism of the shoemakers, tailors, furniture-makers and some building-workers, constituted a temper much closer to that of the fiery workmen of the northern town, than to that of the 'respectables' of moderate Chartism and the LWMA. It has been argued that trades such as these, actively concerned with the restoration of a craftsman status and protected industries, were the supporters of O'Connor, who with his belief in small proprietors, shared their opinions as well as those of the doomed handloom weavers and small independent producers; O'Connor is thus seen as upholding individualism, whereas the new industrial trades are looked upon as potential supporters of socialism. This generalisation, now widely discredited, does not stand up when set against the facts about the Democratic Association and its supporters, for it was the small independent men of the doomed or disintegrating trades, that were 'Socialists' drawing much of their thinking from Thomas Paine, Thomas Spence, Thomas Evans and, to a lesser extent, from Robert Owen.

The Democrats saw that compromise between middle- and working-class interests was impossible – that the victory of the middle classes must mean that middle-class ideas, like middle-class economic interests, would triumph. They wanted 'the Charter and something more' believing that radical social and economic change was the end, and political reform merely one of the means. Harney and some of the younger members appeared temporarily to have bridged the gulf between what, for convenience sake, must be termed the old and the new, by seeking to ally the struggle for the franchise with the struggle for pressing and immediate social reforms and for substantial social change. It was this aspect of the LDA which was to be carried on by Harney and others as a possible programme for the labour movement of the 1840s and 1850s. Initially Marx and Engels opposed this strategy, but were later to give it their support. But by this time the social context had changed. The new trade unionists and working-class radicals were concentrating on coping with, and adapting to, a fast-growing industrial world. If they held the Charter in their hearts, they gave their minds and skills to the strengthening of their own defences.

In the new social scene there could be no support from the doomed trades. As the numbers of these small producers declined so, for a time, did militancy in the working-class movement. The LDA with its programme of social change, class issues and political reform, may claim to have pioneered, to some extent, a way forward for the future labour movement. In another respect, it represented the last significant expression of a working-class radicalism that had excited the loyalties and enthusiasm of the trades of London for over half a century.

NOTES

1. *Prospectus of the East London Democratic Association*, Lovett Collection (Birmingham Central Library) repr. in D. Thompson (ed.), *The Early Chartists* (Macmillan, 1971) p. 55.

2. G. D. H. Cole and R. Postgate, *The Common People* (Methuen, 1938) pp. 275, 276.

3. T. Rothstein, *From Chartism to Labourism* (Martin Lawrence, 1929) p. 133. He writes 'I can claim that I was the first to discover the historical part played by George Julian Harney (one may almost call him) Bolshevik'.

4. M. Hovell, *The Chartist Movement* (Manchester University Press, 1918) p. 126; see also F. Rosenblatt, *The Chartist Movement in its Social and Political Aspects* (Frank Cass, 1967) p. 110.

5. G. D. H. Cole and A. W. Filson, *British Working Class Movements* (Macmillan, 1965) p. 366; G. D. H. Cole, *Chartist Portraits* (Macmillan, 1941) p. 311.

6. A. R. Schoyen, *The Chartist Challenge* (Heinemann, 1957) pp. 30, 32.

7. Rothstein, *Chartism to Labourism*, p. 45.

8. W. Robson, *London Directory 1837* (Robson, 1837).

9. A. Briggs (ed.), *Chartist Studies* (Macmillan, 1959) p. 27. For O'Connor's connections with the ELDA and his later sympathy with the Association in their attempts to elect non-LWMA representatives to the Convention, see J. Epstein, 'Feargus O'Connor and the English Working-class Radical Movement; a Study in National Chartist Leadership' (University of Birmingham, unpub. Ph.D. Thesis, 1977) pp. 75, 276.

10. On Davenport see *Northern Star (NS)*, 5 Dec. 1846: Obituary; *National Co-operative Leader*, 8, 22 March 1861: Extracts from 'Life'; Waddington: Home Office Papers (Public Record Office), 61/22 Police Report, 11 May 1839 (hereafter H. O.) – Waddington was well known in radical circles as the 'Little' Bill-sticker; Preston: A. R. Schoyen, *George Julian Harney* (unpub. Ph.D. Thesis, University of London, 1951); H O 40/4/3, Police Report, 15 November 1816; George: *Place Newspaper Collection* (British Museum) set 56 (July–Dec. 1838) f. 99 (hereafter 'Place 56') – George became a member of the Lambeth Democratic Association; Harper: Place Papers (British Musuem) Add. Mss. 27797 –

Harper was involved in the celebrations when Furzey was acquitted in 1833; Neesom: Place, Add. Mss 27797, f. 193.

11. Luckins was a member of the Surrey Radical Association, (*Radical*, 29 May, 12 June 1836); Ireland and his mother later ran a newsvendors shop near Blackfriars Bridge, (*Post Office London Directory*, 1845 (W. Kelly, 1845)); J. H. B. Lorymer was a well-known editor of unstamped newspapers (P. Hollis, *The Pauper Press, a Study in Working-class Radicalism in the 1830s* (Oxford University Press, 1970) p. 312.)

12. Place 56, f. 76; Place, Add. Mss 27819, F. 88; *London Mercury*, 18 June 1837.

13. See I. J. Prothero, 'Chartism in London', *Past & Present*, no. 44 (1969).

14. Place, Add. Mss, 37773-7, LWMA minute book, 7, 8 Aug., 24 Oct. 1837; hereafter 'LWMA Minutes'.

15. Place 56, f. 56; *London Dispatch*, 26 March 1837.

16. This claim has been supported by several historians, including Schoyen, Ph.D., p. 30; D. Read and E. Glasgow, *Feargus O'Connor* (Edward Arnold, 1961) p. 51.

17. Coombe joined the LWMA in 1836 (LWMA Minutes, 7 Aug. 1836). Both he and Chapman left and joined the LDA at the beginning of 1839 (*Operative*, 6 Jan 1839). On Beniowski, see LWMA Minutes, 18 Sept. 1838 and P. Brock, 'Polish Democrats and English Radicalism 1832-1862', *Journal of Modern History*, vol. 25 (June 1953) p. 146.

18. LWMA Minutes, 9, 16 Jan., 27 Feb., 6 March 1838; *Times*, 13 Feb., 1838.

19. *NS*, 24 March 1838.

20. *NS*, 19 May 1838.

21. HO 44/52, *Constitution of the London Democratic Association*. What follows on the organisation of the LDA is taken from this pamphlet.

22. This structure was significantly similar to that of earlier societies, e.g. the London Corresponding Society, and the Society for Constitutional Information, which had been involved in the Despard Plot (E. P. Thompson, *The Making of the English Working Class* (Gollancz, 1965) pp. 163, 480). Possibly this was why some questioned the legality of the new organisation.

23. HO 44/52, Police Report, 23 Jan. 1839; *Operative*, 10 March 1839; Harney, in an address to his constituents in Norwich, Derby and Newcastle, wrote that the LDA was being denied meeting rooms (*NS*, 30 March 1839).

24. HO 40/44, Police Report, 12 April 1839.

25. *NS*, 15 Sept. 1838. The 'sections' may have been brought together in 'divisions' as suggested in the constitution. Schoyen, *The Chartist Challenge*, states that only three divisions existed: Tower Hamlets, Southwark and the City (p. 32).

26. *NS*, 27 Oct. 1838.

27. *Operative*, 6 Jan. 1839. For the Shoreditch Section see *Operative*, 13 Jan. 1839.

28. HO 44/52, Police Report, 19 Jan. 1839.

29. For information on the WLDA see *Champion*, 27 Jan. 1839; *Operative*, 29 Jan. 1839; Schoyen Ph.D. p. 21; and H O 40/44 Police Report, 19 April 1839. On the Female Association see *Operative*, 14 April 1839.

30. *Operative*, 10 March 1839.

31. Place, 56 f. 80; LDA address 21 May 1837.

32. *Operative*, 13 Jan. 1838; *London Democrat*, 27 April 1839.

33. *Operative*, 27 Jan, 1839.

34. *London Democrat*, 1 June 1839. Coombe was a chemist as his terminology suggested.

35. *NS*, 16 Aug. 1845.

36. Place, 56 f. 416; *NS*, 24 April 1841.

37. *Operative*, 9 Dec. 1838, 20 Jan., 10 March 1839; *NS*, 7 Nov. 1840.

38. Place, 56 f. 4; Rosenblatt contends that the LDA was the mouthpiece of physical force Chartism *The Chartist Movement*, p. 110).

39. For the influence of the French Revolution on the Chartist Movement, see Hovell, *Chartist Movement*., p. 285, Schoyen, *Chartist Challenge*, p. 62, Cole and Filson, *British Working-class Movements*, p. 351. The LDA members saw themselves as playing the same role in the Convention as the pressure group known as the 'Mountain' did in the French Convention of 1792–1793.

40. Place, 56 f. 350; R. G. Gammage, *History of the Chartist Movement* (Newcastle-on-Tyne: Browne and Browne, 1894) p. 95.

41. HO 44/52, Police Report, 15 Feb. 1839; *London Democrat*, 4, 11 May, 9 June 1839.

42. HO 40/44, Police Report, 13, 19 April 1839.

43. *Operative*, 12 May 1839. The schoolmaster was almost certainly Francis Wilbey, who taught at the Pestolozzian Academy, Worship Square; he was arrested with twelve others at Ship Yard (*Operative*, 19 May 1839).

44. See *Champion*, 19 May 1839; *NS*, 18 May 1839; *Charter*, 19 May 1839.

45. *London Democrat*, 18 May 1839.

46. G. Julian Harney to Frederick Engels (1836) in *The Harney Papers*, eds Frank Gees and Renee Metivier Black (Assen, 1969) p. 240. In the same letter Harney cast considerable doubt on his own ability to lead a revolution; he possessed none of the necessary qualities: 'I know nothing of arms, have no stomach for fighting and would rather die after some other fashion than by bullet or rope.'

47. See, for example, *Operative*, 27 Jan. 1839; *NS*, 26 Jan. 1839.

48. W. Lovett, *The Life and Struggles of William Lovett in his Pursuit of Bread, Knowledge and Freedom* (Trübner, 1876) Vol. 1, p. 203.

49. *NS*, 9 March 1839.

50. On Williams, see ibid., 27 April 1839, on Drake *Charter*, 5 May 1939, *NS*, 11 May 1839.

51. *Charter*, 5 May 1839; *Operative*, 17 March 1839.

52. *Charter*, 25 Aug. 1839. Some of the methods which Lorymer suggested for the Chartists to use to achieve the Charter were exclusive dealing, torchlight meetings and attendance in Church.

53. HO 40/44, Police Report, 17 Aug. 1839.

54. HO 40/44, Police Report, 13 Aug. 1839. *Metropolitan Police Papers* (Public Record Office) 2/43. The Chartists discovered Hancock's treachery because, according to Joseph Goulding, he had not been offered sufficient reward for his information and attempted to rejoin the Chartist Movement.

55. HO 40/44, Anonymous letters to Hobler, 15, 16, 18, 19 Nov. 1839; HO 40/4/3, Report, 15 Nov. 1816.

56. *NS*, 22 Sept. 1849.

57. This method was not new in radical circles. Francis Place wrote of the

London agitation during the Reform Bill crisis: 'All that seemed necessary to be done was the making of such various demonstrations as would cause apprehension to the rulers and for the safety of the Metropolis and themselves, compel them to keep the soldiers where they were.' (G. Wallas, *Life of Francis Place*, (Allen and Unwin, 2nd edn, 1918) p. 305). Abortive risings did occur in Bradford, Sheffield and Dewsbury. The *Southern Star*, 19 Jan. 1840, described the risings in the North as 'all apparently acting in concert and for a given purpose'.

58.   For Conway, see *NS*, 25 Jan. 1840; for Stuart, HO 61/24, Letter, 24 Dec. 1839; F. C. Mather, *Public Order in the Age of the Chartists* (Manchester U. P., 1959) p. 205; for Towler, HO 44/52, Letters 16, 22 Jan. 1839; Police Report, 23 Jan. 1839.

59.   HO 41/15, Letter from Normanby to Lord Mayor, 14 Jan. 1840. The anonymous letter is classified under H O 61/25.

60.   *Post*, 15 Jan. 1840; *Southern Star*, 19 Jan. 1840. Other reports are to be found in *The Times*, the *Advertiser*, the *Morning Chronicle* and the *Morning Herald*. The *Weekly Chronicle* wrote 'the wild and truculent spirit that animates small sections of the working classes . . . is truly alarming', and complains of 'brutal attacks on defenceless policemen'.

61.   For information on the arrests and the trials see *NS*, 25 Jan. 1840; *Charter*, 19 Jan. 1840; *Southern Star*, 19 Jan. 1840 and reports in current issues of other newspapers. Neesom, already out of work when arrested, suffered much hardship because of the delay. His furniture was seized to cover bail, and he was forced to go to prison on 6*d* a day (*NS*, 16 May, 6 June 1840). Boggis lost his job as a grocer's assistant because of the arrest (*NS*, 18 April 1840).

62.   LWMA Munutes, f. 103; *Charter*, 17 March 1839; HO 40/44, Police Report, 13 August 1839; C. Reith, *British Police and the Democratic Ideal* (OUP, 1943) p. 240; *Southern Star*, 15 March 1840.

63.   *NS*, 7 March, 4, 18, 25 April 1840.

64.   HO 61/27, Letter, 20, 28 July 1840.

65.   *Operative*, 31 March, 7 April 1839.

66.   *NS*, 28 Nov. 1840.

67.   Ibid., 30 Jan., 6 Feb., 17 April 1841. The new association met, like the old one, at the 'Hit or Miss Inn', Globe Fields.

68.   Briggs, *Chartist Studies*, p. 51.

69.   Democrats in the London Association of United Chartists included Neesom, Rainsley, Boggis, Cater and Peat (*NS*, 4 Jan. 1840); in the Metropolitan Charter Union; Neesom, Savage, Rainsley, Terry and White (*Southern Star*, 22 March 1840).

70.   HO 44/52, Police Report, 26 Aug. 1839; *Northern Star*, 19 Dec. 1840.

71.   Place, Add. Mss 37774, National Association Minute Book.

72.   *NS*, 25 Jan. 1845, 22 June 1844.

73.   Ibid., 24 April 1847, 22 Sept. 1849.

74.   A number of Democrats seem to have remained loyal to Harney. J. Mathias, several years later, gave his support to Harney against Jones; he wrote to Harney: 'My knowledge of you commenced in 1838, when you established the Democratic Association in Bermondsey and of which I was a youthful member' (*NS*, 22 May 1852). Ireland later settled in O'Connorville (*NS*, 30 June 1849).

75.   Drake, an active member of the Democratic Association, is described in

Robson's Directory, (1837), as a beer-retailer. In 1845, the East of London Shoe-makers' Mutual Protection Society met at Drake's public house, as had many clubs and societies before (*NS*, 25 Jan, 1845).

76. *NS*, 27 April 1839; H O 40/44, Police Report, 23 April 1839. The police-man referred to the lack of interest evident in passers-by. The police bias is also shown by reports of the meeting at Smithfield on 6 May 1839. The *Operative* estimated the crowd to have been 6000 (*Operative*, 12 May 1839); a police informer estimated a mere 800 (H O 40/44, Police Report, 7 May 1839).

77. *NS*, 17 Aug. 1839.

78. Gammage, *History of the Chartist Movement*, p. 54; Schoyen, *Chartist Challenge*, p. 31; G. D. H. Cole, *Chartist Portraits*, p. 273.

79. D. J. Rowe, 'Chartism and the Spitalfields Silk-weavers', *Economic History Review* (Dec. 1967) pp. 484, 485.

80. These figures are based on all those members whose occupations were ascertainable, and should be regarded only as an approximate estimate. 160 named individuals have been identified as connected with the Democratic Associations in London – in only 35 cases could direct membership not be verified.

81. *English Chartist Circular*, 30 Jan. 1841.

82. *Operative*, 28 April 1839.

83. The distinction between 'honourable' and 'dishonourable' sections of trades is elucidated by I. J. Prothero, 'Chartism in London', *Past & Present*, no. 44 (1969) p. 83. For a detailed account of the London tailors' situation in the 1830s, see the same author's 'The London Tailors' Strike of 1834 and the Collapse of the Grand National Consolidated Trades' Union: a Police Spy's Report', *International Review of Social History*, no. 22 (1977) p. 65.

84. H O 40/44, Police Report, 8 May 1839; *NS*, 15 Sept. 1849, for a/c of William's death and funeral.

85. *Robson's Directory 1837*, and *Post Office Directory 1845*. One or two members do appear, e.g. William Wilkins, 75 High Street, Poplar.

86. H O Police Reports, 7 May, 13 Aug. 1839.

87. By 1839 there were 23 Precursor Societies in London including branches at Marylebone, Kensington, Holborn, Smithfield, Whitechapel and Moorfields (*Operative*, 13 Jan. 1839). The objects of the societies included loyalty to the queen, safe, prudent and practicable extension of the Franchise, reform of corpor-ations, the ballot, shorter parliaments, no tithes for Ireland and a just proportion of Irish members in a united Parliament (*Operative*, 10 Feb. 1839). A police reporter said that a number of Democrats were leaving their Associations to join the Precursors in January 1839 (HO 44/52, Police Report, 23 Jan. 1839).

88. Briggs, *Chartist Studies*, p. 12.

89. PRO Admiralty papers, 73; *The Friend of the People*, 14 Dec. 1850.

90. *Operative*, 17 March, 28 April 1839; *London Democrat*, 4 May 1839.

91. *Post Office Directory*, 1845.

92. *London Democrat*, 25 May 1839; *Operative*, 16 June 1839. The Democrats rallied to Beniowski's support when the Government cut his grant to £3 a month. He was described as 'Tall, well-looking, slim' (HO Police 40/44, Report, 13 May 1839).

May 1839); and the coalwhipper, James Bettis of John Street, City Road. For the conditions under which coalwhippers worked and lived, see *Weekly Dispatch*, 13 June 1841.

94. *Operative*, 16 Dec. 1838; *NS*, 22 June 1839.

95. *Operative*, 14 April 1839.

96. For example, suppers were held at the 'Sussex Arms' Hammersmith by the Hammersmith, Chiswick and Kensington branch (*Operative*, 13 Jan. 1839) and at the 'Farnham Castle', Queenhithe (*Operative*, 10 Feb. 1839).

97. Place 56, f. 350.

98. Cited Rosenblatt, *The Chartist Movement*, p. 111; see also *London Democrat*, 13 April, 18 May 1839. The *London Democrat* was published from 13 April to 8 June 1839.

99. E. P. Thompson, *Making of the English Working Class*, p. 173.

4. Ireland and the Irish in English Radicalism before 1850[1]

DOROTHY THOMPSON

> Before I reached my nineteenth year (1843) my spare time was divided between three public movements – the temperance movement under Father Matthew, the repeal movement under Daniel O'Connell, and the Chartist or English movement under Feargus O'Connor. In the bewildering whirl of excitement in which I lived during those years I seemed almost wholly to forget myself. Night brought with it long journeys to meetings and late hours, though the day brought back the monotony of the sweater's den . . .
>
> (*Robert Crowe, The Reminiscences of a Chartist Tailor*)

HISTORIANS of English radicalism and Chartism differ on the place which Irish questions played in the various movements, and on the importance of the part played in English radical movements by Irish men and women. The years during which the Chartist Movement dominated English radicalism were also the years of Daniel O'Connell's domination of Irish popular politics. The earlier historians of Chartism tended to see the O'Connellite repeal movement as entirely separate from Chartism, but to allow for a considerable Irish influence in Chartism nevertheless. For many of them, this influence was unfortunate. Mark Hovell, Chartism's first historian, saw O'Connor as an Irish outsider who battened on to English politics after having failed in Irish politics and quarrelled with O'Connell, and who thereby encouraged all that was worst in English popular politics – violence, brutality, and a mindless harking back to an idealised peasant past. Hovell had no time for the Irish in any form. He regarded Feargus O'Connor as the ruin of

Chartism, but interestingly, although he found it difficult to find language base enough to describe Feargus, he nevertheless saw him as 'the best of a rather second-rate lot' when he entered Parliament as one of the Irish members in 1833. The Irish immigrants in Hovell's picture always 'swarm', and serve mainly as shock troops for that turbulent side of the movement for which Hovell had no sympathy or understanding.[2]

Hovell's views were challenged by some later historians, in particular by Rachel O'Higgins, who demonstrated a considerable Irish presence among the Chartist leadership, and a concern for Irish questions which could not simply be ascribed to personal interest on the part of O'Connor.[3] Recently, however, this view has in turn been questioned from a point of view more sympathetic to Irish history than Hovell's, in the work of J. H. Treble. In an influential article he has argued that the Irish immigrants in the industrial areas in Britain were actively hostile to Chartism, and held apart from the movement. In challenging the work of Rachel O'Higgins and J. A. Jackson, he suggests that the large number of Irish among the leadership has been mistakenly assumed to imply a following of Irish in the crowd:

> . . . an untested hypothesis, no matter how plausible, does not begin to serve as a substitute for the rigorous process of historical investigation . . . the view described above presents an essentially misleading picture of immigrant alignments . . . despite the firm grip which individual Irishmen exercised over Chartism's destinies, the vast majority of their fellow-countrymen domiciled in Yorkshire, Cheshire and Lancashire had little contact with the movement until 1848 the 'Year of Revolutions'.[4]

In an interesting and closely argued article, he shows convincingly that the leaders of most Irish organisations in the 1830s and 1840s were actively hostile to Chartism, and discouraged their members from associating with the English movement. His evidence, however, is entirely taken from official pronouncements, and he does not in fact establish the extent to which such pronouncements influenced the ordinary Irish working man. There is no doubt that in the major cities, in particular in Liverpool and Manchester, organisations controlled by Irish politicians and by the Catholic Church had a loyal membership, articulate and organised, if never very large. But in the years before the Famine, there is no proof that these organisations represented the views or commanded the loyalties of the majority of Irish working men and women in Britain, and it is certain that there was always a significant minority of articulate

Irish who were not in sympathy with such pronouncements. Outside these two cities, moreover, there is far less evidence of organised conflict between even the O'Connellite Irish and the English radicals. I will return to these points. Treble's arguments have, however, been taken up and generalised by less scrupulous historians, so that the latest textbook on Chartism contains such statements as that Irish questions 'did not arouse many English proletarian passions' and 'talk of working-class collaboration between English and Irish workers was to cut little ice'.[5]

An examination of the make-up of a crowd in popular demonstrations presents many well-known difficulties. All these apply in an attempt to evaluate the Irish presence in the Chartist Movement. One considerable difficulty is that people do not by any means always identify themselves as Irishmen in this period. To give an example, the former secretary of the Irish Universal Suffrage Association was in Lancashire at the time of the 1842 strikes. He was arrested and tried in the great conspiracy trial in 1843. His name was Peter Brophy, and of course we know that he was Irish, but throughout the trial no reference was made to his nationality. There are many public occasions like this, and very many kinds of record in which no mention is made of birth-place or nationality. Although it is probably safe to assume that a working-class Catholic, in the north of England anyway, is likely to be Irish or from an Irish family, other information can only be obtained by the sort of digging that could take a lifetime if it were to be done for all the Chartists whose names we know. The prison inspectors' reports on those Chartists who were in prison early in 1840 are a valuable source of information. But even here, although prisoners are always questioned as to their religious beliefs, nationality or place of birth are seldom recorded. It is probably safe to assume that James Mitchell, Catholic cotton-spinner tried and sentenced at Preston in 1839 for conspiracy, was Irish. But there is no mention in the trial or the fairly extensive notes on Timothy Higgins, secretary of the Ashton-under-Lyne Working Men's Association, of the fact that he was Irish by birth. He gave as his religion 'no sect or persuasion, has his own ideas upon religion' – the type of answer usually given by unbelievers. But Higgins was Irish by birth, as the Census enumerator's return shows, and certainly on one occasion referred to himself as an Irishman in a public speech. He did not, like O'Connor or Duffy, constantly speak as an Irishman, but was best known for his leadership of the local Chartists and his work among the cotton-spinners.[6] Of the hundreds, indeed thousands, of Chartists whose names and occupations we know, the extra information about religion and birthplace is missing. Apart from the inadequate method of name-spotting, we have no way of telling what proportion even of these were Irish, whilst of the crowds we can tell even less.

The argument of this paper is that there was a very considerable Irish presence in the Chartist Movement. Whereas formal association with the leadership of those organisations set up by Daniel O'Connell was not achieved, either at local or national level, informal association in the smaller manufacturing towns and villages was common, and in any case the clear divisions made by historians and by leaders were not observed by the ordinary members. Kirby and Musson, in their biography of John Doherty, have shown how he maintained through most of his life an allegiance to radicalism and Chartism, a passionate belief in trade unionism, and yet never lost his admiration for Daniel O'Connell, in spite of the latter's attacks not only on trade unions, but also on Doherty himself. Robert Crowe, with whom this paper opens, was an Irish tailor working in London who seemed to find no contradiction between his adhesion to the three different movements, all led by Irishmen, in the early forties, long before 1848. Official condemnation of Chartism by the Church is not a necessary indication of shared hostility. Chartism would not be the first movement to include the devout in spite of ecclesiastical disfavour.

The working people who took part in Chartism lived in the manufacturing districts of the British Isles. These were the districts which had seen a very rapid expansion of population since the beginning of the century. In these districts the Irish were not, as they may have been after the Famine in some districts, a single out-group facing a stable local population. They were one such group among many. In 1839 the magistrate at Barnsley, playing the game that all local authorities played, of blaming 'outsiders' for the turbulence in the town, spoke of the most militant and unruly being 'a deluded portion of the working-classes, who consist . . . of individuals who have come from Ireland, Scotland and Lancashire, and are by occupation linen-weavers'.[7] But the majority of the Barnsley working population were linen-weavers, and as an examination of the well-documented story of Barnsley radicalism shows, they worked together in their trade society and radical organisations with very little awareness of ethnic divisions.[8] Barnsley had a fairly high proportion of Irish-born work-people in 1841, compared with county and with national figures. Other places with high levels of Irish were Bradford, which had the highest (10 per cent) in the West Riding[9] and

Ashton-under-Lyne, which also had a figure of 10 per cent.[10] Barnsley, Bradford and Ashton were probably the towns in the north of England which had the highest levels of Chartist activity throughout the whole period of the movement. There are clear indications of Irish presence among the leaders in all three towns. In Barnsley the local priest for a time was the Revd Patrick Ryan, who became a friend of the Dublin Chartist leader, Patrick O'Higgins, and a member of the Irish Universal Suffrage Association (IUSA). A letter to him congratulating him on joining the IUSA was signed by over a hundred of his former parishioners, names which included some of the most outstanding Chartists of the area such as Aeneas Daly, Peter Hoey, Arthur Collins and William Ashton.[11] In Ashton Timothy Higgins, the outstanding leader of the movement in its early years, was an Irishman, as was the Bradford shoemaker, John W. Smith, who was the most consistent leader of the movement there and represented the town at delegate meetings and conferences throughout the whole of the 1840s.[12] Not only was Bradford one of the earliest and strongest centres of Chartism, but also some of the areas in the city where the first radical groups were established were those of the highest Irish settlement. Sections of the Northern Union were set up in the Wapping and White Abbey districts, which later became Democratic associations and later still localities of the National Charter Association.[13] In 1848 the Commander of the North thought that half the Bradford Chartists were Irish.[14] It is hardly likely that a change of heart on the part of the leadership of the Repeal Association could have made such a sudden change in the personnel of one of the strongest centres of Chartism. It is more likely that the agreement had worked for many years in Bradford. The town was, after all, the chief base of operations of George White, wool-comber, one of the best known of the Irish Chartist leaders. He had been a leader among the combers and had been, with other Chartist wool-combers, responsible for a detailed report on the condition of the Bradford combers produced in 1845.[15]

The population of the manufacturing districts was varied and mobile. But the Irish themselves were not a single, undifferentiated mass. Within each district there could be Irish families from several periods of immigration, some that had come by way of other English or Scottish districts, some who were Protestants, some who had drifted away from the Catholic Church, some who had deliberately broken with the Church. There were people from the textile industries of Ireland which had been destroyed in the 1820s as well as people from the countryside.

After the Famine the Irish community was probably rather more homogeneous, and certainly the tendency for the immigrants to remain grouped around the area in which their priest lived and their church was increased in the second half of the century. It is also apparent that the importance of religion as a defining element in the culture of the working communities increased in the second half of the nineteenth century. The growth of education provided by the denominational bodies, the National and the British and Foreign societies increased steadily until they were absorbed into a national system after 1870. The education, denominational or non-denominational, was uniformly Protestant, and much of it determinedly Anglican. The agitation surrounding the Ecclesiastical Titles episode in 1851-2, as well as the earlier passions aroused among many Nonconformists and Anglicans by the Maynooth grant picked up and exploited a certain amount of latent anti-Catholicism among the working people as well as the middle classes. But in the 1830s and through most of the '40s there is little evidence to suggest that religious affiliations were sufficiently divisive to override the pervasive class loyalties. There was no particular Chartist religious grouping. As far as denominational loyalties can be recovered, the picture, as with occupations, is that Chartists seemed to represent a cross-section of the localities in which they lived. Thus in Barnsley, where there was a large Irish-Catholic population, many of the Chartists were Catholics. In Lancashire there was a high level of non-religious radicalism, but there were also a number of Catholics and members of Nonconformist sects. In the West Riding the majority of the Chartists whose affiliations we know were Nonconformists of one kind or another. But the sample in all cases is small. And although, as Treble shows, examples can be found of priests warning their flocks against associating with the Chartists, such warnings may also be found with great frequency coming from the pulpits of Established and Dissenting Churches. Religion in fact was invoked by the Chartists themselves, including Catholic Chartists, to support their views as well as by their superiors to condemn them. It is therefore clearly not sufficient to demonstrate the articulate hostility of the Catholic Church to Chartism to demonstrate that Catholics necessarily followed that lead.

It has been suggested that concern for Ireland and support for Repeal were grafted on to British Chartism because of a personal foible of its leader, and that this did the movement little service. It has also been claimed that the Irish themselves cared nothing for Chartist politics, but on the contrary accepted the hostility to the movement articulated by Daniel O'Connell and by their Church, and kept well clear of British concerns. A third line of argument, to be found in Carlyle and in many subsequent writers suggests that the ethnic differences of race, religion, language and behaviour that existed between the Irish and the rest of the British population themselves prevented co-operation on any considerable scale. Such analyses need to be examined in the precise context of the 1830s and 1840s.

To understand the concern felt about Ireland, several points have to be made. The first and most obvious is that Ireland, directly ruled and administered from Westminster, contained a third of the population of the British Isles.[16] Any regulation passed by the government with respect to Ireland could well be extended to other parts of the kingdom. The expression 'disturbed districts' used to describe the districts of Ireland in which martial law was to be imposed had also been used in recent times to describe parts of the manufacturing areas of England and Scotland. The number of Irish men and women necessarily included in the labour force throughout Britain meant that anything which affected them, whether legislation, decree or custom came very close to all working people in the British Isles to an extent that has never since been as great. The way Ireland was ruled and the living conditions of her people affected the rest of Britain intimately and immediately.

Before the final achievement of the 1832 Reform Bill, the reformers had a slate of questions on which they hoped a reformed Parliament would act in a more liberal and rational way than the old administration. At the head of these questions was the government of Ireland. Since the Act of Union of 1801 Ireland had been subjected to a series of Coercion Acts, and it was hoped that a new government would end coercion, if not immediately tackling the whole question of the repeal of the union. The disillusion with the actions of the reformed Parliament and the Whig administrations, which was the starting-point of the Chartist Movement, began with the first session. In January 1833 the Suppression of Disturbances Act, a draconian Coercion Act for Ireland was passed – more severe in many ways than any that had gone before.[17] Speaking of middle- and working-class co-operation which had achieved the reform bill, Bronterre O'Brien wrote that 'it barely survived the Irish Coercion Bill, it vanished completely with the enactment of the Starvation Law'.[18] The association between the two acts was often made. The placard issued by the Council of the Northern Political Union calling for a general strike in 1839 included a long list of grievances against the reformed administration:

This brings us up to the passing of the Reform Bill; that Measure, we fondly hoped, would remove our Grievances. For seven years we reposed with Confidence on the Justice and Patriotism of the Middle Classes. Let us examine the FRUITS which the Reform Bill brought forth! 'By their fruits ye shall know them.' First – The despotic and bloody Irish Coercion Bill, which gave to Military Officers the Power to transport or hang the Irish people without either Judge or Jury. Second – the hideous and accurst New Poor Law, which tears asunder the dearest and holiest Ties of the human Heart, which consigns even the Old and Infirm to FAMISH amid the Gloom and SOLITUDE of a Dungeon Workhouse.[19]

Addressing a meeting in 1838, John Fielden declared that:

If the Parliament was composed of working men, they would not have suspended the laws and constitution of the country and have passed a Coercion Bill for Ireland. If the Parliament was composed of poor men, they would not have passed the new Poor Law Amendment Act, but would have first secured to the working class fair remunerative wages.[20]

The passing of the Coercion Act provoked an immediate nation-wide response. Meetings organised to protest against it took place in centres which were soon to become Chartist strongholds, and many of those who spoke at the meetings were soon to become leaders of Chartism. At Leeds the chairman, Thomas Bottomly, and the main speaker, William Rider, were both future Chartists, Rider being a founder-member of the Leeds Working Men's Association and a West Riding delegate to the first National Convention.[21] At nearby Huddersfield the meeting to protest against the act was attended almost entirely by 'operatives' according to the local Tory newspaper.[22] In Halifax Robert Wilkinson, Thomas Cliffe, Elijah Crabtree and William Thornton, all to become leading Chartists, spoke at the meeting.[23] In Manchester a vast open-air meeting heard John Doherty, leader of the cotton-spinners' union, warn the government that '20,000 real, stout, determined Irishmen' in the Manchester district were prepared to assist their fellow-countrymen to resist the act. A petition launched at this meeting was presented soon after by Cobbett in Parliament with 14,000 names attached, calling for the withdrawal of the bill, the abolition of tithes and the introduction of Poor Laws for Ireland.[24] In Nottingham the radicals met to denounce the bill and to relate Grey's Irish policy to their own situation. The matter was, they said, 'a subject of vital importance to the people of Ireland, and scarcely less so to the constitutional liberty of every subject in the British Dominions'. The resolution which they forwarded to the House of Commons declared that: 'Should your petitioners witness these acts of injustice done to Ireland, the most fearful apprehensions will be excited in their minds, that the same odious tyranny will be perpetrated towards themselves'.[25] In Birmingham a meeting on Newhall Hill which exceeded in numbers even the pre-reform rallies in the district was called to protest against the government's Irish policy and in particular the Coercion Act.[26] In February 1834 John Doherty was on the platform at Oldham with John Knight, veteran of Peterloo and founder of Oldham Chartism, to set up an organisation in that town to promote radical reform and the repeal of the union, based on a weekly penny subscription.[27] When he toured the provinces in 1835 and 1836, setting up radical organisations which were among the immediate precursors of Chartism, Feargus O'Connor kept the subject of Irish coercion at the head of his attack on the government.[28] His paper, founded in 1837, was called the *Northern Star* – the name of the journal of the United Irishmen.[29] Repeal of the union and opposition to coercion were important parts of its policy from the beginning, and helped to make it the country's leading provincial newspaper within a few months. But it was not only the northern radicals who made this kind of protest. The London Working Men's Association (LWMA) presented a 'loyal and outspoken' address to Queen Victoria on the occasion of her coronation, and pointed out that: 'The injustice which the Whig and Tory factions have for a long time past inflicted on our Irish brethren has generated and perpetuated the extremes of want and wretchedness amongst them, and calls for an immediate and radical remedy.'[30] The LWMA could never have been accused of pursuing a personal foible of O'Connor's. The British radicals feared both the extension of coercion and the extension of the low standards at which the Irish were forced to live. When the Poor Law Amendment Act of 1834 was passed, which was based on the abolitionist attitude to the Poor Law advocated by the Benthamites, Bronterre O'Brien wrote:

> I have lived in Ireland, was born and bred in Ireland . . . I have seen thousands of Irish who have never tasted animal food, or fish, or wheaten bread twice a year since they were born. I have seen them, whole days together, without even potatoes and salt. I have seen them clothed in rags, their heads full of vermin their legs and hands

covered with scabs, their bodies broken out in sores, and their feet cut and hacked with chilblains and stone bruises until they were unable to walk . . . but you ask 'are we, the wealth-producers of England, to be brought to this?' I answer YES, unless you bestir yourselves in time, there is no escaping the Irish level if the New Poor Law Act be fully carried out.[31]

Well before the publication of the Charter (in May 1838) the radicals among the working people were seriously concerned with the question of Ireland. Before O'Connor emerged as the major leader of British radicalism in the years after 1837, Irishmen were prominent in British radical leadership. John Cleave, who edited and published several of the unstamped journals of the early 1830s, and was a leading figure in the campaign against the newspaper stamp duties, was born in Ireland in the 1790s. He was a founder-member of the London Working Men's Association and a signatory of the original People's Charter. A strong advocate of temperance, he published the *English Chartist Circular and Temperance Record* between 1841 and 1843. He was the chief London agent for O'Connor's *Northern Star* during the Chartist years. Although he is generally regarded as a fairly moderate character, Hovell considered him – possibly because of his Irish nationality – as 'less refined and perhaps less able' than his fellow signatories Lovett, Hetherington and Watson.[32] George Condy, editor and part-owner of the influential radical journal the *Manchester and Salford Advertiser* came of an Irish Methodist family. He was an outstanding campaigner in print and on the platform against Irish coercion, the new Poor Law and the abuses of factory labour. He was a member, with John Doherty and Robert Owen, of the Society for National Regeneration in 1833–4, which aimed at establishing a uniform eight-hour day through industrial action. Condy was a strong believer in independent working-class political action and in universal suffrage. He welcomed Chartism initially, but withdrew his support and that of his paper because of the increasingly violent rhetoric and the Newport rising in 1839. He died in 1841.[33] Bronterre O'Brien, most gifted of the early radical journalists and a key figure in the early years of Chartism, was perhaps at his best in the years before the movement started, especially as editor of the unstamped *Poor Man's Guardian* from 1831 to 1835. He came from a small trading family in Granard, Co. Longford, and was something of a child prodigy while at school in Edgeworthtown. His family were Catholic, but he soon developed more free-thinking views. At his best he had few equals as a political journalist, but he was a difficult personality who quarrelled with every one in the movement with whom he worked. He was probably an alcoholic, and he never completed any of his writing projects which included a short History of Ireland. He got as far as the first volume of his *Life of Robespierre*, and he translated Buonarotti's *History* of the Babeuf conspiracy in 1836.[34] John Doherty has already been mentioned. Leader of the cotton-spinners, leading exponent and practitioner of the ideal of general unionism, he was probably the most important and influential trade unionist in the first half of the century. He managed to combine leadership of his union with support for radicalism of all kinds, including Owenism, and a strong loyalty to Catholicism and Irish nationalism. Apart from the question of loyalty to O'Connell, he found no contradiction in these various courses. Like Cleave, Condy and O'Brien, Doherty was also an editor and publisher, and helped to support himself by running a coffee-house cum book-shop in Manchester.[35]

These men were all nationally known radicals, active supporters of the various pre-Chartist radical campaigns, the reform of Parliament, opposition to the Poor Law, control of factory hours and wages and the battle against the newspaper stamp and paper duties. Mainstream Chartism also included the support of the trade societies and trade unions, and here, since the Irish were so often used as cheap labour or as labour for breaking strikes, more anti-Irish feeling and fewer Irish personalities might be expected. There is no doubt that Irish men and women were often deliberately imported as cheap or strike-breaking labour, as they were in the 1844 coal strike in the north-east.[36] There is clearly, however, a difference between the use of fresh immigrant labour, or of labour deliberately imported to replace or dilute a difficult labour-force, and the behaviour of immigrants already a part of that force. For example, Mr Charles Scott, shipbuilder of Greenock, told the authors of the *Report on the State of the Irish Poor* in 1835 that he had recently used Irish labourers to break a sawyers' strike in his yard. But the striking sawyers, who had been earning, he claimed, between 35s. and £3 a week, included Irishmen among their number, members though 'not the ringleaders' of the union.[37] In Leeds the stuff-weavers were about two-thirds Irish in the early 1830s, and were more intransigent than the English in their struggles to protect the price lists and lengths in 1830.[38] The Glasgow cotton-spinners' strike and the prosecution of their leaders was one of the immediate precipitants of Chartism itself, and the issue which convulsed the manufacturing districts in the winter of 1837-8. Many of the Glasgow spinners were Irish, and two at least of the arrested leaders had been born in Ireland.[39] It is clearly over-simple to see the use of low-paid or un-skilled labour as being necessarily ethnically divisive in the pre-Chartist and Chartist period.[40] There were certainly areas of conflict. Irish migrant labourers came to England during the harvest period, looking to earn enough to carry them over the lean winter months. English agricultural workers and many urban workers also looked for extra work at harvest time, and of course there were clashes. In some agricultural districts the labourers combined to 'run the Irish'[41] at this time of year, but the radicals tried to draw the same lesson from this as from other conflicts. In August 1833 members of the Huddersfield Political Union visited Pennistone to help the local radicals set up their own union. After the official business,

> ...a miscellaneous conversation took place concerning the evils in the agricultural districts, particularly what injury was inflicted by the swarms of Irish who poured in at the harvest season. This, how-ever, was done without any bitterness being manifested towards our Irish brethren, the fault was traced to the government.[42]

Cheap immigrant labour was only one method of attack by the employers and the authorities on the organisations of the working people. The radical response was not to blame the instruments, but to turn their attention to the achievement of political power which they hoped would give them the control needed to protect their jobs and their wages.

The pre-Chartist trade union movement included a number of Irish-men among its leaders. In Lancashire, apart from Doherty of the spinners, John Allison and Christopher Doyle of the powerloom weavers were Irish. The latter had already served a term of imprisonment before the publication of the Charter for his trade union activities, and told the inspector of prisons in 1840 that he had little hope of finding work when he left prison 'through being so well-known as an agitator'. The inspector reported that Doyle was 'self-educated, possessed of a mind of great astuteness' and also that he was 'still resolved to pursue the career of agitation' when he left prison.[43] In this he was correct, for Doyle remained an active and popular leader of the Chartist Movement as long as it continued. Among the linen-weavers of Barnsley, Peter Hoey, who often chaired the weavers' meetings, Arthur Collins and

William Ashton were leading figures in the trade actions as well as in the Chartist Movement. We know, because of the unusually full documentation that has survived, that there were more than a hundred Irish-Catholic Chartists in Barnsley, among who were several prominent leaders of the weavers. They were not, however, a separately organised group, but were part of a much larger Chartist and trade union organisation. It is also interesting to note that a number of the Irish Catholics did not have Celtic names, including Ashton himself, whose religious and national loyalties were inherited from his mother. Ashton had been involved in industrial action before he became a Chartist and had, with fellow-weaver Frank Mirfield, received a sentence of transportation for his part in a weavers' strike. Their return in 1838 was achieved through the money-raising efforts of the Barnsley weavers.[44]

It is among the linen-weavers, cotton-spinners and powerloom operators that most Irish trade unionists are found. This may have been because these were recently grown industries for which formal apprenticeship was no longer required, or it may have been that the Irish who entered industrial occupations, rather than labouring or such casual work as peddling and tinkering, usually came from some kind of textile work in Ireland. The 1820s saw considerable emigration of textile workers from Ireland to Great Britain, with the decay of Ireland's own industry. Doherty had worked in a mill in Ireland as a child, and it seems probable that many of those who entered the textile trades came either from industrial backgrounds, or from some of the many rural districts in which hand-weaving and other textile trades were associated with agriculture. In 1829 there had been in the region of 2000 cotton-weavers in the Bandon district, for example. By 1840 their numbers had dwindled to a mere 150.[45] Some of them had certainly arrived in Barnsley, whence a donation to the defence fund for John Frost was sent in the name of 'a few Bandon [Ireland] men to shew that the traitor O'Connell falsified the character of Irishmen when he said that the Irish in England were opposed to the Radicals'.[46] Chartist shoemakers, tailors and building-workers were less likely to be society men, if they were Irish, as so many immigrants could enter only the lower branches of the trades. John Smith of Bradford, however, visited Ireland on behalf of the shoemakers' union in 1845.[47]

In the ten years preceding the Chartist Movement, there is clear evidence of the presence of Irishmen as metropolitan radical journalists, and as important figures in the provincial trade societies, particularly in the textile industries. However, until 1837 O'Connell himself appeared to be in sympathy with the majority of the radical programme. He was a formidable orator, unpopular with all branches of the Establishment, and his achievement of Catholic Emancipation in 1829, by the lively and imaginative deployment of mass popular pressure had made him a favourite with radicals and reformers. In 1837, however, he made a sharp break with the English radicals, and endeavoured to take the whole of the Irish movement with him. In Ireland, apart from Dublin and a few other centres, he was successful. How far did he succeed in separating the Irish from the British radicals in other parts of the British Isles?

The Glasgow cotton-spinners' case illustrated for the British radicals what the experience of the Dublin artisans had already made clear, the hostility of Daniel O'Connell to trade unionism, and his adhesion to the dogmas of conventional political economy. The London Working Men's Association had secured the support of O'Connell and a small number of other parliamentary radicals for their proposed petition to Parliament for universal manhood suffrage. Francis Place, who had helped to secure this support, had stipulated that the price should be the dropping by the LWMA of any attacks on the Poor Law Amendment Act, the beloved brainchild of the political economists. The support of O'Connell, however, soon showed itself to be conditional upon a denial of the principles of trade unionism. This was too much even for the LWMA, several of whose members were 'society men'. The London radicals were warned by the Radical Member of Parliament for Coventry that O'Connell was making use of them in a cynical way, and at the same time they found themselves under attack from provincial radicals for associating with 'Malthusians' and political economists.[48] The litmus tests of working-class radicalism were opposition to the new Poor Law and support for the trade societies. These were the issues which divided them above all from the Philosophical Radicals in Parliament, and which formed the basis for the alternative radical programme of the Chartists. O'Connell by 1837 was ambivalent about the Poor Law, and had declared his total opposition to trade unionism. When the leaders of the Glasgow cotton spinners were arrested on charges of conspiracy in the autumn of 1837, the whole of the labour movement of Britain rallied in their support. O'Connell, already two years into the Lichfield House compact with the governing Whig party, dissociated himself from the Chartists and the trade unionists, and warned his followers to have

nothing to do with either movement. He dubbed his former associate
Feargus O'Connor, a 'Tory Radical' because of his opposition to the
Whig government.

The split between O'Connell and the radicals of Britain at this time
was not merely a question of English politics: it was also an indication
of differing traditions in Irish popular politics. Some historians have
suggested that the split between O'Connor and O'Connell was personal,
and that O'Connor turned to English radicalism when he was forced out
of Irish politics by his quarrel with his chief. In fact the position was
more complex. The division between the two men was partly one of
tactics. O'Connor believed that the only function of the Irish Members
of Parliament should be to achieve the repeal of the union with Britain.
The first disagreement between the two positions was about the speed
with which a motion for the repeal of the union should be introduced
into Parliament. O'Connell was prepared to do a deal with the government in return for limited concessions, and entered into the Litchfield
House compact in 1835. O'Connor insisted that the repeal issue be put
at once, and that it should continue to be raised at every possible
opportunity.[49] When he was unseated in 1835 on a technicality (the
family income was from leasehold not freehold property) O'Connor
retired from parliamentary politics and entered the arena of popular
radicalism, in the belief that only universal suffrage would achieve the
repeal of the union.[50]

O'Connor was the son of a leading United Irishman, the nephew of
probably the most influential of their leaders. The name of his newspaper was that of the United Irish paper, and the points of the Charter
were in line with the programme of the movement. When he was
elected to Parliament in 1833, it was on a programme of support for
universal suffrage as well as repeal, and from the beginning he pledged
himself to return and offer his resignation to his constituents at the
end of every session – as a kind of personal annual parliament.[51] It
seems clear that many of the other Irish in the Chartist Movement came
from the same tradition. Thomas Ainge Devyr, editorial worker on the
Northern Liberator, was the son of a United Irishman[52], and William
and Walsingham Martin almost certainly came from the Republican
wing of the nationalist movement. The inspector of prisons described
William Martin in 1840 as 'a most dangerous, violent and unprincipled
man, advocating physical force, destruction of property and anarchy in
its worst form. He has been for years a political agitator in Ireland,
Scotland and England.'[53] When Martin left prison he settled for a time
in Bradford, and was put forward as a hustings candidate in the election

of 1841. His proposer introduced him as a man who had been 'born within the precincts of Dublin University and had received the finishing touches to his education at three of the Whig Universities of England. The first was at York Castle, the second at Northallerton House of Correction and the third at Lancaster Castle.'[54] He was a shoemaker by trade and his religious affiliation, Major Williams noted, was to 'the Established Church, according to his own statement, but I doubt his adhesion to any religious sect.'

O'Connell was not a republican. He believed in the continued rule of Ireland by the British Crown, and the retention of control by it of imperial and defence questions. In these matters, as in his hostility to trade unions, he undoubtedly had the support of a majority of his fellow-countrymen but, particularly outside Ireland, a significant alternative existed on both issues.

In 1837 O'Connell was at issue on the question of trade unions with both the artisans of Dublin and the vast majority of English and Scottish radicals.[55] Radical journals in Britain abound with attacks on him for his attitude. In an address to the operative trade unionists of Dublin issued by the Working Men's Association of Newcastle upon Tyne in April 1838, the attack on O'Connell was associated with an appeal to the traditions of the United Irishmen:

... whilst a great proportion of your countrymen appear hopelessly chained to the chariot wheels of the apostate, you asserted the rights of labour, and vindicated them from the grasp of the insatiate capitalists - even though they have managed to enlist in their service that arch-mountebank and hireling, Daniel O'Connell.

... as the first to burst the moral bondage which the heartless apostate has flung over your lovely and much-wronged country, we tender you our ardent and heartfelt thanks for this your past service - as the descendents of men not even yet all departed from among you - who caught the fire of liberty from America and France, we demand, we calculate upon your future assistance. Can we doubt that a tribunal composed of lords and lawyers, bankers, merchants and monopolists, naval and military cut-throats, and all those whom plunder has raised to affluence - can we for a moment doubt that such a tribunal will dispose of Trade Unions in the same manner as the drum-head tribunal disposed of your brave, and patriotic and virtuous fathers, during the bloody era of ninety-eight?[56]

A street ballad about the cotton-spinners made the same connection
between the Glasgow and Dublin operatives:

> Success to our friends in Ireland, who boldly stood our cause
> In spite of O'Connell and his support of whiggish laws,
> Away with his politics, they are not worth a straw
> He's no friend to the poor of Ireland or Caledonia.

> Success to O'Connor who did nobly plead our cause,
> Likewise to Mr. Beaumont, who abhors oppressive laws,
> But after all their efforts, justice and law,
> We are banished from our country, sweet Caledonia.

> Whigs and Tories are united, we see it very plain,
> To crush the poor labourer, it is their daily aim,
> The proverb now is verified, and that you all can know
> In the case of those poor spinners in Caledonia.[57]

Within Ireland itself, certainly outside Dublin, there was little overt
support either for unionism or republicanism until late in the 1840s.
The Chartist Movement had little support, although it was not entirely
absent. The Irish Universal Suffrage Association (IUSA), founded soon
after the National Charter Association early in 1841, had as its aim the
furthering of the six points of the People's Charter and the repeal of
the Legislative Union between Great Britain and Ireland 'which cannot
be achieved without the aid and cooperation of the English Chartists.'[58]
Based on Dublin, where its chairman was the long-standing radical
Patrick O'Higgins, it claimed a paid-up membership of 1000 in 1841[59]
and its secretary, Peter Michael Brophy was selling 400 copies of the
Northern Star weekly in 1842.[60] In Belfast the members collected 2000
signatures to the second Chartist Petition in 1842, and there were groups
in Athboy, Drogheda, Loughrae, Newry and Sligo.[61] Little has been
recorded about the activities of these Irish Chartists, although a lively
pamphlet written by another secretary of the IUSA, W. H. Dyott gives
an idea of some of the problems they faced.[62]

In England, however, the republican tradition was among the aspects
of Irish politics which was greatly respected by the Chartists. Robert
Emmet had been executed within the memory of many Chartists for
his attempted rebellion. His name was constantly introduced into
Chartist speeches, his memory toasted at radical dinners, and represent-

ations of his trial and speech from the dock were regularly presented in dramatic form in all parts of the country. In toasting his memory, Chartists were signalling a challenge to governments and to the continued occupation of Ireland in no uncertain way. R. G. Gammage, historian of Chartism, recalled his first discovery of political matters. Two pamphlets that he came across in his teens made a deep impression. One was Paine's *Commonsense,*

> The other was the speech of Robert Emmet, the eminent Irish patriot – a young gentleman with good promise of success in life, but who before he was 22 years of age led an insurrection in Ireland which proved itself a failure . . .
> So much did I admire the daring courage of the young Irish rebel that I was never weary of reading his speech. I read and re-read until every word was fixed in my . . . memory.[63]

Young Robert Lowery, attacking the sentence on the Dorchester labourers at a mass meeting on Newcastle Town Moor declared:

> They knew what tyrants could effect by law; it was by law that Sydney perished at the block; it was by law that Emmet died upon the scaffold; and it was by law that the field of Peterloo was strewn with unoffending men and women – law it might be called, but never justice (hear, and cheers).[64]

Significantly, perhaps, the editors of the excellent edition of Lowery's writing do not seem to be familiar with the drama of Emmet's court-room defence, or the horror of his hanging and decapitation which, as one writer has said, 'recurred in Irish nightmares for three generations'.[65] Performances of the trial of Emmet were given throughout the British Isles by Chartist groups in Nottingham, the West Riding of Yorkshire and several districts in Scotland, usually touring productions to rouse enthusiasm and raise funds. Treble is surely mistaken in seeing these as unsuccessful attempts to win over the Irish repealers. He records the response made in Manchester and published in the *Freeman's Journal:* 'Although we revere and respect his memory, we view with horror the principle that brought him to an untimely end; and therefore we call on all Irishmen to refrain from attending such a meeting.'[66] It must how-ever be doubted whether this was the view of Emmet held by the repeal movement. The repealers and confederates in Marylebone were organised in the Emmet Brigade between 1843 and 1848[67], and his name was certainly remembered in the nationalist movements after 1848.

The tradition of the United Irishmen was able to have a more open expression in England than was possible in Ireland in these years. The Cheltenham Chartist printer and balladeer, Thomas Willey, published copies of 'The Croppy Boy' - a United Irish balled which James Joyce refers to as the 'national anthem' of Irish nationalism - at a time when it could not have been published legally in Ireland.[68] Some of the many Irish who crossed to the Cheltenham races may have bought copies as well as the local Chartists. In Dublin, however, in 1844 Gavan Duffy was indicted for sedition simply for publishing a poem which started

> Who fears to speak of 'ninety-eight?
> Who blushes at the name?
> When Cowards mock the patriot's fate
> Who hangs his head for shame?[69]

Young Ireland itself had played safe until then by organising an 'Eighty-two Club' - a very much safer date to conjure with. Outside Ireland, however, 'ninety-eight' was remembered and celebrated, with toasts to Arthur O'Connor and Lord Edward Fitzgerald included among the gallery of radical heroes.

It is probable that many of the Irish Chartist leaders and speakers up and down the country came from families with United Irish connections, although this can never now be proved. There were certainly a good sprinkling of identifiably Irish Chartists. Henry Cronin, stonemason's labourer from Bedlington in Northumberland, was dismissed from his employment for his 'outrageous conduct' as leader of the local Chartists and set up a school to which all radicals were urged to send their children.[70] In Wigan, later to be the scene of Irish–English clashes in the 1860s, an Irish handloom weaver, John Lenegan, was leader of the Chartists. Peter Doyle, Catholic building-worker from Newcastle, later recalled some of the more dramatic incidents in the Chartist period, and described the regular outdoor meetings

I will now advert to our week-night meetings. They were generally in front of the old riding school . . . We had then men of warm imagination who aspired to overthrow the tyrants who filled their blessed country with woe. We had Mr Charlton, mason, who always commenced his harangues with the oft-quoted words which

O'Connell recited from Byron – 'Hereditary bondsmen' etc.[71] Mr Charlton contended that Ireland had received nothing but oppression at the hands of England from the invasion of Strongbow down to the Rathcormac massacre.[72] Mr Parker, labourer, said that England called Ireland the Sister Island, but she treated her with the iron rule of a cruel step-mother . . . [73]

Doyle was an admirer of O'Connell, but this did not prevent him from going sufficiently far from the Liberator's Moral Force teachings as to buy a pike and to take part in the stoning of the troops which occurred when the military tried to disperse a meeting of 6000 Chartists in July of 1839.[74] He perhaps illustrates as well as anybody the danger of assuming a kind of ideological purity among the rank and file of popular movements. Leaders who gained the loyalties of the common people may have held views which were mutually incompatible – certainly it would be difficult to reconcile the ideologies represented by Robert Owen, Richard Oastler, Feargus O'Connor and Daniel O'Connell, and yet their followers seemed able to select from the conflicting ideas a radical cosmology which they found consistent. Robert Crowe, with whom this chapter opens, is a good example of this. He came from a strongly nationalist family in Ireland to work with his brother, a skilled tailor, in London. His brother, a skilled master-tailor, was also a heavy drinker, and the younger Crowe left his apprenticeship and became a slop-worker, working for a garret-master. As the quotation indicates, he gave all his spare time to the three movements, for repeal, for the Charter and for temperance. He seems to have found no inconsistency in supporting all three movements until the Young Irelanders repudiated 'O'Connell's peace at any price doctrine', when he and the rest of the London Confederates went with Young Ireland. He was arrested and tried with other London Chartists and Repealers. Cited against him at his trial was a speech he made at the Thomas Davis club in London when false news had been received of a rising in Dublin

So the time has come at last – the time long dreaded by some, but by all true lovers of liberty long hoped for; the time when our own land, our dear land, Ireland, is in arms. At last we throw off the foibles which made our country infantile; scorning any longer to crouch in the attitude of slaves, we stand erect in the attitude of men, resolved to wring from the reluctant grasp of Britain those concessions which, though long delayed, she must at last accord.[75]

John West, Macclesfield silk-weaver was one of Chartism's most popular orators, who was offered tempting fees to use his ability in the cause of more 'respectable' reform movements. He remained loyal to Chartism and repeal, however, and often reported on co-operation between the two movements in provincial districts that he visited. Like his fellow-countryman George White, West was a national and a local leader. Both served on the national executive committee of the National Charter Association, and both also acted as local lecturers and paid agents for the *Northern Star*. White ran for a short time his own journal, the *Democrat and Labour Advocate*. Both men returned to their trades after the end of Chartism, and both died in poverty.[76]

We shall, of course, never be able to measure the participation of anonymous Irish in the Chartist crowds. We know that at least seventeen Irishmen were among the three hundred-odd awaiting trial for Chartist offences in the winter of 1839–40, and we do not know the nationalities of all of those three hundred.[77] There were no Irish among those arrested after the rising at Newport – or at least none was brought to trial. But Lady Charlotte Guest's diary for the following days records:

> It is said to have been lamentable to see droves of these poor tired and defeated men returning from their ill-fated expedition, and the scene at Tredegar was equally distressing owing to the wailing of the women, among whom were many Irish, all ignorant of who had suffered, and fearful lest some of their friends should have been among the number of victims . . . [78]

There is no time here to examine the often-quoted punch-ups in 1841 between the Chartists in Manchester and the Irish 'supporters' of the Anti-Corn Law League. But this brief moment was specifically concerned with local electoral politics, and the Irish, it seems, participated more in the character of 'rent-a-mob' than as supporters of political principle.[79] In fact the fisticuffs of this occasion serve to illustrate the rarity, in an age of violent political confrontations, of other examples of conflict between Irish and British working men in the Chartist period.

The Tory victory in the general election of 1841 released O'Connell to an extent from his compact with the Whigs. He returned again to extra-parliamentary agitation for repeal, and founded towards the end of 1842 the Loyal National Repeal Association. Its story in the next two years is outside the scope of this study, but O'Connell again used the tactic he had exploited so brilliantly in 1829, of a mass peaceful organisation, closely allied to the Church, which was to achieve its ends by the peaceful display of enormous numbers.[80] He was determined that members of his organisation should not associate with the Chartists, and there are many examples of occasions on which such co-operation was discovered and condemned. In Birmingham George White and other local Chartists had their subscriptions returned when their membership became known to the Dublin leadership. When the London repealers invited O'Brien and O'Connor to speak to them, the meetings went off without conflict. However, when the news of the meetings and of the support given by the Chartist leadership reached Dublin, a letter was immediately sent to the London societies, warning them not to associate with the Chartists,

> What could have induced the wardens or Repealers to listen for one instance to the suggestions of any junction with the Chartists? They have mortified and grieved their friends very sadly ... we can countenance no connection whatever with the Chartists ...

They were warned that 'if they intend to act with us and under the guidance of our august leader' they must return all subscriptions and sever all connections with the Chartists.

> The reading of the above letter – commented *The Times* – caused much astonishment, but its adoption was immediately moved and carried without a dissentient voice. It is, however, as well to observe that the document caused more of sorrow than rejoicing ... [81]

This kind of 'official' discouragement, however, does not by any means show that co-operation did not occur at a lower level, and between men and women less easily identified by the leadership. Cleave published a 'memoir' of Emmet in 1843, Bronterre O'Brien's short-lived *Poor Man's Guardian and Repealer's Friend,* published in the summer of 1843 was largely concerned with repeal, and contains some of Bronterre's most interesting writing on Ireland and on Irish history. In February 1844 John West reported from Halifax that:

> The Irish repealers and the Chartists are on the best of terms. The Repealers regularly attend the Chartist meetings, and in turn the Chartists do all in their power to aid and assist them. I had a good meeting at night ... a petition of the repealers which was in the room was signed by every one present ... [82]

After the failure of the Clontarf demonstration in October 1843, the Irish repealers in Britain seem to have moved even more towards the Chartists, a movement which was followed more slowly by Young Ireland on the other side of the Irish sea. At first the Young Ireland leaders echoed O'Connell's distrust. As John Mitchel wrote in 1847. 'We desire no fraternisation between the Irish people and the Chartists, not on account of the bugbear of physical force, but simply because some of their five points are to us an abomination.'[83] W. H. Dyott, of the IUSA, was as suspicious of Young Ireland, whom he considered to be a corporation of literary adventurers':

What they have ever done for the country beyond the production of rhythmical balderdash and one-sided accounts of historical events I know not. They have endeavoured both by writings and speeches to engender and foster a rancorous spirit of irrational anomosity between the laborious classes of the two countries whose interests are identical . . .[84]

As the year of revolutions dawned, however, Mitchel's tone changed. By February 1848 his journal the *United Irishman* was urging the Irish not to reject Chartism: 'Every Chartist is a *Repealer,* to begin with; and all English labourers and artizans are Chartists.'[85]

The full story of 1848 in England remains to be told. All historians are agreed, however, that in that year co-operation between Chartists and repealers was close. Many of those arrested that year were Irish, and it was in those areas in which the co-operation between the two movements was closest that the authorities made the most arrests. The street balladeers like the writer of the verses about the 'gagging act' of 1848 certainly associated the two movements:

> Now you must look before you speak
> And mind what you are after,
> Tis death if you should say Repeal,
> Or, please we want the Charter.
> Sew up your mouths without delay,
> The Government proposes,
> And what the people wants to say
> Must whistle through their noses

CHORUS

Mind what you say by night and day
And don't speak out of season
For everything God bless the Queen
Is reckoned up high treason.

The chartist and repealers say,
In spite of wind and weather,
Both day and night we'll gain our right
By meeting all together
We can whisper where we cannot talk
And speak of might and reason
But they do say, good lack a day,
That everything is treason.[86]

Hostility to the Irish on ethnic and religious grounds certainly existed among the common people, but among the Chartists a feeling of community based on common work experience and a joint feeling of oppression was always very much stronger, and in many cases seems to have produced the opposite effect – that is a great admiration for Irish nationalism. Among the middle classes, however, hostility was much more often enunciated in ethnic terms. Charles Kingsley warned the Chartists against any association with the United Irishmen: 'What brotherhood ought *you* to have with the "United Irishman" party, who pride themselves on their hatred to your nation, and recommend schemes of murder which a North American Indian . . . would account horrible'.[87] Thomas Carlyle, in a famous passage in his pamphlet on Chartism, made a savage attack on the immigrant Irish:

. . . this well-known fact that the Irish speak a partially intelligible dialect of English, and their fare across by steam is four-pence sterling! Crowds of miserable Irish darken our towns. The wild Milesian features, looking false ingenuity, restlessness, unreason, misery and mockery, salute you on all highways and byways. The English coachman, as he whirls past, lashes the Milesian with his whip, curses him with his tongue; the Milesian is holding out his hat to beg. He is the sorest evil this country has to strive with. In his rags and laughing savagery, he is there to undertake all work that can be done by mere strength of hand and back; for wages that will purchase him potatoes . . . The Saxon man, if he cannot work on

those terms, finds no work . . . he has not sunk from decent manhood to squalid apehood . . . the uncivilised Irishman drives out the
Saxon native, takes possession of his room. There abides he, in his
squalor and unreason, in his falsity and drunken violence, as the
ready-made nucleus of degradation and disorder . . . [88]

There is plenty of evidence that Carlyle's pamphlet had a great deal of
influence on those novelists who wrote about Chartism.[89] There is none
that it influenced the Chartists themselves, indeed such influence would
be unlikely, since the language he uses about Chartism itself is hardly
more restrained. Trade unionism, particularly, in the context in which
he was writing, the trade unionism of the Glasgow cotton-spinners, is
referred to as 'Glasgow thuggery', while Chartism is ' . . . bitter discontent grown fierce and mad, the wrong condition, therefore the
wrong disposition, of the Working classes of England. It is a new name
for a thing which has had many names, which will yet have many . . .'[90]
Carlyle was writing in the language of class. His friends in the Young
Ireland movement a few years later did not have 'wild Milesian faces',
or if they did he was prepared to gaze at them across the teacups.[91] For
the Chartists the use of this abusive language was as likely to cement
them in sympathy to the Irish as to divide them, since it was a tone
which was widely, if not universally, adopted towards them also in the
first half of the nineteenth century. To quote a more or less random
example from a contemporary local history, an account describes a
Halifax beerhouse, in which:

the incendiary and the unionist fraternise together; from hence,
under the influence and excitement of their too often adulterated
beverage, they turn out at midnight . . . the one to fire the cornstack
and the barn, the other to imbrue his hands in the blood of a fellow-
workman, or peradventure the man to whom he was formerly
indebted for his daily bread . . . [92]

The wild Milesian faces are almost mild by comparison.

In conclusion, whilst not denying that there were divisive factors in
national and ethnic differences during the Chartist period, I find a
much greater cohesion in a consciousness of exclusion from the
constitution of both Irish and English workmen, in a sense of being
under attack from government and employers, and of being misunderstood and rejected by those with political power in the country. In an
age when the mass of working people who took part in political move

ments - clearly in absolute terms always a minority of the population, although in some areas whole communities participated - believed that their grievances could be solved by political means, the outstanding grievance of the Irish, the union, was also seen as susceptible of a political solution. For those among the Chartists who believed that an armed rising was either desirable or unavoidable, the experience of the United Irish rising of 1798 was always in their consciousness, both as illustrating the possibility of a popular rising, and as illustrating the dangers of lack of preparation and the ruthlessness of British government action. The Chartists always expressed common cause with the Irish repealers. Those Irishmen who were prominent in British radical politics tended to be from the tradition of the United Irishmen rather than from the Catholic Emancipation movement of the late 1820s although in districts in which support was organised for the emancipation movement, as in Leeds, radicals who took part included many who were later to become Chartists. James Duffy was secretary of the Leeds Catholic Association in 1828, was a reformer in the 1830-1 period, became a Chartist and was arrested for his part in the unsuccessful Sheffield rising in 1840. The prison inspector who interviewed him formed the opinion that Duffy had been 'a political agitator most of his life'. Duffy himself claimed at this time that he was 'an O'Connellite and repealer but no Chartist', but he nevertheless continued his Chartist activities after his release from prison until his premature death as the result of his treatment in prison.[93] Many radicals were ambivalent in attitude to Catholic Emancipation. O'Connor saw it as a diversion from the more important emancipation represented by universal suffrage. Doherty paid tribute to the organising power which O'Connell and the Catholic Association had displayed, but vacillated in his own attitude between admiration for the achievement and the view that it constituted a diversion.[94] It is important to remember that the six points of the Charter would have given self-determination to the Irish people, and this was a point which was often made by Chartists, particularly by Irish Chartists. It was also quite often given as a reason for opposing Chartist demands - even Thomas Attwood who came to support the main Chartist programme, dissociated himself in presenting the first Chartist Petition to Parliament from the point demanding equal electoral districts, on the grounds that this would give too much weight in Parliament to the Irish.[95] By the time of the second petition in 1842 the demand for the repeal of the union had been included in the preamble to the petition.

The question of Ireland was continually brought forward by the

Chartists. Neither O'Connell nor the Catholic Church accepted as strong a commitment to a complete rupture with Britain as the Chartists demanded, and later nationalist movements were to reiterate. The Irish Catholic Chartists of Barnsley must, however, have spoken for many of their countrymen in England when they wrote:

> ... our efforts are not directed to the benefit of any one class, creed or locality to the exclusion of another; all are included in the Charter, without distinction of party, sect or colour ... we are all advocates of repeal of the union, but will this give the people any control over the power that oppresses them? Does Mr. O'Connell imagine that a Parliament sitting in Dublin, elected by the present constituency would extend the franchise? but it is absurd to talk about a repeal of the union ever being obtained by the vacillating means he adopts; and if it were possible, it would be a mere delusion, unless the people have control over the action of government which they cannot possibly have without the franchise.[96]

NOTES

1. I am indebted to a number of colleagues and students for illustrations to this paper from their local research. In particular, Nick Cotton, James Epstein, Sieglinde Juxhorn, John Sanders, Jonathan Smith and Robert Sykes.

2. Mark Hovell, *The Chartist Movement* (1918) pp. 92–3 and *passim*.

3. Rachel O'Higgins, 'Ireland and Chartism, a Study of the Influence of Irishmen and the Irish Question on the Chartist Movement' (Trinity Coll. Dublin Ph.D. thesis, 1959) and 'The Irish Influence in the Chartist Movement', *Past & Present*, 20 (1961).

4. J. H. Treble, 'O'Connor, O'Connell and the Attitudes of Irish Immigrants towards Chartism in the North of England 1838–1848' in J. Butt and I. F. Clarke (eds), *The Victorians and Social Protest : a Symposium* (Newton Abbott, 1973).

5. J. T. Ward, *Chartism* (1973) p. 65.

6. For Timothy Higgins's indictment and trial, see TS 11/1030/4424 and for the interview with HM inspector of prisons, HO 20/10. For the information about his nationality I am indebted to Sieglinde Huxhorn.

7. Cited in Treble, 'O'Connor, O'Connell and the Attitudes of Irish Immigrants', p. 41.

8. F. J. Kaijage, 'Labouring Barnsley, 1815–1875' (Univ. of Warwick, Ph.D. thesis, 1975).

9. C. Richardson, 'Irish settlement in Mid-Nineteenth Century Bradford' *Yorkshire Bulletin of Economic and Social Research*, May 1968, pp. 40–57. This article explains some of the problems of making an assessment of the number of Irish families in the pre-1851 period.

10. Figures for Ashton town have been worked out by Sieglande Huxhorn. See also Nicholas Cotton, 'Radicalism and Popular Religion in Ashton-under-Lyne 1815–1836' (Univ. of Birmingham M.A. thesis, 1975).

11. Address to the Revd Patrick Ryan, parish priest of Donabate, from the Barnsley Irish Catholic Chartists, dated Sunday 3 October 1841 (Burland, MS Annals of Barnsley) pp. 186, 187, 188.

12. I am grateful for the information about the nationality of Smith (or Smyth as he was sometimes spelt) to Jonathan Smith of York University.

13. For areas of high Irish settlement, see Richardson, 'Irish settlement'; for Northern Union and Democratic Associations, see *Northern Star* (*NS*) 1838–9 *passim*.

14. HO 45/2410 (4) AB.

15. *Report of the Bradford Sanatory Committee, Appointed at a Public Meeting Held on Monday May 5th, 1845.* Signed by George White, Secretary.

16. Population figures in 1841 were England and Wales 15,929,000

Scotland	2,622,000
Ireland	8,200,000

(B. R. Mitchell and P. Deane, *Abstract of British Historical Statistics* (1962))

17. *3 and 4 William IV cap 4* (1833). The act forbade meetings of more than a very small number, suspended the right of petitioning Parliament in designated 'Disturbed Districts' and imposed martial law, including trial by military tribunal on these districts.

18. *Twopenny Dispatch* 10 September 1836.

19. Placard GENERAL STRIKE, issued by the Council of the Northern Political Union, 8 August 1839. Copy in HO 40/42.

20. R. G. Gammage, *History of the Chartist Movement* (1894 edn) p. 61.

21. *Leeds Times* 14 March 1833.

22. *Halifax Guardian* 2 September 1833.

23. *Ibid.*, 16 March 1833 (this and the two previous references from John Sanders).

24. *Manchester Guardian* 6 March and 6 April 1833; *Manchester and Salford Advertiser* 16 March 1833. Both cited in the very full and detailed biography of Doherty, R. G. Kirby and A. E. Musson, *The Voice of the People* (1976) p. 452.

25. *Nottingham Review* 22 February 1833.

26. *Report of the Great Public Meeting . . . 20th May, 1833* (Birmingham, 1833).

27. Kirby and Musson, *Voice of the People*, p. 452.

28. See for example *Halifax Guardian* 8 October 1836.

29. The *Northern Star,* founded by Samuel Neilson in 1792, ran for six years until its suppression in 1798.

30. William Lovett, *Life and Struggles of William Lovett* (Fitzroy edn) p. 105.

31. *Bronterre's National Reformer* 4 February 1837.

32. Cleave appears in most of the standard histories of Chartism and in accounts of the unstamped press agitation. For a full biography see the entry by I. Prothero and J. Wiener in Bellamy and Saville (eds), *Dictionary of Labour Movement Biography*, vol. IV.

33. Condy speaks for himself in the columns of his newspaper. See also the obituary notices in *Manchester Guardian* November 1841. There is a collection of

cuttings and writings in Manchester Reference Library; see also J. T. Slugg, *Reminiscences of Manchester Fifty Years Ago* (Manchester 1887).

34. A. J. Plummer, *Bronterre* (1971).

35. Kirby and Musson, *Voice of the People*. Among other Irish radical journalists of the early Chartist years, James Whittle, sometime editor of the *Manchester and Salford Advertiser* should be mentioned. Although described by Francis Place as 'the physical force delegate from Liverpool' when he represented that town at the first Chartist Convention in 1839, he was in fact on the moderate wing of the movement, and retired from the Convention in March 1839. He reappears in 1841 as a supporter of Lovett's 'new move', a moderate rival to the National Charter Association.

36. R. Challinor and Brian Ripley, *The Miners' Association, a Trade Union in the Age of the Chartists* (1968).

37. *Report on the State of the Irish Poor* (1835) p. XXVIII.

38. *Leeds Mercury* 1829-30, *passim* (information from John Sanders).

39. For an account of the Glasgow cotton-spinners episode, see Hamish Fraser, 'The Glasgow Cotton Spinners' in *Scottish Themes. Essays in honour of Professor S. G. E. Lythe,* J. Butt and J. T. Ward (eds) (Edinburgh, 1976).

40. Disraeli, the most observant of the novelists who wrote about Chartism, has one of the factory workers in *Sybil* use the word '(h) immigrants' for the country labourers who were being transferred by some Poor Law authorities into the factory districts – 'they're sold out of slavery, and sent down by Pickford's van into the labour market to bring down our wages' (Book 11, ch. 10, Penguin edn p. 130).

41. Examples of this and other clashes between agricultural workers and seasonally migrant Irish can be found in the replies to the questionnaire sent out by the Constabulary Commissioners in 1836 (HO 73); Georg Weerth spoke of the Irish with their scythes moving in to take the work of the Bradford weavers at harvest time in I. & P. Kuczynski (eds), *A Young Revolutionary in Nineteenth Century England* (Berlin, 1971); in 1837 a meeting of unemployed at Leeds complained of the 'swarms of distressed Irish' who took all the haymaking jobs in the district (*Leeds Times* 8 July 1837). Nevertheless the radicals continually preached a political lesson, like that in an anonymous broadside of 1842:

The Irish have got no employment at home,
Then in search of work they are forced to roam;
'Tis forty years since they lost their Parliament
The wealth of their nation abroad is all spent ...

42. *Voice of the West Riding* 10 August 1833.

43. HO 20/10. Doyle was a Catholic, born in Wexford in 1810.

44. For Ashton, see *Dictionary of Labour Movement Biography*, vol. III.

45. Arthur Redford, *Labour Migration in England 1800-1850* (1926; 3rd edn, Manchester 1964) p. 38.

46. *NS* 30 January 1840.

47. Information from Jonathan Smith of York University.

48. Lovett, *Life and Struggles*, p. 95.

49. For this argument, see W. Fagan, *The Life and Times of Daniel O'Connell,* (Cork, 1847-8) pp. 244–51.

50. For an account of Feargus O'Connor's early political career in Ireland and in England, see J. A. Epstein, 'Feargus O'Connor and the English Working-class

Radical Movement, 1832–1841; a study in National Chartist Leadership', (Univ. of Birmingham Ph.D. thesis, 1977).

51. Fagan, *Life and Times of Daniel O'Connell,* p. 249.

52. Thomas Ainge Devyr, *The Odd Book of the Nineteenth Century* (New York, 1882) Devyr was one of a group of able journalists who worked on the *Northern Liberator.* Born in Donegal of a Methodist mother and a Catholic father, he came to England a strong supporter of O'Connell, but moved into the Chartist Movement and became secretary of the Northern Political Union in 1839. Arrested in November of that year, he jumped bail and went to United States, where he had a long career in radical politics until his death in 1887.

53. HO 20/10.

54. *Bradford Observer* 25 November 1905: 'Some famous elections at Bradford'.

55. For the Dublin conflict, see Feargus D'Arcy, 'The Artisans of Dublin and Daniel O'Connell, 1830–47: an unquiet liaison', *Irish Historical Studies,* vol. XVII (1970) 221–43.

56. *Northern Liberator* 14 April 1838.

57. *The Cotton Spinners' Lament* (n.d.) [1838] Newcastle upon Tyne. Printed in full in Roy Palmer, *A Ballad History of England* (1978) pp. 115–16.

58. *Objects of the Irish Universal Suffrage Association* (1841). Copy in TS 11/601 X/L05744.

59. *NS* 20 August 1842. Patrick O'Higgins (1790–1854) was a Dublin woollen merchant, friend and almost exact contemporary of Feargus O'Connor. Accompanied William Cobbett on his Irish tour in 1834. Published the radical journal *The Tribune* in 1834, advocating repeal of the union, the abolition of tithes and a Poor Law for Ireland. Also wrote *Chartism and Repeal* and contributed to the *NS* and other Chartist journals. Was imprisoned for a year in 1848 for having arms in his house.

60. Letter Brophy to Thomas Cooper, TS 11/600. Brophy was originally a wool-weaver, but worked as journalist and lecturer during the Chartist period. Was one of the '58 others' tried with Feargus O'Connor for conspiracy in 1843. He later became a full-time organiser for the Miners' Association.

61. O'Higgins, 'Ireland and Chartism'.

62. W. H. Dyott, *Reason for seceding from the seceders by an ex-member of the Irish Confederation,* R. I. A. Haliday Tract, vol. 2013, no. 2 (1847). Dyott was a small master-printer in Dublin.

63. *Newcastle Weekly Chronicle* 29 March 1884. Gammage was born in 1820, and so would have made these discoveries some time in the eighteen-thirties.

64. *Newcastle Chronicle* 19 April 1834, reprinted in Brian Harrison and Patricia Hollis (eds), *Robert Lowery, Radical and Chartist* (1979) p. 208.

65. Malcom Brown, *The Politics of Irish Literature from Thomas Davis to W. B. Yeats* (1972) p. 22 and *passim* for the importance of Emmet in subsequent Irish nationalism.

66. Cited in Treble, 'O'Connor, O'Connell and the Attitudes of Irish Immigrants', n. 93, p. 225.

67. *NS* 15 January 1845 for one report of a meeting of the Emmet Brigade; David Goodway, *London Chartism* (Univ. of London, Ph. D. thesis, 1979) for a fuller account of the London Irish and Chartism.

68. A collection of Thomas Willey's broadsides is in the Madden Ballads

Collection, vol. 23 (Cambridge University Library). My thanks to Roy Palmer for this information, and for other references to street literature.

69. W. J. O'Neill Daunt, *Eighty-five years of Irish History* (1886) p. 41.

70. Letter Langridge to Lord Howick, 10 June 1839, HO 40/42 X/J 6904.

71. The lines – Hereditary Bondsmen know ye not
   Who would be free, himself must strike the blow?
represent one of several similarly rhetorical slogans which were common to the Chartist and Repeal Movements.

72. An incident in the tithe war of the early eighteen-thirties in Ireland, when twelve people were killed resisting the militarily enforced collection of tithes. According to O'Connor, he secured a verdict of wilful murder against the authorities concerned in the Coroner's Court, but the bills were ignored at the Assizes. (*National Instructor,* vol. 1, no. 10, 27 July 1850)

73. *Newcastle Weekly Chronicle* 27 September 1884.

74. Ibid.

75. Robert Crowe, *Reminiscences of an Octagenarian* (New York, n.d.) [1902] and 'The Reminiscences of a Chartist Tailor', in *The Outlook* 9 August 1902. The editors of the latter journal included a note about the author: 'Mr. Crowe's subsequent life, it may be said, has been a carrying on of the work to which he set his hand when he was a boy . . . He has been in practically all the labour movements of the past two-thirds of a century.'

76. For George White: Ken Geering, 'George White, a nineteenth-century workers' leader and the Kirkdale phenomenon' (Univ. of Sussex M. A. thesis, 1973); for John West: Frederic Boase (ed.), *Modern English Biography* (1921) vol. III. There were many other well-known Irish Chartists, including John Campbell, first secretary of the National Charter Association, George Archdeacon, joint editor of *The English Patriot and Irish Repealer* with James Leach, an Englishman, and John Deegan, card-room hand from Stalybridge, and delegate from there to the first Convention.

77. *NS* 1 February 1840, named O'Brien, Hoey, Martin, Doyle, White, Deegan, Duffy, O'Connor and 'nine others'. I have not been able to identify the two young Irishmen whom Flora Tristan met among the delegates to the Convention.

78. Earl of Bessborough (ed.), *Lady Charlotte Guest's Journal* (1850) vol. 1, pp. 101–2

79. Treble, 'O'Connor, O'Connell and the Attitudes of Irish Immigrants', and Norman McCord, *The Anti-Corn Law League* (1958) p. 102 and *passim*.

80. Angus Macintyre, *The Liberator* (1965) ch. VIII.

81. *The Times* 6 March 1843.

82. *NS* 3 February 1844.

83. *The Nation* 15 August 1847, cited in C. Gavan Duffy, *Four Years of Irish History 1845–9* (1883) p. 450.

84. Dyott, *Reasons for seceding from the seceders,* p. 87.

85. *United Irishman* 26 February 1848.

86. *The Gagging Bill* (broadside: n.p., n.d., 1848).

87. 'Parson Lot' (Charles Kingsley) 'Letter to the Chartists, No. 1', *Politics for the People,* 6 May 1848.

88. Thomas Carlyle, *Chartism* (1839) p. 18.

89.   In particular, Elizabeth Gaskell, *Mary Barton* and *North and South;* Charles Kingsley, *Alton Locke* and *Yeast;* George Eliot, *Felix Holt, the Radical.* Dickens, who did not write specifically about Chartism, was very much influenced in his presentation of working people by Carlyle, perhaps most evidently in *Hard Times* and *Our Mutual Friend.*

90.   Carlyle, *Chartism*, p. 4.

91.   Sir Charles Gavan Duffy, *Conversations with Carlyle* (London 1896).

92.   J. Crabtree, *A Concise History of the Parish and Vicarage of Halifax* (Halifax, 1836) p. 18.

93.   HO 20/10, Thomas Cooper, *Life of Himself* (1872) and *NS passim.*

94.   Kirby and Musson, *Voice of the People.*

95.   *Hansard* 12 July 1839, 3rd series, vol. XLIX.

96.   Burland, MS Annals of Barnsley. In his reply to the letter, Fr Ryan recalled the 'truly Christian piety and devoted attachment and strict attention to the duties of their religion which pervaded my little Flock at Barnsley,' and regretted that he 'had neither the power nor the talent to better your political condition.'

5. Early Chartism and Trade Unionism in South-East Lancashire

ROBERT SYKES

THE early pioneering studies of both Chartism and trade unionism presented a picture of two very separate almost hermetic movements.[1] More recently it has been shown that there was substantial trade union participation in Chartism in London and Scotland.[2] Yet the assumption that the connections between the two movements were minimal and unimportant remains widespread.[3] This proposition in fact forms a central part of what has been called a 'compartmentalist' or 'reductionist' approach to early working-class history.[4] This emphasises the essential separation of various strands of working-class activity, and extent of sectionalism, in order to question the extent of working-class consciousness and working-class support for Chartism.[5] This viewpoint dovetails with a conception of the social composition of Chartism, similarly rooted in the pioneering studies, as essentially a movement of the most depressed outworkers, with the skilled workers in their unions being absent and aloof.[6] In Lancashire Chartism is thus portrayed as quintessentially a movement of the handloom weavers, with the factory workers at best lukewarm and the other trades largely ignored.[7] In consequence, in the momentous Plug Strikes, the 1842 general strike, the evident confluence of Chartists, trade unionists and factory workers has been seen as a novel development, and a momentary aberration.[8]

In fact in south-east Lancashire the connections between Chartism and trade unionism were of considerable importance throughout the early Chartist period, and a meaningful evaluation of the Plug Strikes is wholly dependent upon seeing them in that perspective. There were the informal links of shared ideas, class perspectives, leaders and personnel, but also quite formal expressions of support for Chartism by trade societies acting as societies. Not all trades displayed active, and none wholly continuous, support for Chartism. Yet it would be quite unrealistic to expect them to have done so in a society where economic orthodoxy and wider middle- and upper-class opinion were so vehemently and unanimously hostile to trade unionism. The repeal of the Combination Laws (1824) was such a recent occurrence, and prosecutions of trade unionists, as in the Dorchester Labourers (1834) and Glasgow Cotton-spinners (1837–8) cases, were such live issues. The risks to unions appeared substantial enough even without any explicit alliance with the radicals. 'Their Trades Union was illegal enough at present,' said a London shoemaker making this very point in 1842, 'and they were unpopular enough with the masters without making them more so.'[9] Most unions had rules banning the discussion of political issues. This was partly a defensive accommodation to a hostile political environment which could be easily evaded if necessary,[10] and partly less a calculated rejection of politics than part of a number of reserve rules to prevent disorder and disunion and hence was placed alongside rules banning the discussion of religion, swearing and excessive drinking. Yet it also reflected an obvious difference in function between trade and political societies, and a belief in the utility of separating trade and political action. This belief was in fact enhanced by the considerable ideological and tactical uncertainty about the role of trade unions in radical agitation. In such a context, and given that it plainly needed impressive unanimity within the society to override the 'no politics' rules publicly, any expressions of support for Chartism by trade unions assume considerable significance and provide powerful evidence of Chartist strength amongst those trades.

Moreover a fairly consistent pattern of which trades did support Chartism does emerge. This evidence throws important light upon the extent of class-conscious political attitudes, and the impact of working-class stratification and sectionalism upon political action in the early Chartist period (and thus also provides an important longer-term perspective on the debate about the labour aristocracy in the mid-Victorian period). Distinctions between the skilled and unskilled, and between the factory workers and others,[11] do not provide a useful way of conceptualising a situation where divisions within the skilled sector were highly significant, and where Chartist attachments cut across the divisions between factory and domestic, or small workshop, employment. However the distinction seen in London between the 'upper', better-paid, higher status and more secure skilled trades, and the 'lower' more insecure and threatened skilled trades, with the latter providing the real basis of Chartism,[12] can be fruitfully applied to the cotton district. For the very best paid 'upper' trades, often with the strongest, most permanent trade societies, such as the printers, bookbinders and coach-makers, were consistently aloof from Chartism. Such trades were seen by contemporary working-class opinion as being 'aristocratic'. This did not mean that they were seen as being part of a distinct labour aristocracy, in the sense that the term has been used in the mid-Victorian period to describe not simply aloof craft sectionalism but a coherent unitary social stratum with shared lifestyles, values and institutions cutting across craft boundaries. Instead the term was used in a more limited, and usually pejorative, sense to describe those trades who because of their relatively privileged position remained reprehensibly aloof from inter-trade and political action. However the most numerous groups of adult male workers with some skilled status, both inside and outside the factories were much less secure, not aristocratic in this sense and certainly not aloof from Chartism. We shall find expressions of support for Chartism by trade societies of the largest such groups of factory workers; cotton-spinners, calico printers and dyers, as well as from the largest artisan trades, the clothing workers, especially the tailors and shoemakers and the various building trades. Moreover these trades which faced reasonably similar threats to their status were joined in their support for Chartism, not only by the rather lower status power-loom weavers (amongst whom adult males were a small albeit significant minority) and the depressed textile outworkers, handloom weavers and fustian-cutters, but also by significant numbers of the more advantaged, aristocratically inclined, engineering and metal-working trades. This evidence will be used to indicate the extent to which Chartism in the cotton district was a much more broadly based movement than has often been realised. It will be used to demonstrate how restricted were the numbers of aloof, truly aristocratic trades, to question the postulated indifference of factory workers to Chartism, to criticise the unqualified labelling of those key local workers, the spinners, as labour aristocrats, and to demonstrate that the more obviously aristocratic engineers, at least in Lancashire before the mid-1840s, were not unambiguously aloof.

The radical political action of these trade societies was inhibited by the circumstances we have already mentioned, but it was also securely grounded upon a number of alternative factors. Firstly there was that powerful countervailing force to trade sectionalism, the tradition of inter-trade co-operation. In the textile factories the Factory Movement provided experience of co-operative inter-trade organisation. There had also been important general unions of diverse trades, as in the 1818 Philanthropic Society, and the 1829–32 National Association for the Protection of Labour. Within specific industrial sectors there was also the 1831–3 Operative Builders Union and the United Trades Association established in 1840 and combining the five engineering trades of the smiths, iron moulders, mechanics, millwrights and engineers.[13] Yet arguably such general unions were occasional formal expressions of a wider if more informal process of inter-trade co-operation. Mutual support during strikes was very common, and in key strikes often produced co-operation in the form of combined public meetings and committees. In the years leading up to Chartism such strikes were quite frequent, for example the Ashton spinners 1830–1, the Derby silk-weavers 1833–4, the Manchester fustian-cutters 1836, the Preston spinners 1836–7, the London bookbinders 1838–9, the Stockport weavers 1840 and the London masons 1841. Such occasions often gave rise to proposals to establish more formal general unions, as for example by the inter-trade committee supporting the fustian-cutters 1836 strike.[14] They were an important element in a wider tradition of inter-trade co-operation which is all too easily missed given the emphasis of so much trade union historiography on studying specific trades in isolation over an extended period and on formal institutional development. This tradition, particularly strong amongst the more insecure lower trades, brought factory workers, textile outworkers and artisans together, moderated their sectional impulses and laid a basis for co-operative political action. Secondly an alignment of radicals and trade unions was encouraged by the consistent support for strikes by radical leaders and newspapers, and the consistent misrepresentation and malevolence of middle-class politicians and press. Thirdly the action of the authorities, as in the use of troops in strikes, and what was perceived as the unfair operation of the law encouraged trade union sympathy with those seeking radical reform. Fourthly co-operation between trade unions and radical leaders became especially marked when there was a widely perceived association between the government and the employers. In 1834 the prosecution of the Dorchester Labourers produced a Manchester inter-trade committee closely associated with the radicals.[15] Also in 1834 the apparently Dorchester-style arrest of two Oldham spinners union leaders provoked a spontaneous general strike, and subsequently inter-trade co-operation involving the key local radical leader John Knight.[16] In 1837-8 the prosecution of the Glasgow spinners' leaders again brought radical leaders and trade unions together in a joint campaign. A closer examination of this campaign will provide the starting-point for a study of relations between Chartism and the trades. This will subsequently also lead us through an examination of the trade societies' participation in the first phase of Chartism in 1838-9, the involvement of Chartists with strikes, the relationship between the National Charter Association and the trades in 1840-2, and the Plug Strikes of 1842.

THE GLASGOW SPINNERS CAMPAIGN

In the formation of northern Chartism the importance of the convergence of three great movements, the Factory Movement, the Anti-Poor Law Movement, and the trade unions, was recognised long ago. In recent years, however, the emphasis upon especially the Anti-Poor Law Movement has led to a neglect of the general contribution of the unions, and in particular of the important role of the concurrent, wrongly neglected, national campaign in support of the Glasgow spinners' leaders, prosecuted for offences arising out of their 1837 strike. The south Lancashire campaign fell into two main phases: firstly a series of mainly fund-raising meetings in later 1837, and subsequently in early 1838 a series of protest meetings about their trial and conviction. R. J. Richardson, now emerging as a pivotal figure in the various popular campaigns, who was already the Secretary of the South Lancashire Anti-Poor Law Association, and from April 1838 the Secretary of the new Manchester Political Union, was also as secretary of a joint radical-trade committee in Manchester, a key organiser and speaker in this campaign.[17] It was indeed vitally important in the way it united trade unionists, especially the spinners, and radicals in a joint campaign. The last major campaign of the Factory Movement had already ground to a halt by early 1837, and in so far as the spinners were channelled into Chartism by any sectional issue, the Glasgow cotton-spinners campaign was more important.

The prosecution of the Glasgow spinners, as with the Dorchester prosecutions with which it was frequently compared, also emphasised the extent of the authorities' and middle-class hostility to trade unionism in general and the common insecurity of all unions. As the Manchester masons declared: 'we are all *guilty* of the *great crime* of uniting to protect our labour from the same class of assailants as those who prosecuted the 'Cotton Spinners' and Dorchester Labourers'.[18] It was an essential component in that vital ideological tenet of the first phase of Chartism, the belief in the imminent danger of government repression. Thus the spinners' leader David M'Williams:

> His opinion was, that the government and the manufacturing and commercial interests were determined to bring the working man down to the continental level in their wages. The unions amongst the working men were the great obstacles that stood in the way, and therefore had the determination gone forth to crush them . . . The whigs intended to bring the working classes down to the level of the miserable pauper under the poor law amendment act[19]

This contribution of the Glasgow spinners case to the ideological foundations of Chartism was clearly interwoven with that provided by the movement against the new Poor Law. Both were vital components of the complex of oppressive action against working men, from the prosecution of the unstamped press to the proposed new police, which appeared to justify the notions of 'defensive' and 'constitutional' arming so prevalent in 1838-9. For as a blacksmith commented at a meeting of the Bury trades: 'When the Unions were put down, and the New Poor Law introduced, all moral power would be at an end, and an armed police would be employed to keep the people in subjection'.[20]

Nor should the distinctive contribution of the Glasgow cotton-spinners campaign be underestimated. Although its meetings coincided exactly (with much overlapping of personnel), with those organised by the South Lancashire Anti-Poor Law Association, they were far from dwarfed by them. The vastly more extensive coverage, and especially comment, on the Poor Law issue by the middle-class press was more a reflection of it being a controversial issue *within* the middle class, as the Glasgow case was not, than an accurate reflection of the scale of working-class priorities. Significantly the *Northern Star* paid as much attention to the Glasgow spinners as to the new Poor Law. Herein lay the further important point that even more than with the Poor Law, this was an issue which emphasised class divisions. There was never even the slight hint of 'respectability' which the support of sections of the national Conservative press and of some aristocrats, the frequent reference to apparently plausible historical precedents, and the occasional appearance at public meetings of local liberals or conservatives conferred on the Anti-Poor Law Movement. Indeed as an issue it was consciously used by militant radicals to differentiate themselves from sympathetic liberals. In Manchester it was used to discredit the position represented by the radical-liberal editor of the *Manchester Times* Archibald Prentice, in Ashton to smear as 'Whig' the Reform Association which backed the radical-liberal MP Charles Hindley (and which had already petitioned for universal suffrage and total repeal of the new Poor Law), just as it was used in London by G. J. Harney to attack the Working Men's Association moderation.[21] Support for the Glasgow men was indeed indicative of a degree of class bitterness whether one believed them guilty or not. For either it represented a total disbelief in the case presented by the authorities, a disbelief which speaks volumes for the depth of misunderstanding between the classes, or it meant believing that such was the oppression borne by working men that such violence was sadly inevitable.

THE TRADES AND THE FIRST PHASE OF CHARTISM

A legacy of bitterness was not the only contribution from the trade union world to the gestation of Chartism, for many unions also greatly augmented the organisational base upon which especially Manchester Chartism was grounded. In March 1837 R. J. Richardson, organising a working-class meeting against the new Poor Law, had convened a 'numerous' preparatory meeting of trade delegates. At the subsequent public meeting the chairman, Christopher Dean, 'an honest and intelligent officer' of the Manchester stonemasons, called for the establishment of a Trades Council to consider political issues. Such a body soon emerged with explicitly radical politics and links with the Manchester Universal Suffrage Association, the main working-class radical organisation in Manchester at this time.[22] Richardson acted as secretary of the Trades Council and Dean remained its chairman. They went on to become Manchester's two delegates to the 1839 Chartist Convention. Thus both of Manchester's Convention delegates had been centrally involved in this Trades Council (and indeed both had previously represented their trades at the 1834 Manchester meeting of trades protesting at the Dorchester arrests).

Information on the composition of the Trades Council is rather sparse, but certainly the main textile and building trades were well represented.

The delegates, identified by their trade only, at the first preparatory meeting were a mason, slater, bricklayer, painter, spinner, dyer, silk-weaver, smith and farrier, and at the following meeting in addition a joiner (Richardson), cabinet-maker and a powerloom weaver. In early 1838 the Executive Council comprised two masons, two spinners, a carpenter, a silk-weaver, a fustian-shearer, and a dyer. From September 1837 to March 1838 the Trades Council concentrated upon the Glasgow spinners case, holding five meetings on the subject. The subscriptions they received from trades subscribing as trades were the spinners, dressers and dyers, fustian-shearers, joiners, bricklayers, masons, ladies' shoe-makers and bakers.[23] The growing politicisation of such 'lower' skilled trades was then further intensified by Daniel O'Connell's broadening of the apparent attack upon the unions, in his attacks on the Dublin trades, and by the convening of the 1838 Select Committee on Combinations. This politicisation was channelled through the Trades Council which issued addresses bitterly attacking O'Connell, became the forum for trade union consideration of all these developments, and evolved into the Manchester Combination Committee. The result was that the Manchester trades did not take a narrow view, concentrating upon the specific threat of the select committee (although they did co-operate with the London Combination Committee, and three Manchester spinners' representatives appeared before the committee).[24] Instead they pursued a wide-ranging radical critique of the government which was to lead many of them, as unions, into Chartism.

Two events illustrated the scale of trade union politicisation in Manchester during the summer of 1838; the trades' boycott of the Coronation Procession, and their participation in the first great Chartist demonstration on Kersal Moor. A total of twenty-three trades called for a boycott of the Coronation Procession, as an act of political protest:

We, the Trades Unions have had no encouragement from our national and local rulers to join in any of their schemes, since we find the wealthy, in and out of parliament, conspiring against the labouring poor to deprive them of the rights of industry, and withholding from them the political rights and liberties of free-born British subjects, at the same time they call upon us to testify our allegiance to that very system of government which offers us no protection – which manifests no sympathy for the destitute poor of our country, but upon all occasions takes advantage of the power they possess to treat us as

Table 1
Trade union politicisation 1838–9

	Trades in the Combination Committee 1838–9	Trades in the 1831 but not the 1838 Coronation Procession	Trades attending the Chartist Kersal Moor meeting 1838
Textile factories	Cotton-spinners Dressers and dyers Silk skein dyers Calenderers	Dressers and dyers Silk-dyers Smallware weavers Calenderers	Cotton-spinners Dressers and dyers Calenderers
Textile Outworkers	Fustian-cutters		Fustian-cutters
Engineers and metal workers	National Associated Smiths Smiths and Wheelwrights Smiths and farriers Moulders	Friendly Smiths Farriers Millwrights Tin plate workers Engravers to calico printers	National Associated Smiths Smiths and Wheelwrights Smiths and farriers Mechanics
Building and allied trades	Stonemasons Carpenters and joiners Bricklayers Plasterers Painters Plumbers Brickmakers Sawyers (wood) Marble polishers and sawyers	Stonemasons Marble masons Painters and plasterers Cabinet-makers Upholsterers Sawyers	Stonemasons Marble masons Carpenters and joiners Painters and plasterers Bricklayers
Clothing	Boot and shoemakers Ladies' shoemakers Hatters	Hatters	Men's shoemakers Ladies' shoemakers Tailors
Others	Rope-makers Coach-makers	Rope-makers Sadlers Skinners Organ and piano makers Letterpress printers Brewers	Labourers (of bricklayers?)

The 1838 Coronation Procession consisted of the following marching as trades: the Associated Smiths, plumbers and glaziers, brickmakers, tailors, hydraulic packers, brushmakers, carvers and gilders and bakers, together with three firms of carpenters, three of glass-bottle-makers, two of coach-makers, one slater and one engineer.

SOURCE: for the Combination Committee, Balance Sheet of the Combination Committee, Manchester 1839 (Modern Records Centre, Warwick University); for the Coronation Processions and Kersal Moor, see notes 26 and 27.

slaves, stigmatize us as combinators and persecute us as criminals . . . The forthcoming Coronation will convince the government that the people are becoming tired of the system which encourages luxurious idleness, excessive taxation, constant persecutions of the poor, and the useless squanderings of the hard earnings of the labouring millions.[25]

In the 1831 Coronation Procession, twenty-nine trades of which twenty-two were probably trade societies (the remainder participating as individual firms) marched in the trades section, and in the 1832 procession celebrating the passing of the Reform Bill there were twenty-four trades of which eighteen were probably unions. But in 1838 there were only thirteen trades of which at most only eight were trade societies (see Table 1). The embarrassed organisers were reduced to padding out the 'trades' section with such as 'Mr. Henry Hollins, with a Fire Engine' and 'Mr. H. Jewsby, 103 Market Street with a Soda Water Apparatus'.[26] Yet even of those eight trades attending, the tailors (with a vested interest in such public events because of the extra work it brought them) and the smiths also went to Kersal Moor. This was the second great demonstration of trade union politicisation, for eighteen trades attended the South Lancashire Chartist Demonstration (Table 1). This was an important occurrence for these were genuine and important societies and not simply groups of workmen from the same trade. For example, from press reports it is possible to identify the largest contingent of smiths as being from the largest national union of their trade, the National Associated Smiths, and the 'mechanics' as being from the largest engineers union, the Journeymen Steam Engine and Machine Makers Friendly Society, the society which later became the main basis for that archetypal 'new model' union of the Webbs, the Amalgamated Society of Engineers. Moreover the identification of those trades in the Chartist demonstration and the Combination Committee confirms the pattern which was already emerging from what is known about the composition of the earlier Trades Council (see Table 1). There were the large unions of factory workers, the spinners and dyers, the smiths again but now joined by engineers, the building trades again amongst the traditional artisan trades but now also joined by the tailors and shoemakers. But the best-paid artisans generally do not appear. The absence of the letter press printers from the 1838 Coronation Procession was by accident not design and they otherwise make no appearance in these events, and nor do the bookbinders.[27]

Nor was the trades' attendance at Kersal Moor unique. For there was also trades' participation albeit on a lesser scale at the early Chartist demonstrations in north Lancashire at Preston and in west Lancashire at Wigan, as well as on an extensive scale further afield at the larger cities of Newcastle, and Glasgow.[28] Moreover back in south Lancashire at Bury in 1838 a meeting arranged by twenty-one organised trades established an ongoing committee, and adopted an explicitly radical position, for example advocating the need for universal suffrage and recommending a run on the banks.[29] The occupations of the speakers who were identified, a shoemaker, tailor, cotton-spinner, millwright, blacksmith and stonemason, were a good illustration of the type of workmen who, like the depressed handloom weavers, were entering Chartism. Yet how far such men brought their trade societies with them into Chartism in the smaller towns of the area, is a question upon which the evidence provides only fragmentary clues. There had been a report of a trades delegate meeting at Oldham in 1837, prior to a major Anti-Poor Law and radical election meeting, but there is no evidence of any continuing permanent inter-trade organisation.[30] More generally, it is even unclear from the press reports how far the Manchester policy of boycotting the Coronation Procession was followed, or even attempted, in the surrounding towns. There probably was some trade society participation at Bolton (nine trades identified but none as definite unions), Heywood (where there were trade societies) and Rochdale ('the trades'), but also definite boycotts at Bury and Ashton; with Ashton and Oldham taking the opportunity of a public holiday to hold large open-air radical meetings.[31]

Indeed frequently in the smaller towns, the trade societies can hardly have seemed the appropriate channel for the truly mass Chartist enthusiasm of 1838-9. However they had a real attraction in coping organisationally with the sheer size of the largest cities, especially before large-scale permanent Chartist associations were established. In Glasgow early Chartist organisation was firmly based upon the trades organisations. Moreover in London the failure to mobilise the trades in 1839 goes a long way to explaining the capital's apathy in that year, compared with the 1840s when London Chartism was at its strongest precisely because such a mobilisation was achieved.[32] In Manchester the successful mobilisation of so many key trades in 1838 was a vital factor in the initial very rapid growth of the movement, and there was also some continuing financial support. The following trade subscriptions to the Chartist National Rent were recorded in the *Northern Star* in 1839:[33]

Dressers & Dyers	£10	(30 Mar)
Fustian-Cutters	£3.12s.6d.	(30 Mar)
Spinners	£10 (possibly £20)	(30 Mar)
Spinners shops Nos 4, 7, 12, 17, 38, 42, 74, 78	£2.10s.	(15 June)
Ladies' Shoemakers	£1	(30 Mar)
″ ″	£1	(4 May)
″ ″	£1.1s.10½d.	(29 June)
Brickmakers	£10	(20 April)

As the published accounts were not only incomplete, but also included unattributed sums, so the table may represent an underestimation of union subscriptions. However as all of them came long after the torch-light meetings, the beginning of arming and the discussion of ulterior measures, they surely call into question the hypothesis that such violence alienated all but the most distressed, essentially the handloom weavers.[34] Indeed two trades, the shoemakers and spinners, which were in fact the largest occupational groups of adult males amongst the artisans and factory workers respectively, deserve special mention for their continuing Chartist commitment. The shoemakers trade societies at Manchester and Bolton joined the Chartists *as unions* in June and July 1839, and the only set of published accounts from Stockport (for the August to October 1839 period) reveal an auxiliary Chartist Shoemakers Society from at least August. If the shoemakers radicalism is widely recognised, that of the spinners is not. Yet the Manchester spinners subscribed more than any other trade to the National Rent, and the Stockport accounts similarly reveal spinners union subscriptions in early August. In Bury the political general strike in the mills, on the second day of the Chartist 'National Holiday', was enforced by the unionised spinners.[35]

However, generally the evidence for continuing trade society involvement in Chartism in 1839 is fragmentary. In part this possibly reflects gaps in the evidence, for example in the lack of detailed accounts for the smaller towns outside Manchester, but other factors were involved. Firstly as no government action followed the 1838 Select Committee, and O'Connell turned to attacking Chartists rather than trade unionists, that particular incentive for political action by unions, as unions, was diminished. Also, although the London Bookbinders Strike of 1839 led to inter-trade delegate meetings at Manchester, Bolton and Bury, the issue lacked the emotional appeal and political connotations of the

Dorchester and Glasgow cases.[36] Secondly given the insurrectionary tone assumed by Lancashire Chartism in 1839, the risks to the unions involved in too visible or formal links with a movement so obviously set upon a collision course with the authorities, must have seemed to outweigh the benefits. Hence one should not read too much into the absence of trade societies, as such, at the second great Kersal Moor meeting held to endorse the Convention's projected ulterior measures.[37] Thirdly this was especially so given the lack of any clear conception of the role of trade societies in Chartist action. Chartist tactics in 1839 did not advance out of a familiar, by now almost traditional, framework. Even the proposed general strike, or National Holiday, was conceived in such terms, as a political demonstration by 'the people', and was not a syndicalist scheme envisaging a central role for the trade unions.[38] Finally it does seem that in 1839 Chartist leaders, once having established Chartist associations, were frequently carried along upon a wave of enthusiastic mass meetings and neglected organisational matters of which links with the unions were only a part. This failure later seriously impaired their ability to implement the various ulterior measures. The Manchester Combination Committee made no public political pronouncements in 1839, and there does even seem to have been a failure to consult local unions about the National Holiday. It was left to R. J. Richardson, who had now resigned from the Convention and was campaigning against the general strike strategy, to convene, on his own initiative, an ultimately small-scale and indecisive delegate meeting of trades to discuss the matter only days before the planned date, 12 August.[39] By contrast at Bolton the Chartists had appealed for the unions' 'adhesion in bodies' and according to one report had been answered by several unions 'joining' the Chartists.[40] At Bury the inter-trade committee of 1838 had maintained some sort of existence into early 1839, and the Bury Radical Association secretary John Rawson was planning for action to be taken under 'orders from the Committee of Trades only'.[41] At Bury certainly the spinners acted and in both towns there were successful general strikes. Greater union backing probably was a factor in the greater success in these towns as compared with Manchester, but probably the most important factor was the greater strength of the authorities' forces in Manchester as compared with the smaller towns.

Nationally the failure of the ulterior measures, and the arrests and trials of the summer, produced moves towards more offensive secret insurrectionary strategies in some areas, and ushered in a general period of reassessment and reorganisation in the Chartist Movement. In some places this included making approaches to the trade societies. A 'better organisation of the trades' was specifically recommended by the Chartists of Colne in north Lancashire, and in later 1839 some Chartist trade societies were formed in Newcastle, Chartist trade meetings organised in Birmingham and approaches made (with little success) at Sheffield.[42] However prior to 1842, in England at least, it seems only in London was there any really substantial success in establishing ongoing formalised links with trade societies.

CHARTISTS AND STRIKES

Nevertheless it would be a mistake to concentrate unduly upon institutional links. For if the basis of Chartism lay less in organisation than in the more intangible associations of class, community, neighbourhood, workshop and mill, so frequently did trade action. A great deal of small-scale industrial conflict amongst artisans arose from an instinctive defence of customary practices, founded upon an occupational consciousness which spread well beyond formal permanent trade unionism. The absence of formal trade unionism did not mean the absence of collective industrial action. Both the handloom, and powerloom weavers, in particular, frequently demonstrated this. In such cases 'unions' were temporary creations, or explosive expansions of small-scale existing unions, in a temporary crisis. They were formed immediately before or even during a strike. Nor was this phenomenon restricted to the weavers. The Ashton spinners union which had two thousand spinners on strike in December 1830 had, according to its secretary, contained only twenty members at the start of that year.[43] The pattern of coal-miners' trade unionism, with periodic surges of very extensive and impressive organisation interspersed with periods of apparent inaction, is explicable in the same terms. Hence the lack of institutional links, indeed the lack of any substantial formal radical or trade organisations to be linked, did not mean that there was no correspondence between political and trade action.

Amongst the handloom weavers a number of leaders were bridging figures between radicalism and trade activity. In Manchester, Edward Curran, a leading figure in the Trades Council, was a major ultra-radical leader from the Reform Crisis to the early Chartist period. But he was also involved in the silk-weavers union in the later 1820s and subsequently probably the most important weavers' leader at meetings about trade affairs and government inquiries throughout the 1830s.[44]

At Middleton, Robert Ward, a violent speaker in 1839 and leader in the 1842 Plug Strikes, was a chairman of both silk-weavers' trade, and of Chartist, meetings.[45] In Middleton in 1839 one meeting discussing the Chartist National Holiday scheme broke off to hear a letter read from the Leigh silk-weavers about a wages advance they had obtained.[46] There was no real formal union amongst the Middleton silk-weavers, but there was a very real connection, as elsewhere, through shared leaders, meeting places, traditions, ideas and class attitudes between political Chartist and trade activity. Amongst the cotton factory workers also, the general support for strikes by radical leaders was an additional non-organisational connection between political and industrial action. Established radical leaders were prominent at the meetings supporting the Oldham factory workers during the spinners lock-out of the winter of 1836-7.[47] In Manchester in the winter of 1837-8, a key powerloom weavers' strike at Guest's Mills was led by future Chartists. Christopher Doyle, a leading Lancashire Chartist throughout 1839 and the 1840s, largely organised the union, John Allinson, later a Stockport Chartist and powerloom weavers' union leader, was this union's President. This strike also demonstrated how industrial conflict could develop political overtones. For Doyle and Allinson were arrested for organising the mass picketing and at the protest meeting there were not only other powerloom weavers soon to become major Chartist leaders, but also Feargus O'Connor making sweeping comparisons between the various assaults upon working men, Dorchester, Glasgow and the Bradford Poor Law Riots. Revd J. R. Stephens later even compared the arrested Manchester men with the Glasgow spinners.[48]

However, the number of strikes declined dramatically from 1837, and in the crucial crisis period of early Chartism, from mid-1838 to late 1839, there were no large strikes in the mills, and very few strikes of any kind. The reasons are clear enough. The trade depression ensured that workers would not initiate aggressive action themselves, and the employers by mainly working short time, the option preferred by the operatives, and not reducing wage rates did not provoke defensive action. Indeed in 1839 the one strike in which the Chartists were heavily involved, was geographically on the periphery of the area, at Poynton in Cheshire, and amongst the coal-miners whose traditions of radicalism, in this area, were weaker than the textile workers. It was thus highly significant that the miners' meetings nevertheless became very political, and were dominated by numerous Chartists, none of them miners.[49]

Such was the atmosphere of 1839, that any strike in which the strikers broadened the dispute by holding public meetings, was liable to develop in this manner. But this peripheral strike was the only one where such an appeal was made. However, in early 1840 there were widespread wage reductions in the cotton mills in several towns. At Stockport the reductions produced town-wide mill strikes, centred upon the power-loom weavers, putting an estimated 9000 operatives on the streets and inevitably the violent picketing, assaults, and later victimisation raised class tensions.[50] The political implications of such a strike in the violent atmosphere of 1839 could have been devastating. Large town-wide mill strikes were always liable to develop political overtones. The sheer numbers involved, combined with the widespread economic dislocation, made them such a threat to public order, that the authorities frequently acted in ways in which they could hardly avoid being seen as supportive of the masters, thus heightening and giving a political emphasis to the workers' perception of their class position. Moreover, at times of abnormal political excitement quite strong, explicitly radical, political overtones could be developed. This happened most obviously in the Plug Strikes of 1842, but it had also happened in the great Ashton Spinners strike of 1830–1, coming as it had in the atmosphere of expectancy and excitement after the news of the French Revolution and on the eve of the Reform Crisis. Then the carrying of tricolours, the arming, violence and radical affinities of the strike leadership had very seriously alarmed the authorities.[51]

1839 was a year of almost unprecedented radical strength and political excitement, and I would suggest that the lack of strikes, and lack of any large mill strikes, was a major reason for the relatively limited amount of violence which actually occurred. Both the military and Chartist leadership believed the likeliest catalyst for widespread violence was a 'Peterloo'-style incident, a possibly even accidental clash between soldiers and workers. The careful restraint exercised by the military command, enormously reduced the chances of such an incident being produced by provocative military action. The absence of serious strikes removed the other most likely source of an unpremeditated violent clash between soldiers and workmen. In 1840, at the time of the Stockport strike and afterwards, the Chartists, trying to learn from the mistakes of 1839, were insistent that 'Peace, law and order are inscribed upon our banners', but in 1839 they had just as uniformly been advocating arming and making violent seditious speeches. In 1839 they had not yet learnt the caution taught them by the defeats of that year; and had meetings of strikers then, as they did in 1842, begun to demand the Charter the mixture could have been explosive.

Generally from 1840 to 1842 the round of reductions throughout the cotton industry were received with sullen acquiescence, and a few small-scale, invariably short, unsuccessful, strikes. Victimisation fears ensured that in most instances the strike leadership remained anonymous. In these circumstances however with conventional trade unions contracting or collapsing, the Chartist leadership could play an important role. In Stockport in 1841 turn-out powerloom weavers and spinners both met in the National Charter Association rooms, and indeed the spinners' address was signed by two important Chartist leaders, just released from jail, James Mitchell and Charles Davies.[52] Both men were then beer-sellers, and yet as both were ex-spinners previously active in trade affairs, one can see, on closer examination, just how misleading is any static model maintaining an over-rigid distinction between working-class political and trade leadership, which sees such Chartist involvement as an external force 'capturing' strikes. In situations where formal union structures were weak or non-existent the Chartists could bring leadership and organisational skills, and from positions of relative independence – such as beer-sellers, newsagents and Chartist lecturers – address public meetings without fears of victimisation. In Manchester, Chartists led and organised the powerloom weavers. Chartist lecturers such as Daniel Donovan and Joseph Linney (who had both appeared at the 1837 meeting about the powerloom weavers' strike at Guest's mill) dominated their meetings. The delegate meeting to organise the weavers was held in Chartist rooms. Daniel Donovan was president of whatever existed of a formal powerloom weavers union in 1840–2. Maurice Donovan, who acted as the weavers secretary during the Plug Strikes, was subsequently the Manchester National Charter Association secretary.[53] There was thus ample precedent for the way the weavers accepted Chartist leadership and used Chartist rooms as organisational bases during the Plug Strikes (when after most workers returned to work 6000 weavers remained on strike in their largest and most coherent strike up to that time).[54] At Ashton, where the Plug Strikes began with Chartist leadership of striking millworkers, such leadership had also been provided months before. The Chartists Elijah Broadbent and William Aitken, joined the Irish leader B. S. Treanor, in a meeting asking the masters to work short time rather than reduce wage rates. After a general reduction was imposed, the only three named speakers at the mill workers' protest meetings were three Chartists, Richard Pilling, William Aitken and George Johnson.[55] Moreover the leadership they provided was sensible and responsible, speaking against some angry cries from the floor for strike action, because of the lack of funds and unfavourable economic circumstances. The Chartist leadership of unorganised, or imperfectly organised, mill workers was not a new feature of the Plug Strikes (and most certainly should not be seen as narrow-minded Chartist attempts to exploit them for selfish ends). Nor, as we shall now see, was the association between the Chartists and several of the fairly well-organised trades a new feature of the Plug Strikes.

THE NATIONAL CHARTER ASSOCIATION AND THE TRADES

With the trade unions as with the wider working class it was the hopes raised in 1838-9 and 1842 which brought the greatest support for Chartism. Indeed for much of 1840 and 1841 Chartists were largely concerned with the rather introspective process of rebuilding their organisations in the form of the National Charter Association (NCA). There was some trade union involvement but it was small-scale and patchy. There was, however, in 1840 an active 'National Chartist Shoemakers Society' in Manchester, and from 1841 a tailors' and shoemakers' 'locality' of the NCA. At Bury it was the local shoemakers' trade society which led the way in establishing an active NCA locality there, forming the initial political 'classes' in their own homes, including that of the society's President.[56] In addition, in Manchester some trades did join the largest Chartist processions of these years, those to welcome returned prisoners. The dressers and dyers were at the processions in honour of McDouall in 1840 and O'Connor in 1841, the boiler-makers at McDouall's procession alone, the carpenters and ladies' shoemakers at the Christmas 1840 demonstration on the release of Christopher Doyle, Richardson and other Manchester leaders, and the fustian-cutters, calico printers and bricklayers at both that Christmas demonstration and O'Connor's 1841 procession.[57]

This period from 1840 to 1842 however also saw the development of a more sustained Chartist interest in the possibilities of mobilising trade union support. Unfortunately where historians have at least recognised this development, they have tended to portray it as the personal policy of McDouall.[58] This is misleading, for if the *Northern Star* did not make it a major theme, still the address of the 1841 Convention on

political prisoners, the address of the large delegate meeting at York on
O'Connor's release, the National Executive as a whole on at least four
occasions, and the Executive Secretary John Campbell in his regular
letter to the *Star* another four times, all strongly recommended that
trade societies should join the NCA or praised the London trades who
were already joining.[59] This is not to belittle McDouall's contribution
but simply to set it in context. That context also included the way
(often in response to the arguments of the Anti-Corn Law League) an
'alternative political economy' synthesising familiar themes from the
trade union, Factory Movement, and radical traditions was moved to
the very heart of Chartist arguments. It involved a critique of excessive
competition, over-production, unregulated improvements in machinery,
excessive employer power and the effects of a growing labour surplus.
Its postulated solutions emphasised the role of a ten hours bill to restrict
competition and over-production, the colonisation of the land to ease
the labour surplus (and set a basic living standard below which competitive pressures would be unable to depress workers), increased wages to
stimulate home consumption and, of course, the achievement of
working-class political power. The resolutions of the Bolton spinners
during the Plug Strikes might serve as one illustration of the wide
diffusion of such reasoning amongst the Lancashire working class. They
listed the injustices they faced:

> . . . namely, in the reduction of our wages, in unjust and unreasonable
> abatements, in forcing upon us unhealthy and disagreeable houses, in
> charging us unreasonable and exorbitant rents, and in meanly and
> avariciously employing apprentices to supersede the regular journey-
> men, and in various ways curtailing our wages by not paying up to
> the list that the masters almost unanimously agreed to, thus proving
> their unprincipled meanness and trickery. Third – That this meeting
> is of opinion, that a great deal of the distress in the manufacturing
> districts is owing to the improvements of machinery, which have
> superseded manual labour, and created a redundant and burthen-
> some population. And this meeting is further of opinion, that the
> best means to be adopted, would be to establish an efficient Ten
> Hours' Bill, with restrictions on all moving power; to immediately
> colonize the Crown Lands, which would thus employ the redundant
> population, and at the same time improve and augment the home
> trade. Fourth – That it is the opinion of this meeting that the above
> evils arise from class legislation, and we are further of opinion that

misery, ignorance, poverty, and crime, will continue to exist, until the People's Charter becomes the law of the land.[60]

This alternative political economy, regularly articulated by Chartist lecturers in the early 1840s, represented both a more searching critique of the economic position of working men than had ever been revealed amongst the violent language of 1839, and a more specifically working-class ideological position of more immediate relevance to trade societies.

In south Lancashire, if one must single out one individual centrally identified with both increasing Chartist interest in trade unions, and developing a more thorough, more economic analysis of exploitation, it would have to be James Leach. He was a Manchester Chartist, unlike McDouall from a working-class background, who became the first President of the NCA and emerged as the most important Chartist leader in Lancashire in the early 1840s. He began lecturing on the 'in-efficiency' of trade unions in upholding the value of labour in December 1840. He advocated a two-pronged strategy of strengthening unions in the short term, but advocating radical political change as the only long-term solution.[61] This was in fact a familiar radical viewpoint, advocated by other Chartists, which was in reality only an elaboration of the *Poor Man's Guardian's* criticism of those unionists who in 1834 had decried the importance of political action.[62]

The prevalence of radical assumptions amongst the Lancashire working class helped to facilitate the acceptance of such arguments. There was even, for example, a marked tendency for trade unionists to justify the existence of their unions by reference to the political system. First a hatters' address, then the smiths' *Trades Journal*:

The laws of our country are so framed that they allow the capitalist to ride roughshod over us, which forces us to associate together for common protection.

In Great Britain the only object of the law is, to protect the privileges, the person and the property of the capitalist and the aristocrat; hence the poor, the honest man, hath no protection for his labour, ...[63]

Unions were a necessity in a badly deranged, 'artificial' or 'anomalous' society. Again the *Trades Journal*:

In the present anomalous condition of society, the producers of wealth have been forced, in order to protest their limited means of support from the encroachments of tyranny and avarice and the grinding competition carried on so extensively in the commercial world to form themselves into Trade Societies, . . . [64]

The 1838 Coronation address signed by twenty-three trades declared that unions were:

. . . necessary evils brought into existence by the baseness of our political system, and the consequent tyranny of capitalists, whom the laws allow to ride roughshod over prostrate labour, and drives the labourers to associate for common protection since the law affords them none.[65]

The 'tyranny of capitalists' was 'consequent upon' a corrupt political system. Excessive capitalist competition was an aberration whose permanence, and unions' role within it, had not yet been accepted. It resulted from an unrepresentative government which pandered to the interests of capitalists and ignored the interests of unrepresented workers. Hence the workers' ultimate solution to their predicament lay in political power.

Moreover the circumstances of the trade depression accentuated the relevance of such Chartist arguments. For the point about the 'inefficiency', or limitations, of the strike weapon, was especially pertinent when orthodox trade union action was quite blatantly failing to protect the position of skilled workers. At the onset of 1842 workmen were entering the sixth year of apparently intractable economic depression, coming after many years of a violently fluctuating trade cycle, and it was not obvious that the new industrial society could, or would, emerge relatively unscathed. It was a time when the Anti-Corn Law League was surpassing even the Chartists in publicising an allegedly catastrophic collapse in profits and wages. Indeed the League contributed directly to encouraging the trades to adopt a more explicitly political stance. Under the auspices of the Operative Anti-Corn Law Association, Alexander Hutchinson, the secretary of the National Associated Smiths, organised a meeting of delegates to consider organising a demonstration jointly against the Corn Laws and for the Charter. Despite his dislike of trade unions as such, Richard Cobden backed this initiative and recognised 'the importance of our bringing out the trades if possible'. However, this meeting of sixty-four working-class delegates, held in March 1842, back-fired quite spectacularly, when it voted by fifty-nine to five that the Charter alone was worth agitating for. The delegates were not all from trade societies; three were from the League and fourteen were from eight different NCA localities, but there were also seventeen delegates of ten different workshops and, most numerous of all, twenty-two delegates of thirteen different trades. The latter were the smiths, engravers, glass-cutters (of Hulme), silk-dyers, calico printers (of Pendleton), smallware weavers, fustian-cutters, shoemakers, joiners, bricklayers, sawyers, painters and hydraulic packers. Given the size of the majority virtually all of them must have voted for the Chartist resolution.[66]

Yet further evidence of positive support for the Chartists by the Manchester trades was soon forthcoming. The carpenters society formed itself into a trade locality of the NCA in March 1842. Their example was followed by the fustian-cutters and mechanics (where an amendment in favour of the Complete Suffrage Union collected a derisory three votes) in May, Hutchinson's smiths, the boiler-makers, and painters in June, and the hammermen and bricklayers in July. In August a general meeting of the farriers, scheduled to discuss joining the NCA, was interrupted by the Plug Strike. This process once begun was, in part, self-perpetuating, delegates of trades who had joined accompanying Chartists to meetings of other trades. John Campbell, Secretary of the Chartist National Executive, confidently predicted that in six months all the Manchester trades would have joined and, with the example of the London trades, given confidence for the trades generally all over the country to make a political stance. In a sense the Plug Strike, far from initiating an association between the Chartists and the Manchester trades, actually interrupted an already snowballing process of trades societies' alignment with Chartism.[67]

The pattern was for the trades to establish Chartist localities, theoretically separate from the trade society, but in fact comprising substantially the same body of men, meeting in the same place under the same leaders. These localities then participated fully in the NCA structure. The Chartist National Executive's accounts suggest that it was only Manchester, and above all London, where there was a substantial accession of such trade localities. Elsewhere there were just isolated cases, such as the shoemakers' localities at Northampton and Nottingham.[68] However the contraction of trade society membership in the trade depression must have left branch membership, in the smaller towns especially, so low as to make organisation upon such a basis far less attractive than focusing upon the ties of class and community, particularly in a situation, as in 1842, of a renewed surge in Chartist strength. The organisational benefits of basing ongoing political societies on the trades were most apparent in the largest towns, and especially in London. The National Executive accounts, however, do not provide an exhaustive list of Chartist localities, and in 1842 there was an increasing national interest in securing the alignment of Chartism and the trades.[69] Moreover at Manchester a real breakthrough had occurred, and Chartist arguments had received substantial endorsement from the trades. The joiners, echoing the Chartist argument that trade unions were only a 'temporary' defence, were now convinced:

> . . . from past experience, that Trades' Unions do not possess suf-
> ficient strength to secure to the labourer a just and reasonable re-
> muneration for his labour, and protect his rights; they look upon
> them only as a temporary barrier established in consequence of his
> being denied legal and constitutional protection from the law, which
> right is denied him in consequence of the great bulk of the labouring
> population having no voice in the making of the laws by which they
> are governed, . . . [70]

Even the mechanics emphasised that trade unions were no remedy in the 'anomalous state of things', for 'they had been tried and found wanting', and it was complete organic reform, on the basis of the Charter, which was needed.[71] There was indeed a strong, highly plausible, rational argument for the trades' adoption of political action and alignment with the Chartists, which had already convinced several trades before the Plug Strikes created the exceptional circumstances which produced an admittedly exceptionally strong radical political response from the trades.

THE PLUG STRIKES

In south Lancashire the Plug Strikes provide the best examples of Chartists providing leadership during strikes but there is not room for documentation and discussion here.[72] We must however pursue the theme of the Chartist impulses of the organised trades, for it was a conference of the trades in Manchester which gave the strongest, most coherent impetus towards making the strikes an unequivocal political move for the Charter. This conference originated in a meeting of the five engineering trades (which had recently been involved in the United Trades Association, and amongst whom the Chartists had had such success in forming NCA trade localities) on Thursday morning 11 August, two days after the Manchester strike had begun. This meeting passed nine resolutions, none of them making any reference to engineers' trade or wages demands, but one advocating the Charter, and one calling for a delegate meeting of all the trades. A placard up on that same Thursday convened another delegate meeting of trades and mill-hands on the morning of Friday 12 August. Two hundred delegates were reported to have met and passed two unanimous resolutions, again not mentioning wages, but this time specifically calling for a strike to obtain the Charter. More information is available on the trades delegate meeting on that Friday afternoon, called by the engineers. Delegates from the powerloom and smallware weavers linked the Charter with a demand for a wages advance, but with only slightly varying emphasis the delegates of the other cotton trades, dyers, fustian-cutters, card-grinders and strippers, calico printers, spinners and dressers, joined the tailors, men's shoemakers, bricklayers, carpenters and joiners, sawyers, boiler-makers, iron-planers, spindle-makers and others unnamed and from outside Manchester in wanting to go for the Charter. An amendment in favour of returning to work if the wages of 1840 were obtained 'was so feebly supported that it fell to the ground'. The resolutions in favour of striking for the Charter passed by the morning meeting of delegates were adopted, and a general conference of trades delegates from the surrounding manufacturing area called for the following Monday.[73]

This conference assembled on Monday 15 August under the chairmanship of the smiths' secretary Alexander Hutchinson. They began hearing the delegates' reports and a 'great majority' were for the Charter. Out of eighty-five trades which reported, fifty-eight were for the Charter, nineteen willing to be guided by the conference's decision, a mere seven for a move on wages alone. The conference reassembled the next day and the strategy of striking for the Charter was beset by two amendments, one to return to work and one for free trade. Just before the authorities dispersed the conference, a vote was taken, twelve for the first amendment, seventeen for the second, and a massive one hundred and twenty for the Charter. As the *Manchester Guardian* noted, the majority was quite 'overwhelming'.[74] But it was quite consistent with the result of the earlier trades conference organised by the

Anti-Corn Law League, with the Chartist success in forming NCA trade localities and with the prior trade meetings earlier in the strike. Nor indeed was the decision the result of delegates being carried away with the excitement of the conference, for the massive Chartist majority was clear on the first day when little had been done except hear reports of grass-roots decisions. The strategy of striking for the Charter was, of course, a failure. However, an examination of the most important reasons for the failure would take us beyond the scope of this study. For they lay much less in the deficiencies of support amongst the south Lancashire working class, which though important were not critical, than in the weakness and inevitable delay in the response of other areas, the inherent flaws in such a strategy as an essentially peaceful political strike, in continued Chartist leadership confusion about how to use the strike, and above all in the strength of the authorities. Nevertheless, the sustained pressure for a political strike amongst the trades is a matter requiring more explanation from those historians at pains to discount the political aspects of the Plug Strikes.

WORKING-CLASS STRATIFICATION, SECTIONALISM AND POLITICAL ACTION

The conference of trades in the Plug Strikes was not strictly representative of the regional workforce, but given the very short notice at which it was called, the attendance, and especially that of the Manchester trades, was impressive. Moreover, the occupational analysis of the delegates presented in Table 2 provides considerable information about which trades were willing to be involved in inter-trade political action and which were aloof. The very best paid secure artisans were missing, and the conference was dominated by the largest groups of factory workers and lower artisans, together with a large contingent of engineering and metal-working trades. This picture is quite consistent with that emerging from previous instances of trade society endorsement of Chartism, and together this evidence throws important light upon the extent of class-conscious political attitudes amongst diverse types of workmen and upon the impact of stratification within the working class on political action.

The concept of the labour aristocracy as used by Marxist historians is not normally applied by them to the period before the early 1840s. It is, of course, a vital tenet of a theory seeking in part to explain the dissolution of the greater class consciousness of that earlier period that it should not be applicable.[75] It is true that much Marxist use of the concept has been 'ambiguous and unsatisfactory'.[76] Yet the use of the idea by non-Marxist historians, who frequently do use the term when dealing with the earlier period, has also been ill-defined and unsystematic, and, when used as it so often is to cast doubt upon the existence of any very widespread class consciousness, rather indiscriminate. To portray the terms trade unionist and labour aristocrat as 'almost interchangeable' surely obstructs an understanding of the divisions within the ranks of skilled workers and can lead to a misleading portrayal of the aloof printers as being typical.[77] Trade unions are by their very nature sectional, but, as we have seen, not all unions behaved in ways going beyond this which can be meaningfully described as 'aristocratic'. Similarly to speak of 'occupational groups' such as the low-status shoemakers or poverty-stricken silk-weavers as aristocrats, albeit 'lesser or declining aristocrats'[78] surely denudes the term of any real meaning. When working men employed the term in the 1830s and 40s they clearly did not designate all trade unionists or all skilled men as labour aristocrats, but instead envisaged a more restricted group whose aristocratic aloof attitudes were based upon a privileged economic position. Hence a Manchester Chartist address in 1842:

We wish most respectfully to say to the aristocratical portion of the Trades, who have hitherto stood aloof and treated us with indifference, suspicion, or contempt, that in our opinion, judging rationally from passing events that the same circumstances are at work still which have brought down the wages of, and impoverished other trades, and will continue, if not checked, and operate upon theirs also.[79]

Used in this sense to refer to a minority of skilled trades, which were demonstrably aloof from much inter-trade and political action, the term has considerable descriptive value in the early Chartist period.

Delegates from the most secure artisan trades, those where standard wages of thirty shillings a week or more were not uncommon, were conspicuously missing from the Plug Strike trades conference. There were no delegates from the printers or coach-makers, and the solitary bookbinder was the only delegate publicly disowned by his trade society.[80] These trades, although certainly having strong unions, have been consistently absent from every single instance of trade union backing for Chartism which we have considered. They were also only fitfully in-

Table 2

Occupational Analysis of the 1842 Plug Strike Conference

Textile factories	Textile outworkers	Engineers and metal-workers	Artisan trades	Others
Manchester				
Spinners and stretchers (3)	Silk-weavers (3)	Smiths (1)	Joiners (2)	Labourers (2)
Pierces (1)	Fustian-cutters (2)	Smiths (United Order) (3)	Plumbers and glaziers (1)	Hydraulic packers (2)
Twiners (2)		Wheelwrights and blacksmiths	Stonemasons (2)	
Card grinders and strippers (2)		Mechanics	Bricklayers (2)	
Coarse carders (1)		Steam-engine makers	Plasterers (2)	
Powerloom weavers (2)		Iron moulders	Painters (2)	
Powerloom overlookers (2)		Engravers to calico printers	Sawyers (4)	
Fustian power weavers (2)		Spindle and fly makers	Bootmakers (2)	
Smallware weavers (3)		Spindle-makers	Ladies' Shoemakers (3)	
Silk smallware weavers (2)		Wire drawers and card-makers	Tailors (2)	
Yarn dressers (2)		Boiler-makers	Glass-makers (2)	
Warpers (2)		Metal planers	Bookbinders (1)	
Sizers (1)		Strikers	Skinners (2)	
Dressers and dyers (3)			Rope-makers (2)	
Calico printers (2)				
Total 15	2	13	14	2

Table 2 (continued)

Others

Textile factories	Textile outworkers	Engineers and metal-workers	Artisan trades	Others
Eccles silk-dyers (1)	Eccles handloom weavers (1)	Patricroft mechanics	Eccles plasterers (2)	Eccles miners (1)
Oldham carders (1)	Astley silk-weavers (1)	Oldham mechanics (2)	Leigh shoemakers (1)	Oldham miners (1)
Oldham twiners (1)	Leigh silk-weavers (2)	Oldham roller-makers (1)	Oldham sawyers (1)	Clayton miners (2)
Oldham weavers (2)	Failsworth silk-weavers (1)	Oldham hammermen (2)	Oldham shoemakers (2)	Hopwood miners (2)
Oldham warpers (1)	Middleton silk-weavers (1)	Heywood machine makers (1)	Oldham hatters (1)	(Miners total 4)
Oldham dressers (1)	Heywood fustian-cutters (1)		Ashton hatters (2)	
Royton power weavers (1)			Ashton shoemakers (1)	Crompton people (1)
Lees millhands (1)				Ashton meeting (2)
Hyde factories (2)				Stalybridge meeting (1)
Bolton spinners (1)				Mossley meeting (1)
Heywood spinners (1)				Bury trades (2)
Heywood power weavers (1)				Radcliffe trades (1)
Middleton silk-dyers (1)				Brooksbottom operatives (1)
Middleton calico printers (1)				
Total 14	6	5	7	11
Grand total 29	8	18	21	13

Source: the lists of delegates in MG 17 August; MSA; MT; MC 20 August 1842. The number of delegates is given in brackets.

volved in other exercises of inter-trade co-operation. They exhibited an accentuated aloof sectionalism founded upon relative economic security and can be meaningfully described as aristocratic. But the crucial point is that the implications of such aristocratic attitudes for the extent of class consciousness were severely restricted by the limited numbers of these trades and their isolation, and consequently lack of influence upon the mainstream labour movement.

The engineering and metal-worker sector included the largest groups of workmen with standard wages for many at or above the thirty shillings mark. In mid-Victorian Britain they have been seen as the archetypal labour aristocrats, whose unions were the prime examples of cautious 'new model' unions. In the earlier period they have been represented as being almost entirely aloof from Chartism. Yet as we have seen at least in Lancashire in the early Chartist period this was not so. They were of course not a completely homogeneous group, and some earned lower wages. The smiths, the single largest trade (but one where earnings frequently fell below thirty shillings) have appeared with as consistent a record of support for Chartism as any trade. Similarly the Manchester boiler-makers who marched in the 1840 Chartist procession and formed a trade locality in 1842, had not yet achieved the higher wages, status, and union strength they were later to achieve, when the society the Manchester men began became the dominant and exclusive craft union of the iron shipyards. In 1843 it was said that 'the boiler-makers are looked upon by the mechanics and machine makers as a lower class of men, and have the reputation of being drunken and slovenly in their habits'.[81] Yet on the other hand if the millwrights, the well-paid rather élitist all-round craftsmen, have not appeared especially prominently advocating the Charter, and did not attend the Plug Strikes trades conference, the much more numerous engineers, that is the more specialised but still skilled workmen replacing and already far outnumbering the millwrights, have appeared more strongly and did attend the conference. Indeed it was the five engineering trades of the United Trades Association which initiated the inter-trade co-operation which led to that conference. To a considerable extent the engineering trades were in an 'aristocratic' position with corresponding attitudes before the mid-1840s. This was recognised by contemporary working-class opinion. The *Northern Star's* report after the 'mechanics' formed an NCA trade locality commented that 'This once aristocratical trade has come out boldly for the principles of democracy'.[82] But there were important ambiguities and uncertainties in their position, especially the sheer newness of many of the crafts, and before the mid-1840s the new-ness, fragmentation, localisation and traditional character of their unions. With their horizons circumscribed by customary notions of status and wages they were possibly slow to appreciate the full strength of their bargaining position. That would explain their considerable involvement in the National Association for the Protection of Labour, a general union designed only to prevent *reductions*.[83] Possibly also in the cotton district engineers' radicalism grew out of the deep radicalism of the local communities and the close links between engineering and the strongly radical cotton factories. The crisis produced by the technologi-cal threat posed by the diffusion of new machine tools belonged to the trade depression after 1847, and of course culminated in the 1852 lock-out.[84] But the engineers were still not impervious to the pervasive trade depression in the early 1840s which almost certainly acted as a spur to political action. For example in Bolton where the 'iron trade, consisting of engineers, millwrights, smiths etc.' declared for the Charter in the Plug Strikes, there had been consistent reports of unemployment and wage reductions. In consequence 'the mechanics who a while ago were looked upon as something more than common working men, were now in great distress and paupers of the parish'. If the engineers' radicalism was probably not as deep or consistent as the lesser artisans or factory workers, still in Lancashire before the mid-1840s large sections of them were not unambiguously aristocratic and had not been consistently aloof from inter-trade and mass political action.[85]

The largest group of trades at the 1842 Conference were the cotton factory workers. These included the spinners, those key local workers who had been so important in the first phase of Chartism. The labelling of the spinners as the 'aristocracy of local labour' with their position being compared with the handloom weavers and other workers being largely ignored has been highly misleading.[86] For the insecurity of their position at this time has been inadequately appreciated. The generalised estimates of spinners' wages, giving a range from under twenty shillings to over forty shillings a week can be very misleading, for it was only those spinning the finest yarn in the fine mills who could ever hope to earn wages at the higher levels, and the great majority of the spinners were concentrated at the lower end of the scale. In addition, in the 1830s technological change posed a formidable threat to the spinners' status. Firstly the new long mules and the coupling together, or double-decking, of pairs of mules vastly increased the number of spindles worked by a single spinner. This resulted in substantial unemployment and increased workload for those who retained their jobs. Secondly there were the self-acting mules which spread rapidly in coarse spinning after Roberts's 1830 patent. By making the final stages of the mules' operational cycle automatic, or self-acting, the self-actors removed most of the need for skill and strength. They thus substantially undermined the technical basis for the spinners' skilled status. The wages of fine and coarse spinners fell substantially. In 1841 the local factory inspector estimated self-actor minder wages to be on average between 12s. 6d. and 15s. a week.[87] In other words, the differential over essentially semi-skilled grades, the best powerloom weavers and card grinders and strippers, was totally eroded.

The problems of technological change, unemployment, loss of status and falling wages, combined with strike defeats to ensure that the spinners did not at this time enjoy the level of economic security likely to engender self-satisfied aristocratic attitudes. Nor did they behave as aloof aristocrats. Their strikes were frequent and violent. They were constantly presented as a problem group in the press and local auth- orities' reports. Their unions were not habitually aloof, but on the contrary at the very heart of the most impressive exercises in general unionism in 1818 and 1829-32, and involved in the more informal exercises in inter-trade co-operation. They were too weak to enforce shorter hours by union action and consequently sought this objective in co-operation with other factory trades in the Factory Movement. Moreover radical political action by unionised spinners was by no means unprecedented. The Manchester spinners' leadership Doherty, Foster, Hodgins, Lawton and M'Williams had taken the lead in chan- nelling working-class discontent into radical political activity in 1826-7, and were all present in 1830 when Henry Hunt returned to Manchester. Even the strike addresses of the 1829 Manchester strike contained refer- ences to quite diverse radical issues.[88] The Ashton spinners' secretary, J. J. Betts, was a firm radical who took to wearing a tricoloured sash at strike meetings. At Oldham the veteran radical John Knight was closely involved with the spinners' union and they marched as a body in his funeral procession.[89] Neither in their economic position, nor their radical and trade union traditions were there the conditions out of which, in this period at least, politically acquiescent labour aristocrats were made. Also amongst the adult male factory workers in the finishing sector, the calico printers faced severe unemployment, wage reductions and loss of status with the proliferation of machine printing. The dressers and dyers, with one of the most consistent records of support for Chartism, achieved wages of around twenty shillings in the 1830s. But they were acutely aware that this position was maintained only by union action: wages had previously been much lower and collapsed later when the union broke up.[90]

Indeed there were marked similarities between the situation of such factory workers and the lower artisan trades. They were also striving to maintain their status in the face if not usually of technological change, still division of labour, the competitive pressures of the mass market, the growing surplus of labour and the encroachment of the dishonourable sweated sector. There was considerable class conflict over vital issues *within* their trades in the 1830s. For example in Manchester in 1834 fifty-one master-tailors had combined to smash the tailors' union, which had been attempting to abolish sweating by restricting work outside union-regulated workshops. The shoemakers, who combined a particularly literate craft culture with an economically vulnerable position towards the bottom of the customary hierarchy of artisan trades, fought several strikes in south Lancashire in the 1830s.[91] In 1833 the Operative Builders Union lost its great Lancashire strike against capitalist innovation and the system of general contracting. In the winters of both 1837 and 1838 the Manchester masons faced aggressive combinations of a majority of their masters.[92] At the Plug Strike conference seventeen out of twenty-one artisan trades were from the building and clothing sectors.[93] It was precisely these trades, which not only were the most numerous amongst the traditional artisan trades, but also have consistently appeared supporting Chartism alongside the insecure factory workers, who earned similar wages and faced not dissimilar threats to their status.

Of course an élite portion of such trades, fundamentally those in trade societies, could form an aloof aristocracy within a trade. Mayhew graphically described a situation in London at mid-century, when he estimated such society men constituted on average one-tenth of the trade.[94] But it is vital to see such a division not as a static phenomenon but a product of a dynamic contested process in the earlier period when the situation was more fluid. The 1833 builders' and 1834 tailors' strikes in Manchester over the structure of their trades had involved a clear majority of the workmen. In 1842 the Manchester branch of the General Union of Carpenters and Joiners which formed an NCA locality in 1842, also established a committee of members *and non-members* in response to the desperate position to which they had been reduced by the slump.[95] Similarly the overall occupational consciousness of the spinners ensured that hand spinners and self-actor minders were contained within the same union, and the minders not expelled as they were later in the century. The trade societies of the lower artisans and factory workers were in any case not, in this period, to be found in élitist collaboration with the privileged upper trades, but rather in the mainstream of inter-trade and, as we have seen, Chartist action.

Finally joining these trades at the 1842 conference were a number of the more obviously depressed textile outworkers, not so much the cotton handloom weavers whose numbers in south Lancashire were much depleted,[96] but rather the silk-weavers and fustian-cutters. There were also some miners, who did in fact have much in common with the more insecure artisans, and whose later union, the Miners Association, had very close links with Lancashire Chartism.[97] The trades conference thus consisted of representatives of all the most numerous adult male trades in the area and predominantly it consisted of exactly those insecure trades in the factories and amongst the artisans, together with an admixture of the more radically inclined of the better-paid engineers, which have been consistently showing up in our study backing the Chartists. From this perspective, the fact that a conference composed of these trades should utilise the unprecedented opportunity of a general strike to declare for the Charter seems not at all surprising, but in fact almost predictable.

CONCLUSION

The links between trade unions and Chartism were a matter of real importance in south-east Lancashire throughout the early Chartist period. Moreover a proper understanding of the Plug Strike, so often studied with only cursory attention to prior developments, is wholly dependent upon seeing it in that perspective. As stated at the outset, trade union support was neither unanimous nor continuous. It needed the effervescence of Chartist enthusiasm in 1838–9 and 1842 in order to bring truly substantial trade society involvement. Yet to judge the connections in the light, for example, of those between the Labour Party and the unions, would be to erect an unhistorical standard, inappropriate to the particular stage of development of both the working-class political and trade union movements of the 1830s and early 1840s, and to the hostile environment in which both operated. The connections were there, in shared ideas, personnel, leaders, newspapers and not infrequently expressions of support for Chartism by unions acting as unions. This sup-

port was not unanimous for some of the best-paid trades were consistently aloof. But such truly aristocratic trades were numerically small,
and so many of the largest trades have been shown supporting the
Chartists. This detailed evidence about the participation of diverse
trades is important. For in this period with the complex mix of factory,
small workshop and domestic employment, it is clear that in its economic situation the working class was not a homogeneous 'proletariat'.
Yet it would be wrong *therefore* to discount the existence of any extensive working-class consciousness. There were important *political* forces
moulding class solidarity such as the experience of independent working-
class political action, the definition provided by the 1832 Reform Act,
and the resentment provoked by the 'class legislation' of the reformed
Parliament. Furthermore in the similar nature of their problems, the
similarities in their economic analysis, and the coincidence of a radical-
ising crisis period of structural economic change in several key trades,
(which had previously had a not dissimilar status) there was also an
economic basis for a sense of class consciousness. The evidence provided
in this study has shown that trades, in the new factories and amongst
the traditional artisan trades, and even to some extent amongst the
new engineering trades, *were* able to come together in combined political action, in an intensely class-conscious Chartist Movement. This
evidence provides a powerful indication that the strength of early
Chartism lay much less in the fury of those obvious casualties of the
Industrial Revolution, the handloom weavers, whose relative importance
has been grossly exaggerated in the past, than in its successful ability
to establish a much broader base of support amongst skilled but insecure artisans and factory workers.

NOTES

1. S. and B. Webb, *The History of Trade Unionism*, 2nd edn (London, 1920)
pp. 174–7; M. Hovell, *The Chartist Movement*, 3rd edn (Manchester, 1966) p. 169.
2. I. J. Prothero, 'London Chartism and the Trades', *Economic History
Review*, 2nd ser., XXIV, 2 (May 1971); A. Wilson, 'Chartism', in J. T. Ward (ed.),
Popular Movements c. 1830–1850 (pb. edn London, 1970) pp. 126–7.
3. See A. E. Musson, *British Trade Unions, 1800–1875* (London, 1972)
pp. 45–8 for a convenient summary.
4. F. K. Donnelly, 'Ideology and early English working-class history: Edward
Thompson and his critics', *Social History*, II (May 1976); R. J. Morris, *Class and
class consciousness in the Industrial Revolution 1780–1850* (London, 1979) pp.
44–5.
5. For example Musson, *British Trade Unions*, pp. 19–20, 45–8; and 'Class

struggle and the labour aristocracy 1830–1860', *Social History*, III (October 1976) 336–7; M. I. Thomis, *The Town Labourer and the Industrial Revolution* (London, 1974) esp. chs 7 and 10.

6. For a particularly stark statement of this view, which is implicit in much writing on Chartism, see W. H. Chaloner, the Bibliographical Introduction to Hovell, *The Chartist Movement*, p. iv.

7. D. Read, 'Chartism in Manchester', in A. Briggs (ed.), *Chartist Studies* (London, 1959) pp. 30–2, 48.

8. H. Pelling, *A History of British Trade Unionism*, 2nd edn (Harmondsworth: Penguin pb. edn, 1971) p. 43; G. Rudé, *The Crowd in History 1730–1848* (London, 1964) p. 187; Musson, *British Trade Unions*, pp. 47–8.

9. Quoted in D. Jones, *Chartism and the Chartists* (London, 1975) p. 138.

10. When the Newcastle stonemasons proposed the abolition of the rule against political discussion 'as it is evident we shall have to defend ourselves from the base attacks of intriguing politicians', the central committee replied that the rule would appear as a 'credit' to them in a parliamentary investigation, *Operative Stonemasons Fortnightly Return*, 16 February 1838. It was later noted of the carpenters, tailors and shoemakers that: 'When society business is concluded, and the meeting has been formally closed, it is not unusual for the members to remain sitting, with the same chairman, to discuss social and political questions.' E. S. Beesley, *The Amalgamated Society of Carpenters and Joiners* (London, 1867) p. 8.

11. R. Soffer, 'Attitudes and Allegiances in the Unskilled North', *International Review of Social History*, III (1965); Read, 'Chartism in Manchester', p. 48. Of course skill and skilled status are themselves complex notions, involving not just technical factors such as manual dexterity, but social factors concerned with such as custom and the workmen's control over the work process. In addition there were more similarities in the attitudes and aspirations of the *adult male* factory workers and the traditional artisans than has often been realised.

12. Prothero, 'London Chartism and the Trades', pp. 209–12.

13. R. G. Kirby and A. E. Musson, *The Voice of the People* (Manchester, 1975) pp. 24–7 and chs VI, VII; R. Postgate, *The Builder's History* (London, 1923) esp. chs 3–4; *The Trades Journal, passim* but esp. 1 March 1841.

14. AN APPEAL ON BEHALF OF THE TURN-OUT FUSTIAN-CUTTERS 21 December 1836 (Manchester Public Library).

15. *Manchester and Salford Advertiser* 12 April, 10 May 1834. *Manchester and Salford Advertiser* hereafter *MSA; Manchester Guardian, MG; Manchester Times, MT; Manchester Courier, MC* and *Northern Star, NS.*

16. Butterworth diary (Oldham Public Library) 19 April, 27 June 1834. For this strike see J. Foster, *Class Struggle and the Industrial Revolution* (London, 1974) pp. 109–14, 149–60; Kirby and Musson, *Voice of the People*, pp. 291–4. For a local Chartist study acknowledging the importance of the trade union affairs of 1834 see A. J. Peacock, *Bradford Chartism 1838–40*, Borthwick Papers no. 36 (1969) esp. pp. 7–9, and for a local labour agitator, whose own account of his career proceeds directly from involvement in union affairs in 1834 to Chartism see 'The Reminiscences of Thomas Dunning (1813–1894) and the Nantwich Shoemakers Case of 1834', W. H. Chaloner (ed.), *Transactions of the Lancashire and Cheshire Antiquarian Society* (1947) p. 111 and *passim.*

17. For the Glasgow strike itself see W. Hamish Fraser, 'The Glasgow Cotton Spinners 1837', in J. Butt and J. T. Ward (eds), *Scottish Themes* (Edinburgh, 1976). For the meetings see *MSA* 30 September, 7, 21 October, 4, 11 November, 23 December 1837; *MSA* 27 January, 10 February, 10, 17 March 1838; *Wheeler's Manchester Chronicle* 27 January 1838; *NS* 10, 17 February, 17 March 1838. For Richardson, a carpenter by trade, and an active Manchester radical throughout the 1830s, see the 'political portrait' in *Operative* 3 March 1839.

18. *Operative Stone Masons Fortnightly Return* 15 August 1839.

19. *MSA* 27 January 1838.

20. *NS* 24 March 1838.

21. *MSA* 14 October 1837; 27 January 1838; *NS* 6 January 1838; A. R. Schoyen, *The Chartist Challenge* (London, 1958) pp. 23–5.

22. *Champion* 19 March 1837; *MSA* 15 April 1837: For Dean see *Operative Stone Masons Fortnightly Return* 31 August 1838. For the meeting and address calling for a universal suffrage agitation, see *MSA* 15, 19 April 1837; *Champion* 7 May 1837. The *Manchester Guardian* called their meetings the work of the Spear Street Political and Trade Unionists, Spear Street being the meeting place of the Universal Suffrage Association, *MG* 24 January 1838.

23. *Champion* 19 March 1837; *MG* 12 April 1837; *MSA, MT* 15 April 1837; *MSA* 20 January 1838; Account of the money received for the Glasgow cotton spinners 8 September 1837 to 9 March 1838 (Manchester 1838) (Modern Records Centre, Warwick University).

24. The masons' national union abolished all 'regalia, initiation and passwords' because they thought 'the very existence' of their society was threatened. *Operative Stone Masons Fortnightly Return* 2 February; 2, 16 March 1838. For the attacks on O'Connell see *MSA* 20 January, 17 February 1838. For the committee see *MSA* 10, 17 March, 21 April 1838. Place Collection (BM) set 52 f. 413 Doherty to Place, 5 April 1838 for the initial lukewarm attitude of the spinners, fos. 430, 439 and 441 for the London committee's accounts including Lancashire references, *SC. on Combinations* (Parliamentary Papers (PP) 1837–8 VIII) pp. 251–82 for the three Manchester men.

25. *MSA* 30 June 1838.

26. *MG, MSA* 3, 10 September 1831; 11 August 1832. Further information on which were genuine unions can be found in the letters applying to be in the processions, see Boroughreeve's Letter Book (Manchester Public Library), vol. 2 ff 66–85; 129–46. *MG, MSA* 23, 30 June 1838.

27. *MG* 26 September, *MSA* 29 September, *NS* 29 September, 13 October 1838. For the Trades Council placard calling for attendance see HO 40/38 Wemyss to Phillipps 31 August 1838. The press recognised the significance: 'we cannot blind ourselves to the conviction that to the perfect organisation of the Trades' Unions in this district the meeting owed all the importance which it derived from its magnitude', *Wheeler's Manchester Chronicle* 29 September 1838; 'it was emphatically a meeting of the Trades', *MSA* 29 September 1838. For the general state of trade unionism in the two metalworking trades mentioned see A. Tuckett, *The Blacksmith's History* (London, 1974) ch. 2; J. B. Jefferys, *The Story of the Engineers 1800–1945* (London, 1945) ch. 1. For the spinners' union circular asking for mills to be closed to allow their attendance, see *MG* 22 September 1838. The only obviously dubious group is the 'labourers' but in Manchester there

was a union of bricklayers labourers which had existed for many years, *R. C. on Trade Unions* (PP 1867, XXXII) 3rd Report p. 80, Q6119. For previous joint participation of bricklayers and labourers in union anniversaries e.g. *MSA* 12 July 1834; 18 July 1835. For the printers' absence see *MC* 30 June 1838.

28. *NS* 10, 17 November 1838; D. J. Rowe, 'Some aspects of Chartism on Tyneside', *International Review of Social History*, 16 (1971) 24. According to Gammage 'every trade' including 'the most aristocratic of these bodies', and he mentioned the coach-makers in this respect, attended at Newcastle; R. G. Gammage, *History of the Chartist Movement* (facsimile of 1894 edn, London, 1976) p. 28; seventy trades societies attended the first great Glasgow meeting, itself largely organised by trade delegates: A. Wilson, *The Chartist Movement in Scotland* (Manchester 1970) pp. 47–50.

29. *NS* 24 March 1838; see also Bronterre O'Brien's lavish praise of this meeting; *NS* 31 March 1838 and the address of the 'Trades Union of Bury' *NS* 26 May 1838.

30. It involved the spinners, weavers, dressers, mechanics, moulders, tailors, masons, joiners, shoemakers, hatters and curriers, *MG* 29 March 1837.

31. *Bolton Chronicle*; *MSA, NS* 30 June 1838. For Bury see *MSA* 21 July 1838. At Ashton only the tailors attended, *MSA* 30 June 1838.

32. Wilson, *Chartist Movement in Scotland*, pp. 35, 80–1; Prothero, 'London Chartism and the Trades', p. 203; cf. D. J. Rowe, 'The Failure of London Chartism', *Historical Journal*, XI (1968).

33. The list does not include subscriptions from named factories or workshops which may or may not have been from workers in formal unions. For the spinners see HO 40/53 James Wroe to Richardson 26 February 1839 (an intercepted letter) for an earlier £10 subscription by the spinners on 23 February which may have been subsumed in the accounts (vaguely giving thanks only to 'the trades') in *MSA* 2 March 1839.

34. Read, 'Chartism in Manchester', pp. 45–8. The subscriptions were positive demonstrations of allegiance, and their relatively modest scale should not obscure that fact. Radical organisations had always operated on miniscule budgets and Chartism in 1839 was not in especial need of large, regular subscriptions. The National Convention actually left a large unspent surplus. K. Judge, 'Early Chartist Organisation and the Convention of 1839', *International Review of Social History*, XX (1975) p. 381.

35. *MSA* 15 June, *NS* 20 July, 19 October 1839; HO 40/37 Walker and Hargreaves to Russell, 13 August 1839.

36. *Operative* 17 March, 28 April, 26 May 1839.

37. *MSA* 25 May 1839. The only reference to a body attending as a trade is to the 'Political Society of Fustian Cutters'.

38. I. J. Prothero, 'William Benbow and the Concept of the General Strike', *Past & Present*, 63 (1974). Benbow was actively propagating his political conception of the strike in Lancashire in 1839.

39. *MSA, MG* 10 August 1839. Richardson wrote to the convention against the strike policy, National Convention Letterbooks (BM Add. MSS 34245 B fo. 53–4). An attempt to consult eight unions at Preston, found only 'two or three' in favour of the strike, ibid., fo. 119, R. Walton and G. Halton to Smart, 7 August 1839.

40. HO 40/44 Darbishire to Russell 4 August 1839, enclosing placard dated 29 July 1839; *MG* 10 August 1839.

41. *Operative* 26 May 1839; HO 40/43 Wemyss to Phillipps 23 July 1839.

42. National Convention letter books Add. MSS 34245 B fos. 187–9, Watson to Fletcher 3 September 1839; Rowe, 'Chartism on Tyneside', p. 24. T. R. Tholfsen, 'The Chartist Crisis in Birmingham', *International Review of Social History*, III, 3 (1958) p. 473; J. L. Baxter, 'Early Chartism and Labour Class struggle: South Yorkshire 1837–1840' in S. Pollard and C. Holmes (eds), *Essays in the Economic and Social History of South Yorkshire* (Sheffield, 1976) p. 143.

43. *Wheelers Manchester Chronicle* 19 January 1833.

44. A Huntite opponent of the Reform Bill, he was jailed in 1832 for organising seditious meetings, *MG* 4 February, 17 March 1832. A major figure at radical meetings throughout the eighteen-thirties he was a member of the Manchester Political Union Council in 1839, *Regenerator* 2 November 1839. For his trade activities e.g. *Trades Newspaper* 22, 29 April 1827; *MC* 23 May 1829; *Voice of the People* 24 September 1831; *MG* 28 June 1834; *MG* 4 April 1835; *MSA* 7 April 1838.

45. For trade meetings see *MT* 29 April 1837; *MSA* 26 May 1838; for Chartist meetings see *MSA* 19 January, *MG* 27 July, *MSA* 23 November 1839. All as Chairman.

46. *Bolton Free Press* 2 March 1839.

47. Butterworth diary 30 December 1836; *MSA* 21 January 1837.

48. *MT* 20 January 1838. For Doyle see the interview with him in HO 20/10; for Allinson's later career see C. A. N. Reid, 'The Chartist Movement in Stockport' (Univ. of Hull M.A. thesis, 1974) p. 419; *MSA* 25 November 1837, 27 January 1838.

49. For example the Stockport leaders, Mitchell, Davies, Leah and Essler, Bradley of Hyde, Fenton of Ashton and Revd W. V. Jackson of Manchester; *NS* 22 June, 6, 20 July 1839.

50. Reid, *Chartist Movement in Stockport,* pp. 79–87. 'The Chartist activist Richard Pilling, soon to move to Ashton and gain notoriety as the 'father' of the Plug Strikes, was the major spokesman at public meetings, e.g. *NS* 2 May 1840.

51. For the motivational force of the French Revolution e.g. HO 40/26/1 Bouverie to Phillipps 26 August 1830, Shaw to Peel 4 September 1830, for the political feeling, trivolours, arming and firing of pistols, e.g. ibid., Foster to Melbourne 6 and 12 December 1830; *MG* 6 November, 11, 18 December 1830.

52. *NS* 11, 18 September 1841. Also see the interviews with both in HO 20/10 and Reid, *Chartist Movement in Stockport,* pp. 441–2, 465–8.

53. *MSA* 27 June, *NS* 4 July, 5 September, 10 October, 14 November 1840. Other Chartist lecturers involved were John Campbell, James Leach, Charles Connor, William Tillman and William Thomasson. For Daniel Donovan see *NS* 24 April 1841; 2 April 1842; and for Maurice Donovan *MG* 13, 24 August 1842; *NS* 14 January 1843.

54. Christopher Doyle and Daniel Donovan were prominent, *MSA* 13 August 1842. For descriptions of the Brown Street Chartist room as the weavers' 'headquarters' see *MC* 10 September 1842, *MT* 17 September 1842.

55. *MSA* 15 January, 2 March 1842. All three were arrested both in 1839 and 1842.

56. *NS* 18 July, 19 September 1840, 2 January, 6, 27 February 1841.

57. *NS* 22 August 1840; *MSA, MT* 26 December 1840; *NS* 2 January 1841; *MSA, NS* 2 October 1841. At Glasgow eighteen trades turned out for McDouall, Wilson, *Chartist Movement in Scotland*, p. 119.

58. E.g. Rudé, *Crowd in History*, p. 187; A. Jenkin, 'Chartism and the trade unions' in L. M. Munby (ed.), *The Luddites and Other Essays* (London, 1971) p. 78.

59. *NS* 5 June, 4 September 1841. For the Executive see ibid., 24 July, 7 August, 27 November 1841, 19 February 1842; and for Campbell ibid., 18 December 1841; 9 April, 11 June, 9 July 1842. However McDouall also certainly advocated closer ties with the unions e.g. see his articles in *McDouall's Chartist And Republican Journal*, 17 April 1841; and *English Chartist Circular*, vol. 1, no. 50, pp. 198–9.

60. *Bolton Free Press* 20 August 1842.

61. Esp. see J. Leach, *Stubborn Facts from the Factories by a Manchester Operative* (London, 1844); *NS* 19 December 1840 for the initial lecture, and for its quick repetition in the larger forum of Carpenters Hall and the interest it stirred ibid., 6 February 1841; HO 45/43 Wemyss to Phillipps 31 January and 2 February 1841. He did not obstruct McDouall nor offer 'Chartism as an alternative to unionism'. Cf. J. T. Ward, *Chartism* (pb. edn London, 1973) p. 176.

62. Cf. the Yorkshire lecturer Jonathon Bairstow, speaking in Manchester *NS* 2 January 1841; Macclesfield Chartist John West addressing a meeting of striking ribbon weavers in the Congleton NCA room, *NS* 23 October 1841, and the London shoemakers, *NS* 11 September 1841; *Poor Man's Guardian*, April to June 1834, *passim*.

63. *MSA* 17 April 1841; *Trades Journal* 1 September 1840.

64. Ibid., 4 July 1840.

65. *MSA* 30 June 1838; cf. the comments of two Bury trade unionists, a mill-wright, 'If there had been fair legislation to protect the interests of labour, there would have been no need for unions, for trades or secret societies'; and a stone-mason: 'There were unions of Tories and unions of Whigs, but there was not so much union among Radicals, or Trade Unions would not be much needed (Hear, hear)', *NS* 24 March 1838.

66. *MT* 8 January 1842; Cobden to Watkin 22 January 1842 quoted in E. W. Watkin, *Alderman Cobden of Manchester* (London, 1891) p. 88; *NS* 19 March 1842. The workshops identified were four engineering works, one spinning and one weaving mill, one dye works, one tailors shop and the overlookers of one mill. In addition at a preparatory meeting the smiths had reported a decision for the Charter alone and it was said that all the delegates which included, as well as those listed above, the mechanics and powerloom weavers had reported likewise, *MSA, NS* (3rd edn) 5 March 1842.

67. *NS* 2 April; 28 May, 4, 18 June, 2, 9, 16 July, 6 August 1842 and for Campbell see ibid., 11 June 1842. Certainly not all the trades with strong Chartist sympathies had joined. Campbell said plans were in hand to wait upon the calico printers, dyers and spinners.

68. Ibid., 9 July 1842. The other quarterly accounts for 1842 were published in ibid., 9 April, 12 November 1842; 7 January 1843.

69. For example the proposals for joint Chartist–trades conferences at

Birmingham and in north Lancashire *NS* 26 March; 25 June, 2 July 1842. It was also reported that the Colne shoemakers and Preston cotton-spinners had joined the Chartists as bodies. Ibid., 26 February, 30 April 1842.

70. Ibid., 2 April 1842.

71. Ibid., 9 July 1842.

72. Two existing studies do not exhaust the material or the issues needing discussion. A. G. Rose, 'The Plug Plots of 1842 in Lancashire and Cheshire', *Lancashire and Cheshire Antiquarian Society Transactions,* LXVII, 1957; and F. C. Mather, 'The General Strike of 1842', in J. Stevenson and R. Quinault (eds), *Popular Protest and Public Order* (London, 1974) ch. 3.

73. *MG, NS* 13 August 1842.

74. *MG* 17 August 1842; *NS* 20 August 1842; *MSA* 20 August 1842 had eighteen against. There was little sign of Chartist packing. Indeed those without proper credentials were consigned to the gallery as observers *MG* 17 August 1842. It was only after a discussion that delegates from public meetings were allowed in *NS* 20 August 1842.

75. This is particularly true of the use of the concept in Foster, *Class Struggle*, esp. ch. 7. For more subtle uses of the concept stressing the ambiguity of the labour aristocracy's position see R. Q. Gray, *The Labour Aristocracy in Victorian Edinburgh* (Oxford, 1976) and G. Crossick, *An Artisan Elite in Victorian Society* (London, 1978).

76. G. Stedman Jones, 'Class Struggle and the Industrial Revolution', *New Left Review*, XC (March–April 1975) p. 61, and see the criticisms in H. F. Moorhouse, 'The Marxist theory of the labour aristocracy', *Social History*, III (1978).

77. H. Perkin, *The Origins of Modern English Society 1780–1880,* (pb. edn London, 1972), p. 394; Thomis, *Town Labourer*, p. 133. Professor Musson frequently uses the concept of the labour aristocracy in the earlier period to cast doubt upon the existence of an extensive class consciousness e.g. Musson, *Class Struggle*, pp. 336, 351 and *passim*.

78. Mather, 'General Strike of 1842', p. 140, n. 79. Mather's analysis of the conference in this footnote is based upon the number of delegates, which thus gives undue prominence to those bodies which sent more than one delegate as compared with groups (which included such large, important bodies as the Bolton spinners) which sent only one.

79. *NS* 18 June 1842.

80. The most complete wage statistics are to be found in David Chadwick, 'On the rate of wages in Manchester and Salford and the Manufacturing Districts of Lancashire, 1839–59', *Journal of the Statistical Society*, March 1860; and Proceedings of the Manchester Chamber of Commerce, 27 April 1833 reprinted in A. Redford, *Manchester Merchants and Foreign Trade*, vol. 1 (Manchester, 1934) pp. 237–9. For the bookbinders see *MG* 20 August 1842. (The delegate, Benjamin Stott, was however a genuine member of the society, very active in the efforts to raise money for the 1839 London Bookbinders' strike). For clear documentation of the printers' aristocratic attitudes, see A. E. Musson, *The Typographical Association* (Oxford, 1954) esp. ch. V.

81. J. E. Mortimer, *History of the Boilermakers Society* (London, 1973) *Children's Employment Commission* (PP 1843, XIV), B42. According to Chadwick

boiler-makers earned only 22*s*. in 1839 (with wages rising to 30*s*. in 1849), Chadwick 'On the rate of wages', pp. 17, 25.

82. *NS* 4 June 1842. The engineers were usually termed mechanics in Lancashire, and the most important early engineers' union, the Journeymen Steam Engine and Machine Makers Friendly Society, was called the Old Mechanics. In the United Trades Association it was stated that by the term 'mechanic' was meant members of that union, *Trades Journal* 1 February 1841.

83. E. J. Hobsbawm, 'Custom, Wages and Workload in Nineteenth-century Industry' in Hobsbawm, *Labouring Men* (pb. edn London, 1964) p. 348. See Kirby and Musson, *Voice of the People,* p. 263 for engineers' subscriptions to the NAPL.

84. K. Burgess, 'Technological Change and the 1852 Lock-Out in the British Engineering Industry', *International Review of Social History* (1969).

85. *Bolton Free Press* 20 August 1842. For the mechanics' distress e.g. *MSA* 12 February, 9 April 1842; H. Ashworth, 'Statistics of the Present Depression of Trade at Bolton', *Journal of the Statistical Society*, April 1842, p. 79, and for its impact on their status *MSA* 9 July 1842; Professor Hobsbawm has overstated his case in claiming that 'the engineers failed to take part in the movement for General Union and remained neutral in 1842', E. J. Hobsbawm, 'The Labour Aristocracy in Nineteenth-century Britain' in Hobsbawm, *Labouring Men*, p. 278.

86. For example A. Briggs, 'The Background of the Parliamentary Reform Movement in three English cities', *Cambridge Historical Journal*, X (1952) p. 303. It is as labour aristocrats that the spinners are portrayed in H. A. Turner, *Trade Union Growth Structure and Policy* (London, 1962).

87. The Stockport Chartists had no illusions about spinners' pay and calculated the Stockport average at 18*s* 8*d*. (not far above their figure for four loom power weavers on 16*s* 9*d*. average), National Convention letter Books Add. MSS 34245A fos. 63–4 Leah to Hetherington, 25 February 1839. Long and coupled mules had reduced the number of working spinners in Manchester fine spinning from over 1000 in 1829 to '500 or at most 600', Reports of the Inspectors of Factories (PP 1842, XXII), 31 December 1841, Report of L. Horner, p. 83. For the rapid spread of self-actors see A. Ure, *The Cotton Manufacture of Great Britain* (London, 1861) vol. 2, pp. 153–5; and for minders' wages see Reports of the Inspectors of Factories (PP 1842, XXII), 31 December 1841. Report of L. Horner, p. 92.

88. Kirby and Musson, *Voice of the People*, pp. 41–2. *MT* 21 August 1830, Place Collection, Set 16, vol. 2, fos. 66, 71, 96 for addresses referring to the Corn Laws, bishops' salaries and the expense of government.

89. For Betts see *MT* 18 September, 11 December 1830; *Lion* 29 February, 21 November 1828. HO 40/33/1 Bouverie to Phillipps 3 June 1835 and Foster to Russell 9 June 1835 for his later career. For Knight see, for example, his chairing of the private spinners' meeting reorganising themselves, *MT* 16 October 1830, and for the funeral *NS* 8 September 1838.

90. For the calico printers see J. Leach, *Stubborn Facts*, pp. 45–9. Geoffrey Turnbull, *A History of the Calico Printing Industry of Great Britain* (Altrincham, 1951) esp. chs. 2, 3, 6. For the dyers see the union meeting *MT* 3 March 1832 and

the interview with a dyer who had been a member from 1839 in Webb Trade Union MSS (London School of Economics Library) A. vol. XXXVII fos. 379–80.

91. For the tailors see the masters advertisements *MG* 21 June, 6 December 1834; and for the shoemakers e.g. the strikes in Manchester, Oldham and Bury in 1836 *MSA* 13 February, 9 April, 13 August 1836.

92. Postgate, *Builders' History*, chs. 3–5; and for the masons *Operative Stone Masons Fortnightly Return* 24 November 1837; 22 November 1838.

93. See Table 2. However, the Oldham hatters delegate seconded the amendment in favour of free trade as a question 'superior' to the Charter. *MG* 17 August 1842.

94. Henry Mayhew, *London Labour and the London Poor* (London, 1968) vol. 3, p. 221.

95. *British Statesman* 8 May 1842.

96. D. Bythell, *The Handloom Weavers* (Cambridge, 1969) pp 56–7.

97. R. Harrison (ed.), *Independent Collier. The Coal Miner as Archetypal Proletarian Reconsidered* (Harvester, 1978); R. Challinor and B. Ripley, *The Miners' Association: a Trade Union in the Age of the Chartists* (London, 1968) esp. pp. 15–16.

6. The Crisis of 1842: Chartism, the Colliers' Strike and the Outbreak in the Potteries

ROBERT FYSON

I

IN recent years historians have begun to recognise the crucial importance of the widespread disturbances in Britain in the summer of 1842. In contrast to the older and more traditional Chartist historiography, with its summary and dismissive treatment of the 'Plug Riots' as a brief spasm of unrest,[1] these events have been described as 'a general strike, the first not only in Britain but in any capitalist country' and 'the British equivalent of the 1848 revolution'.[2] F. C. Mather, in a valuable article, has stressed the very wide geographical spread of the disturbances, which affected twenty-three counties between early July and late September, and the seriousness with which the authorities viewed the 'semi-revolutionary strike movement'.[3] Recently the first book on *The General Strike of 1842* has appeared.[4] But with a single exception,[5] the published studies have concentrated almost exclusively on south-east Lancashire and north-east Cheshire, the storm-centre of the strike movement and of the attempts to organise it on a regional, and later national, scale.[6] This concentration can perhaps be justified, for the events in this area, and parts of the West Riding of Yorkshire, most nearly seem to deserve the description 'general strike'. But a wider understanding of the crisis will only be possible when historians have looked more closely at the disturbances in other parts of Britain: as F. B. Smith has said, 'we need to discover much more about the actual spread of the strikes, their local forms of participation, demands and defeats, their leaders and opponents'.[7]

This essay is an attempt to examine and evaluate the crisis of 1842 in the local context of the North Staffordshire Potteries. The 'Potteries Riots' of 15 and 16 August 1842 have long been a well-established landmark in local history and folklore, and feature prominently in two well-known working-class autobiographies.[8] They have attracted some fairly cursory attention from historians writing general surveys of popular disturbances, and the ways in which these were repressed.[9] But the Potteries should be of more than passing interest in contributing to our understanding of the 1842 crisis. Firstly, because the disturbances of that summer began with a colliers' strike against wage reductions at Longton in early June, which became general throughout the North Staffordshire coalfield in July, and was spread by enforced turn-outs, thus setting the pattern which other areas, including the Lancashire and Cheshire textile towns, were to follow. Secondly, because the outbreak of 15–16 August, involving arson and pulling down of houses, was more severely destructive than any similar episode since that at Bristol in 1831, and provoked correspondingly severe punishment. At the Staffordshire Special Commission in October 1842, 276 people were put on trial; 49 men were transported, and 116 men and women imprisoned for offences in connection with the Potteries disturbances.[10] Even if we exclude the 5 transported, and 38 imprisoned for offences in south Staffordshire, this was still, as George Rudé has pointed out, 'by far the largest batch of prisoners arrested, imprisoned and transported for participation in any single event in the course of the Chartist disorders'.[11] This is reflected in the criminal statistics, which show that committals for indictable riotous offences in Staffordshire in 1842 totalled 19.46 per cent of all committals, by far the highest percentage experienced in any county in England and Wales between 1835 and 1870.[12]

Such a phenomenal outbreak of popular discontent deserves closer attention than it has received hitherto.

II

By 1842 the Potteries towns[13] had been the centre of British production of china and earthenware for at least half a century. Factory industrialisation was far advanced; in 1833 130 pottery firms averaged 165 employees each and the seven largest had between 500 and 1000.[14] In the three parishes which encompassed the six towns, 43 per cent of the working population was employed in the dominant industry. Only one-third of this labour force was composed of adult men, one-quarter were boys under the age of twenty, 22 per cent women and 20 per cent girls.[15] The high proportion of young people reflected not only the employers' preference for juveniles, and mortality among adults caused by industrial disease,[16] but also the high rate of population growth: the three parishes[17] increased their numbers during the decade 1831-41 by one-third, from 60,000 to 80,000.[18]

Wages in the pottery industry extended over a wide range: in 1841 a thrower or painter, involved in delicate and precise skilled work, might earn, even in a time of depression, £2 a week and an oven-man, in charge of a kiln, as much as £3; but a transferrer could earn as little as 10s. a week, and children only 1s. or 2s.[19] Working conditions also varied greatly between different 'branches' of work and different factories. Outside the factory, the environment was often appalling, pervaded by noisome and inadequate sanitary arrangements, and overshadowed by the monstrous bottle-kilns belching a pall of black smoke into the atmosphere. In Shelton, the densely packed working-class district adjacent to Hanley, the death-rate between 1838 and 1842 was 28.4 per thousand, only slightly lower than Manchester and considerably higher than Birmingham.[20] A visitor to the district in 1839 remarked on the pervasive smoke, dirt, smells, confusion and squalor and remarked, 'There are, generally speaking, but two classes of houses as of people – the thousands of those in the working order, and the fine massy and palace-like abodes of the wealthy employers.'[21]

During the 1830s the group of wealthy master potters, coal-owners, gentry, clergy and professional men who dominated public life in the district, were increasingly challenged and threatened by the pressure exerted by an autonomous and increasingly self-confident working-class presence, expressing itself in a variety of popular movements. Disillusionment with the 1832 Reform Act led, as elsewhere, to a rejection of middle-class leadership. The missionary work of John Doherty's National Association for the Protection of Labour (NAPL) in 1830-1, and the visits of Robert Owen in 1833, helped to establish the great Potters' Union which posed a fundamental challenge to the power of the manufacturers in the years before its defeat early in 1837.[22] From the ashes of that defeat there arose eighteen months later the militant, and class-conscious politics of Potteries Chartism.

The disturbances of 1842, however, originated not with potters or

Chartists but with the 4000 or so coal-miners who were an important minority among the local population.[23] The North Staffordshire coalfield was a dangerous one, and the death-rate of Staffordshire miners from accidents at work – 7.84 per thousand per year – was in 1851 the highest of any mining area in England and Wales.[24] Wages appear to have varied approximately from 16s. to 24s. a week in the 1830s and early 1840s.[25] Subcontracting, or the butty system, was common, though not universal as in South Staffordshire, and coal-mining was often closely linked with iron mines and furnaces, as in the industrial complexes owned by Earl Granville at Shelton and Thomas Kinnersley at Kidsgrove, and leased by W. H. Sparrow at Longton from the duke of Sutherland. Due to the competing demand for women and children in the pottery industry, there were almost none working in the pits. The mining population was divided between the Potteries towns and the rural hinterland, where some of the largest pits were situated: in 1841 55 per cent lived in the predominantly urban parishes of Stoke and Burslem, the remainder in semi-rural Wolstanton parish.[26]

As elsewhere, the colliers had a well-established reputation for violence and riotousness, most recently manifested during a strike in 1831, when blacklegs were attacked by a crowd of several hundred, an attempt was made to unroof a house, and troops were brought in to restore order.[27] But such action by no means precluded a capacity for disciplined trade union organisation. Like the potters, who supported their 1831 strike, the miners were in touch with Doherty's NAPL,[28] and their short-lived union of 1830–1, initiated by delegates from Lancashire, boasted its own printed rule book.[29] Both the miners' violence and their collective self-discipline were to reappear in 1842 when, as in 1831, they were able to have an effect on the economy of the Potteries out of all proportion to their numbers, simply because without coal to fire the kilns, the pottery industry must grind to a standstill.

III

In the summer of 1842 the Potteries were in the trough of the worst depression of the century: trade was at a low ebb, the workhouses were overcrowded, wages were low and prices high. At about the beginning of June, 300 colliers working for W. H. Sparrow at Longton came out on strike in protest against a wage cut from 3s. 7d to 3s. a day imposed without the legal fortnight's notice.[30] George Mitchison, Sparrow's agent, writing on 9 June to his employer in Wolverhampton, complained that:

> About 200 of them yesterday paraded the Potteries with flags and banners and loaves of Bread on poles. . . their object is to beg. . . They swear vengeance against me – and give it out they will take away my life. . . I am obliged to watch my house every night and the rest of the property.[31]

During the succeeding month the tension mounted throughout the district as, against a background of increasing unemployment and short-time working, the strikers held a series of marches and meetings, and sought moral and financial support from those still at work.

Early in July, John Ridgway, Hanley's leading manufacturer and the chairman of Stoke Parish Board of Guardians, took part in a national Anti-Corn Law League deputation to the Prime Minister: he told Peel that in the Potteries bodies of colliers were patrolling the streets, demanding money or food, and prophesied that 'unless something be done to find employment and cheaper food. . . a struggle will commence, of which no man can foresee the extent and consequences.'[32]

The struggle began two days later: after a second coal-owner, Earl Granville, through his agent, Forrester, gave notice to his men of a 6d. reduction per day, a meeting of colliers in Hanley agreed to call out all the pits in North Staffordshire from Monday 11 July. A central Committee of Operative Colliers was set up, and throughout the next fortnight hundreds of colliers roamed the district in bands, forcibly turning out the pits, and stopping the colliery engines by raking out the fires of the boilers and pulling out their plugs.[33] Almost all the potteries were eventually forced to close for lack of fuel, but the potters showed 'a quiet determination to endure anything, so that the rise of wages asked by the colliers may be gained.'[34] Others gave their support less willingly: in the neighbourhood of Longton, it was claimed, 'The Mob is even taking haymakers out of the fields and compelling them to join them.'[35]

The strike had begun because it was feared that Sparrow's, and then Granville's, reductions signalled the beginning of a general round of wage cuts with which all coal-owners would fall in line. But the demands formulated by the colliers' committee, endorsed by mass meetings, and circulated in handbills now went further than simply the restoration of cuts: by 18 July they were demanding 4s. a day for an eight-hour working day plus a free allowance of coal, weekly payment in cash and that five nights' work should be paid for as six days'. 'Until the whole of the Masters agree to these just and fair propositions, the whole of the Men shall stand out from work, let the consequences be what they may.'[36]

The local magistrates responded to the challenge by calling out the yeomanry and bombarding the Home Office with requests for troops. Two companies of infantry were sent to the neighbouring market town of Newcastle-under-Lyme, and moved into the centre of the Potteries to camp on Hanley racecourse for several days. The soldiers could not guard all the widely scattered collieries in the district, but their presence, and the pressure of empty bellies, combined to undermine the colliers' unity: in Hanley on 18 July there was a meeting of men wanting to return to work, and a Longton meeting on 23 July agreed to open negotiations at works level with individual masters. By the end of the month there was a general drift back to work, and on 2 August the troops were withdrawn.

The uneasy calm was short-lived: on Saturday 6 August there were renewed turn-outs at two pits and during the night a crowd of two hundred colliers attacked Burslem Town Hall to release three of their colleagues who had been arrested for begging, and stoned the windows of the police superintendent and the publican who were responsible for the arrests. Troops and yeomanry were again summoned, but popular restlessness was not dissipated.[37] Many colliers had returned to work on the basis of vague and unfulfilled assurances by employers that their grievances would be examined, and their dissatisfaction soon revived. The Committee of Operative Colliers in Hanley was still functioning, and on 13 August wrote to the owner of Norton Colliery warning him to dismiss four butties accused of unfair treatment of the workmen.[38] Thus matters stood on the eve of the great outbreak of 15–16 August. Over a period of two and a half months, the colliers' dispute had brought a district that was already in the grip of harsh distress before the dispute began to the point of violent conflict and social breakdown.

The orchestration of the wide-ranging bands of turn-outs, the widening of the strike, the escalation of the workers' demands, and the continuation of the struggle even after apparent defeat, are evidence of the determination and capacity for painstaking organisation of the colliers' leaders. Furthermore, the North Staffordshire men were in touch with other coalfields. In the aftermath of the outbreak, it was claimed that 'As early as March 1841 it was intimated to Mr. Forrester that a system of organization had been set on foot among his colliers,' spreading from Lancashire, into Cheshire, Staffordshire and South Wales; and the Home Secretary reported to the Prime Minister that 'The Duke of Buccleuch says that constant communication is kept up between the working colliers in Scotland and those in the neighbourhood of New-castle-under-Lyme.'[39]

During the strike, the North Staffordshire colliers extended their activities into adjacent districts. It was rumoured by 14 July that a party of colliers had gone to Lancashire to extend the turn-out there, and a week later six hundred colliers assembled and marched north twenty-five miles through Congleton and Macclesfield in order to turn out the miners at Poynton colliery, south of Stockport, because they had heard that coal from Poynton was being shipped into the Potteries by canal. They were repulsed by troops, and the Cheshire magistrates were convinced that they had intervened in the nick of time to stop the colliers marching into Manchester and spreading the strike to Lancashire. In Stalybridge in early August the weavers, according to Kitson Clark, were 'excited by the knowledge that the Staffordshire miners were already out'.[40]

Meanwhile other North Staffordshire colliers visited the south of the county, and George Hemmings, the Hanley miners' leader, spoke at meetings in Birmingham, West Bromwich and Bilston; the Black Country miners followed the Potteries' lead in resisting wage reductions by coming out on strike with very similar demands.[41] In Shropshire the coalfield was disturbed by rumours of itinerant agitators and the memoirs of Emanuel Lovekin, a Shropshire miner and Chartist who was arrested in 1842, tell us that 'I formed an acquaintance with a man that came from the Potteries, and it was thought, he brought news of the doings there'.[42] A delegate meeting of the miners of Staffordshire, Shropshire and Cheshire, in Newport, Shropshire, was called by the Hanley miners for 31 July, in order to consider calling a *national* delegate meeting of the miners of England and Wales.[43] Little over three months before the foundation of the Miners' Association in York-shire, the idea of a national union was already being broached; there can be little doubt that in the summer of 1842 the North Staffordshire miners' leaders saw their struggle in a national and not merely a local perspective.

IV

No assessment of the colliers' strike could be complete without reference to Chartism. The relationship between Chartism and the colliers' strike in South Staffordshire has already been the subject of a prolonged academic debate.[44] In order to understand the Chartist role in the events of 1842 in North Staffordshire, an appreciation of the development and strength of Chartism in the Potteries is required.

The Chartist Movement in North Staffordshire had begun in August 1838, in the aftermath of the great rally in Birmingham. A Potteries Political Union was formed, and after three months' vigorous campaigning, a massive open-air meeting took place in November at which Feargus O'Connor was welcomed to the district for the first time, and John Richards, a shoemaker and a veteran radical of sixty-six who had been active in a variety of popular causes since the year 1818, was elected as the Potteries' delegate to the National Convention.[45] 1839 was, as elsewhere, a year of great excitement and rumours of insurrection. In May there were two days' rioting at Longton against the new police force, and barricades were built in the streets; during July arms were being sold; but there was no attempt at a Chartist insurrection and no arrests of local Chartists. Richards' leadership was cautious and realistic: he reported to the Convention that the sacred month was not practicable in the Potteries. By the autumn the crisis had passed, employers victimised known Chartists, and the movement fell briefly into the doldrums.[46]

From the spring of 1840 onwards the Potteries Chartists worked hard and with increasing success to promote a less spontaneous, more carefully organised revival of Chartism through the National Charter Association (NCA). After two years of continuous campaigning, the organisational strength of Chartism had reached an impressive level in the first six months of 1842, and was continuing to grow under the pressure of increasing poverty and distress. In July 1842 there were eight separate NCA branches in North Staffordshire – two in Hanley, one in each of the other five Potteries towns, and one in Newcastle under Lyme – federated in a Potteries District Council. In the election of a Staffordshire delegate to the Convention of 1842 in March, 536 North Staffordshire Chartists voted and John Richards calculated that by 22 May the total paid-up strength was 610.[47] Thereafter the movement was expanding rapidly, and formal membership at its peak may have approached 1000. But the support was more widespread, and the

impact on the working-class communities greater, than formal membership figures alone can indicate. The case of a Tunstall potter who
admitted in court that he had just attended a Chartist meeting, but
insisted that he 'was not a pledged Chartist, who takes a card and pays
a penny a month', must have been typical of very many others. Ten
thousand North Staffordshire men signed the 1842 National Petition.[48]

The occupations of activists can be identified from the lists of
General Council nominations published in the *Northern Star* during
1841-2. Of sixty-two men whose trades were specified, thirty-seven
worked in the pottery industry in various capacities, six were shoemakers, five miners, and of the remaining fourteen about half were
small independent tradesmen. The most conspicuous platform orators
were Richards, Joseph Capper the Tunstall blacksmith, a radical since
the days of the *Black Dwarf*[49] and a popular, humorous speaker, with
a vote and hence more social status than most Chartists, William Ellis
from Burslem, a powerful and talented young Owenite and former
member of the Board of Management of the Potters' Union,[50] Samuel
Robinson, a Stoke china painter whose powers of oratory earned high
praise from Feargus O'Connor,[51] and Moses Simpson the Shelton cord-
wainer who was the secretary of the Hanley and Shelton branch.
Equally essential to the movement were those who filled other roles:
George Mart of Stoke, the chairman of most of the big meetings from
1838 to April 1842 when he retired from the limelight; John Neal, a
shoemaker recently arrived in Hanley, who became secretary to the
District Council and whose Chartist experience included a prison
sentence in Warwick Gaol after the 1839 Birmingham Bull Ring fracas;
and Jeremiah Yates of Shelton, potter turned keeper of the temperance
hotel and coffee-house which was an essential centre for Chartist social
and political activity.

Yates's correspondence with Thomas Cooper from March to June
1842 shows the importance of his role as a Chartist newsagent, with a
regular order for 120 copies of Cooper's paper *The Commonwealthsman*,[52] a variety of other publications, and up to 120 lb. weekly of the
'Chartist Beverage' which was popular with many of his teetotal Chartist
customers. It was through this initial contact that the fiery Leicester
leader made his first visit to the Potteries in April 1842. Such visits by
Chartist lecturers were frequent, due in part to the district's location
between Birmingham and Manchester: in the first six months of 1842
at least a dozen outside speakers visited the area. The most popular
visitor of all was, of course, O'Connor who paid his second visit to the

district in May, and was escorted in triumph through the Potteries in a coach-and-four, in a procession including a band, the usual display of banners, and 300 members of the thriving Upper Hanley and Smallthorne Female NCA.[53]

North Staffordshire Chartists were involved in a wide range of social and political activity, from Chartist tea-parties and balls to political meetings on issues of Chartist controversy, on which they invariably supported O'Connor and the *Northern Star* to the hilt. Some of their greatest successes were scored through involvement in local affairs and their own distinctive interventions on issues posed by others. They regularly disrupted Anti-Corn Law League meetings, even though they collaborated with the Leaguers in opposing Tory candidates and helping to organise the election of Liberal MP J. L. Ricardo in the 1841 general election, or in the burning of Sir Robert Peel in effigy early in 1842.[54] They opposed Church rates, intervened at a meeting to congratulate the Queen on a royal birth, and ensured the election of a Stoke Highways Board composed of working men, in April 1842. In July they took over a Tunstall public meeting called to consider the need for barracks in the town, and defeated the proposal.[55]

Like all vital political bodies, Potteries Chartism had its divisions and internal arguments. Richards, the acknowledged leader in 1839, had perhaps 'blotted his copybook' by spending several months in 1840 as an itinerant lecturer for the Urquhartite 'foreign policy Chartists' and by showing initial sympathy for Lovett's breakaway National Association in 1841 : in the election for a delegate to the 1842 Convention, he received almost unanimous support from the Upper Hanley and Longton branches, but there was equally overwhelming preference for the Black Country nominee in the Hanley and Stoke branches. John Mason, the successful candidate, remarked at the Convention on the divisions in the district, and alleged 'a want of a feeling of charity; many who had dared to give vent to feelings contrary to the majority had been denounced in the Potteries over paltry differences'.[56]

Usually, however, such differences were publicly glossed over or ignored, and the local press seems to have been unaware of them. They appeared insignificant in comparison with the forward movement of Chartism : the *Star* singled out the Potteries district for congratulations on the efficiency of their fund-raising, and John Campbell of the NCA Executive reported with satisfaction early in July that 'Richards and the good men of the Potteries have carried Chartism into almost every hamlet in their district.'[57] Such strength was now to be put to the test for, after the rejection of the National Petition early in May, the movement again had to face the basic problem of Chartist strategy: how to make use of the wide-spread support in a time of crisis in order to win the Charter, in the teeth of a hostile House of Commons?

None of the evidence pre-dating the outbreak in August provides a basis for suggesting that Potteries Chartists were assembling arms or preparing for an insurrection in the summer of 1842, as some of them had done three years previously.[58] Memories of the 1839 débâcle and of the failure at Newport were too recent for this strategy to be seriously considered.

In a climate of mounting desperation, expectation and uncertainty, harsh destitution, millennial hopes and gloomy fears, the Potteries Chartists explored various divergent lines of action simultaneously. One approach was the hope, to which O'Connor had reverted early in 1842, of winning over the middle classes to the Charter. This must have seemed worth pursuing in view of the history of sporadic co-operation in the Potteries between working-class radicals and liberal manufacturers like John Ridgway and his brother William in 1819–20 and 1830–2, and the common concern of both groups with the mounting distress which was affecting manufacturers, tradesmen and shopkeepers as well as working people. John Campbell, visiting Hanley in March, optimistically announced that 'The manufacturers are about to call a meeting to adopt the whole Charter.' Early in July Potteries Chartists held a meeting to 'take into consideration the union of the middle and working classes' without, however, any middle-class participation. At another meeting a month later several manufacturers went as far as to send apologies for their absence. On their side, the Anti-Corn Law supporters similarly hoped to win over the Chartists to become 'repeal men', and in July they set up a branch of the Complete Suffrage Association. But old animosities and suspicions persisted and prevented common action until it was too late; only in the immediate aftermath of the outbreak, on the afternoon of Tuesday 16 August, was an open-air meeting held, in the presence of an overwhelmingly Chartist crowd, at which the Chartist leaders and the Ridgways appeared on the same platform, and this meeting was interrupted and forcibly dispersed by troops acting under the direction of the county magistrates.[59]

The forces making for class conflict were stronger than the tenuous hopes for class conciliation, and the other kinds of Chartist activity during the summer reflected this. First the Chartists intensified their opposition towards the traditional enemies of radicalism, the Tory county gentry and aristocracy. Samuel Robinson of Stoke, for example, inveighed against the monarchy and the duke of Sutherland, the great Staffordshire landowner, in the course of a Chartist speech at Trentham, a village dominated by the duke's hall and estate. Especially astounding to upper-class sensibilities was the visit of a party of Chartists, led by William Ellis, to Stafford in July: they joined forces with the Chartist shoemakers of Stafford to interrupt a meeting of aristocracy and gentry in the Shire Hall, called by the Deputy Lord Lieutenant, Earl Dartmouth, to congratulate the Queen on an escape from assassination. The rulers of the county fled from the hall, and Ellis took over the chair at a three-hour Chartist meeting.[60]

A second Chartist response was the intensification of fierce opposition to the new Poor Law at a time when increasing numbers of working people were having to resort to its provisions. As early as 9 June, the Poor Law Commissioners consented to the suspension at Stoke workhouse of the order prohibiting out-door relief to the able-bodied. By late July, the Burslem and Stoke-on-Trent workhouses were receiving 400-500 new applications for assistance per day. The Wolstanton and Burslem Guardians suspected the Chartists of encouraging able-bodied men to apply in large numbers in order to make the Poor Law unworkable. Early in August the Secretary to the Board complained that 'Hamlet Booth a Chartist one of the able-bodied applicants had been haranguing the men, condemning the Poor Law etc. and using very strong language evidently tending to create dissatisfaction'; the prosecution of Booth was being considered. His agitation was evidently effective, for the Chartists organised two meetings in Hanley at which Booth, with Capper, Ellis and Richards, addressed a crowd augmented by processions of paupers on out-relief from the two workhouses, condemning the operation of the Poor Law and demanding action to end the prevailing distress.[61] Chartist feelings of sympathy and solidarity with the paupers, who included many of their own workmates and supporters, were fortified by the desire to persuade the sufferers of the necessity of the Charter as a cure for their ills.

Thus the pervasive and prominent Chartist presence moulded the climate of working-class opinion and action. It would be absurd to suppose that the colliers' strike could have been immune from Chartist influence.

Only five miners were among the Chartist committee members listed, but they included Thomas Mayer, already a Chartist in April

1841, and George Hemmings, whose name appears in August 1842: these were the two most prominent leaders of the Hanley miners. Certainly the Chartists made a considerable contribution to the organisation and leadership of the colliers' strike, even though there may have been relatively few colliers among their ranks before the strike began. In June, when Sparrow's men first appealed to the public for support, Samuel Robinson, William Ellis, and James Oldham, the leading Etruria Chartist, spoke on their behalf, and Chartist speakers continued to do so throughout the strike.[62] As with the paupers, the ties of working-class solidarity coincided with a magnificent opportunity to make new converts to the cause.

The miners publicly insisted that 'we have nothing to do with any Political question; our dispute is simply upon the Price of Labour', and the local correspondent of the *Northern Star* was equally insistent that 'The Chartists, as a body, have not mixed themselves up with the colliers' turnout, nor will they'.[63] But the involvement of individual Chartists was clear, and the Committee of Operative Colliers had its headquarters in a Hanley pub, the George and Dragon, which was also a Chartist meeting place. John Richards in particular was closely concerned. When the colliers' appeal for support appeared in the *Northern Star* for 16 July, it was signed 'By order of the Committee of Operative Colliers, John Richards, Corresponding Secretary of the N.C.A.' and the letter sent on 13th August by the Committee to the Norton coalowner was said to be in Richards' handwriting. Although himself a shoemaker, Richards had acted as a negotiator for the Potters' Union in the strike of 1836–7; he was an experienced activist and propagandist, and probably put his talents at the miners' service, in drafting statements and perhaps contributing to their overall strategy.

If so, he may have provoked controversy in the Chartist ranks again. When writing to Thomas Cooper on 2 August to accept his offer to speak in the Potteries over the weekend of 13–14 August, Richards added: 'I have to say that owing to the Colliers turn out our organisation is most Sadly Deranged you will therefore be prepared to Enforce the Necessity of Union amongst us.' There was probably little certainty or agreement by this time about the direction which Chartist strategy should take, only a sense of expectation, like that aroused by two Yorkshire Chartists, preaching Samuel Holberry's funeral sermon throughout the Potteries in July, who 'carried conviction to the minds of all present that the time for a great change was fully arrived, and that such change must be brought about by the energies of the sons of toil.'[64]

V

The Potteries were already trembling on the brink of crisis when Thomas Cooper arrived in Hanley on Saturday 13 August. Cooper's account, though written thirty years later, gives a factually accurate picture of his own part in the events which followed: his stirring and calculatedly ironic Chartist sermon, delivered on Sunday evening to an immense crowd in Hanley, helped to raise the emotional temperature of desperate men to boiling point. With a mixture of pride and penitence, Cooper writing in 1872 accepted responsibility for the Potteries outbreak: 'I had caught the spirit of the oppressed and discontented thousands, and, by virtue of my nature and constitution, struck the spark which kindled all into combustion'.[65]

But the news which arrived from Manchester that evening while Cooper was speaking had a greater impact on events than his oratory: the Trades Conference[66] had called a general strike for the Charter, and urged other towns to do likewise. Cooper was, therefore, asked to reconvene and chair the meeting the following morning, Monday 15 August, at which John Richards and George Hemmings, the best-known leaders of the Chartists and the colliers, united in proposing and seconding the motion 'That all labour cease until the People's Charter becomes the law of the land.'

What followed[67] began as an enforcement of the general strike by turning out those at work in the potteries and collieries in and around Hanley. Such familiar tactics, essential if the strike were to become general, necessarily involved breaking the 'Peace, Law and Order' which Cooper had urged. Emboldened by their first easy successes, the crowd attacked the Hanley police office, released several prisoners from the lock-up, tore up books and papers, declaring 'we shall have no more police rates!' and armed themselves with the special constables' staffs. Moving down the road to Stoke, their next targets were the house of the collector of poor rates, and the office of the Pottery Court of Requests,[68] which were attacked and looted. In Stoke the police office was ransacked, a bonfire made of the furniture, the policeman in charge had his arm broken in the mêlée, and cutlasses were acquired by the crowd, before they moved on to the isolated house of Thomas Allen near Fenton, where

They plundered the house – broke the furniture to atoms – emptied beds on the lawn – helped themselves to drink from the cellar – cleared the larder of its contents – took the hams flitches of bacon and cheese without ceremony – and as a climax, they actually burnt a quantity of the old parchment deeds connected with the family.[69]

The pattern had been set for twenty-four hours of a desperate saturnalia by men and women who were hungry, penniless and determined to assert their power through looting and destruction of property. At Allen's house, the crowd divided: one group attacked the house of T. B. Rose, the Stipendiary Magistrate, in the village of Penkhull, and made an abortive attempt on the Stoke workhouse. The larger part of the crowd went to Longton and wrecked the police court and office before descending on the house of the Revd Benjamin Vale, the Rector of Longton, in the afternoon. Vale's house was ransacked and set on fire, and his wine cellar was plundered, so that when the soldiers from Newcastle finally arrived on the scene, they were able to arrest a number of people who were too drunk to run away. Other casualties, late in the day, were the Fenton police office and the house of Charles James Mason, a pottery manufacturer.

After dark, when magistrates and troops had withdrawn to Newcastle and abandoned the Potteries completely to the rioters, the scale of destruction intensified and was centred on Hanley. The office of Forrester, Granville's agent, was an obvious target, and his house was only with difficulty saved from the flames. Later in the night, the crowds, some said to be disguised as women or with blackened faces, gutted and burnt to the ground Albion House, Shelton, the home of the magistrate, William Parker, and Hanley parsonage, where the Vicar of Hanley, the Revd R. E. Aitkens, lived. Other targets during the night or in the early hours of the morning included the homes of Charles Meigh, the master potter, who bought off the attackers, and the Chief Bailiff, where an attack was beaten off by loyal servants. The office of the solicitor, Thomas Griffin, secretary of the Stoke Poor Law Board, was broken into, as were some grocers' and pawnbrokers' shops, where pledges were redeemed without payment.

Early on the morning of Tuesday 16 August (by chance the anniversary of Peterloo) a meeting was held in Hanley, of which reports are confused and vague; but probably its purpose was to organise the large procession of men, many armed with sticks, who set off to Burslem. They may have had two reasons for going there, to extend their control of the streets and attacks on property to the two northern Potteries towns, and to rendezvous with a large body of turn-outs which had originated in Manchester or Stockport and come south via the textile towns of Macclesfield, Congleton and Leek. The rendezvous of the two processions at Burslem, and the renewed violence and intimidation, including an attack on the George Inn, provided the authorities with the opportunity to strike hard at the rioters. A troop of dragoons, backed by special constables, attempted to disperse the stone-throwing crowds with their swords; the Riot Act was read, and when the Leek turn-outs attempted to enter the town, the magistrate Captain Powys gave the order to fire. Only one man is known to have died, but several were seriously wounded. The crowds dispersed, pursued by soldiers, amid scenes of panic: and although for several days afterwards groups of men wandered about the countryside demanding money and food at isolated farms, the outbreak was at an end.

In the immediate aftermath it was widely assumed that what had occurred must have been the result of a carefully organised conspiracy. Rumours of Chartist arming circulated, and of an imminent renewal of popular violence, and the Potteries were said to be in 'a most disorganized and revolutionary state'.[70] But despite the encouragement given to spies and informers by the authorities, and the payment of rewards for evidence leading to successful convictions, no evidence of serious revolutionary preparations, or of the distribution of arms,[71] emerged at the Staffordshire Special Commission in October.

After the initial call to strike for the Charter, a spontaneous explosion of popular anger resulted, for twenty-four hours, in an escalating process of destruction and looting which it was beyond the power of either the Chartists, or the authorities, to control. The most desperate and audacious men, like the brothers George and Isaac Colclough, emerged from the crowd as 'riot captains' to hold brief authority over their fellows, by the force of their personalities and perhaps their physical strength to assume a role of *ad hoc* leadership and to give some direction to the crowd's energies. George Colclough, or 'Cogsey Nelly' to give him his local nickname, a twenty-six-year-old miner, was charged with riot, with attempting to demolish Forrester's house, setting fire to Parker's and Vale's, as well as demanding money with threats from the landlord of the George Inn, Burslem on the next day.[72] Sentenced to be transported for twenty-one years, and not known to have any Chartist connections or to have been a strike leader, he was one of the only 'riot captains' prominent throughout the outbreak who can be identified as such with a fair degree of certainty, but he was exceptional only in the number of his offences.

Only a handful of those charged were Chartist members: the Potteries Chartist Defence Fund committee referred to 'about ten' in the appeal on their behalf;[73] a possible maximum of sixteen can be tentatively identified, three of whom were acquitted. But in one sense it might be true to say that 'notwithstanding there are so few who can be said to have belonged *directly* to the Chartist body, we can state, that the *whole* of them are Chartist in *principle* and at heart!'[74] 'Now lads we shall have the Charter,' one man shouted while demolishing Vale's house, and another said 'he was going to London to raise the Chartists – that he should have the Houses of Parliament down in a week and that everything should be reduced to one level.'[75] This kind of 'Chartism', even though it might have been repudiated by some Chartist leaders, had its foundation in a fundamental class hostility to the rich and powerful, and a readiness to take drastic action in the hope of seeing 'the world turned upside down'.

The liberation of prisoners, the attacks on police stations and court-houses, the search for arms and the ransacking of pawnbrokers' shops fit well with this kind of 'semi-political' consciousness. Whether we can say that the crowd were 'scrupulously discriminating in selecting their targets'[76] is more doubtful. Isolation, vulnerability, the chance whim of a group of looters may have been important determinants, and it would be rash to assume that all those whose property was attacked were necessarily the most hated men in the Potteries. Thomas Allen's house was attacked because it was isolated and because it was wrongly believed that it might hold a store of arms; the house of C. J. Mason, the only master potter to suffer substantial damage to his property, also stood in an isolated position. Rose, the first Potteries stipendiary magistrate, was always deeply unpopular with the working classes; Parker, a lawyer, had recently been in the news as the subject of an unsuccessful Crown prosecution for perjury;[77] both men led the troops around the Potteries in pursuit of the crowds on Monday 15 August. Forrester was an obvious target, but the house of Sparrow's agent, Mitchison, escaped attack, perhaps because Vale's house at Longton was a more tempting prize. Both of the Anglican clergymen concerned were also members of the Stoke Board of Guardians; Vale, with the well-stocked wine cellar, had been advising his poverty-stricken parishioners earlier in the year that they could use dock leaves or broom seed to make palatable substitutes for tea or coffee.[78] The attack on his house very probably suggested the idea of attacking Aitkens'. Working-class hostility to the Church of England was rarely carried to such lengths, but Joseph Whiston, a potter and Primitive Methodist lay preacher proclaimed that he was doing the Lord's work as he helped to fire Vale's house.[79]

George Rudé has provided a brief account of the age, marital status, previous convictions and trades of some of the men transported.[80] As he has shown, they were mainly young men, with an average age of twenty-six. Only twenty-three women were arrested, although according to the *Mercury* 'for plunder, the women were far the worst':[81] fourteen were found guilty, most for offences of looting, though several were involved in the demolition of Vale's house; the longest sentence given was eight months for a woman of forty-eight, more than twice the average age of other arrested women. Finally a further point not elaborated by Professor Rudé deserves notice. Among the fifty-six north Staffordshire men[82] transported, there were twenty-one potters, nineteen miners and sixteen from a variety of other trades. But among the one hundred and sixteen men and women imprisoned for up to two years, there were sixty-seven potters, seventeen miners and thirty-two others. Whereas the rank and file of the crowd in outbreak may have been composed predominantly of potters, as was the working population, among those judged guilty of offences deserving transportation, and therefore more likely to have been ringleaders, there was a disproportionately high number of colliers. This is a salutary reminder that the outbreak of August 1842 in the Potteries cannot be understood unless it is seen in the context of the long-drawn-out industrial struggle which preceded it.

VI

The aftermath of the Potteries outbreak was a period of tension and anticipation scarcely less than that which preceded it. Soldiers swarmed throughout the district, prisoners were rounded up and taken to Stafford jail, and preparations made for the great legal ritual of punishment and revenge, the Special Commission of Assize at Stafford; the ruling élite of the Potteries anticipated this event with pleasure, and it was said 'they are laying bottles of port among the gentry at Hanley that Cooper and Ellis will be hung for treason'. Ellis's name was the first to be mentioned in a witness's deposition received at the Home Office, and Sir James Graham hoped initially to make an example of him by bringing the capital charge of high treason. The Chartists, with almost all their most prominent leaders arrested, were forbidden to hold public meetings and were likely to lose their jobs. Richards, writing to the editor of the *Northern Star* on 22 August, just before his arrest, complained of 'a Tory reign of terror' which was a field day for spies and informers; 'when I reflect on the cause, and see the goodly fabric of Chartism thrown down in these parts, my soul sinks within me and I feel completely unmanned'. The *Northern Star's* local correspondent complained 'we are placed entirely under martial law, and the most absolute despotism is practised upon us.'[83]

When the Special Commission finally sat at Stafford, it took just two weeks, 1–15 October, to deal with 276 accused, often tried together in batches, in three separate courts, each presided over by an eminent judge, one of whom was the Lord Chief Justice, Sir Nicolas Tindal. It was the largest 'Chartist' trial ever held, with the greatest number of sentences of transportation and imprisonment handed down. It has been pointed out by a legal historian that no one was transported for riot or sedition alone, and that by the normal judicial standards of the age the offenders were not treated unusually harshly. Unlike the Bristol trials of 1832 there were no death sentences. But the sentencing of such large numbers of people so hastily, in a context in which there was much bought and perjured evidence, meant that much injustice was inevitably done. Sifting through the evidence, it is impossible to decide with certainty which prisoners were truly the wronged ones, which prisoners' denials were true, or even whether their silence was necessarily proof of guilt, or simply of a bewildered and fatalistic resignation. But even the *North Staffordshire Mercury's* editor was in no doubt that there must be some cases of wrongful identity and mistaken conviction.[84]

In assessing the consequences of the outbreak, the fate of the victims and the impact on their lives deserve to be considered first. Among those transported, William Ellis deserves pride of place. Although he had fled to Glasgow, local opinion was generally convinced of his innocence of the charge of participating in the burning of Hanley Parsonage, of which he was ultimately accused after other charges had been dropped. He established an alibi, but then the weekend recess was used, suspiciously, to procure fresh witnesses against him from the Potteries, against whom he had no opportunity to prepare his case.

Leaving behind him a wife and four children, who sank into destitution, he was transported for twenty-one years and never returned. Although he became a Chartist martyr, often mentioned in the same breath as Frost, Williams and Jones, he never, unlike them, received a pardon. It was widely believed that he had been marked down as a scapegoat.[85]

Another Chartist, whom we may assume to have been 'guilty' since his colleagues made no appeal on his behalf, fared even worse. Richard Croxton, a twenty-seven-year-old engraver from Hanley, married with two children, was a signatory in 1841 of the Chartists' appeal for funds to build a working men's hall. In May 1842, after nearly five weeks unemployment, he was forced to apply to Stoke workhouse for relief, and in return for daily work stonebreaking received his own meals and 9d. per day to support his family. During the night of 15/16 August he led a gang of men extorting protection money from the houses of 'respectables', and the next day was heard to say 'he would rather walk up to his knees in blood than eat his breakfast'. He was transported for life, and in Tasmania committed a long string of offences, mainly connected with drink, which led to his ticket of leave being revoked in 1858. For this man there was no road back from the turning-point of 1842.[86]

Not all of the imprisoned Chartists were more fortunate. William Garrett, a Chartist bricklayer shot through the body by the soldiers at the Burslem confrontation, was nevertheless sentenced to two years' hard labour, and John Ashley, a Newcastle master-tailor and alleged Chartist made the mistake of stopping to watch the sacking of Rose's house for which he received a twelve-month sentence: both men died in the Millbank penitentiary in London. Others survived their ordeals: John Neal, after his second prison sentence of two years, was said to be in 'very ill health', Joseph Capper's two years in Stafford prison, (imposed for charges of incitement in speeches made long before the outbreak, on 24 June and 8 July), broke his spirit and destroyed his commitment to Chartism. Two survived triumphantly: Jeremiah Yates emerged from his one-year sentence (for turning out pottery workers) to resume his Chartist activities, and ultimately to become surveyor to the Chartist highways board in Shelton, until his premature death in 1852; and the indomitable John Richards, after his one-year sentence for incitement at the age of seventy, continued to campaign for Chartism until at least 1850.[87]

It is legitimate to dwell on the fate of the imprisoned Chartists, if only because, apart from the bare facts yielded by Tasmanian convict records, we know so much less about the fate of most of the other, more obscure individuals. By 1868, if not before, George Colclough had returned to the Potteries after serving his sentence, and became a shopkeeper. His experiences had left him 'totally indifferent' to politics, but he had been marked by them no doubt to a greater extent than William Plant, who as a young man of twenty-three was sentenced to two weeks' imprisonment in October 1842 for intimidating a woman into parting with a shilling and who, in later life, 'occasionally at the Liberal Club, Hanley, rehearsed his experiences at Stafford with much pleasantry. The affair by him was treated rather light'.[88]

VII

The 'Potteries Riots' led to swift action by the county authorities: by the end of 1842 the County Police Force had been established and the first Chief Constable appointed. Recriminations as to the responsibility for the outbreak continued for a year or so: Chartists such as Samuel Robinson blamed the Anti-Corn Law League; Tories like Rose blamed the Liberal manufacturers for encouraging the workers to take up subversive ideas; the Home Secretary formally censured Rose for abandoning the Potteries to the mob during the night of 15/16 August.[89] The Chartists had to start rebuilding their movement again, and never regained the combination of mass support with effective organisation which they had previously achieved. The new Potters' Union founded in 1843 was led by William Evans, who had himself been an active Chartist in 1842, but became an outspoken opponent of Chartism.[90] The year 1848 in the Potteries was a relatively quiet affair: the Chartists had become so deeply concerned with the Land Plan that their chief interest lay in persuading the Poor Law authorities to allow the paupers to cultivate vacant plots of land; and the level of Staffordshire committals for riotous offences, at 0.89 per cent of the total committals, was well below the national average for the year of 2.12 per cent.[91]

But it would be a distortion to suggest that working-class activity was severely restricted after 1842. Chartism did revive, even if in a lower key, and the movement was deeply rooted enough in the district to survive until at least 1858. Sparrow's miners, still lower-paid than others, struck again from November 1842 to January 1843, and again in May 1843. Though they were beaten back to work on both occasions, in the autumn the Miners' Association began an active six months' campaign which led to the enrolment of virtually all North Staffordshire miners and another strike of the whole coalfield in April 1844. The 'antiquated forms of action', or 'archaic survivals from the past', as Rudé describes the actions of 15–16 August, 1842 did not preclude a capacity for sustained political and industrial organisation.[92]

The 1842 outbreak had brought to a dramatic conclusion the insurrectionary tradition of working-class protest, so far as the Potteries were concerned; although it was not an organised attempt at revolution, it seemed to show the futility of violence. That it occurred when it did was no doubt in part 'accidental' in so far as it was facilitated by failures of judgement by the authorities, but it also reflected the difficulties of a moment when troops were too stretched by events elsewhere to retain an effective presence in the Potteries continuously.

The contribution of the Potteries to the national crisis of 1842 was a memorable one. Not only was there the most destructive of urban outbreaks – perhaps, as Rudé says, the last great urban riot of the old kind, involving the pulling down of houses – and the most punitive reaction, but also the widespread strikes of 1842 began in the Potteries; the Potteries miners carried their turn-out north to Poynton in July; and the turn-out movement from the textile towns reached its furthest point south when the men from Leek attempted to enter Burslem on 16 August. The Potteries were on the periphery of the 'general strike' and made an important contribution to it, but Mick Jenkins misreads the evidence in claiming that Burslem and Hanley had already 'declared for the Charter' by 31 July.[94] The general strike for the Charter was not declared in the Potteries until 15 August, and it resulted in a moment of dramatic confrontation with authority which only lasted for just over twenty-four hours.

In another important respect, however, the Potteries' experience may confirm some of Jenkins' most interesting findings. The Staffordshire Special Commission took place at a time when the government was still determined on the need for vigorous repression. By March 1843, when the Lancaster Commission sat, a deliberate decision had been made, according to Jenkins, to play down the dangers of the 1842 disturbances and to reach an accommodation with the claims of labour by treating the Chartists more mildly. This may explain why Thomas Tancred's second report of the Midland Mining Commission, based on his visit to North Staffordshire in August 1843, and his inquiry into the cause of the outbreak there, was never published by the government, although it was known to his successor, H. S. Tremenheere.[95] Hence this tumultuous episode was allowed to fade away into the fuzziness of reminiscence without, apparently, any official inquiry into its causes. It became a legend, a symbol for the 'bad old days' in the later Victorian Potteries and clearly, in retrospect, a turning-point. Yet for the working men and women who participated in the events of that summer, it had been the point at which history failed to turn.

Viewed in the national perspective, the Potteries outbreak confirms that the pattern of events in industrial England in 1842 cannot simply be seen as a response to the leadership of the Lancashire vanguard, even in a district so closely adjacent as North Staffordshire. Moreover, what happened in the Potteries bore little resemblance to the nationally organised, centrally directed, General Strike of 1926. 1842 is best understood, not as a distant prelude to the more famous twentieth-century confrontation, but in its own terms, as the supreme moment of crisis in early Victorian Britain, when the State and the existing form of class society were briefly threatened by the challenge of a spontaneous popular resistance.

NOTES

(Place of publication London, except where stated)

1. Mark Hovell, *The Chartist Movement* (Manchester, 1918) pp. 259–63. Unfortunately the latest narrative history of Chartism gives only a similar cursory treatment – see J. T. Ward, *Chartism* (1973) pp. 160–4.

2. R. Challinor and B. Ripley, *The Miners' Association* (1968) p. 24; E. J. Hobsbawm, Introduction to F. Engels, *The Condition of the Working Class in England* (1969 edn) p. 14.

3. F. C. Mather, 'The General Strike of 1842: A Study of Leadership, Organisation and the Threat of Revolution during the Plug Plot Disturbances', in J. H. Porter (ed.), *Provincial Labour History* (Exeter, 1972) pp. 5–27, reprinted in R. Quinault and J. Stevenson (eds), *Popular Protest and Public Order* (1974) pp. 115–40.

4. Mick Jenkins, *The General Strike of 1842* (1980).

5. J. M. Golby, 'Public Order and Private Unrest: A Study of the 1842 Riots in Shropshire', *University of Birmingham Historical Journal* (1968) 157–69.

6. G. Kitson Clark, 'Hunger and Politics in 1842', *Journal of Modern History* (1953) 355–74; A. G. Rose, 'The Plug Riots of 1842 in Lancashire and Cheshire', *Transactions of the Lancashire and Cheshire Antiquarian Society* (1957) pp. 75–112; Mather, 'General Strike of 1842'; T. D. W. and Naomi Reid, 'The 1842 "Plug Plot" in Stockport', *International Review of Social History* (1979) 55–79; Jenkins, *General Strike of 1842*; see also Sykes's chapter 5 above.

7. F. B. Smith, 'The Plug Plot Prisoners and the Chartists', *Australian National University Historical Journal* (7 November 1970) 3–15.

8. T. Cooper, *The Life of Thomas Cooper* (1872; reprint Leicester, 1971)

pp. 186–206; C. Shaw, *When I Was A Child* (1903, reprint Wakefield, 1969 and Firle, Sussex, 1977) pp. 155–71.

9. F. C. Mather, *Public Order in the Age of the Chartists* (Manchester, 1959) *passim*; George Rudé, *The Crowd in History* (1964) pp. 187–91, and *Protest and Punishment* (1978) pp. 131–4; John Stevenson, *Popular Disturbances in England, 1700–1870* (1979) pp. 262–6.

10. PRO ASSI 6:6, Calendar of Prisoners for Trial; HO 27/68; PCOM 2/401, Stafford Gaol Register 1841–5 have full lists of those charged. During the following two years a further seven were transported, and five imprisoned, for offences during the outbreak – see *North Staffordshire Mercury*, 12 November 1842–3 August 1844, *passim*.

11. Rudé, *The Crowd in History*, pp. 189–90.

12. The next highest was Lancashire in 1842 with 12.14 per cent; Stevenson, *Popular Disturbances in England*, pp. 295–6.

13. Tunstall, Burslem, Hanley, Stoke-upon-Trent, Fenton, Longton.

14. S. Pollard, *The Genesis of Modern Management* (1968 p. 121; H. J. Perkin, *The Origins of Modern English Society 1780–1880* (1969) p. 110. But, unlike textile mills, these were 'not so much factories as workshops of craft and ancillary workers under one roof'. I owe this point to Harold Perkin.

15. Figures in this paragraph are calculated from the 1841 Census, Enumeration Abstract for Staffordshire, Parliamentary Papers (PP) 1843 vol. XXII pp. 164–75. There may well have been considerable under-registration, as the Census gives a total of only 14,704 pottery workers in north Staffordshire, compared with reliable contemporary estimates of around 20,000; but there is no reason to doubt the approximate truth of percentage calculations, assuming all categories of people were equally under-registered.

16. For a brief but easily accessible indictment of industrial conditions, see Engels, *Condition of the Working Class*, pp. 232–4, which is based on Samuel Scriven's report to the Children's Employment Commission of 1843, reprinted as *Children in the Potteries* (Staffordshire County Council Education Dept, 1975); see also Shaw, *When I Was a Child, passim*.

17. Wolstanton (including Tunstall), Burslem, Stoke-upon-Trent (including Hanley, Fenton, Longton).

18. W. Page (ed.), *Victoria County History of Staffordshire*, vol. I (1908) pp. 324–5.

19. *Children in the Potteries, passim*.

20. Information from Mr W. E. Townley, see his 'Urban administration and health : a case study of Hanley in the mid-nineteenth century', (Univ. of Keele M. A. thesis, 1969).

21. *North Staffordshire Mercury* 30 November 1839.

22. See H. Owen, *The Staffordshire Potter* (1901, reprint Bath, 1970) pp. 19–46; W. H. Warburton, *The History of Trade Union Organisation in the North Staffordshire Potteries* (1931) pp. 34–101; F. Burchill and R. Ross, *A History of the Potters' Union* (Stoke-on-Trent, 1977) pp. 58–74.

23. PP 1841 Census Occupation Abstracts for Staffordshire, 1844 gives the figure of 2850, or 8 per cent of the total labour-force in the three parishes. But, as with the potters, under-registration seems likely: it was claimed at the 1844 conference of the Miners' Association that there were 4000 members in north

Staffordshire (*Northern Star (NS)* 30 March 1844) and H. S. Tremenheere, Government Inspector of Mines and Collieries, thought there were 4500 miners in north Staffordshire (PP 1844, vol. 16, Report on Mines and Collieries, p. 60). Clearly numbers were growing, and some collieries were outside the three Potteries parishes. For some illuminating general considerations on the history of mining communities see the editor's introduction to R. Harrison (ed.), *Independent Collier* (Hassocks, Sussex, 1978) pp. 1–16. For evidence on the north Staffordshire miners, see PP 1842, vol. 15, Children's Employment Commission (Mines), report by S. Scriven; PP 1844, Report on Mines.

24. P. E. H. Hair, 'Mortality from Violence in British Coal Mines 1800–1850', *Economic History Review* (1968) 546. But this figure may conceal a lower death-rate in north Staffordshire compared with the much larger Black Country coalfield.

25. Such calculations are fraught with difficulty, and averages may be a poor guide. I have based mine on references cited above, and on the demands made in the strikes of 1831, 1842, 1844.

26. PP 1844, Occupation Abstracts. This calculation excludes the small rural coalfield around Cheadle, several miles to the east.

27. *Staffordshire Mercury* 28 May 1831.

28. Ibid., 4 June 1831; R. G. Kirby and A. E. Musson, *The Voice of the People: John Doherty 1798–1854* (Manchester, 1975) pp. 175, 231.

29. *Staffordshire Mercury* 4 December 1830, 29 January 1831; Stoke-on-Trent City Museum, Enoch Wood scrapbook, f. 206[A].

30. *NS* 16 July 1842: Letter from the Colliers of North Staffs. says they have been out for 'more than six weeks'.

31. Wolverhampton Public Library, Local Collection, Archives DX/84/18.

32. *North Staffordshire Mercury*, 16 July 1842.

33. Ibid., 16, 23, 30 July; PRO, HO 45/260.

34. Ibid., 23 July 1842.

35. Staffs. CRO, Sutherland Collection, D593/K/1/30, letter of William Steward to James Loch, 15 July 1842.

36. HO 45/260, f. 153.

37. See HO 45/260 and *North Staffordshire Mercury,* July–August 1842 for these events.

38. PRO, TS 11/602, copy of letter from the Committee of Operative Colliers to Mr Dean of Norton Colliery, 13 August 1842.

39. TS 11/599, prosecution brief, Queen *v.* Thomas Roberts and others; BM, Peel Papers, Add. MSS 40, 447, Graham to Peel, 20 November 1842.

40. HO 45/242 fos 1–12; Rose, 'Plug Riots of 1842', pp. 85–6; Kitson Clark, 'Hunger and Politics', 362.

41. *NS* 30 July and 6 August 1842.

42. Golby, 'Public Order and Private Unrest'; J. Burnett (ed.), *Useful Toil* (1974) p. 291. For the indictment against Lovekin, see PRO ASSI 6/5.

43. *NS* 23 and 30 July 1842.

44. *Bulletin of the Society for the Study of Labour History*, nos 19, 20, 22–5, 27 (1969–73): contributions by J. E. Williams, R. Challinor, C. P. Griffin, G. J. Barnsby.

45. *North Staffordshire Mercury,* 11 August–17 November 1838. The local press

records Richards's activities only from 1830, but see *NS* 24 September 1842: Address of the Defence Fund Committee for the Staffordshire Potteries.

46. For these events, see *NS* and *North Staffordshire Mercury*, 1839; HO 40/48; BM Add. MSS 34, 245; D. Vincent (ed.), *Testaments of Radicalism* (1977) 'Reminiscences of Thomas Dunning', p. 136.

47. *NS* 5 March 1842; TS 11/596 – John Richards's notebook.

48. *North Staffordshire Mercury*, 13 August 1842; *NS* 30 April 1842.

49. *North Staffordshire Mercury*, 24 June 1837.

50. Ibid., 31 December 1836.

51. *NS* 28 May 1842.

52. TS 11/600-1. There are two issues of the *Commonwealthsman* in HO 45/260.

53. *NS, Staffordshire Mercury*, 28 May 1842.

54. Ibid., 23 July, 26 February 1842.

55. *NS* 27 November, 20 November 1841; *North Staffordshire Mercury* 2 April, 30 July 1842.

56. *NS* 5 March, 23 April 1842.

57. *NS* 5 March, 9 July 1842.

58. HO 45/260, fos 94-103, 106-108, contains some letters suggesting conspiracy, which T. B. Rose, the Potteries stipendiary magistrate, considered to be forged by the man who allegedly found them. I share his opinion.

59. *NS* 5 March, 1842; *North Staffordshire Mercury*, 9 July 1842; *NS* 20 August 1842; *Staffordshire Mercury*, 16, 23 July, 20 August 1842.

60. TS 11/596, Queen *v.* Samuel Robinson and others, evidence of Thomas Smallwood; *NS* and *North Staffordshire Mercury*, 18 June 1842.

61. PRO, MH 12/11196 and 11460; *NS* 20 August 1842.

62. *North Staffordshire Mercury*, 18 June, 9 July 1842. Etruria was the Wedgwoods' factory village near Hanley.

63. HO 45/260, f. 127; *NS* 6 August 1842.

64. TS 11/602; *NS* 9 July 1842.

A note on terminology: I have been persuaded, after discussions with colleagues, that 'riot' is an indiscriminate and legalistic term, most often used by the 'respectable classes'. I have therefore tried to avoid using it, where possible. The word 'outbreak' is, I hope, value-free and has the advantage of being a contemporary usage, e.g. Cooper, *Life*, p. 197; TS 11/601, John Cleave to Thomas Cooper, 17 July 1842: 'A report has just reached us that the Potteries are in outbreak – it may only be rumour.'

65. Cooper, *Life*, pp. 187–92, 197.

66. Cooper, *Life*, p. 190, wrongly says 'the Chartist Committee in Manchester'. The strike call must have come from the meeting described in Jenkins, *General Strike of 1842*, p. 145.

67. The fullest and most accurate narrative of the events of 15–16 August, which I largely follow, is in *North Staffordshire Mercury*, 20 August 1842.

68. Cf. Gwyn Williams, *The Merthyr Rising of 1831* (1978) for the unpopularity of these courts for the recovery of small debts.

69. *Staffordshire Mercury*, 20 August 1842.

70. See the report of J. A. Wise to the Home Office on 22 August, HO 45/260, fos 329–32.

71. Pistols were fired during the outbreak, according to some reports, but there was no suggestion that anyone suffered injury as a result.

72. ASSI 6:6; Calendar of Prisoners for Trial.

73. *NS* 24 September 1842.

74. *English Chartist Circular*, 132, August 1843 on the Lancashire prisoners, cit. Smith, 'Plug Plot Prisoners', 12.

75. ASSI 6:6.

76. Rudé, *Protest and Punishment*, p. 52.

77. *North Staffordshire Mercury*, 30 July 1842.

78. Ibid., 22 January 1842.

79. TS 11/596, Queen *v.* Joseph Whiston etc.

80. Rudé, *The Crowd in History, passim.*

81. 20 August 1842.

82. Including seven who were sentenced after the Special Commission.

83. *English Chartist Circular,* no. 146 (n.d.); HO 45/260, fos 287–8, 374; *NS* 20 August 1842 (4th edn).

84. Sir Leon Radzinowicz, *History of the English Criminal Law,* vol. IV (1968) p. 250; *North Staffordshire Mercury,* 22 October 1842.

85. Thomas Cooper, 'A Brief Memoir of W. S. Ellis, The Chartist Exile', *English Chartist Circular,* nos 145–150, 152, (n.d.), *c.* November–December 1843.

86. *NS* 24 April 1841; MH 12/11460; ASSI 6:6; Tasmania RO, CON 33/38 9102.

87. *NS* 23 December 1843; *North Staffordshire Mercury,* 17 June 1843, *NS* 10 May 1845; *North Staffordshire Mercury,* 5 October 1844; *People's Paper* 16, 23 October, 1852; *NS* 8 June 1850.

88. William Scarratt, *Old Times in the Potteries* (Stoke-on-Trent, 1906; reprint Wakefield, 1969) pp. 131–2; ASSI 6:6.

89. HO 45/260, fos 474–85.

90. *NS* 13 August 1842; *Potters' Examiner and Workman's Advocate, passim.*

91. *NS, Staffordshire Mercury,* 1848, *passim;* HO 45/2410; Stevenson, *Popular Disturbances in England,* pp. 295–6.

92. *People's Paper, passim; Staffordshire Mercury;* 1842–3; *NS* 1843–4; Rudé, *The Crowd in History,* p. 190.

93. Rudé, *Protest and Punishment,* p. 243.

94. Jenkins, *General Strike of 1842,* p. 62.

95. Ibid., pp. 219–39; PP 1844, Reports of Commissioners into Mines and Collieries, Staffordshire, pp. 54, 62. I have not located Tancred's report on North Staffordshire.

7. Some Organisational and Cultural Aspects of the Chartist Movement in Nottingham

JAMES EPSTEIN

THE Chartist Movement came together with great speed and intensity in 1838, although the agitation was rooted in an established tradition of working-class radicalism and emerged from a series of overlapping struggles dating from the years of the reform agitation. Early Chartist protest was characterised by a high degree of spontaneity along with a sense of imminent and decisive class confrontation. However, in the wake of the first National Convention and Petition, the 'monster' demonstrations and abortive risings, it became increasingly apparent that the campaign for working-class political rights was destined to be a protracted affair. While the movement never fully recaptured its earlier spontaneity or confrontationalist tone, in the 1840s Chartists turned to the task of building an effective national organisation, establishing the National Charter Association as the first working-class political 'party'. At the same time, local Chartists gave increased expression to the cultural side of their radical commitment. Throughout the country they formed Chartist schools and democratic chapels, co-operative stores, burial clubs, temperance societies. A constellation of leisure activities was provided locally: regular lectures, debates, newspaper readings, soirées and tea-parties, annual dinners to celebrate the birthdays of such radical luminaries as Paine and Hunt. This cultural broadening, the creation of what might be termed a 'movement culture', was crucial to binding Chartism together in the 1840s.[1] It provided a context within which the potential for creating a society based upon alternative social values to those becoming dominant under industrial capitalism might be suggested.

While Chartism's more insurrectionary moments (1839–40, 1842, 1848) have captured the attention of historians, relatively little interest has been shown in the movement's self-sustaining cultural and organisational achievement. In general, Chartism's challenge at this cultural level was complementary rather than antithetical to the movement's more overt challenge through mass protest and direct action. Mass political action was itself dependent upon cultural forms and community solidarities established over many years. Certainly many Chartists who advocated the need for working-class education, co-operation, temperance or religion assumed leading roles in the turbulent events of 1842 and 1848. Moreover, it would be mistaken to view Chartism's cultural dimension as simply a holding operation. The cultural sphere was one of vital class self-definition and continual conflict. Bourgeois efforts to assert control and influence over a range of cultural activity were integrally linked to the complex process of reproducing relations of economic, social and political dominance within early Victorian urban society. This is not to deny that an artisan tradition which stressed the importance of collective self-help and 'moral' improvement often remained ambiguously poised between revolutionary class politics and a more gradualist, or at times even class-collaborative orientation. But the 'moral' face of Chartism cannot be regarded merely as a prefiguration of Gladstonian liberalism. The strong emphasis many Chartists placed upon the desirability of working-class self-improvement did not in itself represent an accommodation to middle-class liberalism, an acceptance of middle-class social values or concepts of 'respectability'. What needs consideration is the content, the meanings with which working-class radicals endowed their political and cultural activity. Some estimate must be made of the extent to which such activity constituted an oppositional alternative to middle-class cultural initiatives and values, a form of counter-hegemony.

The broadening of Chartism's cultural involvement was central to the flourishing of the movement in the early 1840s, especially in countering tendencies towards sectarianism. It could, however, also create difficulties in maintaining both national and local Chartist unity and direction. Such concerns could divert radicals away from the central thrust of Chartism, away from the primary demand for working-class political power and the agency of the mass platform. On the other hand, the incorporation of working-class co-operative, educational or temperance tendencies within the framework of the local Chartist Movement proved important in undercutting the attraction which alternative movements of working-class improvement held for many radicals. Activists were able to fulfil a wide range of political and cultural goals within one movement. The key, however, was the subordination of various social and cultural objects to the political agitation for the suffrage, and the continued openness of the movement to 'members unlimited'. Only in this way could they avert the twin dangers of fragmentation and of retreat into an introspective artisan élitism.

This essay sets out to discuss the character of local Chartist protest in one locality, with particular reference to the early 1840s. It seeks to suggest something of the texture of local radical culture and organisation, to celebrate its achievement and to offer some indication of its limitations. No locality can be regarded as 'typical' during the Chartist period. The Chartists at Nottingham and the surrounding district established one of the country's staunchest centres of support for the National Charter Association. They also sustained a vibrant local movement which offered a diverse range of cultural and political activity. However, the highly integrated cultural achievement at Nottingham was not an isolated phenomenon. Nor was it a form of working-class radicalism peculiar to impoverished domestic workers, although it may have been more typical of Chartist protest in localities where the movement drew its strength primarily from workers engaged in one industry. Above all, Chartism at Nottingham, as elsewhere, represented the culmination of a tradition of artisan culture and radical protest.

I

The Chartist Movement at Nottingham took its character to a large degree from the framework knitters of the town and district. Somewhere between 20 and 25 per cent of the town's population of 53,000 was economically dependent upon the framework knitting industry. The surrounding knitting villages – Arnold, Old Basford, Bulwell, Calverton, Carlton, Hucknall Torkard – demonstrated an even higher degree of economic dependence upon the knitting trade.[2] The framework knitters, or stockingers, were among the most impoverished sections of the English working-class, comparable perhaps only with the Lancashire handloom weavers. Framework knitting was a domestic industry in which the entire family often co-operated in the various stages of production. Sons still followed their fathers into the trade, although apprenticeship was virtually extinct. The struggle to preserve some measure of the stockinger's artisan status, to maintain some form of craft control and protection, had been lost several decades before. Technically framework knitting had changed little since the seventeenth century. Labour had been subordinated to the power of capital upon the technical basis of handicraft, and this remained the case into the second half of the nineteenth century. The ever-increasing dominance of slop work, particularly 'cut-up' hose, however, rendered most of the finer skills of the stockinger redundant, reducing much work to a semi-skilled level. In the face of unregulated competition, branch after branch of the trade succumbed to the power of spurious manufacture.[3] At Nottingham there was a concentration of both 'cut-up' work and the most highly skilled, and most highly paid, work making silk hose and gloves.

Despite the total openness of their trade and the absence of nearly all aspects of craft control, many knitters retained vestiges of an artisan consciousness, a continuing sense of craft pride and aspirations to re-capture some measure of their former independence. Knitting continued to be regarded as a 'trade'; and stockingers continued to form and sustain trade union associations. As one stockinger giving evidence to the Royal Commission on the condition of framework knitters (1845) observed: 'There is that feeling amongst us, low as we are, that if we could maintain our independency any way, we would willingly do so.'[4]. The gulf, how-ever, between such aspirations and the realities of the knitters' condition was enormous. Dependency was the mark of the stockinger. Very few knitters owned their own frame. Frames usually had to be rented from one or another species of middleman, often acting for a merchant hosier, who also supplied the raw materials for production. Not only did this allow the hosier to pass on a substantial part of the cost of production to the worker, but also it gave hosiers and middlemen a critical means of control over the stockinger and his trade. The hosiery industry was dominated by a handful of large and long-established family firms, some of which employed several thousand frames. The price schedules of these large merchant hosiers tended to set the standard wage rates throughout the trade. These prices were subject, however, to constant reductions and undercutting by hosiers, middlemen and small manufacturers, particu-larly the infamous bag hosiers who operated in the industrial villages. The trade suffered from a state of chronic under-employment, as well as seasonal and cyclical unemployment. While in effect stockingers were wage labourers, their form of payment remained that of a price for commodities sold rather than for labour power sold. This, along with other aspects of industrial organisation – for instance, stockingers often had to pay for their articles to be finished – perhaps helped to sustain a consciousness among stockingers of themselves as artisans, petty commodity producers, rather than strictly proletarians.

Knitters did retain of course some control over their hours and pace of work. 'Saint Monday' was still commonly observed; and some manufacturers complained of the stockingers' independence and their 'loose abandoned habits'. One hosier observed:

> the men are all independent of you. They work at home, and work when they like; and they are so perfectly independent of you, that you have no control over them. It is one of the most convenient trades, and in consequence of its convenience it is abused . . . it brings that sort of independence on the part of the men, that when they have got your work, they can do just as they like with it.[5]

But the overwhelming impression left by the statement of stockingers upon their material and moral condition is that of acute crisis often verging on despair. Benjamin Humphries, leading Chartist and secretary to the Nottingham knitters' trade association, described how stockingers after working through the night on Thursday and Friday and standing with no work from Saturday to Monday returned to their frames.

> Then they go to it again in the same frame, and work all hours. This all deteriorates the mind of man; he becomes as it were, I do not know what; more like an ass than a man, from his excessive labour, and want of time to study, and to learn, to intermix with social society.

'It is true that they [stockingers] *exist*', commented Nottingham's Revd James Orange, 'but it is in a manner utterly inconceivable to a stranger.'[6] In any assessment of the politics and culture of Nottingham Chartism we must always remember the dire conditions of existence which governed the lives of thousands of working people, and the material, cultural and psychological limitations this imposed upon working-class organisation. The knitters' experience, however, was merely an extreme example of a more general process taking place at varying paces over the whole spectrum of artisan trades. The increased control of merchant capital over labour, the advance of free competition, the rise of mass production, the undermining of traditional trade skills and overstocking of labour, the increased division and intensification of labour were all interrelated aspects of the development of nineteenth-century industrial capitalism. Similarly Nottingham's knitters brought to Chartist protest a sense of 'moral' economy, a concern to limit competition and an insistence upon the need for regulation, underpinned by notions of a 'fair' wage for their labour, which was part of a widely held working-class critique of industrial capitalism.

Machine lace manufacture was Nottingham's other major industry.[7] An offshoot of the stocking frame, lace machinery had been adapted to steam-power and factory production, although before 1850 the units of production remained relatively small and hand machinery continued to predominate. The large, steam-powered lace factories were located outside Nottingham in the surrounding suburbs of Carrington, New Lenton, New Radford and New Basford. Smaller workshops using hand machines were situated in Nottingham and the suburbs. Most fancy lace still had to be produced on hand machines. A high level of skill was needed in the manufacture of lace on both hand and steam-powered machinery. Lace hands were considerably better-off than stockingers, although wages in the lace trades declined sharply after the heady days of the early 1820s. There was a general move to larger-scale production and an increased concentration of capital ownership. The eclipse of the independent machine owner was particularly marked in the plain lace branch. Many lace hands in the factories outside Nottingham had been recruited from either the knitting trade or from hand lace manufacture; many no doubt returned to the stocking frame or hand lace machinery when their eyesight no longer met the severe demands of factory lace making. The extent to which lace hands formed a separate élite stratum within Nottingham's working-class during the Chartist period is questionable.[8]

There was, of course, a high degree of interrelatedness between 'traditional' and innovatory forms of industrial organisation, between steam-power and hand technology in the development of British industrialisation.[9] The lace industry created many more jobs outside the factory than inside. The women employed as outworkers in the finishing sections of the trade (mending, embroidering or running) which were centred in the town of Nottingham far outnumbered the men employed in lace factories. Female labour was integral to both the lace and knitting trades. In knitting, as in lace, most women were employed in finishing (seaming, stitching, embroidering or chevening). Some women worked stocking frames alongside their husbands. In lace factories and workshops with hand machines women and children were employed winding, threading and removing lace from machines. An exceptionally high proportion of Nottingham's female population was employed. This was due both to the large demand for female labour in Nottingham's two major industries and the necessity for women to supplement their husbands' meagre earnings. Along with their children, labouring women represented the most exploited section of Nottingham's working-class and played an important part in the local Chartist Movement.[10]

Chartism at Nottingham drew its strength from a working-class community dominated by two closely related trades; a community packed into the back streets and courts of perhaps the most overcrowded town in England. Nottingham's working-class had a mixed residential and industrial character. The ties of occupation, kinship and neighbourhood were brought into the local Chartist Movement which became the political expression of this working-class community.

II

As Nottingham was a major organisational centre of the hosiery trade and a county town, so it became the centre of a Chartist district. During the early Chartist days, the Nottingham Chartists helped to organise Chartist groups in the surrounding villages and suburbs. During the National Holiday of August 1839 and again during the general strike of August 1842 working people from the outlying knitting villages converged on Nottingham. With the threat of serious riot or possible insurrection in early 1840, General Napier cut off the roads into Nottingham from the villages of Arnold, Sutton-in-Ashfield and Mansfield.[11] At any of the mass Chartist demonstrations at Nottingham the surrounding villages and suburbs were well-represented. When the movement was reorganised in the early 1840s around the National Charter Association (NCA), regular delegate meetings were held for the Nottingham district. Much of the central planning of the Nottinghamshire movement went on at Nottingham. The Nottinghamshire NCA supported a series of full-time lecturers - John Mason, William Dean Taylor, E. P. Mead.

The hosiery industry dominated the lives of thousands of working people in Nottinghamshire, Leicestershire and Derbyshire, and provided an ever larger network of association. A sense of occupational identity was as important to the stockingers of the three counties as any strictly local identity. They shared the same grievances and suffered the same poverty. They had often come together in their trade union organisations to voice common demands and to resist the undercutting of their wage rates. At the end of 1838 the Three Counties Framework Knitters

Union was revived; at the same time political links were renewed. Contact between the Chartist leaders of the three counties, particularly the Nottinghamshire and Leicestershire leadership, was close, as were the political sentiments of the stockingers. As early as March 1839 delegates came together at Nottingham to form the Three Counties Chartist Association; it was also resolved to start a Chartist journal for the east Midlands based upon co-operative share holding. In 1840 the Chartists of the three counties formed the Charter Association for the Midlands Counties as part of the NCA; they held regular delegate meetings and maintained an executive council at Nottingham. Plans for a Chartist journal eventually materialised in 1841 with the publication of the excellent but short-lived *Midland Counties Illuminator*, published from Leicester by Thomas Cooper.[12]

The Nottingham Chartists played an active role in the reorganisation of the national movement in the early 1840s. They were firm supporters of the NCA, the *Northern Star* and the national leadership of Feargus O'Connor. According to the Revd George Harrison of Calverton, the Nottingham district's representative at the National Convention, by spring 1842 there were between 1000 and 1200 NCA members at Nottingham organised in eight localities meeting at local taverns, in addition to the group meeting at the Chartist Democratic Chapel. Harrison estimated that there were between twenty and thirty Chartist associations in Nottinghamshire's industrial villages and between two and three thousand NCA members in the county. The question of Chartist 'membership' is, however, problematic. It is unclear exactly what NCA membership meant in practice. Certainly many working-class radicals at Nottingham would have found it difficult to meet the requirement of regular weekly subscriptions no matter how small – a point which George Black, a local knitter, stressed at the founding conference of the NCA. On the other hand, the NCA executive commended the Nottingham NCA members for being one of the few localities to maintain regular national subscriptions. In early 1842 the *Nottingham Mercury* reported that at nearby Sutton-in-Ashfield, 'a remarkable stronghold of the Chartists', more than 800 workers were subscribing a penny a week to the Chartist funds, 'notwithstanding the great distress' and the fact that the local stockingers were 'steeped in poverty'. Still, sending delegates to conferences, supporting local lecturers, and renting meeting places cost money, and there must have been a material threshold to formal Chartist 'membership' which many Nottingham workers could not cross. Jacob Bostock, a local knitter and active Chartist, noted that many would support the Convention (in 1842) financially who did not regularly contribute to the NCA.[13] At best NCA membership provides merely a very rough comparative index of local Chartist strength. Of towns of comparable size only the Leicester Chartists, under the direction of the remarkable Thomas Cooper, boasted a larger membership.

The influence of a movement like Chartism cannot be gauged by counting dues-paying members. The latent support for Chartism, the powerful force of dreams too long deferred, dramatically reasserted itself at moments like the summer of 1842. Writing to Thomas Cooper, in late July 1842, George White, one of the movement's most steadfast leaders, scoffed at the 'card retailers' of the NCA Executive: 'Poor Campbell [NCA national secretary] always estimated the progress of the movement according to the number of cards sold and paid for . . .' White reported that he was addressing immense meetings in the Birmingham district, 'and the universal cry is "we must have the Charter" – and Wonderful! oh Wonderful, not one in a thousand has got a *Card*.'[14] There is, however, a useful distinction to be drawn between working men and women who attended Chartist demonstrations, signed the National Petitions, stayed away from work during the National Holiday or the 'general' strikes of 1842 and a smaller group who attended weekly meetings of one of the Chartist associations, paid regular subscriptions, remained active during lulls in mass activity, sent their children to the Chartist school, attended Chartist teas and dinners and for whom Chartist involvement became part of a life-style. Obviously no rigid barrier separates these two levels of support, there was a fluid relationship between them.

General working-class support for the principles of the Charter at Nottingham is hardly in question. While estimates vary, the largest Chartist demonstrations at Nottingham drew between 20,000 and 30,000 people, including a large number of women and children (a point often stressed in the middle-class press). Nottingham contributed 17,000 signatures to the first Chartist Petition and the county of Nottinghamshire over 40,000 to the second Petition. Funds for the national rent to support the Convention and for the National Defence Fund were collected from all the surrounding villages and suburbs of Nottingham, with Mansfield and Sutton, Hucknall, Carrington, Arnold, Old and New Basford donating the largest sums relative to population. Taverns, reading-rooms, political associations, factories and workshops all appear in lists for the national rent and defence fund. If signing the Petition, attending outdoor demonstrations and occasionally contributing a copper to the cause constituted being a Chartist, then there was a sense in which the Nottinghamshire working-class was by and large Chartist. In 1839 John Tomlinson, sinker-maker and secretary to the Sutton-in-Ashfield WMA, commented: 'in no place is there more unanimity with regard to the principles of the Charter for nineteen-twentieths of the population are in favour of them.'[15]

While it is difficult to penetrate the anonymity of the mass support for the Charter at Nottingham, something can be discovered about the occupations of local activists and those who joined the NCA. Through a sample (n = 176) based primarily on nominations to the NCA council, some idea of the occupations of the most active Chartists from the town of Nottingham emerges. The results of this occupational breakdown are not surprising. Stockingers dominate, representing 34 per cent of the sample (21 per cent of employed males over twenty years old at Nottingham were knitters according to the 1841 Census). As in other localities, shoemakers (5.5 per cent of employed males over twenty) were particularly prominent, composing 17.6 per cent of the sample. The shoemakers formed their own branch of the NCA at Nottingham, and the local shoemakers' society affiliated to the NCA.[16] Tailors, cabinet-makers, workers involved in the building trades and trades linked to the hosiery industry – needle-makers, sinker-makers, framesmiths – are all represented.[17] Lace-makers (9 per cent of the employed males over twenty in the *town* of Nottingham) compose 18.8 per cent of this sample. Most of these lace workers presumably worked large hand machines in the town's workshops. The NCA samples from the factory districts on the outskirts of Nottingham – New Radford, New Lenton, Carrington – are too small to draw any firm conclusions; however, of the twenty-nine names we have, the majority (seventeen) are lace hands. The Chartist Movement in the lace suburbs, particularly in the populous Radford area, appears to have lacked the cohesiveness and strength of the Nottingham movement. The relatively high proportion of NCA members at Nottingham who were lace-makers, however, suggests that residential segregation, moving out of the older neighbourhoods of the town, was more important in determining the character of organised Chartism in these districts than the mere circumstance of the lace workers' higher wages relative to stockingers.[18] Another index of Chartist support, contributions to various Chartist funds, indicates that the lace hands at Fisher's New Radford factory (the largest in the district), Robinson's New Basford factory and Birkin and Biddle's New Basford factory were clearly supporters of Chartist principles.[19] These were among the factories which Chartists tried to turn out in the summers of 1839 and 1842, with only mixed success. It must be remembered, however, that factory hands operated under a much higher degree of direct employer control and surveillance than knitters. Finally a sample of members of the Chartist Land Company (1847–8) from the Nottingham district demonstrates an even more diverse spectrum of working-class support than the NCA lists, with lace hands constituting 26.5 per cent of members.[20] Thus, contrary to the view of several Nottinghamshire historians, there was widespread support for Chartism among the lace hands of the district.

The Chartists in the knitting villages outside Nottingham – Arnold, Bulwell, Old Basford, Calverton, Hucknall and Lambley – were nearly all stockingers.[21] A sample of NCA membership (n = 76) at Sutton-in-Ashfield and Mansfield reflects a similar overwhelming predominance of stockingers (77.6 per cent). In all these localities there was an extraordinary degree of economic dependence upon the knitting trade.

The lower-middle-class element in the NCA samples at Nottingham and the surrounding districts – bakers, publicans, butchers, and so on – perhaps indicates that Chartist appeals to shopkeepers to support their cause found a few receptive individuals.[22] Some of these 'middle-class' Chartists directly serviced the movement: for instance, James Sweet's barbershop and booksellers, Mrs Smith's radical newsagency at the 'Tradesman's Mart', or the landlords of several Chartist drinking establishments who were also NCA members. Many of the Chartists who ran various business concerns had been, and were shortly to become again, working artisans: William Swann who ran a temperance hotel where Chartists met had been a cabinet-maker; Elmer Rollett who ran a newsagency and Chartist coffee-rooms had been a knitter; Henry Dorman, knitter, opened another temperance hotel in 1843, where Chartists congregated; and even James Sweet had worked as a tailor. The leadership of the Nottingham movement was drawn almost exclusively from the ranks of the working-class. There were a few middle-class men active in leadership roles: Samuel Fletcher, a lace agent who emigrated to the United States in 1840; James Sweet who was among the movement's most trusted leaders; George Harrison from Calverton who was one of the most popular local Chartist speakers. Sweet and Harrison often served as Nottingham delegates to national Chartist conferences in the 1840s. But generally the local leaders, Chartists who regularly spoke at meetings, attended delegate conferences and served on various committees, were drawn from the same occupations as were NCA members, although there was an even more pronounced dominance of stockingers at the leadership level. One of the striking features of the Nottingham movement was its continuity of leadership. Many of the men who assumed leadership roles in 1838-9 continued as prominent Chartists into the 1840s.[23] Although Nottingham had a long-standing tradition of revolutionary politics, most of the town's Chartist activists emerged from the struggles of the post-1832 period: the campaign for an unstamped press, the defence of the Dorchester Labourers, the various attempts to form a general trades union, the opposition to the new Poor Law, the universal suffrage movement and O'Connor's Radical Associations.

There is a general lack of information about the occupations of the women who took an active part in the local Chartist Movement. In late 1838 the Female Political Union was established at Nottingham to co-operate with the Birmingham Female Political Union, 'and to aid their husbands, brothers, &c., in their present arduous struggle to establish the People's Charter.' A group of Chartist women from Nottingham joined the NCA and sent in nominations to the NCA council, in itself somewhat unusual, but they did not include their occupations. It must be assumed that the majority were seamers, stitchers, lace runners, menders or knitters. Quite a few, such as Martha Sweet, appear to have been the wives of active Chartists.[24]

The ages of Nottingham Chartists nominated to the NCA council also tell us something about the Chartist commitment. The median age was thirty-five (average age 36.8). The large majority were between the ages of twenty-five and forty. We also have the ages of twenty-five workers (nineteen knitters, four lace-makers, one labourer and one nail-maker) brought to trial for their part in the 1842 general strike, all of whom were given financial aid by the local Chartists. Their average age was just over thirty. From a sample of forty-seven NCA members forty were married, of whom thirty had children (average number of children 2.7). Clearly the movement was not made up of youths, but 'mature' adults, with something to lose through their involvement in radical politics.[25]

III

In March 1840 James Sweet remarked in confidence: 'They [the Chartists] are completely beat by having too much force against them. If there had not been so much, there would have been something done to be talked about.' The same month, following the Manchester conference at which the Chartist Movement registered a decisive shift away from insurrectionist action towards national reorganisation, it was reported that George Black, Nottingham's delegate to this conference, 'actually *cried*, saying he could not face his constituents, who had expected a movement immediately.' The knitter William Kibbey sold his gun.[26] The Nottinghamshire Chartists, particularly the group which met at the King George on Horseback and which included the knitters Black, Kibbey, John Peters and the shoemaker William Lilley, had been closely involved in the plans for insurrection which surfaced in the dark winter months of 1839–40. The failure of the Chartist Movement to win working-class political power in the summer of 1839 led to schisms within the Nottingham movement over the question of 'ulterior' action. The quarrels did not last long, but were illustrative of the frustrations of Chartist men and women who had hoped for more – Chartists temporarily divorced from a mass following. At a meeting of the female Chartists in April 1840, one woman observed: 'the times were dead again'en', but she hoped they would soon have the opportunity to come out again for universal suffrage and annual parliaments.[27]

In November 1839 the Nottingham Chartists obtained the Democratic or Chartist Chapel which had formerly been a Methodist and then Primitive Baptist Chapel. The Chapel which held around 800 people became the most important centre of Chartist activity and organisation in the early 1840s. In 1841 a letter from 'A Chartist Shopkeeper', published in the *Midland Counties Illuminator*, described the range of activity organised around the Democratic Chapel.[28] Firstly the writer noted the problems which working-class radicals faced in finding a regular meeting place.

> Like our brethern in most other towns, the Chartists of Nottingham had great difficulty in obtaining a room to hold their meetings in; all the large ones being in the hands of persons whose minds were prejudiced against us on account of our being called 'Chartists'.

On Sundays the Chapel was opened for religious services 'and the whole truth is fearlessly preached there in.' The writer assured readers that at the Democratic Chapel: '*There is no letting of seats*; those who come first sit where they please. *No poking of a plate under your nose in the pews; and no paid parsons!*' The democratic character of the proceedings at the Chartists' Chapel was in marked contrast to most middle-class religious and educational institutions in Nottingham. Even the Primitive Methodists had a very high ratio of rented pews. On Monday evenings the Chartist Association transacted its business. The Chartist Total

Abstinence Society met at the Chapel on Tuesday evenings. Wednesday evening was devoted to Chartist singing practice. On Saturday evenings Chartists met for 'mutual instruction' and the reading of Chartist newspapers. A tract society was being formed to spread political information among the labouring population and a library 'which will materially assist us in our onward progress to establish practical religion and liberty' had already been established. During the day the Chapel was occupied 'by one of our brethern', William Russell, who conducted the Nottingham Democratic school. On Sundays Mary Ann Abbott organised the Chartist Sunday school.[29] The Chartist concept of education was highly political. Children were to be taught their historical rights and learn of the struggles of their forefathers for democratic principles, in preparation for engaging their political opponents in debate.

> There [at the Democratic school] the children are taught their duty to one another, and to society in general; and will be taught to put a proper value upon *men and things*. In due time they will hear *when and how* their forefathers were plundered of their liberty and property; – of the struggles which have taken place from time to time to regain their rights! – of the rise and progress of the Chartist movement; and the principles which are embodied in that document entitled 'the People's Charter', will be fully shewn them. The excellent little tract, 'What is a Chartist?' will be their daily study until they are made quite conversant with the subject; and by the time they leave the school, they will be enabled to meet either Whig or Tory in fair argument, and beat them into the bargain.

An adult school had also been formed and met two or three evenings a week to receive instruction in reading, writing and the principles of Chartism. The expenses of this adult school were to be met through voluntary contributions from members.

One of the most important achievements of the local Chartist Movement at Nottingham, as elsewhere, was the challenge it presented to the existing social order not merely in terms of riot and insurrection, but in terms of providing alternative cultural institutions and activities for working people. From the outset the Nottingham Chartists had emphasised the need for working-class education and information. The objectives of the Nottingham WMA, published in summer 1838, included the promotion of the education of the rising generation, the formation of a Chartist library, the support for a cheap and honest press and the collection of information concerning the wages, conditions and habits of labour.[30] James Sweet, the local movement's foremost advocate of educational and moral improvement (as well as being a staunch O'Connorite), signed his regular column in the *Midland Counties Illuminator* 'A Chartist and Something More'. He urged readers:

> *Prepare your minds*, then, my countrymen, to encounter opposition and calumny . . . Be ready, upon all occasions, to give a reason for the faith that is within you; and tell those who inquire what you want, that you are seeking after truth . . .[31]

The appeal to 'reason' was characteristic of a certain style of working-class radical discourse. The call for Chartists to prepare their minds was not merely in order to convince others of the justness of their claims, much less to prove their fitness for the suffrage, but to ensure that once the Charter was won that working people would be in a position to use their political rights in the best interests of democratic society and to guard against the reimposition of tyrannical government. The Chartist Movement provided a context within which articulate, self-educated working men might employ their talents. The local movement was by no means dependent upon the services of the district's full-time NCA lecturer, as local Chartists toured the district lecturing on political and historical topics. The needle-maker Joseph Burbage and the tailor Cornelius Fowkes lectured at the Democratic Chapel on subjects such as 'Finance and the Funding System' and 'The Robberies committed at, and subsequent to, the Reformation, on the Poor of England'. Jonathan Brown, a lace-maker, lectured at Dorman's Temperance Hotel on the 'History of the Rise and Progress of Jacobinism in Nottingham'. In addition to the library at the Democratic Chapel, the Chartists who met at the King George on Horseback established their own library. Chartist schools and libraries were also formed at nearby Arnold, Calverton, Mansfield and Alfreton.[32]

The Chartist Movement offered a mixture of formal and informal educational modes: schools and lectures, communal newspaper readings, debates and free discussion. However, as Richard Johnson has noted, the 'key feature' of working-class radical educational experience was its 'informality'. 'The typical forms were improvised, haphazard and therefore ephemeral . . . Educational forms were closely related to other activities or inserted within them, temporally and spatially.'[33] A typical Chartist gathering consisted of a group of radicals reading from the

Northern Star or one of the other Chartist or local papers, followed by a discussion of the contents. Nottingham's working-class taverns, coffee-houses and reading-rooms provided meeting places for such discussion groups. The Chartists who formed an NCA branch at the Sign of the Feargus O'Connor announced that every Sunday evening at seven o'clock the *Northern Star* and *Evening Star* (O'Connor's short-lived daily journal) would be read aloud. These readings would end at nine o'clock and the rest of the evening be devoted to free discussion. Members were asked to give one week's notice of any topic which they wished to have discussed. In the summer of 1842 the *Evening Star* was read between seven and nine on Monday evenings at the Democratic Chapel; admittance was free, although there was a one penny voluntary subscription. Tuesday evenings were given over to 'democratic discussion' and the reading of other daily papers and the local press.[34] The low, voluntary subscriptions to educational activities at the Democratic Chapel contrasted with the mandatory, higher subscriptions demanded at most middle-class educational institutions set-up for the working-class. Chartist activities at Nottingham were usually scheduled for the weekend or the early part of the week, rarely on Thursday or Friday evenings when stockingers often worked late into the night. The Chartist press was central to much Chartist activity. Local Chartists exercised considerable influence over the fortunes of the radical press. On several occasions the Nottingham Chartists burnt copies of radical journals as a symbol that they had withdrawn their support from a paper which they felt had reneged upon radical principles, and called for such papers to be banned from working-class reading-rooms.[35]

The Chartist and other working-class educational institutions at Nottingham were established in opposition to middle-class efforts to provide 'useful' knowledge and propagate a middle-class conception of the virtues of self-help.[36] Of course most working-class children did not attend the Chartist day school or Sunday school, but received the only formal education they were to acquire at Sunday schools associated with the town's various religious denominations. Nottingham's bourgeoisie shared in 'the early Victorian obsession with the education of the poor', in the attempt to assert control through educational means over working-class patterns of thought and behaviour.[37] However, their success at providing educational institutions for working-class adults fell short of their ambitions. For instance, both the Artisans' Library, founded in 1824, and the Nottingham Mechanics' Institute, founded in 1837, were under the firm control of the town's Whig élite; both institutions failed to attract working-class membership. A new Mechanics' Institute, 'which forms one of the ornaments of the town', was completed in 1845 at the cost of over £6000. Thomas Wakefield (hosier, former mayor and one of the most prominent representatives of the town's Whig oligarchy) 'expressed his confidence that the working classes felt grateful for all that had been done for them'.[38] Whether they felt grateful or not, few working men found their way into the Grecian corridors of the Nottingham Mechanics' Institute. Working men still preferred their own reading-rooms and libraries centred on various taverns throughout the town. The Chartist Henry Dorman at a meeting called to establish an Operatives' Hall stressed the need for having a place where working people could meet. He explained that the great obstacle to taking rooms at the Mechanics' Institute was the ban on the discussion of political subjects:

> he held this to be a barrier at once to their occupation by the operative classes. (Hear.) He considered the question of politics to be paramount in importance to them . . . that the doings of the body of working men, and this salutary check could not be available, unless some place of meeting were in the hands of the people. (Hear.) At the same time, he would not for one moment have a political or party tinge thrown upon the undertaking generally – he merely wished to make it understood that politics were to be discussed for the general benefit of all . . . party feeling and sectarian differences would be kept in the background . . .[39]

In contrast, the Operatives' Library was established in 1835 at the Rancliffe Arms by a few working men who reacted against the proscription on the discussion of political and religious topics at the Artisans' Library. They came together to purchase a copy of William Howitt's *History of Priestcraft* and began meeting regularly in order to buy, read and discuss books. By 1845 there were eight Operatives' Libraries at Nottingham, New Sneinton, Radford and New Lenton. Political discussions were conducted 'under judicious regulations' at several of these libraries. All the libraries were housed in taverns; several libraries held anniversary dinners and free-and-easies during the year. While these libraries enjoyed the patronage of a few wealthy local worthies, they remained under the control of working men. The libraries also sponsored lectures by middle-class radicals such as Thomas Beggs and the Revd William Linwood, both supporters of the Complete Suffrage Union. The entrance fees (usually 6*d*.) and weekly subscriptions (1d.) contrasted to the higher fees of middle-class educational institutions. The annual budget of the Operatives' Library number one (1843) was £55; there were 275 members and over 1500 books.[40]

The exact relationship between the Operatives' Libraries and the town's Chartist Movement is unclear. The statements of the libraries were moderate in political tone. On the other hand, a fair number of Chartists were prominent in the affairs of the libraries. When Dr Peter M'Douall, member of the NCA executive, visited the town he expressed particular pleasure at the progress of the Operatives' Library at the Rancliffe Arms: 'Oh, for 10,000 others like this library.' When local Chartists organised a subscription for John Frost they called upon the members of the Operatives' Libraries, the town's working-class news and reading-rooms for assistance. Most of the taverns at which the libraries were located also served as Chartist meeting places. As John Rowley has commented: 'it is clearly not without significance that both forms of activity centred on the same circle of pubs, forming part of a resilient and independent working-class sub-culture . . .'[41] In 1843 the Chartists at the Democratic Chapel initiated a plan to consolidate the holdings of the Operatives' Libraries – over 3300 books – into one institution, to be called the Working Men's Hall and Library. R. T. Morrison, a commercial traveller and for a time one of the town's leading Chartists, noted that the working-class at Nottingham 'had long seen the necessity of having libraries under their own management'. He called on the more than 700 members of the Operatives' Libraries to join with others to build a Working Men's Hall for the general use of the local working-class community. When the Chartists revived this proposal (in 1845) there was support from the Operatives' Libraries; although no hall was built, 1000 five-shilling shares were taken out.[42] No doubt many Chartists and members of the libraries shared political, as well as educational, cultural and 'moral' goals; they also shared a belief in the need for working men to control their own cultural institutions.

The failure to establish a Working Men's or Operatives' Hall at Nottingham serves to underscore the tensions which often existed between Chartist ambitions and actual achievement. It serves also as a reminder of the material constraints upon the creation and sustenance of working-class political and cultural institutions in this period. When a People's Hall was finally established at Nottingham in 1854 it was largely the result of middle-class money and initiative.[43] In the 1840s the issue of popular education might provide an area of contact and co-operation between working-class and middle-class radicals, although it should not be assumed that their motives were necessarily the same. The proposal to establish an Operatives' Hall attracted the support of several middle-class radicals, men like Thomas Beggs (a stationer) who had a strong interest in temperance as well as educational improvement. By the mid-1840s the education of the working-class, their 'moral' improvement, had taken on particular importance for many middle-class liberals at Nottingham. Thus the *Nottingham Review*, a radical middle-class journal which supported the demand for universal suffrage, declared: 'the MORAL must FORERUN the POLITICAL victory in connection with the thorough emancipation of the working-classes ... We therefore regard education as the subject of subjects at the present moment ...'[44] While many Chartists recognised the need for working-class education, few could accept this formulation.

IV

Teetotalism, like education, came within the orbit of Nottingham Chartism. The Chartist Abstinence Society met regularly at the Democratic Chapel. The Chartist leader Henry Vincent found an enthusiastic Chartist welcome at Nottingham in 1841 on his temperance tour. The town's female Chartists presented him with a cap, gloves and other articles produced at Nottingham for his wife. Despite such enthusiasm, the attitude of the Nottingham Chartists towards the temperance question had been established as early as summer 1838. William Hall, then secretary of the Nottingham WMA, stated that while Chartists condemned drunkenness, they questioned whether teetotalism could alleviate the grievances of the working-class. He called on teetotal supporters to join the ranks of Chartism. By the early 1840s Nottingham's official temperance movement was under middle-class control. While several of Nottingham's leading Chartists acknowledged the virtues of temperance as part of the struggle for working-class dignity and self-respect, temperance was neither obligatory nor regarded as the panacea for working-class social and economic ills. Thomas Cooper captured the distinction between teetotal reformers and teetotal Chartists rather neatly: 'To them, Teetotalism is both *the means and the end:* with *us*, it is only the mean *to* an end ...' The demand for universal suffrage, for political power, remained at the centre of Nottingham Chartists' radical commitment. When it appeared as if the 'New Move' and the advocates of 'Church Chartism, Teetotal Chartism, Knowledge Chartism and

Household Chartism' might threaten the national unity of Chartism, the Nottingham Chartists gave unequivocal support to the leadership of O'Connor and the NCA. Concentration upon the splits within the movement's national leadership, however, has often tended to obscure the unity forged within the local Chartist Movement. The Nottingham Chartists' support for O'Connor and condemnation of William Lovett and the other leaders of the New Move did not signal an abandonment of their own commitment to working-class self-help and mutual improvement. At the 1842 Chartist Convention Nottingham's delegate, George Harrison (a fierce opponent of the New Move or any tendency towards an accommodation with middle-class radicalism) reported that he represented two Chartist groups: 'the one teetotal, the other not, but they were both good Chartists'.[45]

The Democratic Chapel, Dorman's Temperance Hotel and the various Chartist coffee-houses at Nottingham were clearly Chartist alternatives to the public house. Social teas and balls, 'rational' entertainment, were popular forms of Chartist leisure activity. The concluding comment in the *Northern Star* report of one such Nottingham gathering was typical: 'a more rational convivial meeting of the working-class could never be held. The songs were of a chaste character, and all breathing a pure spirit of freedom'.[46] While such 'respectable' behaviour contrasts with a more boisterous, 'rough' working-class culture, it should not be regarded as evidence of an accommodation by working-class radicals to middle-class social values, part of a diffusion of middle-class cultural influence. Many Nottingham Chartists shared areas of cultural concern with middle-class reformers, but they maintained differing class perspectives on the central issue of social and political change. Social class remained the fundamental rift in Nottingham society of the 1840s. If Chartists often failed to defend traditional, 'rough' sports or denounced heavy drinking, this was, at least in part, because they believed that such pastimes disarmed the working-class, served to obstruct the formation of a disciplined political force.[47]

Nottingham was one of the most open constituencies in England. Drink was a powerful political weapon used by both Whigs and Tories to bribe working-class electors. It is hardly surprising that a teetotal Chartist like James Sweet should regard drunkenness as a major obstacle to working-class political emancipation.

Remember the moment you cease to be bribed – to get drunk – to shout and do the dirty work of the factions – that moment you shew

your intelligence, and that you have made up your minds to be free –
and then your political emancipation will be sure.[48]

At the local by-election of April 1841, an election upon which
national Chartist attention was focused, the Nottingham Chartists supported John Walter, Tory owner of *The Times*, solely upon the basis of
his opposition to the new Poor Law. Three hundred Chartist electors
marched to the polls together before ten o'clock, in order to avoid
charges of bribery, and voted for Walter. In a constituency renowned
for corrupt elections, impoverished stockingers forewent bribes in order
to score an impressive political victory. The Chartist votes were the
margin by which Walter won the election. Working-class radicals had
managed to break thirty-five years of Whig dominance at Nottingham.
This was the kind of political power to which Chartists like Sweet
looked in the struggle to secure political rights, a power contingent upon
disciplined working-class action. However, Chartists were not resigned
entirely to such 'moral' force. The highlight of the Nottingham by-
election of August 1842 at which Chartists supported the universal
suffrage candidate Joseph Sturge against Walter was the fierce street
battle between Chartists and the Tory 'lambs', notorious roughs employed to intimidate electors. The Chartist crowd refused to let the
once-popular, Tory-radical Revd J. R. Stephens speak. 'The crowd were
assailing Stephens with the vilest epithets, and tearing up his portrait
which had formerly been issued with the *Northern Star*, and throwing
the torn fragments at his face.' Thus provoked, the Tory lambs attacked.
The Quaker pacifist Sturge, along with Henry Vincent, retreated from
the liberal waggon as O'Connor led the Chartist forces in a victorious
counter-attack.[49]

The 'rational' tea-parties, working-class libraries and teetotal associations were characteristic features of Chartism in the 1840s. But there
was a less 'respectable' face to Chartist protest, the face of the Chartist
crowd. Working-class women were often in the forefront of radical
crowd protest at Nottingham, looked to as agents of working-class community censure. During the National Holiday of August 1839 the
Nottingham Mercury, reflector of dominant local bourgeois opinion,
was outraged by the conduct of Nottingham's working-class women –
'most flagrant and wicked in the extreme'.

> every inducement or threat that could be held out to goad forward
> the men was fully applied by these harpies, whose expressions on

every occasion, whose oaths and blasphemy, groans and yells, really made us blush for the feminine sex of England ... In Lees close, when the Mayor read the riot act, the scene was truly horrifying: a decided majority in number of women, many with children, were assembled, and attempting, by all the means in their power, to raise a disturbance or promote a riot against the authorities. 'I wish I was a man', said one, 'I'd soon put the — police to rout.' Another exclaimed, 'What are they running at! why don't they cut them to pieces now they have them here ...' - while shouts of 'At 'em lads', and 'Down with them', burst from the mouths of the mothers of families and wives of hard-working men ... We do not hesitate to say, that the men would never have met in the Market Place or on the Forest on Monday were it not for the women; the taunts and revilings at their conduct in not turning on the soldiers, and sticking up for their rights cannot be described.[50]

Following the failure of the National Holiday it was the Nottingham female Chartists who organised a system of exclusive dealing, designed to intimidate shopkeepers unsympathetic to Chartist principles. During the general strike of 1842 large crowds assembled in defiance of the prohibition of the magistrates to hear Chartist speakers. For four days Chartist crowds toured the town and suburbs turning out factories and workshops and skirmishing with police and soldiers. The strike culminated in the 'Battle of Mapperley Hills' where the military dispersed a peaceful gathering of 5000 working people holding a 'feast' on the commons outside the town and took 400 prisoners.[51]

V

Despite the reservations which some Chartists had about meeting at drinking establishments, the town's taverns, inns and beerhouses became indispensable centres of Chartist association. This is clearly reflected in a list of Nottingham district NCA branches and meeting places: the Rancliffe Arms, King George on Horseback, Peacock, Noah's Ark, Dove and Rainbow, Nag's Head, Tiger's Head, Queen Caroline, Butcher's Arms, Britannia, Seven Stars, Fox and Hounds, Robin Hood, Feargus O'Connor, T. S. Duncombe Inn, King of the French were all centres of Chartist activity. Several of these taverns were associated with particular trades: Chartist shoemakers met at the Dove and Rainbow, Britannia and Butcher's Arms; lace-makers formed an NCA branch at the Nag's Head.

The addresses of NCA members show that the majority usually lived within the immediate vicinity of their respective meeting places. Thus while the Democratic Chapel was used for more centralised activities, larger meetings and delegate conferences for the town and district, taverns and coffee-houses provided meeting places for smaller, more localised or occupation-based groups. The centrality of working-class taverns to popular radicalism is well-illustrated by the activities organised around the King George on Horseback. Not only was the King George an important Chartist centre, but also it housed an Operatives' Library, became the headquarters from 1843 of the framework knitters' central committee for the co-ordination of the great framework knitters' petition, provided a meeting place for the Nottingham district committee of the National Association of United Trades in 1846–7 and offered its premises for a co-operative store established in 1847.[52] John Gibson, landlord of the King George until 1842, was a member of the NCA. He had formerly been the proprietor of the Sir Isaac Newton's Head, perhaps the most prominent centre of radical activity at Nottingham from the Luddite years through the 1830s. Samuel Mellors who succeeded Gibson at the King George was a Chartist sympathiser, as were William Thornton at the Seven Stars, Joseph Cooke at the Noah's Ark beerhouse and John Ellis at the King of the French, all of whom acted as branch treasurers for the Chartists who met at their establishments.[53] In February 1848 the King of the French underwent republican redecoration.

> The representation of Louis Philippe which, for some years past, has adorned the front of the public-house in Woolpack Lane, was mutilated . . . by some unknown parties, and the ex-monarch is now represented with his head detached from the body with a broad streak of red paint.[54]

At Sutton-in-Ashfield the proprietor of the Chartist Robin Hood Inn was James Turner, brother of William Turner who was executed in 1817 for his part in the Pentrich rising. Nottingham's working-class taverns and radical reading-rooms represented one of the most direct organisational and cultural links between Chartism and earlier working-class protest.[55] Through selective patronage Nottingham's working-class radicals and trade unionists had established a network of drinking places where they could meet among trusted comrades. This was a vital area of working-class cultural and political control.

Most Chartists envisaged their protest as part of a continuing radical tradition which went back at least to the 1790s. The transmission of this radical tradition and culture was of great importance. The toasts, songs and recitations delivered at Chartist dinners give some idea of the richness of the heritage to which Chartists laid claim and the interweaving of old and new loyalties. Throughout the Chartist period, working-class radicals gathered at the Seven Stars tavern at Nottingham to celebrate the birthday of Thomas Paine. James Sweet, teetotal Chartist, was usually called upon to preside. As chairman Sweet proposed the toasts which were then responded to by different radicals:

'The sovereignity of the People' . . . 'The People; may they well study the first principles of government, and never relinquish the struggle for social and political rights, until the People's Charter becomes the law of the land;' . . . 'The memory of the immortal patriot, Thomas Paine – may the principles he advocated become universally studied, and reduced to practice;' spoken to by the old veteran reformer, Mr Thomas Roper, at great length. 'The *Northern Star,* and the whole of the democratic press – may it continue to advocate the rights of man, and be supported in its warfare with the oppressors of the human race, by every true lover of his country;' . . . 'The speedy downfall of kingcraft and priestcraft;' . . . 'May all mankind become brethren, and to do good be their rule of faith;' (spoken to) by Mr Baker, who gave – 'Robert Emmet's defence.' 'T. S. Duncombe, Esq. M.P., the only man in the British House of Commons who has the honesty to demand justice for the whole people;' spoken to by the Chairman, and drunk with all the honours. Song by Mr Gisby, 'The four-leaved Shamrock.' 'Feargus O'Connor, Esq., the people's friend and the tyrant's foe – may he live to see the men for whom he struggles socially happy and politically free.' Drunk with all the honours. Song by the whole of the Company – 'The Lion of Freedom.' 'W. P. Roberts, Esq., the people's attorney-general – may the working-classes cheer him in his onslaught against tyrant magistrates and bloated capitalists.' . . . 'The Executive of the National Charter Association, and the Trustees and Directors of the Land Company . . .' Recitation – 'The Black Slave,' by Mr Baker. 'The speedy return of Frost, Williams, Jones, Ellis, and every other political martyr.' Song by Mr Clarkson, 'Frost, Williams, and Jones.' 'The memory of Henry Hunt, and the illustrious dead of every age and nation, who while living struggled for the freedom of their fellow-men.' Various songs and recitations were given by Miss Blatherwick and others . . .

The evening concluded with votes of thanks 'to the ladies for their attendance upon the occasion', 'to the aged democrat, Mr Thomas Roper' (who had been active in popular radical politics in Nottingham since the days of the Luddites and Jeremiah Brandreth), to Patrick O'Higgins 'for his exertions in the cause of his oppressed countrymen', and to the chairman 'for his past services'.[56]

There existed a sense of communality and equality within the local Chartist Movement. Before a crowded meeting at the Democratic Chapel, the *Nottingham Mercury* noted disapprovingly, 'many pipes were steaming away, and both ladies and gentlemen passed them to each other to take a whiff'. If the role of Chartist women remained subordinate to that of the Chartist men, it constituted more than a passive presence. Besides organising the social teas and balls, Chartist women attended and sometimes addressed Chartist gatherings, formed their own political associations, established the Chartist Sunday school, signed petitions and engaged in exclusive dealing.[57]

Both nationally and locally Chartists sought to provide a working model of democratic organisation. At the Democratic Chapel, for instance, a new presiding council was elected every three months. Delegates to national conferences were held strictly accountable to the local Chartist body. Such procedures were of course in line with the governance of other working-class institutions, such as trade unions and friendly societies.

The local movement was often called upon to support comrades who had suffered for their radical commitment, either through imprisonment or employer victimisation. The knitter James Woodhouse and his family were paid a guinea a week by the local movement in autumn 1839, when no employer would hire the former Convention delegate. Woodhouse opened a Chartist co-operative store in an attempt to find employment within the movement. The knitter George Black had his frames removed by his employer and remained unable to find work because of his reputation as a violent Chartist agitator. Eventually Black, a former Primitive Methodist preacher, turned to the uncertain career of a Chartist lecturer. Jonathan Barber, arrested for his part in the National Holiday in 1839, told a meeting in 1847 that he was out of work, 'but having taken an active part in public for the working man, and being one of the proscribed, he had an allowance, a very small one, from the Working Men's Association, or he must have starved'.[58] Besides such individual cases of hardship, the local movement had to sustain the large cost of the defence, support and sureties for the twenty-six working men imprisoned from two to six months at Southwell House of Correction for their part in the 1842 general strike. For the next three years proceeds from Chartist teas and balls, concerts and amateur dramatic performances, lectures and sermons, went to relieve the debt incurred in support of these 'victims of magisterial oppression', as well as to support other Chartist victims throughout the country.[59] Thus while such convivial activity was important in providing low-cost entertainment for working people, it was also essential to the finances of the movement.

In the spring and summer Chartist agitation moved outdoors, into the market-place and onto the commons outside the town. These were the months of the 'monster' demonstrations, the National Holiday, the general strike. At Nottingham the *Northern Star* was read regularly in the market-place. On Sundays Chartists preached on the Forest. Following a Sunday evening gathering on the Forest addressed by Dr M'Douall in summer 1842, several thousand marched through the streets singing Chartist hymns and songs. According to the *Star*, this behaviour 'astonished some of the natives very much, especially the Sabatonian canters'. The streets were a non-exclusive space, open to a variety of influences. As E. P. Hennock has commented, it was the difficulty of controlling these influences which alarmed Victorian moralists.[60] In summer 1844 a memorial was presented to Nottingham's mayor and magistrates calling upon them to ban preaching to large bodies of people in the market-place on Sundays. This move was directed primarily against Chartist and Owenite lecturers. The *Nottingham Mercury*, after wrestling with its Whig conscience, supported the memorialists:

> We are no advocates for interference with the civil or religious liberties of the people ... but when we find preachers of politics, Mormonism, and infidelity, availing themselves of the facilities thus afforded, for giving publicity to their dangerous doctrines, we are sure that the religious and moral portion of the community will unite with us in the opinion, that it would be far better to do away with all 'out-door' preaching than to inflict so great an evil ...[61]

In spite of such middle-class importuning, the Nottingham authorities chose not to interfere with Chartist meetings. The town's authorities generally avoided confrontation with Chartists over the use of urban public space. In fact during the 1840s the town's mayors often granted Chartists the use of the town hall, while declining Chartist requests officially to convene such meetings. However, during moments of Chartist crisis, such as the 1842 general strike, the authorities dropped such non-confrontationalist tactics and moved to ban public meetings.

For several years after 1842 Chartists held anniversary celebrations upon the site of the 'Battle of Mapperley Hills', as a reminder of the county magistrates' and military's transgression against popular rights.

> The Chartists are determined it shall ever be held in remembrance, by holding yearly meetings upon the spot where it took place . . . (and to demonstrate) by their presence, their detestation of tyranny, in every shape, and their determination to enfranchise themselves.[62]

Nottingham's unenclosed commons were particularly important to the local working-class, providing an escape from the overcrowded town, an area for working-class leisure and recreation. Thomas Cooper, who spoke on several occasions at Chartist camp meetings on the Forest, observed, 'the people . . . were proud of their unenclosed "Forest" . . .' The *Nottingham Review*, in contrast, complained: 'these plains are disgraced by dog-fighting, badger-baiting, tossing, boxing, and other disreputable practices'.[63] The celebrations on the anniversary of the 'Battle of Mapperley Plains' took on the character of a Chartist fair.

> The plains were studded with camps, marquees, and stalls; several bands of music were in attendance, and the parties amused themselves with dancing and various rural sports, and appeared to enjoy the fun amazingly. Mr Feargus O'Connor and several other persons addressed the people, consisting of from two to three thousand men, women and children, who kept up the 'anniversary' to a late hour.[64]

Chartism's great outdoor demonstrations were popular festivals, celebrations of working-class solidarity and creativity. The demonstrations offered a mass exhibition of the rich cultural traditions of working-class radicalism. They were not spontaneous gatherings, but events which required much local preparation, expense and regional co-ordination. Flags and banners had to be made and borrowed from nearby localities, bands hired and the detailed order of procession drawn up. On a Monday in late July 1842, Feargus O'Connor, the 'People's Champion', arrived at Nottingham. Tens of thousands met him in the town's market-place with bands and banners. After a short speech, O'Connor set out, accompanied by a grand procession, on a two-day tour of liberation through Nottinghamshire. From Nottingham they marched six miles north to the 'tory ridden village' of Calverton, met on the way by Chartists from the villages of Bulwell, Carrington, Arnold, Basford and Hucknall. A mile outside Calverton O'Connor was welcomed by members of the Calverton Charter Association, the Sutton-in-Ashfield band, more banners, flags and garlands with fresh flowers. At Calverton the Revd Harrison had arranged a great outdoor Chartist tea. A tent, marquee and stalls had been set up in a large pasture. At one time, according to the *Northern Star*, there were as many as 5000 people 'at this moral fete in honour of O'Connor'. Nearly 1000 'sons and daughters of toil' took tea, plum and plain cake, bread and butter. There were 'all sorts of innocent amusements – kiss in the ring, country dances ... [and] a Nigger, a real Nigger, accompanied by two fiddlers, dancing Jim along Josey in real Nigger style'. At seven O'Connor spoke from a waggon in the meadow. This was followed by recitations and Chartist songs composed by the Arnold Chartist John Hardy. Politics were mixed with pleasure, amended forms of traditional popular recreation mingled with aspirations of a new socio-political order. As advertised:

"The youthful and gay will be favoured with a dance on the green; while the old and more sedate will devise the best means possible to cause the Charter to become law, and hasten the day of freedom.

The following day was even more impressive, as O'Connor proceeded to Mansfield and Sutton-in-Ashfield. Outside Mansfield a procession of 2500 greeted O'Connor:

Each man wore his rosette, or green ribbon; the leaders of the procession had wands of office, and the boys had papers round their hats, of different colours, bearing on them the inscriptions 'Welcome to O'Connor', 'Remember Holberry the Martyr', 'More Fat Pigs and less Fat Parsons', Frost, Williams, and Jones' ... The flags in the procession were exceedingly good, and many of them new for the occasion. The first flag was a large black one, having on one side 'Thou shalt do no murder', and on the other 'Vengeance is mine, saith the Lord, and I will repay it. Remember Clayton and Holberry, the Martyrs for the People's Charter'. This presented an exceedingly imposing appearance. Pink, blue, red, green, and hosts of all coloured flags met the eye ... [we] give the inscriptions of all we could make out ... 'Unity is Strength' ... 'Triumph Justice, and Cease Tyranny', 'Peace, Plenty, and Happiness', 'National Charter Association, Skegby',

'He that will not work, neither shall he eat', 'Mansfield Chartist Association' – 'Feargus O'Connor, the Tyrant's Enemy', 'The Friendly Institution of Cordwainers' (a splendid flag, with figures on it as large as life), 'The Judgment of Heaven is Labour and Food, but the Judgment of Kings is Toil and Starvation' . . .

Two miles from Sutton the procession, which had grown to 20,000 strong, was met by the Sutton female Chartists carrying a large black flag which read 'A tear of sympathy for the martyred Clayton and Holberry'. The women were dressed in white muslin, with black scarfs and ribbands, 'being in mourning for Holberry'. Sutton itself presented a grand Chartist spectacle:

O! heavens, what a sight! Doors, windows, and walls presented hundreds of Chartist mottos, *Star* portraits, flags, garlands, oak-boughs, and evergreens, and roofs, windows, and walls were crammed with human beings. The shouts, as we passed the streets, rent the welkin. In our passage down the hïglin [sic], we passed under several triumphal arches, which were suspended across the street from house to house.

The working-class had taken hold of Sutton for one day as a form of symbolic gesture, a prefigurement of Chartist victory. The local magistrates who had severely repressed the Chartist agitation in 1839 were gathered in the town hall. From the platform O'Connor proclaimed the town's main thoroughfare renamed 'Charter-street'. He assured the huge crowd, 'let them go on, and finally, ere it was long, they would obtain that which they much sought for – the assertion of the rights of labour . . .' The meeting adopted a remonstrance to the Queen, calling on her to dismiss her ministers and accept the National Petition. According to the *Nottingham Review*'s reporter, 'many walked between forty and fifty miles that day to follow in the train, and form parts of the procession'.[65]

VI

In his report to the 1842 Convention George Harrison, himself a Primitive Methodist preacher, drew attention to the strong religious aspect to Chartist agitation in Nottinghamshire:

We here perhaps carry on our agitation different to what they do in some parts of the country; we know the strong religious feelings which actuate a large portion of the community, and we endeavour to prove to them that our principles are those advocated in the Bible, and hitherto we have done so with complete success.[66]

Nottingham had been an early stronghold of Primitive Methodism. Methodism remained an influential force, particularly in the industrial villages of Nottinghamshire.[67] The relationship between working-class radicalism and Methodism was complex and contradictory. The moral earnestness, discipline and crusading zeal which Methodists and ex-Methodists brought to Chartist protest were of great importance. The organisational skills, particularly that of public speaking, which such men had acquired were of inestimable value. On the other hand, Methodists constituted a community which to a large degree had turned in upon itself, separated and sheltered from the working-class at large through a sense of moral superiority. Chartism was essentially a non-sectarian, inclusive movement which sought to appeal to a larger sense of class solidarity. There were obvious points of antagonism. Not only did Methodism oppose involvement in radical politics, but also much of Chartism's convivial activity – the tavern culture, the men and women smoking pipes before meetings, the country dancing on the common, the balls and political preaching on the Sabbath – was offensive to Methodist, as well as to much middle-class, moral sensibility. In a letter of 1842 to Thomas Cooper, himself an ex-Methodist, E. P. Mead, Nottingham's NCA lecturer, reacted to the Methodist charge that he was a 'profain swearer': 'If saying in plain blunt terms that the Methodists as . . . a body are a damned canting set of hypocrites be swearing – I plead guilty.'[68] In 1841 the Nottingham Primitive Methodists expelled a member on the grounds that he was 'a bad man, fond of ale, a desperate tobacco smoker, and a great Chartist'. In the same year, Henry Dorman was instructed to cease delivering political lectures. When Dorman quit the connection in 1843, it was recorded: 'though H. Dorman left of his own accord he had caused great trouble to the members and leaders by taking an active part with the Chartists'.[69]

Whatever the relationship, however, between individual working-class radicals and organised religion at Nottingham, the Chartist Movement adapted religious forms to its own purpose. The powerful rhetorical force of popular religion was brought to the Chartist platform. At Nottingham's first Chartist demonstration in the autumn of 1838, the knitter James Woodhouse denounced as hypocritical the professed

Christian beliefs of their 'social betters', and appealed to the principles of Christianity to justify the poor man's cause.

Is this [the discrepancy between the poverty of those who worked and the wealth of those who did not] . . . to be endured in a Christian country? – in a land where the Bible is read, where great churches stand in the midst of our towns and villages, raising their towering heads above the rest of the buildings? . . . He would say, certainly not; and yet they saw notwithstanding the extensive circulation and use of the Bible, from which they all professed to take their creed, and in which they read that Christ himself chose the poor for his followers, that distinctions were made, and some amongst them were called Lords and Dukes, who while pampered themselves, keep the working-classes in a degraded situation, toiling from morning until night, having nothing to wear, their wives beggared, their children in rags, their grates without fire, and their houses without furniture. He considered this state of things a disgrace to a Christian country, and would say arise and demand their rights.[70]

The appeal to Christianity, like the appeal to the ancient constitution, served as a powerful source of legitimation for Chartist action; it represented an appeal to what was regarded as a recognised, absolute standard of moral and social values, a standard which transcended the existing social order. The concept of a democratic religion, a religion which claimed the spirit of early Christianity as its model, had great attraction for working people, especially when contrasted to the corruption, privilege and exclusiveness of the religious establishment. The incorporation of certain religious modes and forms of rhetoric within the Nottinghamshire Chartist Movement offers perhaps the clearest example of the way in which working-class radicals turned one of the most important ideological props of early Victorian society against that society's dominant set of values.[71]

During the early Chartist period, the brand of primitive, political preaching pioneered by the Revd J. R. Stephens on the northern Anti-Poor Law platform found widespread support in Nottinghamshire. The clarity with which the Anti-Poor Law campaign posed the question of social justice was brought into Chartism. Religion which drew the line so clearly between good and evil, the damned and the saved, the children of the Lord and His enemies, in the mouth of a political preacher like Stephens was an exhortation to revolutionary action. Revd Harrison told the Nottingham Chartists that he believed 'religion and politics were united as soul and body'. He supported Stephens

> because I profess to be a Minister of the same gospel, and have been a preacher of it for twelve years. (Hear, hear.) . . . In the days of old, the preachers of truth were murdered and imprisoned; and for what? for preaching the truth. The same cause has produced the same effect, with respect to their friend, Joseph Rayner Stephens. He then instanced the prophets Nehemiah and Joel . . . and insisted that it was the duty of every Christian to become part and parcel of the present agitation, and that Radicalism was consistent with the word of God. (Hear, hear.)

Woodhouse declared that Stephens

> had shown the people of England that the Bible when opened and read aright would teach them to get their political rights. (Hear, hear.) . . . If they read that book aright, they would see it was their duty to cast down oppressors, and in this manner, as St Paul says, 'he that will not work, neither shall he eat'.[72]

In spring 1839 thousands congregated on the Forest every Sunday for the three services at which Harrison and other Chartists preached and read Stephens' political sermons. The meeting which assembled on the first day of the National Holiday at Nottingham began with a Methodist hymn, followed by a prayer with particular reference to the children of Israel in Egypt and their deliverance from bondage. With the suppression of working-class radicalism by local authorities following the holiday, the Nottingham Chartists ceased holding public meetings, but the Sunday prayer meetings on the Forest continued with increased support. At the Manchester national conference held early in 1840, George Black, Nottingham's delegate, invoked the text: 'He that hath no sword let him sell his garment and buy one'. His meaning was unmistakable, although most Chartists had lost their enthusiasm for insurrectionary action.[73]

During the early 1840s religious modes remained a permanent feature of Nottinghamshire Chartist protest. At Arnold and Calverton Chartist chapels were established. At Nottingham's Democratic Chapel sermons were delivered on Sundays by Harrison, Black and other leading Chartists. J. Dean, a stockinger from Lenton, told Chartists 'to consider Jehovah as their only King, and if they heard anything about politics, to test it by the Scriptures'. He continued: 'The man who had property and called it his own had no religion, for "the earth is the Lord's and the fullness thereof" . . .' The theme of retributive social justice was a common one. James Simmons, a Nottingham knitter, spoke to the text:

Ye shall not afflict any widow or fatherless child.
If thou afflict them in any wise, and they cry at all unto me, I will surely hear their cry;
And my wrath shall wax hot, and I will kill you with the sword; and your wives shall be widows, and your children fatherless.

Sermons demonstrating that Chartism was in accord with the principles of Christianity were frequently preached.[74] During the spring and summer, at least until 1844, Chartists preached on Sundays on the Forest. In summer 1841 the Nottingham Chartists convened a series of all-day camp meetings for the East Midlands district on the Forest at which sermons were delivered and hymns sung. An estimated 10,000 people assembled on the Forest to hear Harrison deliver a funeral sermon for Samuel Holberry.[75]

Chartist hymns were particularly popular. 'Get some Hymns in the Pioneer if possible', Sweet urged Cooper. The knitter Samuel Boonham informed Cooper that the Nottingham Chartists had formed a choir and were collecting hymns from back issues of his journals. There was an underlying class content to Chartist hymns and songs. For example, in these two verses from a popular hymn sung at the Democratic Chapel:

The seasons toll at thy command
And plenty crowns the soil,
But Avarice spreads his grasping hand,
And mocks our fruitless toil.

Abundance in a flowing tide,
Fills all the realm with good.
But Labour's share is seized by pride,
And Labour pines for food.

An itinerant Methodist preacher on the Nottingham circuit, fearing young converts might be drawn into the Chartist ranks by such singing, composed a hymn entitled 'The Lion of Judah' to the tune of Chartism's most popular ballad, 'The Lion of Freedom'. Whether this attempt to turn the tables on the Chartists had the desired effect may be doubted, but it is a testament to the powerful attraction Chartist hymns held for working people. There was also a rash of Chartist christenings at Nottingham in the early 1840s. Zephaniah Williams Frost Greensmith, Feargus O'Connor Lester, William Feargus O'Connor Ellis were living evidence for another generation of their parents' Chartist convictions. This adaptation of religious ritual was a conscious affront to the religious establishment, an attempt to infuse traditional forms of ritual with radical content.[76]

The Chartist assumption of the mantle of 'true' Christianity was a response to working-class experience; it rallied support through a shared idiom, a common point of moral and cultural reference. It is doubtful, however, whether it represented some measure of shared identity with middle-class religious sentiment. The religious establishment, in particular, came under constant attack. Joseph Souter, a local knitter, put it simply: 'The bishops and parsons told them to put their trust in God, while they robbed.' Jonathan Barber, a free-thinker and highly class-conscious Chartist, dwelt on the same theme at greater length, arguing the need for working-class political power.

This was a land of Bibles and parsons. There were whole armies of parsons going forth to teach man his duty to his fellow, yet the greatest amount of misery and destitution existed. If the parsons were sincere, why did they not set about in real earnest to bring about a better state of things? . . . They preached against worldly riches; but they take the 'dangerous stuff themselves, and leave heaven for you'. If the people had political power, they would not have bishops with their tens of thousands a-year composing prayers for the people to offer up to Almighty God, to avert a famine they themselves had created . . . He thought that if the people had political power all classes would be banished.[77]

Sections of the middle-class had a somewhat different perspective on the need for churches and parsons. At a town meeting called to form a Church Building Society in 1841, it was stated with extraordinary candour:

The most effectual mode of making men good subjects, was to make them good Christians; and if a statesman looked at the question in no higher point of view, he must at least regard the clergy as an efficient Preventative Police, who, by inculcating Christian principles, purified the sources of human action, and thus restrained men from the violation of the laws.

One of these 'Preventative Police', the Revd J. Brookes, vicar of St Mary's, noted 'the sullenness of manner' he encountered among Chartists and socialists on his missions of Christian purification; 'when he entered their houses they would whistle, or take up O'Connor's newspaper, or go away'.[78]

VII

Chartist politics were infused into working-class struggle from within, integrated into the fabric of working-class culture, traditions and language. The leadership of Nottingham's Chartists was rooted in the everyday experience of working-class life. This allowed Nottingham's Chartist leaders to assume more generally the role of representatives of the local working-class. Repeatedly they came forward as the spokesmen for working-class interests on a wide-range of issues: conditions at the poor-law workhouses in the district, enclosure of the commons, the high price of bread, church rates, night work at factories, the Master and Servant bill, bribery at local elections, Graham's Factory Education bill.[79] Nor were they merely self-appointed spokesmen. Their leadership outside the strictly political struggle for universal suffrage is well-illustrated by the involvement of many leading Chartists in local trade union activity, particularly the framework knitters associations. No doubt many working-class radicals shared Jonathan Barber's conviction, that his trade union experience had 'proved to him clearly that he can do nothing to ameliorate his sufferings, and secure to him permanent benefit without the possession of the franchise'.[80] This did not, however, prevent Barber from taking an active part in the framework knitters movement in the 1840s. Benjamin Humphries, a founding member of the Nottingham WMA and active NCA member in the 1840s, was secretary to the plain silk glove knitters and grand secretary to the Nottingham knitters committee in charge of organising the framework knitters parliamentary petition. Humphries had been a union leader since at least 1827.[81] John Macduff, leading member of the Democratic Association and then of the Nottingham NCA, was secretary to the committee of two-needle framework knitters. The local Chartists John Peters, Henry

Dorman and John Buckland, active in pre-Chartists attempts to form a general union of the working-class, continued as Chartists to combine political involvement with leadership within the knitters trade associ- ations. With the national re-emergence of widespread trade union activity in 1843, the Nottingham Chartists played a prominent role in the reorganisation of the Three Counties Framework Knitters Association and the campaign to present the knitters' petition to Parliament. At least sixteen Nottinghamshire Chartists were delegated to give evidence before the Royal Commission on the condition of framework knitters. Samuel Parr who had been arrested for his part in the 1839 National Holiday represented the Radford fancy silk branch. George Woodward, an early member of the Nottingham WMA committee, represented the plain silk hose branch; in 1836 he had been the principal unionist in the negotiations to revise the 1825 price statement for the trade. Thomas Emmerson, a leading Chartist at Arnold who had been secretary of the Arnold knitters union, was delegated to give evidence to the Commission. The Chartist George Kendall gave evidence in his capacity as secretary of the Sutton-in-Ashfield Anti-Truck Association.[82] Almost certainly a large proportion of Nottinghamshire Chartists were or had been unionists. Chartists called upon the trades of Nottingham to attend their demonstrations. Various societies, for instance the knitters and shoemakers, marched to Chartist rallies under trade banners. During a lace-runners' strike in late 1840, in which over 400 women organised themselves into a union (if only temporarily), the female strikers met at the Democratic Chapel.[83] During the general strike of 1842 delegates from the stonemasons, dyers, joiners, coach-makers, lace-makers, smiths, shoemakers, tailors and knitters all met at the Chapel and resolved to strike for nine days. The political nature of their action was manifest in their resolve

to co-operate with their fellow workmen in other parts of the country, in their endeavours to emancipate the working classes from the grasp of those who legislate for their own exclusive benefit, instead of that of the whole community . . .[84]

The Chartist leadership within the framework knitters movement is of particular significance, as it serves to highlight what was perhaps the major area of ideological conflict between working-class radicalism and bourgeois liberalism, that of political economy. Thus the framework knitters' petition of 1843 called for the revival of protections accorded under the 1663 Charter of the Framework Knitters Company. The petition requested wide-ranging governmental regulation of the industry: control of quality of goods manufactured, statutory limitations upon frame rent, prohibition of foreign imports, increased penalties for truck payment, the delivery of tickets with work describing the employer's price, the regulation of wages and prices.[85] Such attempts to regulate manufacture found no support among either liberal or radical sections of the middle-class. As Benjamin Humphries explained, the opponents of state intervention were concerned solely with 'production', but the knitters' concern was with

> a corresponding amount of comfort to society, and not to individuals; and as the present system of competition has the reverse effect, we are desirous to have such altered, for, as at present, thousands of worthy operatives have been deprived of the means of comfort from being deprived of their labours.[86]

The position was essentially a moral one. In a similar vein, Jonathan Barber asked, 'what ought to be the first duty of governments?'

> Certainly to protect the weak against the mighty – to dispense even-handed justice; but it seems to be the opinion of some that every species of property ought to be protected but *labour*, the only *property* of the working man. Property in horses, asses, and dogs is protected; the property of the miserable owner of some five or six independent frames is to be protected, while the working man, the producer of all wealth, is to be left a prey to every mean, petty-fogging 'bagman', who may think proper to oppress him, because forsooth no one is allowed to interfere in these matters . . .[87]

It is worth noting that much of the knitters' moral outrage was directed not against the large merchant hosiers, but against the bag-hosiers and middlemen in the trade.

Liberal middle-class opinion was at odds with the position of Chartists like Barber on three fundamental counts. In the first place, the agreement between employer and worker was regarded as having been freely entered into, and was, therefore, not subject to government interference. Thus the radical *Nottingham Review* argued:

The contract between master and workman is entered into from the feeling that for the time each is doing the best he can for himself; there is no compulsion in the matter; it is a simple bargain between man and man . . .

In 1844 the local Chartists withdrew their support for the Nottingham MP Thomas Gisborne, a supporter of universal suffrage, because of his opposition to the ten hours bill. The *Review* came to Gisborne's defence: 'We do not understand this jumbling together of questions of political economy . . . with constitutional principles.'[88] Secondly upholders of bourgeois political economy, rejected the humanitarian or moral basis of the working-class claim for protection of labour. Prices and wages must be determined by the inexorable laws of supply and demand. The true course towards economic well-being for both workers and manufacturers lay in total freedom for trade and manufacture.[89] Thirdly they rejected the assertion that members of the working-class were the sole producers of wealth. In response to a statement of the framework knitters committee (which included the Chartists Barber and Thomas Kerry) in 1847, the *Review* noted:

> there is one assertion . . . a very common one, and which we notice, as it involves a fallacy that is very injurious to this class. A highly important portion of the community no doubt is the labouring class; but the working man is not, as he asserts to be, the 'producer of all wealth'. Wealth cannot be produced without the co-operation of his labour; but there must be other equally important elements at work . . . Money, capital, integrity, knowledge, and enterprise. A workman, as such, does not necessarily possess or exemplify any of these qualities.[90]

In contrast, Chartists and unionists stressed the primacy of the working-class as producers of wealth and the dependence of the other classes in society upon their labour. The labour theory of value was a key component of Chartist ideology. Barber told a meeting in 1846:

> (he) contended that the working classes, if they were well-informed – if they were united – would produce wealth for themselves instead of for those who use it to oppress them, and then they could force their claims upon any Government.[91]

The striving for an assertion of working-class self-sufficiency found expression in various, often short-lived, schemes for co-operative retailing and production associated with the local Chartist Movement. Both the Chartist land plan – directed at alleviating the problem of surplus labour – and the National Association of United Trades – an attempt at general union with an emphasis on co-operative production – found considerable support at Nottingham.[92] Political economy was rejected in both theory and practice.

In the early 1840s the Chartist Movement at Nottingham reached the zenith of its strength and influence, as working-class radicals moved towards creating more regular and diverse forms of political organisation. The movement sustained a highly integrated cultural and political challenge to bourgeois society. From the mass demonstrations to the small groups for stockingers reading the *Northern Star*, Chartists sought to exert a measure of control over their daily lives. The Chartist Movement offered a context within which the creative energy of working-class men and women could be expressed, together with a commitment to the creation of an alternative social and political order. In conclusion, however, it must be noted that by the mid-1840s the Nottingham movement had lost much of its momentum. Significantly in late 1845 the Chartists were forced to give up the Democratic Chapel. For an historical moment Chartism had managed to fuse a radical working-class concern for mutual improvement and collective self-help with a highly class-conscious political movement, without losing the spirit of the mass demonstration or the aspirations for fundamental socio-political change. By 1846 the *Nottingham Review* rejoiced in what it perceived to be the new tone of Chartist protest.

For our own part, we attach very little importance to a noisy, brawling Radicalism, which spouts invective by the hour, and 'mid soaring assemblies pours forth its wordy tirades against things which are . . . There may be numbers, rant, and show, without any large amount of intelligence . . .

Compare the Chartism of past days with Chartism as it exists and operates now, and how vivid the contrast – how wonderous the change. Once a thing of noise, of bands, of banners, meeting by torchlight, and the worship of leaders; it has grown into a thing of thought and earnest meditation.[93]

While offering an insight into what middle-class radicals found objectionable about Chartist protest, there was clearly a hint of wishful thinking in such middle-class assessments. This was demonstrated with the resurgence of mass Chartist agitation in 1847–8. In a sense, the local movement's greatest achievement came in 1847, with the return of Feargus O'Connor as MP for Nottingham. Yet any comparison between the movement of 1848 with that of 1839 or 1842 reveals the diminished strength of Chartism.

This change was apparent throughout the country. However, if the decline of Chartist influence is clear, the reasons for this change are less obvious. Some answers must be sought at the national level. The failure to advance a strategy which went beyond mass petitioning campaigns, the demoralising effect of the defeats of 1839 and 1842, the splits within the national leadership over the proffered middle-class alliance with the Complete Suffrage Union and over the organisation and direction of the NCA in late 1842 and 1843 all had repercussions at the local level. The 'economic recovery' of the mid-1840s was no doubt of some importance, although it was less significant in a locality like Nottingham where stockingers continued to suffer appalling poverty. The lines of fragmentation within the labour movement, so apparent in the 1850s, were already beginning to show by the mid-1840s. Perhaps significant sections of the working class were already becoming resigned to the permanence of industrial capitalism. There was also a shift in the ruling-class response, both nationally and locally, the beginnings of a mellowing of tone and a somewhat more accommodative posture. John Foster has drawn particular attention to the impact of the process of 'liberalisation' upon working-class radicalism – although the process was almost certainly less conspiratorial, sudden and free from internal contradictions than Foster has implied.[94] At Nottingham there are some indications of an increased concern within the middle-class to provide cultural institutions for sections of the working-class – for instance, the establishment of the new Mechanics' Institute (1845) and the People's College (1847).[95] There may also have been a growing middle-class responsiveness to the needs of the urban poor.[96] On the other hand, the repression of 1842 had a damaging effect upon the local Chartist Movement. Yet the following year, William Hill, former editor of the *Northern Star*, praised the Nottingham authorities for allowing Chartists the use of the Exchange Hall.[97] There was a subtle interplay between control and accommodation. As 1842 and 1848 demonstrated, the authorities were prepared to act decisively when they felt threatened. Still, there was a softening of attitudes among sections of the middle-class in the

1840s, particularly as Chartist protest lost much of its more overt revolutionary tone. From summer 1842 there was a series of initiatives from middle-class radicals at Nottingham directed at finding areas of political co-operation with Chartists.[98] From the mid-1830s middle-class radicals had been notable for their absence from the movement for working-class political rights. The re-emergence of limited class co-operation was, therefore, significant, although it is difficult to gauge the effect of such co-operation, or the more accommodative posture of the local authorities, upon the force of Chartist protest. In 1848, while prepared to volunteer as special constables, a considerable section of the town's bourgeoisie advocated the need for political concessions to the working-class.[99]

This is not to suggest that Chartism ceased to be an important political and cultural force from the mid-1840s. On the contrary, we know that in many localities, including Nottingham, the movement retained substantial working-class allegiance into the 1850s. It is to suggest, however, that 1842 may have been as critical a turning-point in the course of working-class radicalism as 1848, and that the subtle redefinitions of class relations and the reorientations of the labour movement in the mid-1840s, both locally and nationally, remain in need of further study and illumination.

NOTES

1. The term is borrowed from Lawrence Goodwyn's remarkable study, *Democratic Promise: The Populist Movement in America* (New York: Oxford Univ. Press, 1976).

2. D. M. Smith, 'The British Hosiery Industry at the Middle of the Nineteenth Century: An Historical Study in Economic Geography', no. 32 (1963) pp. 125–42; Parliamentary Papers (PP) 1844, XXVII, pp. 142–5. The account of the framework knitting industry here is based on: *Report of the Commissioners appointed to inquire into the Conditions of Framework Knitters*, PP 1845, XV, pts 1 and 2; W. Felkin, *A History of the Machine-wrought Hosiery and Lace Manufactures* (1867; reprint Newton Abbot: David and Charles, 1967); W. Felkin, *An Account of the Machine-wrought Hosiery Trade and the Condition of the Framework Knitters* (London, 1845); F. A. Wells, *The British Hosiery and Knitwear Industry; Its History and Organization*, (Newton Abbot: David and Charles, revised edn, 1972); R. A. Church, *Economic and Social Change in a Midland Town, Victorian Nottingham, 1815–1900*, (London: Frank Cass, 1966), chs 1 and 2.

3. 'Cut-up' hose, as opposed to fully wrought hose which was shaped on the frame, was produced without narrowings in the material. On the wide cut-up frames, a stockinger could produce three 'stockings' at once. For a vivid chronicle

of the decline of skill, quality and fashion in the trade, see Gravener Henson's comments, *Report . . . into the Conditions of Framework Knitters*, pt 1, pp. 92–3.

4. *Report . . . into the Conditions of Framework Knitters*, pt 1, p. 219. I'm concerned here primarily with the way in which stockingers perceived themselves and their trade. For a useful discussion of the various definitions of the term 'artisan', see M. Hanagan, 'Artisan and Skilled Worker', *International Labor and Working Class History*, no. 12 (1977) pp. 28–31.

5. *Report . . . into the Conditions of Framework Knitters*, pt 2, pp. 89, 96; *Report to the Commissioners on the Employment of Children*, PP 1843, XIV, pf. 84.

6. *Report . . . into the Conditions of Framework Knitters*, pt 2, p. 46; J. Orange, *A Plea on Behalf of the Poor* (Nottingham, 1841), p. 13.

7. For the best account of the lace industry, see Church, *Economic and Social Change*, chs 3 and 4; also Felkin, *History; First Report of the Select Com. on the Laws affecting the Exportation of Machinery*, PP 1841, VII, appendices 4–6; F. A. Wells, 'The Lace Industry', in H. A. Silverman (ed.), *Studies in Industrial Organization* (London: Methuen, 1946); D. E. Varley, *A History of the Midland Counties Lace Manufacturers Association* (Lace Productions, Long Eaton, 1959); N. H. Cuthbert, *The Lace Makers Society: A Study of Trade Unionism in the British Lace Trade* (Amalgamated Soc. of Operative Lace Makers, Nottingham, 1960).

8. Cf. Church, *Economic and Social Change*, pp. 121–2, 153, 157, 165; J. D. Chambers, 'Nottingham in the Early Nineteenth Century', *Transactions of the Thoroton Soc.*, XLVII (1943) p. 36. In the 1840s the average wage for factory hands in the plain lace branch was around 16*s.*; hands doing the best work in the trade could make up to 40*s.* a week. Lace-makers working narrower hand machines, declining in number, suffered poverty equal to many stockingers. By 1836 two-thirds of the lace machinery was in the hands of 6 per cent of the owners. Felkin, *History*, pp. 331–4, 341, 344, 552; *Report . . . on the Employment of Children*, 1843, XIV, ppf. 49–50, 80–2.

9. See R. Samuel, 'The Workshop of the World: Steam Power and Hand Technology in mid-Victorian Britain', *History Workshop Journal*, no. 3 (1977).

10. See I. Pinchbeck, *Women Workers and the Industrial Revolution, 1750–1850*, (London: Frank Cass, 1969), pp. 209–19; E. Nicholson, 'Working-Class Women in Nineteenth-Century Nottingham' (Univ. of Birmingham B.A. dissertation, 1974) ch. 1; D. Wardle, 'Working Class Children in Nottingham from the Blue Books, 1842–62', *Transactions of the Thoroton Soc.*, LXX (1966) pp. 105–14.

11. W. F. P. Napier, *The Life and Opinions of General Sir Charles Napier*, 4 vols (London 1857) II, p. 110.

12. Felkin, *History*, p. 453; *Nottingham Review* (*NR*) 17 December 1838; *Northern Star* (*NS*) 13 April 1839, p. 8; 14 November 1840, p. 2; *Operative* 31 March 1839; T. Cooper, *Life of Thomas Cooper*, (1872; reprint Leicester Univ. Press, 1971) pp. 145 ff.

13. *NS* 23 April 1842, p. 6; 25 July 1840, p. 1; 11 December 1841, p. 5; 9 April 1842, p. 1; *Nott. Mercury* 25 February 1842; *NR* 28 January 1842, p. 3 (Bostock).

14. PRO, TS 11/602, White to Cooper, 27 July 1842.

15. Add. MSS 34, 245 A. fo. 84, Tomlinson to Wade, 1 March 1839.

16. *NS* 23 July 1841, p. 2; 14 September, p. 1; 5 March 1842, p. 5; 13 August, p. 5; 12 November, p. 8.

17. In the following numbers: three needle-makers, three framesmiths, one sinker-maker, four tailors, one dyer, three cabinet-makers, two bricklayers, two plumbers, one joiner, three labourers.

18. Around 30 per cent of employed males over twenty in the parish of Radford (pop. 10,800) were employed in lace manufacture; 17 per cent in hosiery. Residential segregation was here primarily a function of the location of industry.

19. *NS* 23 March 1839; p. 4; 13 April, p. 4; 13 July, p. 3; 3 August, p. 5; *NR* 1 March 1838, p. 4; *Nott. Journal*, 26 July 1839, p. 2; *Nott. Mercury*, 9 August 1839, p. 256.

20. This sample (n=223) is based on records of the Land Company, PRO, BT, 41/474. 31.8 per cent of Land Company members from the Nottingham district (including: Nottingham, Carrington, Basford, Radford, Hyson Green, Sneinton, Lenton, Sherwood) were knitters. There are problems, however, with equating Land Plan membership with Chartist membership and support.

21. Of seventy nominations to the NCA council from these villages, sixty-four were knitters.

22. The Nottingham sample includes ten shopkeepers, (four bakers, two butchers, one hairdresser, one bookseller, one coffee-house keeper, one druggist), as well as four publicans or beer-sellers, two teachers, one lace agent, one clerk, one corn-keeper, one farmer, one commercial traveller, one lace manufacturer. For the hairdresser James Sweet, see John Rowley's entry in J. Bellamy and J. Saville (eds), *Dictionary of Labour Biography* (London: Macmillan, 1977) IV, pp. 171-3.

23. The majority of the leaders of the WMA (founded in late 1837) and the Democratic Association, the two earliest Chartist associations at Nottingham, continued as local leaders into the 1840s – this included the knitters Benjamin Humphries, Jonathan Barber, Jacob Bostock, John Wright, George Woodward, John Peters, Henry Dorman, J. R. Macduff, the lace hands John Barratt and William Burden (who moved to Leicester), the tailors Cornelius Fowkes and Charles Roberts, the hairdresser James Sweet and the shoemaker William Lilley. Thomas Roper (sinker-maker) and Charles Merry (knitter) seem to have been the only prominent Chartists in the 1840s who traced their radical careers back to the days of the Luddites.

24. *NR* 26 October 1838, p. 4; 2 November, p. 5; 9 November, p. 3; *Operative* 25 November 1838, p. 57; *NS* 6 May 1843, p. 3.

25. Information concerning the age, marital status and number of children of NCA members (n=47) is based on the notebooks of the Census enumerators (1841). The age distribution was as follows: under 20, 2; 20-29, 6; 30-39, 27; 40-49, 7; over 50, 5. *NR* 21 October 1842, p. 3, for 'strikers'; also see C. Godfrey, 'The Chartist Prisoners, 1839-41', *International Rev. of Social History*, XXIV (1979) pp. 193-9.

26. PRO, HO 40/55, fo. 742; fos 60-1, Heywood to HO, 16 March 1840; HO 40/58, fo. 258, Napier to HO, 8 April 1840.

27. *Nott. Mercury*, 24 April 1840, p. 133. For the plotting of winter 1839/40,

see ibid., November 1839–March 1840; Napier, *Life and Opinions*, II, pp. 95 ff; PRO, HO 40/53, 40/58, reports of Napier; HO 40/55, reports of Rolleston and Roworth; HO 40/44, deposition of James Harris.

28. *Midland Counties Illuminator* 27 February 1841, p. 9; also 17 April, p. 38.

29. *NS* 6 May 1843, p. 1; 27 May, p. 4; 1 June 1844, p. 1.

30. *NR* 10 August 1838, p. 8.

31. *Midland Counties Illuminator* 13 March 1841, p. 1.

32. *NS* 26 December 1840, p. 1; 13 February 1841, p. 2; 10 April, p. 2 (Mansfield); 6 March 1841, p. 1 (King George); 20 March 1841, p. 1 (Democratic Chapel); 24 April 1841, p. 1 (Arnold); 27 November 1841, p. 2 (Alfreton): *Nott. Journal*, 23 August 1844, p. 3 (Sutton); *NS* 23 October 1841, p. 8 (Burbage); 13 November, p. 1 (Fowkes); 19 August 1843 (Brown). For radical working-class education more generally, see B. Simon, *Studies in the History of Education, 1780–1850*, (London: Lawrence and Wishart, 1960) ch. 5.

33. R. Johnson, '"Really Useful Knowledge"; Radical Education and Working-Class Culture', in J. Clarke, C. Critcher, R. Johnson (eds), *Working-Class Culture: Studies in History and Theory* (London: Hutchinson, 1979) p. 79.

34. *NS* 26 July 1842, p. 6; 24 September, p. 1; 3 December, p. 1.

35. *NR* 19 October 1838, p. 4; *Nott. Mercury* 26 July 1839, p. 237; 27 March 1840, p. 98; *Northern Liberator* 21 March 1840, p. 1; *NS* 24 December 1841, p. 1.

36. As Engels observed: 'Here the children receive a purely proletarian education, free from all the influences of the bourgeoisie . . .' *Condition of the Working Class in England*, in *Marx and Engels on Britain*, (Moscow 1962) pp. 274–5.

37. R. Johnson, 'Educational Policy and Social Control in Early Victorian England', *Past & Present*, no. 49 (1970) 119. For educational provision in Nottingham, see D. Wardle, *Education and Society in Nineteenth-Century Nottingham* (Camb. Univ. Press, 1971); R. J. Smith, 'Education, Society and Literacy: Nottinghamshire in the Mid-Nineteenth Century', *Univ. of Birmingham Historical Journal*, XII (1969) 42–56.

38. J. W. Hudson, *The History of Adult Education* (London 1851) p. 147; *NR* 31 January 1845, p. 3; J. H. Green, *History of the Nottingham Mechanics Institute* (Nottingham 1887); W. H. Wylie, *Old and New Nottingham* (Nottingham 1853) p. 342, gives a complete breakdown of the MI's membership: of 984 members only 45 came under the category of journeymen lace and stocking-makers.

39. *NR* 2 May 1845, p. 8.

40. Wylie, *Old and New Nottingham*, pp. 350–1; Wardle, *Education and Society*, pp. 183–4; *Catalogue and Rules of the Operative Library Number One*, (Nottingham 1843); Hudson, *Adult Education*, p. 148; J. J. Rowley, 'Drink and the Public House in Nottingham, 1830–60', *Transactions of the Thoroton Soc.*, LXXIX (1975) 78–9; *NR* 6 January 1843, p. 4.

41. *McDouall's Chartist and Republican Journal* 24 July 1841, p. 131; *NR* 12 June 1846, p. 8, Rowley, 'Drink in Nottingham', 79. The Chartists John Goodson (cabinet-maker), Henry Cope (secretary of the Radford Library), Joshua Carrington, James Bucknal, John Christie (knitters) and Joseph Burbage (needle-maker) were all active in the affairs of various Operative Libraries.

42. *NR* 27 January 1843, p. 4; 6 December 1844, p. 4; 1 February 1845, p. 1;

28 February, p. 4; 11 April, p. 4; 2 May, p. 8; 23 May, p. 6; 13 June, p. 4; 12 September, p. 4; 7 November, p. 4; 10 April 1846, p. 4.

43. Ibid., 13 October 1853, p. 4; Rowley, 'Drink in Nottingham', 84.

44. *NR* 13 November 1846, p. 8.

45. *NS* 8 January 1841, p. 3; 10 April, pp. 1, 4; 17 April, p. 1 (Vincent); *NR* 31 August 1838, p. 6 (Hall); *Midland Counties Illuminator* 1 May 1841, p. 46 (Cooper); *NS* 1 May 1841, p. 1; 8 May, p. 1; 29 May, p. 2 (New Move); *NS* 30 April 1842, p. 6 (Harrison); also see B. Harrison, 'Teetotal Chartism', *History*, LVIII (1973); J. J. Rowley, 'Drink and Temperance in Nottingham, 1830–60' (Univ. of Leicester M.A. thesis, 1974). I am also indebted to Mr Rowley for sharing his knowledge of Nottingham Chartism with me.

46. *NS* 1 January 1842, p. 1.

47. See G. Stedman Jones, 'Class Expression versus Social Control? A Critique of Recent Trends in the Social History of "Leisure"', *History Workshop Journal*, no. 4 (1977) 169–70.

48. *Midland Counties Illuminator* 17 April 1841, p. 38; also 27 March, p. 26.

49. Ibid., 24 April–15 May 1841; *NS* 24 April–1 May 1841; Cooper, *Life*, pp. 156–8.

50. *Nott. Mercury*, 16 August 1839, p. 264.

51. *NR* 23 August 1839, p. 4; *Nott. Journal*, 30 August 1839, p. 3; *NR* 19 August–2 September 1842; PRO, HO 45/254.

52. *NR* 2 February 1844, p. 8; 18 October, p. 4; 19 September 1845, p. 4; 19 December, p. 4; 23 April 1847, p. 4; 10 December, p. 4; *NS* 1 June 1844, p. 8; Rowley, 'Drink in Nottingham', 75–8.

53. *NS* 12 March 1842, p. 7; 28 May, p. 2; 3 June 1848, p. 5; 29 July, p. 1.

54. *NR* 3 March 1848, p. 4.

55. *NS* 8 April 1843, p. 5; 17 June, p. 8; Rowley, 'Drink in Nottingham', 76. The pre-Chartist radical movement at Nottingham was organised around working-class reading-rooms in taverns. See for instance *Black Dwarf* 21 August 1822, p. 267; *Lion*, 15 August 1828, p. 195; M. I. Thomis, *Old Nottingham*, (Newton Abbot: David and Charles, 1968) ch. 10.

56. *NS* 13 February 1847, p. 1.

57. *Nott. Mercury* 6 December 1839, p. 392. Eliza Blatherwick lectured regularly at the Democratic Chapel during the mid-1840s. For Chartist women more generally, see D. Thompson, 'Women and Nineteenth-Century Radical Politics: A Lost Dimension', in J. Mitchell and A. Oakley (eds), *The Rights and Wrongs of Women* (Harmondsworth: Penguin, 1976).

58. PRO, HO 40/50, fo. 752; *NR* 24 January 1840, p. 4; 31 January, p. 5; 10 July, p. 4 (Woodhouse); *NR* 6 March 1840, p. 80 (Black); 14 May 1847, p. 3 (Barber).

59. *NS* 15 October 1842, p. 1; 5 November, p. 6; 31 December, p. 8; 18 February 1843, p. 8; 8 April, p. 5; 15 April, pp. 1, 5; 25 May 1844, p. 1. The Nottingham Chartists put on the 'Trial of Robert Emmet' and the play 'John Frost' to raise funds for the local victims. *NS* 29 July 1843, p. 2; *NR* 16 February 1844, p. 5.

60. *NS* 13 August 1842, p. 5; 'The Working Class and Leisure: Class Expression and/or Social Control', conference report, *Bull. of the Soc. for the Study of Labour History*, no. 32 (1976) 7.

61. *Nott. Mercury* 23 August 1844, p. 135. Emma Martin, the Owenite lecturer, had been speaking in the market-place.

62. *NR* 9 August 1844, p. 5.

63. Cooper, *Life*, pp. 174–5; *NR* 10 April 1846, p. 4.

64. *Nott. Mercury* 30 August 1844, p. 139.

65. *NS* 23 July 1842, p. 5; 30 July, pp. 4, 1; *NR* 29 July 1842, p. 6.

66. *NS* 23 April 1842, p. 6.

67. See G. M. Morris, 'Primitive Methodism in Nottinghamshire' (Univ. of Nottingham Ph.D. thesis, 1967); Morris, 'Primitive Methodism in Nottinghamshire, 1815–32', *Transactions of the Thoroton Soc.*, LXXII (1968).

68. PRO, TS 11/601, Mead to Cooper, 30 July 1842.

69. Minutes of the Nottingham Circuit Quarterly Meeting, June 1841; December 1841; December 1843 – cited in Morris, 'Primitive Methodism' (Ph.D. thesis), pp. 246–8; *NS* 10 April 1841, p. 1. On occasion Chartists were allowed to meet at Methodist chapels in the industrial villages; more often they were denied such access.

70. *NR* 7 September 1838, p. 4.

71. Cf. H. Gutman, 'Protestantism and the American Labor Movement: The Christian Spirit in the Gilded Age', in H. Gutman, *Work, Culture and Society in Industrializing America* (New York: Vintage, 1977), particularly pp. 84–90, 107.

72. *NR* 29 March 1839, p. 7.

73. Ibid., 7, 14 June 1839; 26 July–16 August; PRO, HO 40/53, fos. 531, 593–7, 607–10, 636–7, HO 40/47, fos. 350, 525; *NS* 14 March 1840, p. 7.

74. *NS* 19 December 1840, p. 1; 17 April 1841, p. 1; 24 April, p. 1; 24 September 1842, p. 2; *NR* 9 December 1842, p. 4; *Nott. Mercury* 27 March 1840, p. 98 (Dean); *NS* 14 May 1842, p. 2 (Simmons); also see R. T. Morrison, *Class Legislation Exposed; or, Practical Atheism Identified with the Advocates of Property Qualifications for Legislative Enfranchisement* (London, 1841).

75. *NS* 28 August 1841, p. 7; 12 March 1842, p. 1; 30 July, p. 3; 6 May 1843, p. 8; 27 May, p. 4; 14 June 1844, p. 1; *NR* 5 April 1844, p. 4.

76. PRO, TS 11/601, Sweet to Cooper, 16 July 1842; Boonham to Cooper, (n.d.); *NR* 19 July 1844, p. 6; B. A. Barber, *A Methodist Pageant* (London: Holbern Publishing House, 1932) pp. 74–5 – cited in Morris, 'Primitive Methodism' (Ph.D. thesis) pp. 246–7; see E. Yeo, 'Robert Owen and Radical Culture', in S. Pollard and J. Salt (eds), *Robert Owen, Prophet of the Poor* (London: Macmillan, 1971) pp. 99–103, for inversion of ritual.

77. *NS* 24 October 1846, p. 5. For Barber, see John Rowley's entry in *Dictionary of Labour Biography*, IV, pp. 6–7.

78. *Proceedings of the Meeting called . . . for the purpose of forming a Church Building Society, for the County and Town of Nottingham* (Nottingham, 1841) p. 2; *NR* 6 October 1848, p. 5.

79. *NS* 20 May 1843, p. 6; 30 March 1844, p. 1; 20 April, p. 6; 15 August 1846, p. 5; *NR* 2–23 February 1844; 15 March, p. 4; 29 March, p. 4; 5 November 1847, p. 2 (Poor Law and local government); *NR* 7 May 1845, p. 2 (enclosure); 14 May 1847, p. 3 (distress); 24 June 1842, p. 4; 27 January 1843, p. 2; 21 February 1845, p. 6 (church rates); 19 January 1844, p. 2; 10 April 1846, p. 8 (night work); 12 May 1843, p. 2 (education bill); 3 May 1844, p. 3 (Master and

Servant bill); 4 November 1842, p. 3; 10 November 1843, p. 3; 7 June 1844, p. 6; 21 November 1845, p. 8 (election bribery). In effect, the local Chartist leaders formed a group of what Gramsci termed 'organic intellectuals'.

80. *NR* 7 December 1838, p. 8. In 1847 Barber was secretary to the Nottingham knitters. *NR* 23 April 1847, p. 4.

81. PRO, HO 40/22, fo. 44, handbill dated 8 March 1827, signed by Humphries, as secretary to the striking silk-knotted knitters, an office he was to hold for the next twenty years.

82. *Report . . . into the Conditions of Framework Knitters*, pt 2. Other known Chartists included: John Buckland, Thomas Kerry, Benjamin Humphries, Henry Dorman, William Carrington (Nottingham), Thomas Grainger (Arnold), William West and Thomas Allsop (Radford), William Parker and Thomas Crompton (Sutton), Samuel Winters (Carlton), John Hickling (Basford).

83. *NR* 25 December 1840, p. 4; *Report . . . on the Employment of Children*, 1843, f. 43.

84. Ibid., 26 August 1842, p. 4; *NS* 27 August 1842, p. 1: *Address to the Magistrates, Gentlemen, Manufacturers, and Tradesmen of Nottingham* (1842, handbill, Nottingham County Library). Local Chartists supported both the great stonemasons' strike in 1842 and the miners in 1844. A. R. Griffin, *Mining in the East Midlands* (London: Cass, 1971) pp. 72–3, suggests that the organisation which sprang up so quickly in support of the miners was provided by the Chartists.

85. *House of Commons Journal*, LXLVIII (1843) 3 July, p. 445; *NR* 21 April 1843, p. 8.

86. *NR* 12 May 1843, p. 2. For a classic working-class statement of 'moral' opposition to bourgeois political economy, see *A Reply to 'A Manufacturer's Remarks' on the Hosiery Bill . . . by a Workman* (Nottingham, 1847).

87. *NR* 26 March 1847, p. 2.

88. Ibid., 6 February 1846, p. 8; 24 May 1844, p. 4 (on Gisborne).

89. Ibid., 21 January 1842, p. 4; 1 March 1844, p. 4; 29 March, p. 4; 6 February 1846, p. 8; *Nott. Mercury*, 28 April 1843, p. 970; 3 April 1846, p. 273; 17 April, p. 281; also see *Hansard*, 3rd series, LXLIII, 9 June 1847, cols. 261 ff. (debate on the Hosiery Manufacture Bill).

90. *NR* 2 April 1847, p. 6.

91. *NS* 24 October 1846, p. 5.

92. For co-operative retailing, production and the NAUT at Nottingham, see *NS* 19 February 1842, p. 8; 9 March 1844, p. 2; 8 February 1845, p. 5; 22 February, p. 1; 29 March, pp. 7–8; 14 November 1846, p. 5; 13 February 1847, p. 5; 23 March, p. 4; 29 May, p. 6; 30 October, p. 1; 6 November, p. 7.

93. *NR* 16 October 1846, p. 4.

94. J. Foster, *Class Struggle and the Industrial Revolution: Early Industrial Capitalism in Three English Towns* (London: Weidenfeld and Nicolson, 1974), pp. 3, 186–94, ch. 7, *passim*. See Stedman Jones's chapter 1 above.

95. The People's College was largely the work of George Gill (a wealthy hosiery agent, Unitarian, temperance reformer and radical). While more 'liberal' than the MI, the College was ultimately under the control of leading local merchants and manufacturers.

96. Revd James Orange's paternalistic scheme to provide allotment gardens

for working-class families is perhaps an example of such concern, despite the near total failure of the plan. See R. A. Church, 'James Orange and the Allotment System in Nottingham', *Transactions of the Thoroton Soc.*, LXIV (1960).

97. *NS* 29 July 1843, p. 5.

98. *NR* 2, 9 September 1842; 11–25 November; 18 August 1843, p. 5; 1 December, p. 4; 12 January 1844, p. 8; 1 November, p. 6; 14 March 1845, p. 8.

99. *NR*, 14 April–5 May 1848; 23 June. The People's League, like the Complete Suffrage Union, found considerable middle-class support at Nottingham.

8. 1848: Feargus O'Connor and the Collapse of the Mass Platform

JOHN BELCHEM

I

A study of the national structure of popular protest, a study concentrating on the national leaders and public image of the Chartist
Movement, might appear a somewhat backward step in historiographical
terms. True, there has been some concern at the dominance of the local
studies approach since the appearance of A. Briggs's *Chartist Studies*.
But now that local studies have begun to highlight the 'cultural'
dimensions of radical commitment, showing how at the branch level at
least, Chartists were able to experience an alternative way of life in
their own lifetimes, it would seem rather perverse to define the Chartist
challenge in terms of political pressure, of national campaigns and mass
platform agitation.[1] Furthermore those historians who see strong
insurrectionist impulses within the movement are little concerned with
the national leaders and evanescent crowds at the great mass meetings,
but seek to draw our attention to leaders and activists 'below the
platform' and to more permanent 'cells of opposition.'[2] In short, to
concentrate on the platform smacks too much of a 'spontaneous' or
reductionist interpretation of popular protest, concluding investigation
at the very point at which it becomes of interest to the social historian.[3]

What must be understood here is that this is a study of Chartism in
1848, the last great mass platform agitation. In every sense the campaign

was a conscious revival of earlier agitations: in every aspect failure was more obvious than ever before. Economic indices, charts of 'social tension', all the devices of economic reductionism, can explain neither the ageing structure of protest in 1848 nor the quality, intensity and complexity of the debate which was to produce a fundamental redirection of radical endeavour in the ensuing years. 1848 witnessed the last display of the strength of the mass platform: afterwards radicalism lost both its confrontationalist stance and its resistance to meliorist alternatives and cultural assimilation. This does not imply that 1848 represents a Chartist climax: rather that it marks the end of an era in popular radicalism. It was the decisive and somewhat ignominious failure of the basic radical tactic which was to call the whole pattern of radicalism into question. A functional analysis of the mass platform in 1848 should shed light on the earlier structure of popular protest and suggest some approaches to understanding the transition to mid-Victorian radicalism.

The potential of the mass platform, barely glimpsed in the 1790s, was established in the post-Napoleonic period, when open constitution-alism brought thousands to the radical cause, posed considerable problems for the authorities and stirred middle-class 'public opinion' out of its war-time compliance.[4] Extra-parliamentary 'constitutional' agitation by all for a 'constitutional' programme for all, remained the very essence of mainstream popular radicalism, continuing to serve these three functions – uniting the working class, pressuring the govern-ment, and courting public opinion. The legitimacy of both tactics and programme was heavily stressed, the 'culture of constitutionalism' being so open to radical interpretation, with the rulers, as Edward Thompson has noted, 'whether willingly or unwillingly, the prisoners of their own rhetoric.'[5] Birthrights, the rule of law, constitutionalism, provided the radicals with a court of appeal that was held in popular reverence and which the ruling class could not ignore, save by shedding too much of its legitimising ideology and unmasking its class rule. As such consti-tutional exactitude and punctiliousness was not the besetting sin of a radical movement overburdened with artisan autodidacts and lapsed lawyers all anxious to display their pedantry, but a forthright strategy for popular radicalism, very much in line with the modern 'politics of protest', in which the inter-action between the protesters and the authorities is recognised as all important.[6] Early nineteenth-century popular radicalism operated beyond the communal framework and direct action of the 'pre-industrial' crowd. The mechanism of the mass platform was more protracted, but its pressure was cumulative.

Petitions, remonstrances, memorials, appeals to the nation, not only facilitated a progressive display of national solidarity, but also could – as Peterloo had shown – unnerve the authorities, and secure the radicals moral ascendancy.

Seen in these terms, the mass platform represented a real challenge, and was the unquestioned tactic of radicals of all shades. So-called 'ultra-radicals' looked to the constitutional mass platform as the means of engineering confrontation and harnessing popular indignation – as 'a good means of beginning a revolution.'[7] 'Moral force' radicals appreciated the opportunity both to demonstrate the legality of the radical cause and to outmanoeuvre the authorities in the wider contest for public opinion. As for the great popular leaders, Henry Hunt and Feargus O'Connor, the platform served to facilitate such a display of overwhelming mass support and preparedness as would coerce an otherwise inexorable government. This policy of forceful intimidation underlined the threat of violence implicit in the platform and capitalised on the essential ambiguity of open constitutionalism, with Hunt and O'Connor punctuating their exhortations to legal behaviour with dire threats of what might happen should the people's will be denied.[8] Finally even the insurrectionists, or 'real conspirators' as they have been called, the small minority who actually crossed the threshold of violence, chose not to act until after the whole gamut of extra-parliamentary machinery had been tried. Vanguard groups operating outside this 'constitutional' framework and prepared to use 'extra-legal, anti-system tactics' do not figure prominently in radicalism during this period.[9]

The mass platform remained largely unchallenged as the fundamental radical tactic. In times of 'distress' there still seemed no quicker way of attracting numbers and of binding sectional interests together. Although increasingly aware of just how transient such support could be, few radicals were prepared to shun the platform altogether. Hard-bitten Chartists continued to calculate on the dynamic of 'excitement' which the platform generated, once a campaign had got off the ground. Furthermore of course, extra-parliamentary activity had been seen to succeed in 1829 and 1832, promoting the very highest hopes of what a genuine mass platform campaign could achieve. The Chartists of 1848 had lost much of their naïve optimism, but it was still to the mass platform that they turned.

II

The impact of revolution abroad, it is generally assumed, resuscitated

Chartism in 1848. The assumption is shared by, on the one hand, those historians who view the agitation of 1848 almost as an unnecessary postscript, the movement having been defeated to all intents and purposes, by the social legislation and increasing economic stability of the 1840s; and on the other hand, by the growing number of historians who see the period 1848-51 as a satisfying coda, the initial external stimulus adumbrating, as it were, the tardy but welcome infusion of continental social theories and ideas. As it was, the machinery of the mass platform creaked into motion well before the outbreak of the French Revolution. The campaign was a revival in every sense with the old leadership and the old tactics very much at the centre.[10]

There seemed little prospect of a revival as 1848 opened. Neither the commercial crisis nor the general election of 1847 had done much to rekindle Chartist spirits, and political indifference characterised the members of the Land Company. The 'Chartist Intelligence' columns of the *Star* suddenly sprang to life, however, when the localities learnt that O'Connor's return as MP for Nottingham was being contested. So favourable, indeed, was the response to the call to help defend O'Connor's seat that the Executive decided to mount a petition campaign for the Charter itself.[11]

For once, London was in the forefront of the movement, with the Chartist Council arranging a series of meetings to promote the new campaign. At the Royal British Institution on 11 January, Ernest Jones announced the tactics to be adopted:

> I conceive we are assembled here to assist in passing a Coercion Bill against the government, and to produce such a 'pressure from without', as shall squeeze poor little Lord John into something like a decent and statesman-like shape.

He then detailed a programme of forcible intimidation:

> We must agitate and organise! One simultaneous meeting, at one hour of one day all over the United Kingdom, to shew our organisation. One vast petition, to prove the people themselves how strong they are in numbers. One vast procession of the men of London to present it, while a Convention watches the debate, and keeps piling the pressure from without, till every town in England and Scotland rallies with the same spirit ... we are not men of non-resistance and

passive obedience; we will not be the aggressors – but if we are struck, will return the blow and they must stand the consequence.

He was seconded by Harney, by now a veteran campaigner, who underlined the need for organisation and preparation to accompany platform agitation: 'any petition will be the very vanity of vanities, unless the people exhibit the will and determination to take other steps to enforce their claims.' Convinced that political and social monopoly could be shattered by the numerical force of the working class, Harney and Jones were drawing up the battle lines for 'The War of Classes.' Jones, in particular, was anxious to avoid earlier errors and weaknesses, not least the false and debilitating division into moral and physical force camps. Moral force and physical force, Jones contended, were 'twin cherries on the stalk', the essential point being that 'by showing a bold physcial front, they would prevent the necessity for physical action.' Physical organisation was thus the order of the day: without organisation, Jones elucidated, 'a people is a mob; but with it, it becomes an army.' There were two ways of using physical force, he explained to a Halifax audience on 24 January: 'the one is to be strong enough to strike – that is but a poor way and a wrong one. The other is: to be strong, *that none dare strike you! Become so!*' Harney even suggested that the Chartists lecturers should forgo 'traversing the great-trodden path – the beaten round of the towns in the manufacturing districts' in favour of enlisting the physically strong part of the working population, the railway labourers, miners, soldiers and the like: 'those masses of physical force, which, even at present, though deplorably wanting in mental power, strike alarm into the minds of the supporters of the existing system.'[12]

In their advocacy of 'pressure from without' Harney and Jones looked upon the constitutional machinery of petitioning as useful only in so far as it facilitated the development of an organisation which no government would dare to resist. At last it seemed, the threat of overwhelming numbers would have something firm behind it. The necessary discipline and organisation, however, were not easy to achieve. Many agitators were still content to rodomontade about the power of the platform, indulging in thrilling oratory and ominous threats, without ensuring that their audience actually enrolled in centrally co-ordinated, ongoing organisation. Dr Peter Murray McDouall, for example, the most popular peripatetic orator in the provinces, was the master of instant dramatic involvement – the procession, the emotive pledge and 'exciting oratory.' 'In seeking for the regeneration of our country', he told a large audience in Nottingham Forest,

> we must go through certain forms, and after we have done every-thing, such as signing the petition, then if we fail, I trust we shall either conquer or die together (hear, hear) . . . We pray for the people's Charter: if they dare us to take it, we will take more than the people's Charter (Cheers) . . . We cannot tolerate aristocracy any longer. If we cannot remove it peaceably then there is one more appeal: are you prepared to answer that appeal? (loud cries of 'yes').

He then led the crowd in a procession to the market-place where they swore their allegiance 'not to the Queen, BUT to the People's Charter' and registered a 'vow to God, that we shall sacrifice life, liberty and property, till the country shall be free.' This was marvellous-sounding stuff, but McDouall's rhetoric of emotive ambivalence, like so much radical oratory in the past, made it difficult to restrain some groups until the 'certain forms' had been tried, whilst at the same time providing no clear guideline as to when or how the threshold of violence should be crossed.[13] More damaging still, as far as the successful application of pressure from without was concerned, was the reluctance of some Chartists to discuss ulterior measures at all at this stage. Leading figures like Philip McGrath were determined to preserve the constitutional image of the movement. As forceful as McDouall in his denunciation of aristocratic usurpation and class legislation, McGrath was critical of those who belittled the process of petitioning, particularly as he sensed 'the revival of that spirit which triumphed at Runnymede.' Although he conceded the Petition would probably be rejected, he stigmatised any discussion of ulterior measures as premature and harmful, and insisted that such matters be reserved for the Convention.[14]

McDouall's extravaganza, McGrath's attention to constitutional propriety, Jones' promotion of physical organisation, all operated within the uncontroverted framework of the mass platform. Until the National Petition was discredited, the movement was firmly united. O'Connor's leadership was unquestioned. His credentials, of course, were enshrined in the past history of the movement, in 'our wars, our struggles, and our conquests.' The scourge of the 'poor gentlemen' and 'coward brawlers' who had infested earlier campaigns, O'Connor was now determined to use his 'legitimate position as your trusted leader' to implore the Old Guards 'not to allow our holy purpose to be marred, retarded, or stopped, by treachery, imbecility or folly.' With news of revolution abroad having brought a tremendous injection of strength, and with the Convention and the presentation of the National Petition duly moved forward a month, O'Connor was determined to retain the generalship of the platform, to take his rightful place on 10 April 'at the head of the mind of England, followed by the sinews of England, in procession to the House of Commons, for I will allow no man to go before me.' At the same time, O'Connor was busily engaged in presenting the movement in a somewhat different guise. Chartism, he explained, had now reached the final stage of agitation, the direction of public opinion. With the people now 'prepared to hear and discuss what they were to do with the Charter when they got it', O'Connor was anxious to convince the lower-middle class of the necessity and practicality of Chartism's programme of 'social regeneration.' After April this second course was to predominate, and whilst this vitiated the efforts of those who still looked to the mass platform, it can hardly be described as an abnegation of leadership. Rather, it was the forceful assertion of a redirection of radical endeavour.[15]

Details of O'Connor's programme for practical social regeneration appeared in a lengthy 'manifesto' in the *Star* in mid-March.[16] The timing is most significant. On the one hand, O'Connor was responding to the new language of the 'organisation of labour' introduced by the revolution in France and rapidly all the rage. O'Connor was not going to allow the Land Plan – his 'god-like scheme of releasing your wives and little children from the abodes of pestilence, famine, immorality, disease and death, and placing them in their own paradise' – to be up-staged. Since the very beginning of the campaign he had insisted that the Charter and the land were inseparable. They now benefited, he insisted, by having 'both a political and a social wedge': indeed, 'he would not give a pin for the Charter tomorrow, if the land was locked up from them.' Having created and organised Chartist opinion, he was now, so he claimed, directing its mind towards a new and secure social system 'based upon social happiness, arising from individuality of possession, and cooperation of labour, protected by the possession of political power.' The French approach to political and social reform, he never tired of explaining, was quite inappropriate for English purposes. The platform made recourse to physical force unnecessary, while serving too as a forum for instruction 'in the value of a new social system, of the fruits of which you have resolved that you will not be robbed.' Lacking this solid base of instruction in the 'Labour question', the French had spawned visionary schemes of social reform all of which, he confidently predicted, were doomed to disaster and would end in a revolution against the labourer.[17] But O'Connor's practical plan to make 'the rich richer and the poor rich' was less a bid to fore-stall the intrusion of continental notions than an attempt to capitalise on the domestic political situation. Circumstances seemed particularly propitious for the radicals to appeal yet again to their economic if not political allies, the lower-middle class. The 'manifesto' reflected a pervasive Chartist conviction that the financial ineptitude of the Whigs would shatter the specious unity which Cobden had given the middle classes completely divorcing the small shopkeeper and the like from what Samuel Kydd dubbed the 'mushroom millionaires' of 1846. So-called Free Trade, the 'manifesto' explained, had seen home trade, the shopkeepers' bread and butter as much as the working man's wages, sacrificed to foreign trade, the exclusive monopoly of the capitalists, the 'great moneyocracy.'[18] O'Connor's programme offered an end to the excesses of the national debt, indirect taxation, church rates and poor rates, the last being redirected towards the purchase of land, 'my mode of setting all the springs of industry at work.' Self-support-ing agricultural schools and colleges were to replace the Poor Law Bastilles. The unwilling idler would become the happy man in his own labour field and, as the shopkeeper would appreciate, 'a better customer, a better friend, and a better subject, than the system-made pauper who is consigned to the workhouse and made a burthen upon their industry.'

O'Connor's hope for an alliance with the shopkeepers exemplified the Chartist propensity to overrate middle-class discontent and the vicissitudes of Westminster politics.[19] More egregious still in this particular instance, was the absence of any estimate or consideration of the social and political polarisation generated by the mass platform in this 'year of revolution.' O'Connor never realised that the contest for public opinion had been lost before Kennington Common, before indeed the publication of his 'manifesto'. The mass platform was to fail so miserably in its effort to compel Parliament to accept the Charter in 1848, because it fell so short in its other functions. McGrath's traditional constitutional moderation, O'Connor's emphasis on practical social regeneration, made no impression on public opinion, 1848 witnessing, as John Saville has noted, 'the first example on any extended scale of that extraordinary unanimity which comes over the English press in face of social revolutions abroad which threaten to export their dangerous ideas.'[20] Nor for all their awareness of what was lacking in the past could Jones and Harney bring sufficient discipline and organisation to the platform to make it an effective expression of working-class grievance.

The débâcle of the anti-income tax agitation and the Poor Law riots of March illustrate the complementary failure of the platform to harness the riotous disposition of the crowd and to secure public approbation. The clamour of the 'Bees of Society' – 'Professional Gentlemen, Bankers, Merchants, Manufacturers, Tradesmen, and all who constitute their numerous train of aides, assistants, or dependants'[21] – along with the prospect of parliamentary defeat by an alliance of protectionists and radicals, prompted the Whigs to relinquish plans to increase the income tax. Charles Cochrane, a middle-class demagogue still saw fit to continue with an anti-income tax meeting, but at the last minute 'fled – disguised as a respectable man' leaving Trafalgar Square to G. W. M. Reynolds, a 'frequent bankrupt' who now 'jumped into Chartism at Charing Cross.'[22] The Chartist Executive were scornful of Cochrane's parody of Odillon Barrot, and were considerably disturbed by Reynolds' maverick behaviour. Reynolds, indeed, had won the meeting for the Charter, but at the cost of identifying Chartism with riot, disorder and crime. The meeting, it appears, was rather a field day for the capital's petty criminals, whilst the ensuing procession and rioting gave the crowd a chance 'to show their Republicanism by breaking all the Crown glass that they can get a shot at unseen by the authorities.' As a result of the 'Trafalgar Square Revolution', *Punch,* an accurate barometer of opinion, 'felt it to be his duty to exert all his powers of ridicule, even to a pardonable exaggeration, in the cause of order and loyalty'. The efforts of the Chartist Executive to set the public record straight were unavailing: from this point on, the press refused to distinguish between rioter, revolutionary, criminal and Chartist.[23] Attempts to convince the crowd of the need for discipline and organisation were no more successful. Care was taken to ensure that the official Chartist line was propagated at the flurry of outdoor meetings which followed Trafalgar Square. Ernest Jones was deputed by the Executive to attend the largest of these gatherings, at Kennington Common on 13 March. But the day ended as something of a repeat performance of the previous week's proceedings, a 'mob' of about 400 foraging its way through Southampton Street, relieving the pawnbrokers and shopkeepers there of a thousand pounds-worth of their stock.[24]

This 'turmoil' in London did not fit into Chartist tactics at all. Those involved were primarily youths: only 9 of the 127 apprehended between 6 and 8 March were over thirty. There was no concentration on particular or traditional radical artisan groups. The occupation of 23 of the 27 apprehended on 13 March is known: no less than 18 different occupations are listed ranging from a ginger-beer maker to a hawk-boy. According to the *Annual Register*, at least two of the number were known thieves, having been convicted twice before. The contrast with those involved in 'conspiracy' later in the year is striking.[25]

Events in the provinces took a similar turn. In those areas where the economic dislocation precipitated by the French Revolution had swollen the numbers of unemployed, the Chartists were accounted responsible for the various riots and disturbances in and around the workhouses. In fact, in every case the local Chartist leadership kept well distant from events and reprobated such 'foolish and criminal exhibitions.' Here too youths seemed to make the most of the occasion. The Manchester riot, the Chartists insisted, was all the work of 'mischievous imps and lads': of the fourteen people apprehended, only four were over twenty.[26]

The disorderly behaviour of youths, the unemployed, and the metropolitan lumpenproletariat, rightly or wrongly, tarnished the public image of Chartism. The sumptuary radicalism of the middle class disappeared: the inequities of taxation, the soaring burden of poor relief, were overshadowed by the need to maintain order. And with the press warning of the spread of the continental revolutionary contagion, the Chartists stood little chance of establishing the legality of their campaign and the legitimacy of their demands. The *Annual Register* correctly assessed the implications of the March riots: 'The nuisance had, however, one favourable effect, in rousing the inhabitants of London to meet the more formidable dangers of the 10th April.' 'Borderline' occupational groups, shopkeepers, clerks, the lower-middle-class elements O'Connor so earnestly invoked, hurried to enlist in the ranks of the special constabulary.[27]

Much the same can be said of Chartism's express identification with the Irish agitation in 1848. The union in no way enhanced the public image of the movement: to the press and the juries the subsequent riotousness of the Irish was the final confirmation of the essential violence of Chartism. However, against the backlash of public opinion, and the ultimate failure to impose a disciplined, organised framework, must be set the excitement and anticipation the alliance generated. The long-hoped-for union was a considerable accretion of physical strength. To O'Connor, of course, this had always been the desideratum. 'For now thirteen years', he chided the audience at the Free Trade Hall on St Patrick's Day, 'I have have advocating the very union which you have thus tardily confirmed.' So began 'three glorious days' of celebration in Lancashire, culminating in a great demonstration on Oldham Edge, where a solemn vow was sworn to set England and Ireland free – it was O'Connor's most impressive performance of the year.[28]

The Irish alliance sharpened the Chartist challenge. Throughout the north Confederate orators restored an ominous literalness to the otherwise devalued talk of the 'last petition.' Dr Reynolds, indeed, introduced himself to a Liverpool meeting as 'a Young Irelander – one of that class of men who detested and hated, and spurned the word "petition".' The need rather than the right to arm was heavily stressed. 'The only way to proceed', Matthew Somers insisted, 'was with a musket over the Shoulder and a pike in the hand.' These instruments, it seems, were obtainable from Dr Reynolds at modest cost.[29] As in early Chartism, there was strong expectation, even an eager anticipation of governmental violence,[30] with Somers promising 'the martyrs dying on the scaffold or on the plain . . . the consolation in looking up to Heaven to see the skies reddened with the blaze of the Babylons of England.' To watch for provocation, an Observation Committee of Chartists and Confederates was set up in Manchester, prepared to 'dare all and risk all even life.'[31]

In the build-up to 10 April, the Irish alliance certainly seems to have strengthened the Chartist platform. The 'press gang', of course, could score the easy point, *The Times* categorising Chartism as 'a ramification of the Irish conspiracy. The Repealers wish to make as great a hell of this island as they have made of their own.'[32] But the union did give Chartism a more formidable visage. The possibility of the military being overstretched by simultaneous outbreaks in England and Ireland perturbed many magistrates. The rhetoric of open constitutionalism had been revitalised and taken at least to the very verge of legality. It remained for the Convention to provide central co-ordination and leadership.

III

The Convention assembled at John Street on 4 April, with the delegates all reporting that this was to be the 'last petition', and that they were pledged not to leave London without the Charter. Subsequent discussion, however, soon revealed an all-too familiar hesitancy and diffidence.[33] G. W. M. Reynolds insisted that 'this should be the last petition to the House . . . its refusal would be a declaration of war against labour . . . A few drops of blood were as nothing in the scale.' Ernest Jones had no time for such bluster: in fact only Cuffay was prepared to support Reynolds's precipitate bellicosity. What disturbed Jones even more, however, was the temporising programme outlined by the Executive. Should the National Petition be rejected, they were to address a memorial to the Queen, which was to be adopted at simultaneous meetings to be held on Good Friday. In the interim, the Executive insisted, the Convention should be dissolved, the country agitated from end to end, and then a new more fully representative convention or national assembly should be held 'to carry out the measures now recommended.' Jones considered this an unnecessary and debilitating circumspection of the present Convention's competence. He had hoped, indeed, that the Convention would declare itself permanent straight away, thereby providing much-needed central co-ordination and direction to 'pressure from without.' Determined that the platform should retain the initiative at the critical moment of escalation from petitioning, Jones demanded that, at the very least, the Convention remain sitting until the National Assembly convened:

> it was absolutely necessary the organisation should go on instead of going back – grow larger instead of smaller – and the nucleus must be kept in London. The Convention must be kept sitting – and while they ought to be acting in the capital, they might be only electing in the provinces.

It was only after some discussion and several jibes of despotism that Jones succeeded in amending the Executive programme. After 10 April and the discrediting of the National Petition, he was to find it harder still to convince the Chartists that the programme remained operative.

Jones's policy of progressive, cumulative pressure took for granted the smooth operation of the first stage of the extra-parliamentary mechanism – the display of strength and the presentation of the Petition. It was just such a demonstration that the government was determined to prohibit. Chartism in 1848 was faced by a supremely confident government, so assured of public support that any deference towards constitutional fair play was quite unnecessary. Only too aware that it would not be exposing its own limited professional forces of coercion on 10 April, the government proscribed the Chartist challenge. The percipience not the moderation of the Whigs is remarkable.[34] They seized the opportunity of overpowering a somewhat decrepit protest movement by exploiting the hysteria of the middle class and its lengthy swishing tail, whilst ensuring that precipitate or risky confrontation was avoided. In the midst of the mummery of preparation for 10 April, at the very moment when the Palace of Westminster was being secured against any attack, they rushed through legislation specifically designed to silence the mass platform. The Crown and Government Security Bill introduced the new charge of felonious sedition, a charge which extended to 'open and advised speaking.' The traditional and even Tory-respected distinction between the written word (a felony) and the spoken word (a misdemeanour) was brought to an end. The misleaders rather than the misled, the government explained to warm approval, would at last feel the full force of the law.[35] As for 10 April itself, Stuart legislation against tumultuous petitioning was retrieved from desuetude to prohibit any mass procession through the streets. The government was adamant on this issue as was promptly discovered by the deputation from the Convention sent to the Home Office 'to acquaint the government that they have no intention, and never had, to make an armed display.' Bronterre O'Brien was the first to voice misgivings about persevering with any demonstration, for which transgression he was compelled to resign from the Convention. What disturbed O'Brien was not just the strength and determination of the government, but the adverse effect a demonstration was likely to produce on public opinion, since it 'would let loose hundreds of rogues and thieves upon society, thus bringing down upon themselves the indignation of the reflecting people of this country.' In secret, it seems, Harney arranged a series of meetings with various delegates on 8 and 9 April, at which he advocated the abandonment of both the procession and the meeting on Kennington Common itself. Given the 'alarm' that the press was so industriously creating, Harney opined that operations should be restricted to the mere presentation of the Petition by a small official deputation.[36] Finally McGrath, as chairman of the Convention, wrote to the Commissioners of Police in the hope of reaching a last-minute compromise: 'The car on which will be placed the National Petition, will leave the procession at Regent's *Circus,* and proceed unaccompanied by the people to the House of Commons.' At 8.45 a.m. on 10 April, Inspector Lund showed McGrath a memo from Richard Mayne, stating that no procession whatsoever would be allowed.[37] It was left to O'Connor to find a way out of the impasse.

O'Connor served the movement well at this moment of crisis for which it was largely unprepared, although 'Feargoose' is never given credit for the fact that some display of Chartist strength took place and that an unpropitious clash was avoided.[38] The Convention looked to O'Connor as the only person who had both a sufficient standing with the people and a sufficient command of oratory to extricate the movement from the difficulty posed by the intractability of the government. It was O'Connor who insisted that the meeting, at least, should take place: it was O'Connor who ensured that all went peaceably. His speech on Kennington Common – 'wonderfully silly rot', Henry Solly called it[39] – was in the best tradition of gentlemanly leadership, the rhetoric of mutual flattery being the very thing needed for such an exigency. The death motif, Henry Hunt's favourite device,[40] established the essential indentification of leader and movement:

> I have received at least 100 letters, telling me not to come here today, for that, if I did, my own life would be the sacrifice. My answer was this – 'I would rather be stabbed to the heart than resign my proper place at the head of my children.' (Shouts of 'Bravo!') . . . Will you obey my counsel, and follow my advice? ('Yes, yes.') I will remain among you as a hostage, for, so help me God, I will not desert your cause until life deserts me. (Loud and prolonged cheering) . . . How should I feel if I thought that by any act of mine I had jeopardized the lives of thousands, and thus paralysed our cause? (Hear, hear.) How, I ask, would you feel if you were conscious that you had been parties to my death? What would be our trouble and our sorrow, how great would be our loss!

By such means, O'Connor was able to call off the procession without a murmur of dissent, and to proclaim the meeting 'a great and glorious step achieved', allowing him to 'read the government a lesson in citing your courage and your resolution, but in telling them also of your love for order, and your respect for the law.'

O'Connor, indeed, ensured that 10 April would go down in Chartist annals as 'a day which was neither disfigured by cowardice nor disgraced by turbulence.' As Thomas Frost later wrote, despite the 'wonderful unanimity' which had banded in close phalanx the swindler, the gambler, the pugilist, the brothel-keeper, the stock-jobber, the biller discounter, the profitmonger, the usurer and the factory ogre, the real victory of 10 April 'remained with those who had asserted and maintained the constitutional right of meeting on the one hand, and saved the Proletarians from the vengeance for which their oppressors thirsted on the other.'[41]

IV

O'Connor heralded 10 April as a great triumph, but his reading of the day's outcome served to enervate the Chartist platform. Kennington Common, he maintained, represented a decisive moral victory:

> Chartism – heretofore under a bushel – laughed at by the Press, and mocked in the House of Commons, now finds a place in every newspaper, and haunts every man's brain: whereas, if Chartism had made a feeble resistance to an armed force, the principles would have been destroyed.

O'Connor's tactics were now determined by his conviction that the Chartists had scored a constitutional triumph on 10 April. The movement, he contended, had emerged from Kennington Common in an 'exalted position' and 'augmented in force', having secured the support of the shopkeepers (the jury class) and the trades, the very groups to whom he had addressed his March 'manifesto.' To retain this valuable support, strict adherence to constitutional procedure was imperative.[42]

A further pressing consideration here was the discredited National Petition, the real 'fiasco' of 1848. O'Connor was subjected to much unwarranted contumely in the Commons when the Committee on Petitions reported that the National Petition had not been signed by 5,706,000 as the Chartists alleged, but by 1,975,496, a figure which included many bogus, fraudulent and obscene signatures.[43] Reporting back to the Convention, O'Connor impugned the Committee but insisted that, as things now stood, he would not be justified in moving a motion for the Charter. He suggested further petitioning, hardly a feasible policy with so many delegates committed to the 'last petition.' Militants like Cuffay were undisturbed by the turn of events and 'did not consider that it mattered much what was the real number of the signatures attached to the petition.' Some delegates welcomed Harney's advocacy of a National Guard, 'the most convincing answer they could give to those who denied the numbers.' The majority, however, were anxious for dissolution, thereby deferring any contentious discussion of ulterior measures. As the delegates began to leave for their localities to seek guidance, Jones warned of the danger of losing the initiative. He called upon the delegates 'to act in accordance with previous resolutions which they had come to.' The Petition, he maintained, 'had been virtually rejected, and they were, therefore, justified in coming to the conclusion that they ought to memorialise her Majesty.' The adoption of the Memorial proved to be a parting gesture. The Convention was not actually dissolved but, with its numbers dwinding daily, 'it may be said to have closed its labours.' The exodus to the provinces betokened uncertainty and uneasy unity, just as it removed effective central direction. To many Chartists the next step was not immediately apparent, having been outnumbered on Kennington Common and embarrassed by their own petition. Constitutionalists had been denied the requisite display of righteous public opinion. Confrontationalists had been prepared for repression and resistance, not public ridicule. It was not long before doubts were raised as to whether Parliament's virtual rejection of a discredited unpresented petition afforded sufficient grounds for the step up to the Memorial. O'Connor, indeed, was soon to insist that both the Memorial and the National Assembly should be given up, thereby confounding Jones' policy of mass pressure.

After the 'triumph' of 10 April and the 'unfortunate affair of the National Petition', O'Connor was no longer prepared to endorse and direct a policy of intimidation, to persevere with tactics which necessitated his appearing far more insurrectionary than he in fact was. His intention now was 'to take the stink off Chartism'.[44] This was no retraction, no abnegation of leadership: O'Connor was as determined to head a movement directed towards practical social regeneration as he had earlier been resolute to retain the generalship of platform agitation. Behind his qualms about the Memorial and his spurious legal objections to the National Assembly, lay a genuine commitment to Chartism as a 'labour movement', a determination to extend discussion of the 'labour question.'[45]

The events of April provided the opportunity not the cause for O'Connor's attempted redirection of Chartist endeavour, serving to compound his earlier misreading of the political and social structure. With the middle classes now 'tendering their hearty co-operation to the popular cause', enthusiastic language and extra-parliamentary assemblies were out of place. 'Will you allow', O'Connor demanded, 'the madness of the intemperate to baulk us of the service of these recruits, and once more throw them into more deadly hostility?' Whether legal or not, the National Assembly, he opined, would court disaster and opprobium. Rather than run such risks, and in the absence of a definitive petition, he would wait to see 'how far the combination of shopkeepers, trades, and Irish Repealers, led by their legitimate leaders, and how far liberals and free traders in the House of Commons will go with the people.' Throughout the remainder of his active political life O'Connor entertained extravagant hopes of a new political conjunction, a regrouping of the forces of popular reform, representing the alliance of the 'industrious classes.'[46] In no sense did this imply any diminution in his political and social programme. Whilst determined to expedite the disintegration of the Whigs, O'Connor was no unqualified supporter of the parliamentary radicals: indeed, he delighted in being 'the bugbear of free traders and middle-class deceivers.' Similarly his overtures to the 'veritable middle classes' – 'those of the middle classes who live by agency – buying from the producer and selling to the consumer' – were always accompanied by unequivocal proscription of the capitalist employers, 'the traffickers in human blood and in infant gristle.' The artificial labour system, upon which the power of these 'speculators in unrepresented labour' was built, remained his principal target of attack. In his first major speech of the 1848 campaign at the 'Resurrection of Birmingham' back in January, he had demonstrated how the competitive labour market was the source of working-class misery and disunity:

> we have been most frustrated by those who have measured labour's right by the comparative, instead of the positive scale – by those aristocratic tradesmen who, receiving thirty shillings and two pound a week themselves, scoffed at my battalion of fustian jackets, blistered hands, and unshorn chins, who had but the alternative of entering the competitive labour market, or the Poor Law bastille.

This artifical system, O'Connor appreciated only too well, accounted for the fluctuating fortunes of Chartism, with the labourers 'in the hour of comparative prosperity' deaf to those 'silly enough to foretell the coming cloud and the storm', yet moved to 'frenzy and impetuosity' with the inevitable onset of adversity. Heartsick of the repetition of this pattern, O'Connor called for a new kind of movement: a movement based around discussion of and education in the 'labour question.' In place of the National Assembly, he suggested a convention to propound 'a code of social laws', convinced that 'the flood of Chartist mind will compel the middle classes to fraternise with us, for the animal, name and all .' Immediately after his most virulent attack on the National Assembly, he published his 'Treatise on Labour', a lengthy exposition of his practical programme of social amelioration, punctuated with swingeing attacks on the nascent Little Charter movement.[47]

Whilst his commitment to radicalism remained unmitigated, O'Connor must stand accused of inconsistency. His apostasy over the National Assembly was a crippling blow to those still hoping to pile on the pressure from without. The dissolution of the Convention, and the small crowds at the Easter demonstrations were discouraging enough, but it was O'Connor's sudden and unexpected injunction which all but nullified the National Assembly, the last vestige of the anti-parliament as an operative idea in British radical politics.[48] It was a sorry end to the policy of forcible intimidation.

The sparsely attended Assembly proved to be a bitter disappointment to Ernest Jones, provoking dissension which, he always maintained, could have been avoided had the Convention declared itself permanent in the first place.[49] Inevitably positions had hardened over physical and moral force. The Scottish delegates, who culpably misled Jones with their exaggerated reports of the state of physical organisation in Scotland, asserted

> That moral force was all a humbug
> That nothing persuades like a lick in the lug.[50]

Kydd and Clark countered with an address making it clear that 'the Assembly recommended lectures, tracts, and public meetings as the only means by which that document (the Charter) might be made to become the law of the land.' Jones tried to curtail further discussion and division by insisting that delegates concentrate on what was the task at hand – the presentation of the Memorial. Jones, indeed, still hoped to go on with a policy of cumulative pressure as if the events of April had raised excitement and expectation rather than hesitancy and doubt. The Memorial was to be the next ploy, the mass exercise of this constitutional right serving to remind the government that 'though the physical power of the country might at present slumber, it needed but a touch to make it rush forth like a volcano.' Few delegates appreciated the urgency: most indeed, preferred to discuss 'Great Social Grievances' before giving any consideration to the Memorial.[51] Jones found himself called upon to remind the delegates that they 'were not sent here to discuss abstract principles, but to adopt measures for the enactment of the Charter.' Those who hoped to conciliate the middle class by discussing vague social theories should realise that 'Agitation, action – not talking – could increase the pressure . . . by the time the middle class got hungry enough to swallow the Charter, the people would be starved into their graves.'

Further valuable time was lost during the debates on organisation. To Jones's dismay, the Scottish delegates insisted on introducing personality. Harley began with a tirade against the present 'system of hirelingism.' 'As long as they called themselves the Chartist Association,' Adams elucidated, 'it would be called O'Connor's Association.' The other delegates rallied to the defence of the NCA and O'Connor. Letters of confidence flooded into the Assembly and Harley was soon forced to resign. The *Star* of 13 May was dominated by 'The People's Verdict': fifty meetings which had passed votes of confidence in O'Connor were listed; the next week another forty-six were registered. The Scottish delegates were supported, however, in their call for greater local autonomy within the movement. As at the Convention, Jones's insistence on strong central direction provoked charges of despotism. The new organisation, for the most part 'a return to the good old plan of 1839 of having class leaders', introduced provincial commissioners to keep the Executive in touch with the wards and the classes. Jones, of course, believed that the Executive and the commissioners should be appointed there and then by the Assembly. The delegates rejected this out of hand, and gave short shrift to a compromise proposal suggesting the appointment of a provisional Executive whose election would later be 'ratified' by the country. It was finally agreed that a provisional Executive be appointed only to fill the vacuum until proper elections could be arranged, as the result of which, ironically enough, O'Connor was to be returned president of the NCA.[52] A similar course was adopted for the commissioners, with Jones again being accused of dictation when he tried to impose an Intendant-like function and criterion of selection. He wanted local leaders excluded from consideration since the commissioners 'would have to examine, mediate, and report on the state of the various districts, according to the instructions of the Executive, and they ought therefore to be independent of all local influences.' Inevitably too there were financial issues – the passing-on of local membership fees to the NCA, a proposed increase in salary for the London-based Executive – which exacerbated the tension between the centre and the localities, and consumed still more of the Assembly's time. Detrimental as this was to the rapid and effective application of mass pressure, the vigilance displayed by the provincial delegates over such matters was to remain a major feature of late Chartism. As agitation merged into movement, the details of organisation were of overriding interest in the localities, such concern representing a substructure of constant radical commitment and debate little affected by the ideological fissures which so fascinate historians of the period. Provincial grievance, indeed, became O'Connor's major plank in his subsequent attack on Harney and the 'drones' and 'poor gentlemen' of London – the socialist Fraternal Democrats – who captured control of the NCA in early 1850.[53]

Eventually the Assembly came to discuss the Memorial. Once again the Chartists were hesitant and disunited, the government firm and adamantine. Many delegates echoed O'Connor's earlier reservations, deeming it necessary to test the opinion of the House before memorialising the monarch. They were dismayed to learn, however, that O'Connor still felt unable to bring in a bill for the Charter without the support of petitions. Predictably there was the disturbingly familiar talk of dissolution once it became clear that the authorities would not allow a mass presentation or indeed any presentation of the Memorial to the Queen herself. Jones persisted with the vain hope that further correspondence with the government would secure the people their undoubted right to make their grievances known to the chief magistrate personally. For this he was duly ridiculed by the Scottish delegates – 'mere blusterers on physical force' Gammage labels them – who insisted that they should proceed with a mass demonstration and presentation. With the discussion becoming heated they reminded Jones that it was he who had earlier spoken of both the legality and desirability of such a course of action. A saddened Jones replied: 'circumstances had since altered, and what he now recommended was a thorough organisation of the country before they attempted to come into collision with those rebels in high places.' In the ensuing speeches, as Gammage notes, 'no very amiable feeling was manifested.'[54] Eventually it was decided to shelve the issue: the Memorial was left in the hands of the Provisional Executive. Clearly dissolution was the next step. McDouall in his closing address, and Jones in his 'funeral oration' tried to salvage something, insisting that the Assembly, whilst the target of much attack, had preserved the unity of the movement. Vernon, a future 'red republican' would have none of this, explaining that he could not understand

Mr E. Jones when he talked about there being division but not disunion. He said that they were disunited. The 10th April was not a victory, as had been asserted but a signal defeat . . . There were many of them who did not believe that the Charter was to be got by petitioning and agitation . . . in fact, they must fight for it.

V

The collapse of the National Assembly represented the end of a determined effort to work through the traditional extra-parliamentary machinery of the mass platform to obtain the Charter. Hope remained, however, of marshalling a display of overwhelming public support by some means or other. It was not until such hopes were finally dashed that 'conspiracy' developed.

At the local level Chartist activity had been on the decline since 10 April, convincing Lt-Gen. Arbuthnott of 'the diminished interest of the people.'[55] Chartist commitment and militancy intensified however in areas where the persistence of economic distress and the presence of a strong Irish influence counteracted any hesitancy or languishing discussion of tactical and constitutional niceties. Bradford is a near perfect paradigm of the support Chartism could elicit at the community level. The working class were subjected to distress and displacement. Unlike other towns, the number of recipients of poor relief continued to increase after April. Depression in worsted-manufacture coincided with the introduction of machinery in wool-combing. The Irish influence, personified by George White, was particularly strong, Bradford having the highest concentration of Irish-born in the West Riding. The local authorities were inept but provocative. The Bradford Chartist Council soon took control of events. They demonstrated the inadequacy of appeals calling for the use of certain machines to be discontinued. They prevented 'suicidal' partial rioting and insisted on the need for organisation. They strengthened links with the Irish Repealers – 'the same Government that oppresses them, is also the Enemy of our Rights.' They promoted the formation of the National Guard. With open drilling taking place in the streets of Bradford, the magistrates panicked. A pattern of bungled arrests and crowd rescues was soon established. The Chartist Executive decided to despatch McDouall to Bradford in the hope of capitalising on this outburst of militancy. McDouall held two 'tremendous meetings' on 22 and 23 May: the *Star* commented

all terminated in peace and good order – for a very sufficient reason, that no power was greater than that of the people. If you wish to have the Charter, then let every district do openly, and therefore legally, what Bradford has so nobly done.

The fervour rapidly engulfed the region. The Halifax Chartists marched to McDouall's meetings 'with music playing, banners flying, and the glittering pikes flashing in the sun.' Open drilling spread to Leeds and Bingley, where the most spectacular 'rescues' were effected. Matters finally came to a head at Bradford on 29 May when an intoxicated police constable botched the arrest of two local Chartist leaders, David Lightowler and Isaac Jefferson, better known as 'Wat Tyler'. 'Let us do the Chartists justice', *The Times* reported, 'if fighting with pluck against Special Constables and the police could make a revolution, those who fought at Bradford ought to have succeeded.' After a protracted mêlée, the police eventually emerged the victors and secured nineteen arrests. At last in some control of the situation, the magistrates prohibited a pro-Mitchel procession on 31 May, and followed up this act of 'insolent tyranny' with more arrests. At the same time Ferrand, the Tory factory reformer, asserted his authority at Bingley.[56]

At the national level Chartism was unable to mount such a display of strength, although a determined effort was made to establish the movement's numerical preponderance. The occasion for a national demonstration of strength was provided by the 'insults' of Lord John Russell and Richard Cobden. In the Commons Russell had insisted that the working class did not favour organic reform, and Cobden had dismissed O'Connor as the leader of an insignificant number of 'myrmidons'. To put the record straight, the Provisional Executive called for nation-wide simultaneous meetings on Whit Monday at all of which the Chartists were to stand in rows, thereby facilitating an exact count of heads.[57] The meetings on 12 June were to be the great moral demonstration so far denied the mass platform: here was an opportunity to make good the discredited Petition. This was a forlorn hope. The government was now in a position to direct the full force of its monopoly of legitimate violence against the movement.

The crucial demonstration had, of course, already taken place back in April. 'The Chartists', J.M. Ludlow, the Christian Socialist, explained, 'chose to stake their cause upon a display of physical force, and by a display of physical force they were overwhelmed. They made number their argument and it recoiled upon themselves.' *The Times* calculated that for every Chartist on Kennington Common there were fifteen special constables and insisted that this 'settles the question. In common fairness it ought to be regarded as a settled question for years to come.'[58] After 10 April the government was clearly countenanced to employ coercion should the Chartists refuse to submit to the logic of Kennington Common. Reinforcing the government's resolve and its sanction to deal peremptorily with any Chartist resurgence was the behaviour of the Irish. It was at this eleventh hour that the Chartists' failure to impose a disciplined organised framework was particularly telling.

The Irish connection had been an important factor in Bradford. Maj.-Gen. Thorn, despatched by Arbuthnott to verify the magistrates' alarmist reports, discovered that half the Bradford Chartists were Irish and made no secret of their intention 'to make a diversion should Mitchel be convicted, in order to prevent the government from sending more troops to Ireland.'[59] Mitchel, editor of the *United Irishman,* was the first victim of the Crown and Government Security Act. News of his conviction and transportation was greeted with anger and a show of force throughout the midlands and the north. There were nightly processions through the streets and talk of 'private assassination and Moscowing.' Such conduct was generally disavowed by local Chartist leaders, busy preparing for the great Whitsun demonstrations.[60] Even where the Mitchel protests were co-ordinated and organised, as in the Manchester area, similar disapprobation ensued. At meetings at Oldham, Stalybridge, Stockport and Newton on 29 May, it was resolved to march to Stevenson's Square, Machester on 31 May, a demonstration organised by the Repeal Delegates in Manchester Assembled. This body, chaired by George Archdeacon, the Irish orator who had opened the proceedings at the Free Trade Hall on 17 March, included local Chartist leaders like Edward Clark Cropper and Daniel Donovan. The demonstration was declared illegal and the authorities took possession of the Square early in the day. News soon came of processions from Ashton, Oldham and Mosley, all of which were turning out the mills by drawing the plugs. Then a placard was spotted announcing that the meeting had been adjourned to Failsworth, to which venue Arbuthnott hastily repaired only to find that all the mills had been turned out and that the meeting had been transferred yet again. There were minor incidents in Manchester itself in the evening but, as *The Times* reported, 'no serious breach of the peace is anticipated, the leaders of the Chartist and Repeal parties being at issue with their followers with reference to some of today's proceedings.' In his subsequent reports Arbuthnott expressed some concern. He had received reliable information that 'secret' arrangements for 12 June had been made at a meeting somewhere between Failsworth and Oldham. Whit Monday, he regretted, was a Bank Holiday: the 'enthusiastic' warehouse clerks, so much in evidence on 10 April, would be 'away in the country amusing themselves.'[61]

In the provinces the reaction to Mitchel's conviction resuscitated Chartism, although often at the cost of a division into moral and physical force camps. The insurgent temper of the Irish in their midst, the tightening repression, pushed some towards conspiracy whilst thwarting the efforts of others to stage an open display of strength. In London Chartism had remained far more vigorous after 10 April. The news from Dublin heightened feelings considerably: the task facing the Executive was to align this vehemence with discipline and organisation, thereby aggrandising the Whitsun demonstration.

Chartist and Irish open-air meetings, a regular feature of the East End Sunday, became a daily occurrence. On 29 May huge meetings were held at Stepney Green and at Clerkenwell Green. The former can be designated Chartist: it was addressed by Ernest Jones, Bezer, Macrae, McDouall, McCarthy and Mander May. From it a peaceable procession was formed which met up with an even larger body from the Irish meeting on Clerkenwell Green. The authorities were caught napping: as Thomas Frost observed, 'the procession of May 29th came upon them like a thunder clap in the dead of night.' When the police eventually arrived on the scene they were drenched with boiling water thrown down on them from top-floor windows. For the next few days battle was joined around Clerkenwell Green, the forces of order wreaking their rage in a graduated display of force. Police mobilisation prevented any procession on 30 May, but provoked several incidents of stone-throwing as the meeting dispersed. The next day the meeting was declared illegal and a troop of Life Guards took possession of the field. Undeterred, a crowd of 3000 gathered, only to be promptly dismissed by 'hard truncheon blows' aimed so indiscriminately that the government reporters had to apply to the Home Office for damages.[62] All this was a flexing of muscles for 4 June when Ernest Jones addressed a large meeting on Bishop Bonner's Fields, cautioning the crowd against any hot-headed impetuosity, partial outbreaks or rioting. 'Show us your organisation,' 'Jones exhorted, 'and you will have a glorious opportunity on the 12th':

Only preparation – only organisation is wanted, and the Green Flag shall float over Downing Street, and St. Stephen's. Only energy is wanted – only determination – and what will be the result? Why?

That John Mitchel and John Frost will be brought back, and Sir George Grey, and Lord John Russell will be sent to change places with them.

It was not until after Jones had left the meeting to catch the mail-train north that the violence began, although there had been 'collisions' between the authorities and crowds throughout London all day. As the crowd dispersed, a vast police force, concealed in a nearby church, emerged with ferocious violence. A whole file of the Metropolitan Police records is full of complaints against the police, all from non-Chartists. On 6 June twenty-two people (average age twenty-four) were brought before the magistrates accused of riotous behaviour.[63]

The Chartist Executive wrote to the Prime Minister repudiating the violent language and mushroom orators of the Clerkenwell Green meetings, whilst trusting that there would be no repetition of police aggression on 12 June. By way of reply, the government declared the Whitsun demonstration illegal and categorically refused to allow the Executive to present the Memorial. 'The Whigs *à la Jack Ketch,* "finished" "The Constitution"', Harney expostulated, 'the reign of terror is established. We live under Martial Law!' The Executive still intent on a numerical display, decided to give up Whitsun meetings planned for Clerkenwell Green and other busy and populous areas: all efforts were to be concentrated on Bishop Bonner's Fields. When McDouall arrived early in the day, he found the authorities in possession of the ground. Assured by the magistrate in attendance that a demonstration would be prevented at all costs, McDouall called the meeting off. *The Times* commented: 'The "peaceful demonstration", unavoidably postponed from April 10 to June 12, stands adjourned *sine die*.'[64]

The *Star* reported the Whitsun activities under the heading 'Suppression of Public Meetings in the Country.' In Manchester and several other areas magistrates prohibited any meetings: elsewhere meetings were permitted on the strict understanding that no procession would be attempted. O'Connor, who spent 12 June touring the Land Company estates, even found himself prohibited from addressing a meeting at Loughborough two days later. The Executive, again denied a display of strength, tried to salvage some respect by emphasising the enormity and culpability of the government's unconstitutional conduct: 'The Whigs having chosen a false and most odious position, let us pin them to it, and let the people decide the issue by a most rapid, unprecedented, and overwhelming organisation of numbers.'[65] This was futile counsel. The 'reign of terror' proceeded apace, an interdict of open display, an inducement to conspiracy.

The government was now determined to crush what remained of the Chartist challenge. The calumny of the press and the compliance of the courts facilitated repression. The unannounced nocturnal events of 29 May, Thomas Frost maintained, 'created a deeper feeling of uneasiness among the middle and upper classes than even the demonstration of April 10th.' Certainly as far as the press was concerned Chartism had been transmogrified on Clerkenwell Green. In 'The Song of the Seditionist', *Punch* portrayed the Chartists revelling in rapine, pillage and massacre. *The Times* was appalled by 'that extravagance of wild sedition which, for want of any other adjective, must be denominated "Irish".' Bradford Chartists had at least displayed the English predeliction for 'a stand-up fight': London was endangered by 'the Irish love of knife, dagger and poison bowl.'[66] The courts saw no cause to distinguish between official Chartist gatherings and the mêlées in Clerkenwell and the East End. Predictably it was Fussell, an impassioned Clerkenwell Green orator and advocate of 'private assassination' who was first to face the London jury in a series of trials which culminated in the conviction of Ernest Jones for his speech on Bishop Bonner's Fields. Jones, it was admitted, had spoken in more measured tones than other orators, but 'his station and education served but to give the greater weight to his erroneous instructions.'[67]

Bereft of its most able tactician, Chartism was soon to lose other major figures as arrests continued apace. McDouall was the next to feel the full rigour of the law, the court deciding to make a 'severe example' of him. Immediately after cancelling the London demonstration on 12 June, McDouall had gravitated towards conspiracy, becoming a member of the committee formed to 'appoint the day and hour when the final struggle is to take place.' Two days later, however, he sent the delegates a note stating that the Executive refused to sanction either the existence or the plans of the committee. From this point on, McDouall was perhaps the most industrious advocate of Executive policy, the proselyte of open organisation. In an extensive tour of the north, he drummed up support for the new organisation adopted by the National Assembly, being 'what I call moral force backed by physical force.' It was for these speeches that McDouall was apprehended at Ashton and brought to trial. The prosecution made great play of the fact that an extract from Mitchel's *Irish Felon* had been found on McDouall's person. This, together with the unwarranted but now standard allusion to the 'perfectly revolting' events in France, more than compensated for the acknowledged inadequacy of the police reports of what McDouall had actually said.[68]

The arrest of popular leaders like Jones and McDouall inflamed passions and provoked further contention over moral and physical force. Each stage indeed in the tightening of repression, precipitated an increased commitment to violence.[69] This was the familiar tremulous path to insurrection. Although the mass platform always possessed the potential for popular insurgency, the threshold of violence tended to be crossed by an ardent embittered few, dismayed with the caducity of mass support and enraged by the onrush of repression. Superimposed on this pattern in 1848, however, was the excitement generated by the Irish situation. As was the case before 10 April, the Irish connection, however much it stigmatised the movement in the press and in the courts, inspirited the Chartist challenge. The news from Ireland – first Mitchel's conviction, then the Suspension of Habeas Corpus, and finally Smith O'Brien's rising – accelerated and strengthened moves towards insurrection. At the same time, the vigorous response to events in Ireland served in a way to counteract the ignominious failure of the Chartist platform, thereby preserving hopes of a great numerical display. Two new papers appeared in Lancashire, hoping to succeed where Jones had failed in channelling indignation into disciplined organisation. In the *Truth Teller* Bernard Treanor, president of the Stalybridge Confederates and local Chartist leader, proved a willing amanuensis for the NCA Executive, insisting on the need for 'full and perfect organisation', reprobating any talk of fighting, and promoting the Defence Fund. Far more strident in tone was the *English Patriot and Irish Repealer.* This paper, edited by James Leach the leading Manchester Chartist, with the assistance of George Archdeacon and George White, the most able and peripatetic exponent of the National Guard, captured the heightened mood induced by the 'reign of terror' in England and Ireland. The extent of English sympathy with Ireland's wrongs was heavily underlined: attempts to create division between the English and the Irish were strongly denounced. The first issue contained an emotive appeal by Archdeacon to all Irishmen resident in England to join the newly formed Irish League, and a powerful leading article which enjoined: 'Organise! and *then* —— .' In the next issue, details of the Executive's new plan of organisation followed the injunction: 'Prepare, prepare.' 'Touch Ireland if you dare!', the government was challenged, following the Suspension of Habeas Corpus in late July: 'Try the first shot, and your reign is ended for ever: you will find to your shot, that it is not Ireland alone you have to deal with.'[70]

As with news of Mitchel's transportation, the response to the Suspension of Habeas Corpus in Ireland was prompt and vehement, suggesting organisation and communication outside formal Chartist and Confederate machinery. Very little of the activity of late July was reported in the *Star*. An initial display of strength was rapidly followed by moves towards secrecy, as all informers' reports attest. Only in Liverpool had the authorities anticipated trouble. A pre-emptive display of force prevented any flare-up in the city, although on 24 July Joseph Cuddy, a leading Confederate, was arrested for possessing thirty-one pikes. A week later a cache of 500 cutlasses and several cannisters of gunpowder was discovered in a cellar.[71] Elsewhere large crowds gathered completely unannounced to march in procession through the streets. Often no speeches were made, the crowd dispersing once Mitchel had been given three cheers, a pattern followed at Birmingham, Manchester and Bolton.[72] A London-based informer straightway detected a move towards secrecy in Chartist and Irish circles and reported that: 'measures are being arranged to cause an outbreak in the North of England the moment any demonstration shall take place in Ireland – and this outbreak, they expect, will become general throughout the land.' From Oldham, William Dawson reported in similar vein, adding that even if the Irish 'failed', the English would move by August.[73] News of Smith O'Brien's rising in Ireland emboldened many orators up and down the land, and raised the emotive question: 'IS IRELAND UP?' In an environment in which insurrectionary language was not immediately suspect and in which some system of secret organisation existed, the provocateur found his task all the more easy. It was at the end of July, when plans on how to capitalise on the deployment of so many troops across the Irish Sea were rife, that Powell began taking notes.[74]

'Treachery' *The Times* explained when exonerating the infamous Powell, 'is the natural and providential antidote for treason.' There was no doubt, as another informer reported apprehensively, that Powell 'has been offering for Sale Cutlasses, Guns, Pistols and other implements of destruction and instigating the Chartists on to all manner of mischief.' Powell had infiltrated Chartist circles shortly after Kennington Common and had ingratiated himself with the more militant elements by continually referring to O'Connor as 'a – coward, for he recommended peaceable measures, and that the National Assembly should be postponed.' He soon became one of the leaders of the Cripplegate branch from whence, under the name of Johnson, he progressed to the secret committee at the Black Jack. At the same time he sat on committees at Saffron Hill, the Lord Denman, the Orange Tree and the Crispin beer-shop, and he was a member of the Bride Lane 'Ulterior Committee'. As a member of the Lord Denman committee he attended the meeting there on 15 August which appointed Ritchie, Mullins, Brewster, Cuffay, Lacey and Payne as a subcommittee to head the rising then fixed for the following night. Whilst the meeting was in progress local groups, primarily composed of Irish Confederates, assembled at Shouldham Street and Praed Street to await instructions from 'delegates.' On the evening of 16 August four delegates were due to report to Ritchie at the Orange Tree to receive final instructions. In the event it was the police and not the delegates who turned up. The police reports can be found in the aptly headed file: 'Reports of Anticipated Disturbances on Wednesday Night.'[75]

By comparison with those apprehended in the March riots, the August conspirators were old hands. Cuffay, a tailor, and a 'nigger' as *The Times* frequently pointed out, was over sixty. Lacey, a bootmaker and keeper of the Charter Coffee-House, was thirty-eight. At twenty-four, Dowling, a portrait painter and prominent Confederate, was by far the youngest of the leading figures, although he always protested that he was not an English factionist, but an Irish nationalist. The average age of those apprehended at the three principal venues – the Orange Tree, the Angel and the Charter Coffee-House – was thirty-three, thirty-one and thirty-three respectively. O'Connor claimed that the great majority were unknown to the leading Chartists, but those involved were certainly not the youths who had caused the movement so much trouble earlier on. They came from traditionally radical artisan groups. Of the twenty-seven apprehended at the three main venues, ten were shoemakers. *The Times* commended: 'A dozen or two shoemakers, tailors and joiners are discovered to constitute the nucleus and mainstay of that Chartism which last spring was to upset and remodel this Empire.'[76]

Provincial involvement in the August 'conspiracy' is difficult to assess. In the north where magistrates instituted a ban on confederated clubs, the move towards secrecy did not necessarily imply a commitment to insurrection. At the private meetings at Hannah Scholefield's house in Rochdale, for example, physical-force oratory was discountenanced. A delegate meeting in Manchester on 13 August poured scorn on the tenor of the Rochdale meetings. Thus rebuked, militants like Gill, anxious to 'do a 1842 again' came into the force at the next meeting at Hannah Scholefield's. But arguments immediately broke out, with the majority insisting that they should wait and abide by the Executive.[77] Furthermore there is evidence of continuing contention between Chartists and Irish over the use of violence. On 14 August Arbuthnott reported that many of the Bolton Chartists were 'withdrawing' because the Irish amongst their number wanted 'an immediate outbreak of a serious nature.' The same was true in Ashton, Arbuthnott reported the next day, following the rioting of 14 August and the murder of Police Constable Bright. In Manchester also, Arbuthnott continued, there were heated disputes between the Chartists and the Irish over the latter's determination on violence.[78] The riots of 14 August reveal a complex number of forces at work, making an accurate assessment of Chartist intentions almost impossible. Ashton and Hyde were traditional strongholds. The arrest of McDouall, a great favourite in these parts, had provoked considerable indignation. The visit in early August of G. J. Mantle, the militant Birmingham-based orator, fanned the flames. But, as subsequent evidence makes clear, the Ashton Chartists were not responsible for the depradations of 14 August. Bright, the policeman, was not killed by Joseph Radcliffe, leader of the Ashton National Guard, but by one of the disreputable witnesses who testified against Radcliffe and the Chartists and who were hurriedly given a free passage to Australia, while at Hyde, the turn-out crowd which visited the mills was headed by a spy.[79]

All things considered, there is much to suggest that Manchester was intended to be the centre of co-ordinated action on either 15 or 16 August. Lacey assured the London insurrectionists meeting at the Lord Denman on 15 August that Manchester, whence he had recently returned, would be 'up' that night. The Oldham authorities informed the Home Office that the surrounding towns intended to march on Manchester during the night of 15 August: Manchester was to be burnt and its magistrates shot. In the event only seventy men set off from the Working Men's Hall, Oldham, in the direction of Manchester. The authorities intervened and arrested one of the marchers, but his only weapon was a few stones in his pocket. Across the Pennines three informers had infiltrated Chartist circles in Bradford, now arranged in 40-50 sections of 100-200 men. A letter from Manchester had been expected during the night of 13 August: as none was received, Smyth was sent to Manchester for instructions. He returned on 16 August and showed one of the informers a letter: 'it said that all was broken up and come to an end.' On the night of 15 August the Manchester magistrates had struck a 'decisive blow', arresting fifteen Chartist and Confederate leaders. This was the beginning of an exhaustive round-up of prominent Chartists.[80]

Seizing upon the events of mid-August, the authorities cast the net as wide as possible. The Manchester magistrates sent a bill before the Grand Jury at Liverpool listing 'all the leading agitators who have for some time past infested this City and the neighbouring Towns.' The Birmingham magistrates were just as diligent. Throughout 15 and 16 August they kept a close watch on 'the violent men in the Clubs' and made several arrests. On 18 August the mayor was pleased to report the committal of George White and the apprehension of G. J. Mantle, 'the most strenuous in recommending violence.' Mantle was the one notable omission from the Manchester magistrates' 'monster indictment': the Birmingham authorities, were instructed by the Home Office to spare no pains in collecting evidence against him. In the West Riding the Bradford authorities, primed by the irascible Ferrand, decided to apprehend all the forty-odd members of the local Chartist council. 'Owing to the watchfulness of the parties', they reported, 'we only succeeded in arresting ten men.' Early in September, however, they at last managed to effect the arrest of Isaac Jefferson: their last attempt in mid-July had precipitated a riot which lasted a couple of days.[81]

The subsequent trials followed the established pattern, with convictions promptly secured even in those cases where the prosecution was forced to withdraw the discreditable testimony of its venal witnesses and to concede the selective nature of the police evidence. Harney poignantly summarised the procedure:

Place *Fustian* in the dock, let *Silk Gown* charge the culprit with being a 'physical force Chartist', and insinuate that he is not exactly free from the taint of 'Communism', and forthwith *Broad Cloth* in the jury box will bellow out 'GUILTY.' [82]

VI

In the autumn of 1848, with the movement sadly depleted, O'Connor reasserted his leadership. Ever since April he had chosen to act cautiously in the country. In the sanctuary of Westminster, however, where the 'Felon Act' did not apply, he had treated the Commons to 'repeated doses' of Chartism, he reported in the *Star*, and had served as 'the scourge of the Quadrupeds', Hume's Little Chartists who 'were marshalling the working classes as a means of enforcing a reduction of taxation from which the labourers would not derive a farthing per cent.' Actually O'Connor was at his most impressive over Irish matters, a brave and ultimately solitary voice of protest against coercive legislation.[83]

Following the shambles of August, O'Connor's letters in the *Star* were shot through with self-righteous indignation. What was poor Cuffay, he demanded, but the victim of the rash language and the applause of the informers in the gallery at the National Assembly? Reaffirming his credentials for leadership, O'Connor added a new chapter to his well-established chronicle of the movement. Kennington Common, the latest and most dramatic illustration of his bravery, represented a great triumph. The National Assembly, the most horrendous example of the 'treachery and treason' to which the movement had been so prone, had 'destroyed the effect of that triumph, and laid the foundation of the present prosecutions.' As ever, he was prepared to act a generous part, and made sure that the Chartists were fully aware of the expense to which he was put in defending 'honest Chartists' like Jones, Vernon and Cuffay, men who had been ensnared by those who looked to 'traffic in abuse of Feargus O'Connor' as the last hope of profit. On top of all this, O'Connor was able to cite the recent report of the Select Committee on the Land Company which had shown him to be £3000 out of pocket. 'Your principal security', he concluded convincingly, 'lies in my being YOUR UNPAID SERVANT.'[84]

With the point established, O'Connor was able to return to his plans for 'the amelioration of the condition of the working classes'. He toured Scotland to discuss the labour, social and land question, 'showing that the People's Charter is the only possible means by which labour can be emancipated, social happiness secured, and peace, contentment and reform ensured.' He took time out, of course, to give a 'good drubbing' to those Scottish delegates who had 'vilified' him at the National Assembly where too they had inveigled poor Ernest Jones with their 'base and shameful falsehoods . . . as to the state of preparedness and resolution of their several districts.' Characteristically he opened the columns of the *Star* to them, when they complained that they had been denied a fair hearing. They laid some thirty charges against him, the tenor of all being that he had vitiated the excitement of the spring by advocating the policy of 'wait, wait, wait.'[85]

O'Connor left Scotland to attend the Land Company Conference at Birmingham. In the evenings a group of delegates met at the Ship Inn to decide upon a plan of Chartist reorganisation, the organisation adopted at the National Assembly having recently been pronounced illegal. Throughout the movement, and certainly amongst the delegates, there was a strong desire 'to fall back upon the old organisation' and to try to repair the damage wrought by the rash and the enthusiastic. Adopting a broader perspective, the delegates concluded that their major fault had always been a preoccupation with mere numerical force: 'they were in times of excitement too eager to admit members regardless of their character or condition.' After much had been said against 'mushroom Chartists', it was unanimously resolved to return to the old organisation and to concentrate energies on lecturing and tract distribution. Kydd, who took the leading role at the Conference, was delighted: at last the movement would be able to turn its attention to the discussion of social issues.[86]

The Ship Inn Conference appears a definite regression: one historian has characterised it as a 'violent swing to the right.' In fact it represented something of a new departure. The abandonment of the mass platform, the concentration on education and propaganda, presaged the extension of the Chartist programme. O'Connor was certainly delighted with the outcome of the Conference and hailed the 'new-birth of Chartism.' Throughout 1848 he had sought to supplement the antique radical programme with a practical solution to the 'Labour Question – the question of questions.' Now the movement was firmly committed to the discussion of social reform. 'We have been censured by the most enthusiastic Chartists', he wrote in the *Star*, 'for having attached a SOCIAL SYSTEM to our POLITICAL CREED.' The great merit of the Ship Inn Conference was that it had 'relieved the social question of the political odium sought to be cast upon it.' O'Connor had had enough of those who 'denounced the Land Plan as the destroyer of Chartism, while those who did not join in the social move were only prepared, upon the depression of trade and bad times, to assist in the Chartist movement, and then only with cheers.' The Ship Inn Conference, he was determined, would take Chartism along the path he had outlined in his March 'manifesto' and his 'Treatise on Labour.'[87]

There was the same indomitable commitment to the Charter, the six points being 'indispensable for the obtainment of social regeneration.' There was the same indignant exposure of middle-class dodges. Throughout the autumn O'Connor was engaged in a running battle with the promoters of the Financial Reform agitation, culminating in a spirited attack on Cobden, the paymaster of Alexander Somerville, the vitriolic anti-Land Plan propagandist. O'Connor exhorted the Chartists 'not to be bought by talk of financial gain': Cobden's 'People's Budget', whilst a useful weapon with which to whittle away at Whig patronage, was nothing other than a capitalist-inspired tax juggle. Furthermore, of course, there was the same repudiation of socialism and communism, theories 'at variance with the ruling instinct of man, which is selfishness, self-interest, self-reliance and individuality.' With the unwilling idle located on the land and in possession of the franchise, free trade and machinery would become 'man's holiday' and 'man's friend', instead of his curse and his oppressor. There was no need for those visionary social theories favoured by reformers in continental countries which had been denied political education. France, indeed, was now witnessing the emergence of Louis Napoleon, the 'King Constable' who had armed himself in London on 10 April:

> not to resist anticipated violence, but to cow public opinion . . . an opinion which sought not the destruction, but the renovation, of the veritable British constitution; an opinion which promised sustenance from Labour, and not Luxury in idleness; an opinion which was not the bubble of theoretically excited enthusiasts but the adopted conviction of thoughtful and reasoning men.[88]

VII

By the end of 1848 O'Connor looked upon himself as the leader of a labour movement at its highest stage, directing the public mind towards a programme combining the traditional radical political catechism with a practical scheme for social regeneration. Rash political behaviour, visionary social theories, spurious middle-class schemes were all proscribed. Throughout the year he had been striving to lead Chartism in this direction, although in the early months he had willingly adopted the requisite bellicose posture for the policy of forcible intimidation. His abjuration of the National Assembly, coming so unexpectedly and devastatingly after his militant stance in the Convention and his fortitude on 10 April, certainly impaired the Chartist challenge. O'Connor, however, can hardly be held responsible for the decisive defeat of the mass platform in 1848. Nor should he be excluded from studies of the Chartist epilogue, that protean period of radical reappraisal necessitated by the total failure of 1848. An incomparable leader of mainstream popular radicalism, O'Connor became acutely conscious of the inadequacy of the mass platform. The experience of 1848, of course, convinced everyone of the inefficacy of traditional tactics. This did not necessarily occasion shamefaced retreat, although a good number could no longer resist the middle-class embrace. The renunciation of the mass platform was both the proximate cause of the 'Charter and Something More' and a necessary precondition of mid-Victorian 'consensus and cohesion.'[89]

1848, George White rued, had witnessed nothing more than 'the mere ebullition of momentary feeling very little superior to animal instinct.' The conclusive failure of the platform to secure the enduring adherence of those 'whose every interest would benefit by the triumph of Chartism', convinced Harney and other 'men of the future' of the need to expound the social benefits of the Charter, to incorporate a programme of social rights, and above all to eschew the bluster of traditional extra-parliamentary agitation in favour of 'an efficient propaganda of the principles of Democratic and Social Reform.'[90] Thenceforward, with the movement progressing 'from green flag to red', O'Connor is generally dismissed as an exploded force. To many Chartists, however, O'Connor remained the cynosure of the movement, although some considered his repeated proposals for prize-essay competitions and conventions on the rights of labour 'too advanced.'[91] In fact in the late Chartist period, O'Connor played what can best be described as a central role, leading the way in calling for a redirection of radical endeavour and in denouncing the great capitalists and the aristocracy of labour, yet refusing to sanction socialism and always keeping the option open for an alliance with the 'veritable middle classes.' Certainly his conduct became more tortuous as he tried to reconcile his commitment to social reform with his ire at the advance of socialism, his sanguine expectations of lower-middle-class radicalism with his animadversions on the reform programmes of 'the money manufacturing middle class – those who live upon labour, who coin your sweat, marrow, and bones into gold.'[92] But other Chartist leaders became just as entangled in the labyrinthine structure of the Chartist finale, the prelude to mid-Victorian radicalism.

For all its failings, the mass platform had given shape and protection to working-class radicalism, rendering it impervious to any diluent. Following the abandonment of the mass platform, Chartism was permeated by a miscellany of reform groups all of whom repudiated confrontation, intimidation and the exclusive nature of working-class protest. Radical renegades, 'middle-class literati', social reformers and divers faddists, presumed that the rejection of the platform was an act of contrition, a recantation of the Chartist shibboleth. Harney's efforts to incorporate the various advanced social reform groups in a programme for the 'Charter and Something More' foundered on their interpretation of Chartist overtures as an avowal of former error, their refusal to accord primacy to the six points in any joint manifesto, and their homilies on the need for strict conformity to accepted standards of social decorum by the advocates of oppositional values.[93] Concentration on education, discussion and propaganda, commitment to the power of reason rather than the force of numbers, proved indeed, less an advance beyond the evanescence of the platform into alternative ultra-radical 'élite politics', than an acceptance of gradualism, moderation, expediency and self-improvement, a fudging of the differences between radicalism and liberalism, and a kind of deference towards the 'legitimising tendencies inherent in the mid-Victorian ethos.' Without the protection of the mass platform, working-class radicalism became vulnerable to what Tholfsen calls amiable middle-class versions of consensus values. The 'active attempts by the bourgeoisie to win back mass allegiance', an integral part of 'liberalisation' as described by Foster, were surely assisted by the disquietude and uncertainty in working-class radical ranks following the decisive failure of the time-honoured mass platform in 1848. Without the platform indeed, the 'working-class vanguard' was not so much 're-isolated' as assimilated to patterns that presupposed subordination and inequality.[94] Harney quickly fell in with the times, endorsing liberalism and palliative social movements. His only critic was Ernest Jones, the proud and worthy successor to Feargus O'Connor, 'the worn-out warrior.'

NOTES

1. E. Yeo, 'Robert Owen and Radical Culture' in S. Pollard and J. Salt (eds), *Robert Owen: prophet of the Poor* (London, 1971) pp. 104–8.

2. J. Foster, *Class Struggle and the Industrial Revolution* (London, 1974) p. 31.

3. E. P. Thompson, 'The moral economy of the English crowd in the eighteenth century', *Past & Present*, 50 (1971) 76–9.

4. J. C. Belchem, 'Henry Hunt and the evolution of the mass platform', *English Historical Review*, XCIII (1978) 739–73.

5. E. P. Thompson, *Whigs and Hunters* (Peregrine edn: London, 1977),

pp. 258–69. J. C. Belchem, 'Republicanism, popular constitutionalism and the radical platform in early nineteenth century England', *Social History,* VI (1981).

6.   'Introduction' in R. Quinault and J. Stevenson (eds), *Popular Protest and Public Order* (London, 1974) pp. 20–1.

7.   I. J. Prothero, 'William Benbow and the concept of the 'general strike', *Past & Present,* 63 (1974) 141 and 149–55.

8.   T. M. Kemnitz, 'Approaches to the Chartist movement: Feargus O'Connor and Chartist strategy', *Albion,* V, (1973) 67–73.

9.   For a contrasting view, see Foster, *Class Struggle,* pp. 99–100.

10.   For a comprehensive study of Chartism in 1848 and its historiography, see J. C. Belchem 'Radicalism as a "platform" agitation in the periods 1816–1821 and 1848–1851; with special reference to the leadership of Henry Hunt and Feargus O'Connor' (Univ. of Sussex D. Phil. thesis, 1974) pt 2, ch. 1, pp. 181–269.

11.   *Northern Star (NS)* 1 January–5 February 1848.

12.   Jones's speeches at Royal British Institution, *NS* 15 January, Halifax and the National Hall, *NS* 5 February, John Street, *NS* 26 February and 1 April, and Kennington Common, *NS* 8 April; Harney, 'The War of Classes', *NS* 19 February.

13.   Clerk to the magistrates at Nottingham, 3 April, Home Office Papers: Public Record Office (HO) 45/2410 (3). See also the reports of meetings and processions in Sheriff of Lanarkshire, 8 March, HO 45/2410 (5) AG, and Town Clerk, Leicester, 6 April, and Clerk to the Justices, Loughborough, 8 April in HO 45/2410 (3). In his weekly reports in *NS* McDouall showed a strong appreciation of the need for organisation: 'There is no organisation now, and I find my labour quadrupled; but I must get through it, and endeavour to leave something like a system and order behind me', *NS* 19 February.

14.   Speeches at the National Hall, *NS* 5 February and John Street, *NS* 1 April.

15.   O'Connor's speeches at Birmingham, *NS* 29 January, and at the National Hall. *NS* 5 February; and his letters 'To the Old Guards' *NS* 26 February and 4 March. J. Saville insists that O'Connor abnegated the leadership, see 'Some aspects of Chartism in decline', *Bulletin of the Society for the Study of Labour History,* 20 (1970) 16–18 and his introduction to the 1969 reprint of R. G. Gammage, *History of the Chartist Movement,* pp. 34–5 and 65.

16.   'To the Imperial Chartists' *NS* 18 March.

17.   See in particular his letters 'To the Old Guards' and 'To the Imperial Chartists' in *NS* 1 April.

18.   See 'Our Charter' *Labourer,* III (1848) 183–6; P. M. McDouall, *The Charter . . . an address to the middle classes* (London, 1848); and speeches by Kydd at Greenwich and Jones at Halifax in *NS* 5 February. Jones was always precise in distinguishing between the small shopkeepers and the great moneyocracy.

19.   J. A. Epstein, 'Feargus O'Connor and the English working-class radical movement, 1832–1841; a study in national Chartist leadership' (Univ. of Birmingham Ph. D. thesis, 1977) pp. 417–60. The militancy of the middle-class anti-income tax agitation is often underestimated, see Belchem, 'Radicalism', pp. 289–94.

20.   J. Saville, 'Chartism in the Year of Revolution (1848)' *Modern Quarterly,* new series, VIII (1952–3) 1, 23–33.

21.   W. Drabwell, *Short Treatise on Equitable Taxation* (London, 1848), p. 16.

22. *Puppet Show,* I, (1848) 1, 8. Reynolds was to remain one of the most controversial figures in late Chartism, see Ward's speech at John Street, *NS* 23 March 1850, and T. Clark, *A Letter addressed to G. W. M. Reynolds, reviewing his conduct as a professed Chartist, and also explaining who he is and what he is, together with copious extracts from his most indecent writings* (London, 1850).

23. 'The Trafalgar Square Revolution', *Punch,* XIV (1848) 112 and 'Introduction', XV (1848); *NS* 11 March.

24. *Times,* 14 March, and *NS* 18 March.

25. Records of the Metropolitan Police Officers: Public Record Office (Mepo) 2/63 and 2/64. Commissioner Mayne, 4 April HO 45/2410 (2). *Annual Register,* 48–50. For a convenient summary of Gurr's three classifications of domestic political violence – turmoil, conspiracy and internal war – see W. H. Maehl 'The dynamics of violence in Chartism: a case study in north-eastern England' *Albion,* VII (1975) 105–6.

26. Posting-bill issued by the South Lancashire and Cheshire Delegates, enclosed in Magistrates, Oldham, 19 March, HO 45/2410 (1)A. D. Read, 'Chartism in Manchester' in A. Briggs (ed.), *Chartist Studies* (London, 1959), p. 63. Poor Law riots and disturbances occurred in early March at Manchester, Edinburgh, Glasgow, Kilmarnock, Ayr, Airdrie and Newcastle upon Tyne. For an excellent analysis of the Scottish riots, see A. Wilson, *The Chartist Movement in Scotland* (Manchester, 1970), p. 218 onwards.

27. *Annual Register,* 43. Mepo 2/65 'Swearing in of Special Constables, protection of Public Buildings etc.'

28. *NS* 25 March; *Times* 21 March; Oldham magistrates, 19 March and Revd T. S. Mills, 25 March, in HO 45/2410 (1)A.

29. *Times,* 10 April; and reports enclosed in Rushton, 15 November, HO 45/2410 (1)A, when Somers offered to turn Queen's Evidence; Dr Reynolds had by then fled to America.

30. D. Thompson, *The Early Chartists* (London, 1971), pp. 18–21.

31. *NS* 1 April. James Leach was the chairman.

32. *Times,* 10 April.

33. This account is based on *Proceedings of the National Convention* (London, 1848) which includes a full report of the Kennington Common meeting on 10 April. T. M. Parssinen 'Association, convention and anti-parliament in British radical politics', *English Historical Review,* LXXXVIII (1973), 504–33.

34. F. C. Mather considers the behaviour of the government was characterised by 'forbearance and restraint', see 'The Government and the Chartists' in Briggs (ed.), *Chartist Studies,* 395.

35. *Parliamentary Debates,* 3rd series, XCVIII.

36. See the letters from Harney and Thomas Clark in *NS* 2 February 1850.

37. McGrath's undated letter and Mayne's memo can be found in Mepo 2/65.

38. For a full discussion of the injustice done to O'Connor in all accounts of 10 April, see Belchem, 'Radicalism', 206–13. 'Feargoose' was the sobriquet favoured by *Punch.*

39. H. Solly, *James Woodfood, Carpenter and Chartist,* 2 vols (London, 1881) II, 208–12.

40. Belchem, 'Henry Hunt', p. 757.

41.   T. M. Wheeler, 'Sunshine and Shadow', ch. 34; in *NS* 15 September 1849. T. Frost, 'The Secret', ch. 7, *National Instructor* (1850) 66-7.

42.   'To the Imperial Chartists' *NS* 15 April and his letters in *NS* 22 and 29 April.

43.   'The Chartist Petition – Messrs O'Connor and Cripps', *Parliamentary Debates*, 3rd series, XCVIII. See also 'How signatures were obtained to the Petition', HO 45/2410 (2).

44.   See O'Connor's letters and articles in *NS* 22 April – 27 May.

45.   O'Connor always insisted that the opinion of Parliament needed to be tested before the monarch could be memorialised. He provided a less convincing case against the National Assembly, and soon dropped his argument that any assembly of over forty-nine delegates was contrary to law, a wise decision for one who had earlier agreed to the Assembly because the need was for a large, representative gathering.

46.   The hope was nothing new, see Epstein, 'Feargus O'Connor', 457-61. It remained central to his later career, 1849-51, see Belchem, 'Radicalism', pt 2, ch. 3.

47.   'A Treatise on Labour', *Labourer*, III (1848) 251-90. See also 'Resurrection of Birmingham' *NS* 29 January, 'To the Imperial Chartists' *NS* 18 March, 'To the Fustian Jackets, Blistered Hands and Unshorn Chins', *NS* 29 April, 'To the Old Guards' *NS* 13 May and 'To the Members of the Land Company' *NS* 29 July.

48.   For a full list of the various Easter demonstrations, see Belchem, 'Radicalism', Appendix E. Parsinnen, 'British radical politics', 531.

49.   E. Jones, 'To the Men of Halifax' *NS* 20 May. The National Assembly was fully reported in *NS* 6, 13 and 20 May.

50.   Jones was given wildly exaggerated reports of the growth of the National Guard, particularly at Aberdeen, during his brief tour of Scotland immediately following the Convention. At the National Assembly he extolled the example of Aberdeen where there were '6,000 Chartists, all good men and true, armed to the teeth and waiting for the fray', see Gammage (Merlin reprint 1969) 336. The Scottish delegates, well aware that the figure was not even 600, made no attempt to set things straight. The various ensuing recriminations are summarised by Wilson, *Chartist Movement in Scotland*, p. 232.

51.   The Assembly adopted an Address on the Labour Question, drawn up by Kydd, which closely followed O'Connor's writings on the subject.

52.   O'Connor, McCrae, McDouall, Jones and Kydd were elected, see *NS* 1 July.

53.   Belchem, 'Radicalism', 370-4 and 390-471.

54.   Gammage, *History of the Chartist Movement*, pp. 336 and 329.

55.   Lt-Gen. Arbuthnott 12 and 22 April, HO 45/2410 (4)AB.

56.   Letters and enclosures, Mayor and Magistrates, Bradford 16 May-1 June, and the Statement of the Justices in Quarter Sessions, 19 May, HO 45/2410 (4)AC; *NS* 20 May-3 June; *Times* 31 May. For poor relief figures, see *Parliamentary Debates*, 3rd series, CVI, 1183-4. For Bingley, see Ferrand 24-31 May, HO 45/2410 (4)AC, and Lt-Gen. Arbuthnott, 28 May, HO 45/2410 (4)AB. For drilling at Leeds, see Clerk to the Magistrates, 26 May, HO 45/2410 (4)AC; at the

camp meeting near Wilsden, *NS* 3 June; at Manningham, Clayton, Horton, Drighlington, and Tong Moor, see the reports of the York Assizes in *NS* 5 August and 23 December.

57. *Parlimentary Debates,* 3rd series, XCVIII, 1310–2; NS 27 May.

58. 'The Suffrage', *Politics for the People,* no. 1; *Times* 11 April.

59. Thorn's reports enclosed in Lt-Gen. Arbutnott, 19 and 23 May, HO 45/2410 (4)AB.

60. The reports and enclosures in Mayor of Nottingham 7 June, HO 45/2410 (3), suggest a split in Chartist ranks. See also Mayor of Birmingham, 29 May and 7 June, HO 45/2410 (3)P. *Times* 2 June.

61. Reports and enclosures in Lt-Gen. Arbuthnott 29–30 May and 1, 6 and 9 June, HO 45/2410 (4)AB. *Times* 1 June.

62. *Times* 31 May–2 June. *NS* 3 June. T. Frost 'The Secret' ch. 12, *National Instructor* (1850) 133–4 and *Forty Years' Recollections* (London, 1880) p. 49. Letters from Faulk and other government reporters in HO 45/2410 (2) and in Mepo 2/66.

63. *NS* 10 June; the June section of HO 45/2410 (2) and Mepo 2/66. For details of the various meetings and clashes throughout the day, see Belchem, 'Radicalism', Appendix F.

64. Executive Committee of the NCA to Russell and to Grey in HO 45/2410 (2). 'Martial Law' *NS* 17 June. See also Frost *Forty Years,* pp. 157–61. *Times* 13 June.

65. For details of the Whitsun activities, see Belchem, 'Radicalism', 244–6 and Appendix E. 'Executive Committee to the People' *NS* 17 June.

66. T. Frost, 'The Secret' ch. 12, *National Instructor* (1850) 133–4. *Punch* XIV (1848) 240. *Times* 2 June and 8 July.

67. 'The Trials' *NS* 8 and 15 July. See also E. Jones, *Letter to Chief Justice Wilde* (London, 1848).

68. For London conspiracy, see the information of George Davis 12 and 14 June, Reading to Mayne 12 June, 'F' Division report, 15 June and 'Y' Division report, 17 June, in HO 45/2410 (2). At McDouall's trial, a pocket book was produced listing the places visited in his tour; several letters from the Executive were also found on his person, one of which rebuked him for 'running about trying for meetings' instead of sticking to an agreed programme, see *An authentic report of the trial of Doctor Peter Murray McDouall* (Manchester, 1848). Police reports enclosed in Clerk to the Magistrates, Ashton-under-Lyne, 18 July, HO 45/2410 (1)A. *Punch* XV (1848), 13.

69. According to Davis's evidence, the series of meetings which was to produce the August 'conspiracy', began when George, Mullins, Rose and Payne drew the old Whitsun Committee aside and suggested rescuing Ernest Jones, see the report of the trials in *NS* 30 Sept. At Leicester there was a clear division into moral and physical force camps when the official Chartist body accepted the magistrates' ban on meetings and processions: Buckby and Warner formed a rival, militant group, the Working Men's Charter Association, see Town Clerk, 13 and 14 June, HO 45/2410(3)R.

70. *Truth Teller,* no. 2, 5 August and no. 3, 12 August; *English Patriot and Irish Repealer,* no. 1, 22 July and no. 2, 29 July. For details of White's tour pro-

moting the National Guard, see 'Chartism in Lancashire and Yorkshire' *NS* 22 July, which also contains details of the Irish League.

71.   Report of the Committee of Magistrates, 8 July, Rushton 24 July, and the Mayor, 25 July and 3 August, in HO 45/2410 (1)A. See also Lt.-Gen. Arbuthnott 2 August, HO 45/2410 (4)AB and *Times* 24 and 26 July.

72.   Mayor of Birmingham, 27 July–1 August, HO 45/2410 (3)P. Lt.-Gen. Arbuthnott, 26 July, HO 45/2410 (4)AB. Reports and enclosures in Clerk to the Magistrates, Bolton, 28 July–1 August, HO 45/2410 (4)AB. Similar reports were received from Loughborough, Stockport and Edinburgh.

73.   Paterson, 24 July, Mepo 2/62. Dawson's reports enclosed in Duke of Portland, 21 July–10 August, HO 45/2410 (1)A.

74.   Shaw, Bryson, Shell, Crowe and Bezer, the prominent Chartist, were brought before the courts for their speeches at a London meeting advertised with placards, 'IS IRELAND UP?', see the reports of trials in *NS* 2 and 23 September. See also Powell's evidence at the examination of W. Dowling, *NS* 26 August.

75.   *Times,* 29 September. Paterson 19 August, Mepo 2/62. Powell's evidence at the first examination of the prisoners, *NS* 26 August, and at Cuffay's trial, *NS* 30 September. The police file includes daily reports from Davis, HO 45/2410 (2).

76.   *Times* 18 August and 29 September. For full details of those apprehended, see Belchem, 'Radicalism' Appendix G.

77.   Police reports enclosed in W. Heaton, 5 September, HO 45/2410 (1)A.

78.   Lt-Gen. Arbuthnott, 14 and 15 August, HO 45/2410 (4)AB.

79.   J. C. Belchem, 'The Spy System in 1848: Chartists and informers – an Australian connection', *Labour History* (November 1980).

80.   Magistrates, Oldham, 15 August, HO 45/2410 (1)A. Magistrates, Bradford, 15 August, HO 45/2410 (4)AC, and the evidence of Shepherd, Emmet and Flynn at the York Assizes, reported in *Times* 25 December and *NS* 30 December. Manchester, Electric Telegraph Company, 16 August, HO 45/2410 (1)A; Lt-Gen. Arbuthnott 20 August, HO 45/2410 (4)AB; and *NS* 19 August.

81.   Mayor of Manchester, 22 August, HO 45/2410 (1)A. Mayor of Birmingham, 17 and 18 August, HO 45/2410 (3)P, and Waddington to Mayor of Birmingham, 19 August, HO 41/19. Ferrand, 16, 21 and 24 August, and Mayor of Bradford 21 July and 24 August, HO 45/2410 (4)AC. Jefferson's arrest, and that of John Smyth, secretary to the Bradford Chartist Council, was reported along with many others in *NS* 16 September.

82.   'L'Ami du Peuple' *NS* 23 December. The trials are reported in *NS* 23 December–6 January 1849.

83.   O'Connor's letters in *NS* 15 April, 29 July–9 September, and the report of his putting himself up for 'annual re-election' at Nottingham, *NS* 23 September.

84.   O'Connor's letters in ibid., 29 July, and 9 September–7 October.

85.   O'Connor's letters and reports in ibid., 30 September, 28 October and 4 November. He replied point by point to the charges, see *NS* 2 December. 'Wait, wait, wait!' were the 'delusive words' O'Connor would not allow his lips to utter, see his stirring letter 'To the Imperial Chartists' on the eve of Kennington Common, *NS* 8 April.

86.   *NS* 11 November. Throughout the winter Kydd was busily engaged in a tour of Yorkshire, lecturing on the labour question and promoting the formation

of 'people's colleges', see, for example, his letter from Bingley, *NS* 23 December.

87. Saville, 'Chartism in the year of Revolution', p. 32. 'Political and Social Regeneration' *NS* 18 November, and 'To all who live by industry' *NS* 25 November.

88. O'Connor's attack on financial reform began with his letter to 'Poor Douglas Jerrold' *NS* 16 September; he was particularly severe on Cobden in his letter 'To the industrious classes', *NS* 30 December. See also his speech at Nottingham, *NS* 23 September; 'Our Anniversary' *NS* 18 November; and 'King Constable' *NS* 25 November.

89. For an analysis of Chartism in the years 1849–51 in these terms, see Belchem, 'Radicalism', pt 2, chs 2 and 3.

90. 'The Peace Congress, and Democratic Progress', *Democratic Review,* no. 5, October 1849. 'L'Ami du Peuple' *NS* 6 January 1849, and 'To the Working Classes' *Democratic Review,* no. 4, September 1849. Harney had referred to Marx as 'one of the great men of the future', a term which annoyed O'Connor, and was consequently often adopted by Harney and his supporters.

91. See reports of meetings at Glasgow, *NS* 20 January 1849, and at John Street, *NS* 24 February 1849.

92. See for example his speech at the People's Institute, on the eve of the Manchester Conference, *NS* 1 February 1851.

93. For interesting insights on the ultra-conformity of the public demeanour of middle-class radicalism, see F. Parkin, *Middle Class Radicalism* (Manchester, 1968), pp. 21–32.

94. For an interesting discussion of the conflict over élite politics, see D. Jones, *Chartism and the Chartists* (London, 1975), pp. 64–70. T. Tholfsen, *Working Class Radicalism in Mid-Victorian England* (London, 1976) chs 5–8. Foster, *Class Struggle,* ch. 7.

9. Late Chartism: Halifax 1847 – 58

KATE TILLER

WHAT happened to Chartism and Chartists after Kennington Common and the National Petition of April 1848? This essay looks at the important evidence provided by a study of events in Halifax, where a local working-class movement was firmly rooted in a community-based Chartism. The essay provides a retrospective look at Chartism, concentrating on the years 1848 and after. This is in contrast to the great majority of Chartist studies, which concentrate on the early years of the movement, and it may provide a corrective to impressions that late Chartism did not exist, or was at most a predictable and insignificant part of the Chartist experience. As events in Halifax demonstrate, it could have considerable substance and be an important influence upon the development of the labour movement in the 1850s and after.

In Halifax, and in the out-townships and rural hinterland which were an inseparable part of the setting of local Chartism,[1] political intervention had long been regarded as the primary means to social change. This theme had figured strongly in local working-class movements since the late eighteenth century and on through the Paineites, the United Englishmen of 1801, the Luddites, Owenism, the reform agitation of 1831-2, the Factory Movement and the Anti-Poor Law campaign, to pass directly into Chartism in 1838. The resulting movement proved strong and persistent up to and beyond 1848. It focused, and grew from, the diverse groups it encompassed – the factory reformers, the trades, the Owenites and co-operators, and the Anti-Poor Law campaigners. It achieved considerable formal membership.[2] In 1847-8 there were about 500 members of the Chartist Land Company in Halifax.[3] This was just the tip of the iceberg with a large informal body of support in Halifax, in the scattered groupings of cottages in the surrounding uplands and in the fringe townships. Halifax Chartism was a movement involving all sections of the working-class community with small local and great regional summer camp meetings, women activists, social events, tea-parties, temperance groups, schoolrooms, Chartist literature and exclusive dealing with sympathetic tradesmen.[4]

The primacy of a radical political tradition was a particularly powerful element in Halifax Chartist experience, both early and late. Comparison with other local communities[5] shows that for many Chartism was not the dominant feature of working-class activity throughout the years 1838–48, and certainly not thereafter. The relative strength of Halifax Chartism, and its close links with national developments, make it an excellent case study of the course of the movement after 1848. However it is important to note several features that added distinctive local emphases, the strong continuing faith in political solutions, often in terms of the existing political system, being one of them. Halifax had no parliamentary representation before 1832. Unlike many towns already represented, and where formal politics were discredited as a genuine representation of the people, Halifax parliamentary politics were free of established patterns of influence, the achievement of reform was a focus of working-class political activity and parliamentary elections were occasions for organising and articulating demands across a wide range of themes. Extra-parliamentary constitutionalism was an accepted mode of expression, before and after 1848.

A second reason for the political rather than, for example, trade unionist complexion of Halifax's working-class movement lies in the area's industrial structure. Its industry was diverse, including wool, worsted, cotton, carpets and coal. The major work-force was traditionally one of craft handworkers in wool and worsted. As Defoe recorded in the 1720s[6] they lived in scattered moorland settlements around Halifax, combining the trade of small-scale clothier with working smallholdings. Carding, spinning and weaving were carried out on a domestic basis with Halifax as the centre of trading. The increasing prosperity of the woollen and worsted industries in the eighteenth century meant that farming became a secondary occupation and the combers and weavers formed a well-paid, self-confident group, with a strong craft identity asserted through apprenticeship and restrictive craft practices. From the late eighteenth century these groups of handworkers suffered a series of dislocations of economic and social position which brought them to the forefront of Chartism. First came the development, by large clothiers, of a capitalised putting-out system which undercut the handworkers' prices, and then mechanisation and the subsequent growth of factory units, first in spinning, then weaving and finally (still continuing in the 1850s) in combing. These changes destroyed the economic prosperity, the craft status and strong sectional organisations of the woollen and worsted handworkers and drove them from a sectionally conceived, craft-based position to one weak in terms of industrial bargaining but strong in articulating wider, non-union-orientated working-class aims. Underlying all of these was the desire for the prized attributes of the traditional handworker – independence and self-determination at home and at work. Thus throughout the pre-Chartist, Chartist and late Chartist periods displacement of numerically large and politically significant groups of handworkers continued, and was generating a broadly conscious and extremely articulate base for working-class discontent and organisation of a political nature.

A third facet was the militant Dissenting tradition of the area. Halifax parish was the largest and one of the richest in the country, with a large tithe income. This produced strong anti-Church feelings in local radicalism. Membership of a Dissenting chapel was one assertion of independence for many working-class people, a road to self-education through classes and meetings, a way of gaining experience of self-government and public speaking. Many leading Halifax Chartists had such a background, often Methodist. Dissent was also the principal platform of the middle-class radicals of Halifax. Their pleas for non-sectarian education and Disestablishment of the Church in the cause of individual liberty evoked considerable sympathy from the Halifax working-class movement, especially when coupled, as in the case of leading middle-class radicals at the 1847 parliamentary election, with the support of Chartist policies. Dissent took on a particular importance during the peak years of Chartism and after as a potential area of co-operation between working- and middle-class politicians. It appeared either as an area through which Chartism might influence the existing political system, or as a point at which the undermining of autonomous working-class politics and middle-class takeover might begin.

Many of these characteristics found expression during 1847-8 when Halifax Chartism reached new peaks of activity, and when many of the relationships and personalities that were to influence late Chartism emerged. Activity centred first on the 1847 parliamentary election. It was at this election that a national Chartist campaign to make their claims heard in the existing Parliament began. O'Connor's election at Nottingham proved the tactical potential of the exercise and Halifax was one of the handful of other constituencies chosen to be contested by a Chartist candidate.[7] He was Ernest Jones, at first glance an unlikely figure, a recent (summer 1846)[8] recruit to Chartism, from a military and landowning background, and with no prior connections with industry or the north of England.[9] He brought an extreme radical-political philosophy, with as yet none of the wider social and political aspects he later developed.[10] He was a popular and self-confident orator and injected a new international note into local Chartism, apparent in Halifax's election of a delegate to the proposed International Congress of Nations, proposed by Marx and Engels.[11] Jones was to prove a vital figure in the Halifax working-class movement, bringing it to the forefront of national developments and also appealing to the liking of Halifax working men for figures in the gentleman-leader mould of Hunt and O'Connor. Jones provided the inspirational oratory, the guiding principles and the national framework that generated such enthusiasm for him, as it had for O'Connor, and would to some extent for Gladstone.

Jones's arrival coincided with major changes in the orthodox political scene locally. No conventional two-party system prevailed. The decisive factor was the relationship between the two wings of Whig Liberalism, and in 1847 the pressing claims of the 'new' Dissenting, radical Liberals finally ruptured the uneasy alliance with the traditional Whig landowning leadership, driving them into the arms of the Tories.[12] In Halifax parliamentary politics the fortunes of the Chartists and Tories were largely a by-product of the Whig–Liberal relationship, so when this was broken new opportunities to gain a foothold in the system were offered. The sitting 'Radical' MP, Protheroe,[13] was no longer sufficently radical and withdrew from the poll. Sir Charles Wood, the Whig MP, sought a new alliance with the only local candidate, Henry Edwards, a Tory magistrate, founder of the local Yeomanry Cavalry during the Plug Plot, a Church and State man, but with a record on factory reform in his mills superior to many Liberal employers.[14] This left Jones and Edward Miall, a militant Dissenter and the 'new' Liberal candidate. They too formed an alliance, Miall accepting the six points of the Charter in his programme and Jones including Anglican Disestablishment and a voluntary system of education in his.

It was a heated campaign.[15] The orthodox candidates concentrated on 'the religious question', but Jones constantly called for political reform through the Charter. To the six points he added others, producing a manifesto including almost every major demand to be campaigned for by Halifax working-class and radical politicians for the next three decades. The demands were Disestablishment of the Church; voluntary educational provision free of government control; the abolition of capital punishment and of the 1834 Poor Law; the repeal of primogeniture, entail and game laws; direct, not indirect, taxation policies; the availability of small holdings to the people; and the pursuance of Free Trade principles.[16]

At the hustings, when Jones undertook to be publicly accountable to his constituents at an annual meeting, he was clearly elected on the show of hands, with Miall coming second.[17] The official poll, with a total registered electorate of 1022, showed:

Henry Edwards	Conservative	511
Sir C. Wood	Whig	507
Edward Miall	Radical	351
Ernest Jones	Chartist	280

It was apparent that the assault from the left had driven many electors not just to support Wood, but to vote Conservative. Edwards had by far the highest number of plump votes (108 to Wood's 60), suggesting that some voters felt that even Wood was tainted by his Liberal connections. The vast majority of Jones' votes came from those (245) who also voted for Miall. Only three electors voted for Jones alone.[18] His support[19] came primarily from shopkeepers (79), particularly from grocers, general dealers and drapers; and from craftsmen (59), including several trades where Jones' votes outweighed any other, (machine makers, cloggers, tailors, light-metal workers and building trades). Neither Jones nor Miall derived appreciable support from the drink trade (with some 60 votes), despite the potential susceptibility of inns and beerhouses to influence from radical customers.

The election had immediate and long-term repercussions. The Chartists continued exclusive dealing, begun during the campaign and directed against Jones' opponents.[20] Some firms were reported to be turning off his supporters in August, when some 7000 non-electors held a meeting to consider cases of victimisation. They heard that Crossleys, at the enormous Dean Clough carpet mills, were willing to take on the victims.[21] Francis Crossley had spoken for Jones at the election and built up much good will for his own subsequent parliamentary career at this time. The Chartist Election Committee continued to operate during the acute distress and unemployment of the winter of 1847–8, when relief committees and public works schemes were instituted in Halifax.[22]

The momentum was also increased during this period by a succession of other factors – the enthusiasm in Halifax for the Chartist Land Plan; participation in the local campaign for an efficient and democratic local government which culminated in the incorporation of Halifax in 1847; the organisation of the new National Petition and Chartist Convention; and the enormous spur given by the news of the French Revolution in February 1848. The débâcle of the petitioning of 10 April 1848 in London did little to stem this momentum in Halifax Chartism, rather spurring it on. On Good Friday 1848 a great West Riding demonstration was held at Skircoat Green, confirming Halifax as a leading centre of Chartism in the county. An estimated 20,000 people met to hear speakers including Ben Rushton, Kit Shackleton and Isaac Clisset of Halifax. They were apprehensively watched by over 500 special constables and units of Henry Edwards's yeomanry. The political day of reckoning was widely thought to be imminent.

Ernest Jones, as Halifax delegate, was playing a major role at the National Convention and meetings in the localities. He reflected a growing mood when he told the Convention that 'his constituents wanted to observe the laws that protected life and property, but determined to break those that restricted liberty and justice'.[23] It was Jones who later proposed a successful resolution recommending the people to arm.[24]

The collapse of the Chartist National Convention in May confirmed local misgivings over the indecisive leadership of 10 April and threw the weight of continuity more than ever onto the localities. As O'Connor's influence waned Ernest Jones emerged from the Convention as a national Chartist leader committed to the use of physical force where necessary. It was to his tried basis of support that he turned and Halifax became a hard core of Chartist organisation in the increasingly isolated West Riding stronghold of the movement. This was the situation that moved one of the most militant Halifax working men, George Webber, to propose the 'Republic of Lancashire and Yorkshire', in what seemed to be the only real areas of resistance. Nightly Chartist meetings were held.

When the town's first comprehensive local government was introduced in May 1848, the Chartists played a major role. The first town's meeting passed resolutions, submitted to Parliament under the mayor's signature, declaring the Commons unworthy of public confidence (proposed by Ald. Dennis and John Snowden, Chartist) and calling for 'every member of the community' to be fully represented according to the Charter, (proposed by Francis Crossley, and Christoper Shackleton, Chartist).[25]

The local radical paper *The Halifax Reformer* assessed the make-up of the new council as seventeen radicals, four Chartists, six Whigs and three Tories.[26] The Chartists again campaigned through their own committee, based on Nicholls Temperance Hotel. Three members of the Akroyd family were defeated at the polls. As in 1832 in parliamentary politics Halifax's new municipal politics represented a fresh start, untrammelled by fossilised forms of corporate rights and with strong radical and working-class influence established from the first. Chartist intervention forced middle-class participators in the political process to take notice, either from sympathy or fear. Circumstances forced a complete breakdown of the 1834 Poor Law. Yet the fact remained that political participation was still largely by proxy, indirectly exercised through men like Crossley or Jones' shopkeeper supporters of 1847. The first municipal electorate totalled only 1610 voters.[27] Despite unprecedented changes in the local political balance of power Jones had not been elected. Moreover the Poor Law administration had foundered chiefly because of the magnitude of the destitution amongst the very people who *were* Halifax Chartism, the populations of the out-townships, the handworkers in the declining employments whose resentment and self-respect were the backbone of the movement, and to whom the need to apply for relief represented final defeat. In their immediate memory every political tactic had been employed – direct political campaigning, tactical alliance, exclusive dealing, petitions and external pressure groups – and had failed to win sufficient change to bring political power or restraint upon industrial development and economic hardship.

It was in May 1848 that the arguments for the use of physical force became predominant. Men like Ben Wilson accepted the need for force and bought a gun, and listened to unambiguous advocacy of armed action by Ben Rushton, Bill Cockcroft, Isaac Clisset, Kit Shackleton, George Webber and others.[28] This course meant the sacrifice of any tactical initiative the Chartists held in terms of existing political structures. The events of April and May frightened those in government, nationally and locally, and middle-class concession found its limits. The prospect of physical confrontation clearly defined basic underlying divisions afresh. Widespread arrests and displays of official force were made in the West Riding towns to counter Chartist drilling.[29] A major spur to local Chartists was the arrest and imprisonment for two years of Ernest Jones (June 1848). Depleted leadership, threatened reprisals and waning support in other areas put them on the defensive. The spontaneous courage and resolution generated between February and June could not be sustained indefinitely and official Chartist recognition of the case for the use of force came too late to effectively harness it.[30]

II

By late 1848 Halifax Chartism had undoubtedly lost its momentum. Degrees of disillusionment and forms of response varied. There was no easy recognition that 1848 was the end of the movement. The sort of strength, of numbers, organisation and feeling, demonstrated in that year could not be dissipated overnight. Fluctuation, renewal and re-organisation were familiar themes and many Halifax Chartists looked forward to new phases of the movement. The climactic political experiences of 1847–8 had both confirmed the position of the majority of people outside the existing political system, and illustrated in an exciting way their ability to influence it. It was to be another ten years before Chartism in Halifax was reduced to a handful of disillusioned enthusiasts with little to concentrate on but past glories.

At the end of 1848 the future directions of Halifax Chartism were by no means clear. Local Chartist leadership was heavily identified with physical-force policies. Some Chartists had never accepted them, others discarded them now. Any initiative on the use of force had been lost months before, and even then overbearing odds on the official side had been clear. Yet force was to have been the Chartists' ultimate sanction. Now it had failed a bankruptcy of tactics existed. Established activists were isolated by their stand on force. There was no question of being able to implement a strike policy as in 1842. In the mills the bitter imperatives of the handworkers' situation were lacking. Now in late 1848 they experienced a sudden and very considerable improvement in trade, which strengthened the swing away from desperate measures for change. This relative prosperity was to persist over the next years[31] which were crucial to any possible restoration of Chartism to its former strengths. It sapped sources of political urgency and was complemented by longer-term trends for younger men and juveniles not to enter the collapsed, traditional woolworking industries, but to go into the mills. The vital power base of Chartism in the handworking crafts was steadily contracting.

Signs of Chartist decline were quick to appear. Despite collections for Ernest Jones and the exhortations of lecturers support and finance waned. The Chartist hall had to be abandoned.[32] The very intensity of political involvement in 1848 produced strong reactions. Continuing energies were often channelled in new directions, reflecting various analyses of the reason for past failures. It was at this time that the first post-Owenite co-operative movements in Halifax were started, largely by Chartists.[33] Working-class members of the Mutual Improvement Society, recently amalgamated with the middle-class dominated Mechanics Institute, made their presence felt in the administration and tone of the new body. Temperance principles and organisations received increased support and a new priority in the eyes of many working men, among them Benjamin Wilson, who forswore drink and tobacco in 1849, 'as an example to others' and to allow no diversion of effort or money from the need to maintain his family and further the working-class cause.[34]

No major change occurred until the release of Ernest Jones (in July 1850) once again recalled the aims of the political movement. Jones's individual links with Halifax had never lapsed and were now revived more strongly. The fact that he had been harshly treated in prison brought added sympathy from those who had admired Jones in 1847 and 1848. A revitalised Chartist organisation in Halifax centred on providing a hero's reception for Jones on his release. On 14 July 1850 several thousands attended a Chartist rally on Blackstone Edge and heard speeches by Ben Rushton and Kit Shackleton of Halifax. On 15 July Ernest Jones returned triumphantly to Halifax in a carriage drawn by four greys and provided by local Chartists, and to the cheers of a large crowd. On this and the following day three great open-air meetings of welcome were held in West Hill Park.[35]

The return marked Ernest Jones's deliberate choice of Halifax as a power-base for himself, and thus for the projected revival of the Chartist Movement. He deliberately appealed to the kind of occupational groups which had provided his most vehement support in the past, and particularly to the wool-combers who, because of differing paces of mechanisation, were only in the 1850s suffering the effects of machinery and factory organisation. Jones in his national publications, *Notes to the People* and from 1852 *The People's Paper*, often addressed himself to the working people of Halifax. Thus he exhorted the wool-combers there, who were striking against wage reductions in the winter of 1851–2:

Wool-combers! place not your trust in the 'Kindly feelings and gentlemanly manner' of any capitalist. Impute no bad motives to Mr. Akroyd, more than the general policy of the whole capitalist class – to depress

labour and pay wages as low as possible . . . Working men, arise! and
learn to know yourselves and your foes.[36]

Jones did not confine his appeals only to those motivated by their own
miseries, but spoke also of a pride in the radical reputation of the town.
It was the Halifax Chartists, 'who kept the democratic principle erect
and pure . . . and impregnated its political energies with the long-neglected
germs of social knowledge.'[37] Jones had to recognise the diverse non-
political channels into which local popular political interest had flowed
since 1848 as it became clear that a working-class movement could no
longer survive merely on a political platform, even in Halifax where
Chartism had previously comprehended other issues. 'Social Knowledge'
took on a primary importance. Jones was disturbed by the growth of
other forms of working-class organisation. He disapproved of the most
important of these in Halifax, co-operation, because he saw in it inherent
dangers of fragmenting working-class unity.[38] Jones's first formulations
of policy on leaving prison were to repudiate any middle-class alliance,
and to direct his efforts towards the development of a social programme
which would include the various aspirations of groups like the Co-
operators within the new Chartism. He hoped for fruitful ground in
Halifax, but also for a much bigger expansion of support from this and
similar strongholds. In this context the Chartist social programme was
justified by Jones with solid realism. 'I believe there is little use in holding before them the Cap of Liberty, unless you hold THE BIG LOAF by
the side of it.'[39]

Jones played a major part in drawing up a manifesto aimed at the
social as well as the political emancipation of the people, and in getting
it accepted as national Chartist policy. As a member of the executive of
the National Charter Association (NCA), he figured prominently in the
Convention, which met in London on 31 March 1851 and which accepted
the new programme.[40] The achievement of the six points of the Charter
was still seen as the essential prerequisite of economic and social change,
but for the first time the winning of political power was related to a
specific programme of policies. This consisted of the nationalisation of
land; the Disestablishment of the Church; the provision of free national,
secular and compulsory education; the development of co-operative
manufacture and the participation of existing Co-operative Societies in
the movement (Jones, acting as Halifax delegate, was the 'special pleader'
of this clause); the right to State poor relief (including the unemployed,
the aged and infirm); the levying of taxes on land and accumulated

property; the liquidation of the National Debt and currency reform; the democratisation of the Army, with a people's militia; and the removal of taxes on knowledge. This was an impressive programme, which more nearly approached later developments in English socialism than anything that had gone before in popular politics. Jones's biographer, John Saville, describes the 1851 programme as 'a blue print for a social democratic state,' and regards Jones's individual contribution very highly,

> It was one of the great achievements of Jones that, after 1848, appreciating the 'connecting link' between 'politics' and 'economics', he wrote into the Charter the assumptions and social programme upon which the modern socialist movement has been largely built . . . although this had to be independently rediscovered by later generations.[41]

Halifax's close ties with Ernest Jones meant that these policy developments were well-known there and that Halifax Chartists influenced Jones in his formulations, for example over co-operation. In the national councils of Chartism leadership disputes, notably with Harney, meant that by 1852 Jones was the leading figure and directing force.

The years 1852 and 1853 were the heyday of Jones's influence in Halifax. There was an appreciable revival of Chartism. Many of the old figures had persisted in political activity since 1848 among them Kit Shackleton,[42] Bill Cockcroft, Ben Rushton, Benjamin Wilson and Isaac Clisset. Others became prominent, notably Thomas Wood, Harrison Holt, Plinny Barrett and Alexander Stradling. Meetings of the NCA were held weekly. West Riding delegates met, drawing mainly on the Halifax and Bradford districts. Activity was generated by various associated causes - in May 1852 a fund to support the ailing O'Connor, in September 1852 a regular subscription to support the *People's Paper* (the Chartists' own national paper, founded and edited by Ernest Jones); and in November 1852 the Halifax Short Time Committee. The main focus of energies, however, was Jones's second parliamentary candidature of July 1852.

In contrast to 1847 this was the only Chartist candidature that actually came to the poll.[43] Despite events elsewhere (with a number of abortive attempts at Chartist candidatures), Jones' campaign was as rhetorically optimistic as ever and won considerable support. The West Riding Executive, which included Bill Cockcroft and Isaac Clisset, issued a circular reminding their 'Brother Chartists' that, 'The example of France fully teaches us that working men alone are capable of representing labour.'[44] In Halifax a network of non-electors' committees campaigned for Jones. The campaign was valuable as a well-publicised platform for Chartist programmes and boosted the morale of local Chartists and hitherto inactive working-class sympathisers. However, it was not forgotten that Jones actually polled 280 votes in 1847 and the campaign was directly aimed at winning the middle-class vote, especially from those groups – the small tradesmen and craftsmen, and the radical Liberals – which supported Jones in 1847. They canvassed likely supporters and circularised every elector in Halifax:

> The offer of union and fraternity was made by the working men to the small shopkeepers, if the latter, out of two votes that each elector possessed, would give one to the working men's candidate, and one to their own.[45]

Despite these overtures the canvassers found a discouraging situation. The pressures which the Chartists, at a peak of their influence in 1847, had been able to apply now worked the other way. It was clear that 'small tradesmen were canvassed by their largest customers, and in many instances great pressure was brought to bear upon them.'[46] This was not the only reason for the breakdown of the pattern of Chartist-radical alliance. The events of 1848 and the spectre of violent confrontation had intervened to deter the radicals from association, even in a tactical electoral sense, with the local Chartists amongst whom the same men who had talked of arming were still prominent. It was the Chartists who, despite Jones's continued rejection of any class alliance within the political movement, were forced to seek a tactical and electoral compromise. The radicals had no such need. Their split with the Whigs in the 1840s had jolted both sides out of complacency. By 1852 the radicals had found themselves a particularly strong candidate in Francis Crossley. Crossley had the advantage of being local, being firmly identified with the fortunes of the whole town as its largest employer and being in his own life the epitome of a successful and commercially adept self-made man. His humble origins gave him an added reputation for the common touch, and this was confirmed by his political and industrial record. Moreover he was a devout and politically aware Nonconformist. He epitomised the main features of the developing Liberalism of the industrial areas. By 1852 the Whigs had recognised and accepted this, and their candidate Charles Wood had severed his electoral links with the

Tory Edwards, and now stood with his 'fellow' Liberal Crossley. This pairing could attract almost every shade of elector in the Whig–Liberal spectrum.[47] It left the associated bases of support for the Tories and the Chartists on either wing of the electorate with no support. The conciliatory Chartist approaches in 1852 got them nowhere and their campaign was increasingly thrown back on obtaining impressive but electorally insignificant displays of popular support for Jones. These came from the Chartist townships, and the borough itself, where open-air meetings of several thousand people were seen for the first time in four years.

The nomination took place on 7 July in the great quadrangle of the Halifax Piece Hall, a building symbolic of the lost prosperity of the small men of the cloth industry. The crowd of 20,000 heard the uninspiring oratory and expedient policies of the sitting Conservative MP, Edwards. Free trade and its benefits were the main theme of both Liberals. Only Crossley bothered to mention the issues of political reform which remained the Chartists' primary concern, a striking contrast with their enforced prominence in 1847. He spoke for a household, rate-paying suffrage and the ballot.

Ernest Jones's speech was undoubtedly the highlight for the crowd, in terms of entertainment and content.[48] They heard themselves hailed as the reality of universal suffrage, whose sole representation for the next seven years would be settled by only 500 people the following day. Jones undertook to expose free trade in relation to the conditions of working people. He eloquently argued the reality of unrestrained competition in home and foreign markets, which necessitated buying cheap and selling dear.

> The employer buys the labour cheap – he sells and on the sale he makes a profit; he sells to the working man himself – and thus every bargain between the employer and the employed is a deliberate cheat on the part of the employer.

In order that the employer might continue to sell cheap, especially overseas, wages would inevitably be depressed, and machinery, female and child labour increasingly used, and unemployment created. In this lucid outline Jones saw the worker as first sufferer, but appealed to other groups by extension – to shopkeepers, who were losing custom from the impoverished and unemployed; to ratepayers, who would be burdened by costly poor relief; and to the newly prosperous working men, who should take warning from the evidence of a continuing process. ('The low paid trades of today were the high paid once – the high paid today will be the low paid soon.')

Jones's approach showed that Chartism had to appeal not just to displaced craft-workers, but to their successors in the mills and small workshops. It was to this theme that Jones tied the development of the Chartist social programme, as the means of liberation for the unemployed and the petty-bourgeois taxpayer alike from the restrictions of the economic structure imposed by the 'money mongers' of both parties. Here he specified land nationalisation as a means to relieve the misery and expense of unemployment, and co-operative production as an independent and equitable alternative to capitalist manufacture. The ten-hour day was to be an immediate mitigation of the worst evils of industrial employment.

Jones's whole approach was laced with lively, often extravagant language, which delighted his supporters. It was a blend of Biblical resonance and the down-to-earth satisfaction of hearing their 'betters' thoroughly lambasted. Thus he exhorted the crowd to adopt the means to be – 'Industrious, healthy, happy, free – the sons of God instead of the victims of the devil.' There was no doubt as to the identity of the devil. Here he was incarnate in the person of Charles Wood, a member of the government which had imprisoned Jones, and on this theme his victim developed a final rhetorical crescendo:

> I summon the angel of retribution from the heart of every Englishman here present (An immense burst of applause) Hark! you feel the fanning of his wings in the breath of this vast multitude!
> The Whig, there he sits, turn him out! Turn him out, in the name of humanity and of God! Men of Halifax! Men of England! the two systems are before you. Now judge and choose!

This plea, the antithesis of the ponderous tones of the party politicians, aroused enormous emotion amongst the crowd. At the show of hands, taken immediately afterwards, Jones was elected by a large majority, with Henry Edwards as runner-up.

After this great occasion the official poll the next day formed a stark contrast:

Sir C. Wood (Liberal)	596
Francis Crossley (Liberal)	573

Henry Edwards (Conservative)   521
Ernest Jones (Chartist)   38

Both the Conservatives and the Chartists claimed that the Liberals had
made extensive use of corrupt methods, treating electors and 'bottling',
but there was little doubt of the temper of the electorate. The pattern
of Liberal voting displayed in 1852 was not seriously disturbed again
until the Reform election of 1868. Neither the Tories nor the Chartists
seriously challenged the dominance of the Liberal party as it had evolved
between 1847 and 1852. Through its internal alliance the party consistently returned two MPs one representing each wing of the party – the
Whigs and the middle-class radicals. It was the latter whom Ernest Jones,
in the light of his defeat, considered the more dangerous, and in this he
showed considerable foresight. The local record of a man like Crossley,
with his continued support for a political reform in advance of most of
his contemporaries even if short of the Charter, had definite attractions
for working-class politicians following their failure to achieve a realistic
intervention in the existing system. Jones sought to expose Crossley in
his post-poll speeches, because as a 'Manchester Reformer' and free
trader he was essentially a perpetrator of the tyranny Jones had described
at the hustings. Such men, he said, were 'hypocrites and traitors, who
make of political liberalism a cloak under which to carry on social
tyrannies unquestioned.' Again it was not so much his traditional supporters but the growing number of millworkers whom Jones sought to
impress: 'You men of the mills! What boots it if a dozen of you get a
vote, and fresh hundreds of surplus hands are cast before the millgate
by that Liberal Reformer.'

The Halifax election of 1852 again showed the reserves of popular
support on which an independently expressed working-class political
programme could draw. The crowds in the Piece Hall, in the reassuring
safety of numbers, were for once on top in expressing their opinions and
derision. But 1852 also showed that the middle-class radical alliance was
now barred to the Chartists, and without it they could achieve nothing
in existing political terms. The danger of eroded political support was
clear, and Jones's post-poll pledge – 'I will contest this borough until I
represent it. And you know the time will come' – expressed bravado
rather than political realism.

Jones was not the only optimist. The period immediately after the
election saw continued Chartist enthusiasm. James Finlen, the Chartist
lecturer, was heard by an audience of 5000 behind the Unitarian Chapel

and concluded that, 'This appears to be the centre of Northern Democracy from which must ultimately radiate liberty's clear and refulgent light, to penetrate the surrounding gloom of ignorance.'[49]

The thirty-eight electors who had 'voted for the people' were enthusiastically recognised. They came from the groups which had provided Jones's hard-core support in 1847, predominantly grocers and other small shopkeepers and dealers. Beer retailers, a wire drawer, machine-maker and pipe-maker were also included. Chartist strengths in the out-townships were indicated. Eleven of a total of fifty-three voters in Northowram township voted for Jones. Only four voters plumped for Jones. For the rest an alliance with the radical Liberal did not win automatic acceptance – eighteen voted for Crossley and Jones, but fifteen for the Tory, Edwards and Jones.[50]

On the basis of post-electoral enthusiasm, the organisation of a Lancashire–Yorkshire Chartist rally on Blackstone Edge, to recall the days of the 1840s, was attempted in August. This was wholly a Yorkshire, largely a Halifax, initiative. It found little response over the Pennines, and it was decided not to risk a possible fiasco by relying solely on West Riding attendances.[51]

Local indoor meetings continued, focusing mainly on the issue of the management and maintenance of the *People's Paper*. Halifax's first contribution of £3 in September was equalled only by Bradford Chartists.[52] Perspectives and participation were narrowing again. More than ever the conviction of the primary importance and realism of political aims was wavering. In October a Halifax correspondent to the *People's Paper* urged his townsmen to eschew the misery of agitation and,

> Get hold of capital – capital now improperly directed and expended in beer-shops, spirit vaults, and stopped into tobacco-pipes. Employ it in your emancipation, and political freedom will follow, it always has followed commercial liberty.[53]

Again the themes of co-operation and temperance were prominent at a time when Liberal dogmas of free trade were being pressed upon the popular consciousness. The lessons of 1852 were a powerful impulse. In November Kit Shackleton, veteran Chartist and then county secretary, joined the movement for limited political reform and was described as 'a paid agent of the middle classes.'[54] His example was a dangerous one. There was a general return to more fragmented working-class efforts, for example in the Halifax Short Time Committee, whose address to Richard Oastler in November 1852 demonstrated a heavily retrospective viewpoint, redolent of paternalism in its appreciation of 'our good old king ... our kind father [who] can still think and care for his children.'[55]

III

By early 1853 old areas of support in the Halifax district were becoming inactive, for example at Queenshead, Ovenden, Ripponden, Elland and Stainland. Despite this, attempts were made to organise a traditional summer-camp meeting in the hills. At the end of June Ben Rushton the sixty-eight-year-old Chartist stalwart died. His death and funeral proved an ideal focus for this latest revival of Chartism, uniting memories of the heyday of Rushton's generation with the present campaign. Rushton, like so many of the Chartists, came from an out-township – Ovenden, a mile down the valley from Halifax. His body was borne in procession through the town centre of Halifax to the local cemetery. It was drawn by two horses on a beplumed hearse and escorted by 140 Odd Fellows, by Ernest Jones and R. G. Gammage of the Chartist National Executive, and by thousands of local Chartists. The procession was joined by a contingent of Bradford Chartists, led by their band, and veteran leader Joseph Alderson. Jones's own description of the scene conveys a potent atmosphere:

> A more imposing spectacle of self-created order was never witnessed ... a continuous wall of human beings was ranged for the length of two miles on either side of the road, while still up the openings between the houses, fresh streams were seen pouring. The very hills on the opposite side of the valley were crested with people.

As the procession passed through Halifax all traffic was stopped. In the cemetery there were some 15,000 people who heard a secular funeral service with orations by Chartists and Odd Fellows. Rushton's legacy, Jones emphasised, was the realisation that 'the working man is the benefactor of the world ... the working man is the charioteer of progress' and must act independently of the capitalists, of whose resources he was the sole producer. At a later meeting in West Hill Park Ernest Jones graphically summed up his message. Why the Charter? Look around at this park:

There is a panorama of Labour's history. At one end it is bounded by a factory, at one end by the workhouse – and opposite by Bellevue, the mansion of a capitalist employer (Francis Crossley) ... There, on the left, in that factory, the wealth is created; there opposite to that mansion, all the wealth goes; and there to the workhouse, go the men who created the wealth.[56]

At the same time Halifax was hearing of Chartist meetings in many other areas. Halifax itself was able to readopt a district organisation, holding delegate meetings with representatives from Ripponden, Hebden Bridge and Midgley. In August, thus encouraged, the local leadership, who had been meeting at Bill Cockcroft's own house, decided to hire a meeting room.[57] However, where in 1848 the Chartists had their own hall and co-operation locally amounted to little more than a few active Chartists and a tiny shop in a cottage, now the Chartists went to the co-op, and asked for the use of one of their rooms. They also arranged a number of public lectures and enrolments.

Events in Halifax were increasingly superseded during the autumn of 1853 by developments elsewhere. There was an upsurge of industrial discontent with many areas experiencing major strikes. This generated developments in the labour movement nationally which took it in alternative directions to those adopted by the political working-class movement in Halifax, and which, until this date, had placed Halifax Chartism in the forefront of mainstream developments, an example of working-class activism and consciousness. Now this continuity was broken. The clearest indication of this was the wavering of the link between Halifax and Ernest Jones who, despite his protestations, had been unavoidably aware after the 1852 election that a realistic and effective working-class movement could not rest solely on a political programme. Now he seized on developments as an opportunity to harness support to a working-class movement more attuned to the participation of the industrial worker in the mills, the mines and the prospering crafts. He became committed to the idea of a Labour Parliament. His efforts were predominantly Lancashire-orientated and Manchester-based.

These events were symptomatic of a climate of class relations in which trade unions, rather than a directly political organisation, were increasingly seen as the 'typical' expression of working-class opinion. Halifax, by contrast, had little surviving trade union tradition within its working-class movement. The trade unionism of the handcrafts had its heyday in the late eighteenth century, for example in wool-combing the effective end of an already depleted union organisation had been the strike defeat of 1825 thirty years before. No appreciable unionisation among Halifax factory workers, many of whom were women and children, was to occur until the first decade of the twentieth century and this owed much to influences from the Lancashire cotton industry.[58] Only one strike of mill workers was recorded in the area in 1853.[59] Jones's search for new solutions and new tactics, which meant the reshaping of Chartism, took him increasingly further from Halifax.

From October 1853 Jones prepared for the Labour Parliament, canvassing support for the Mass Movement which was to be the vehicle of working-class participation in the Parliament and the source of funds to implement policies of strike support and nationalisation of land and production. For six months Halifax Chartists held aloof despite visits by lecturers, and the March 1854 Labour Parliament had no Halifax representative. In Halifax there was more concern with the NCA executive elections which drew 126 votes in February 1854.[60] Only at the end of May was a branch of the Mass Movement formed and its secretary, Joseph Noble, was not one of the leading Chartists. They remained passively resistant. The most active of them, Thomas Wood, who was also West Riding secretary, summed up their attitudes in reply to a suggestion from the south Lancashire district for a traditional Blackstone Edge meeting for summer 1854. Wood wrote:

It is unwise at any time to try and force a movement, ours has too long been forced. The few that have laboured have become exhausted. For a time various measures have been proposed, without apparently producing any results. The Lancashire strikes took place, and in consequence the Labour Parliament was proposed. Those of the active men that did not take part in it at least threw no barrier in its way. Nevertheless, some believe as I myself do, that if it succeeds, it will swallow up the Political Movement . . . I am of this opinion, that no man, at the same time, can give his attention to two movements and do them justice . . . Yorkshire would not contribute very largely to such a demonstration this summer.[61]

Despite this realistic local assessment Ernest Jones went ahead with his plans for a Blackstone Edge meeting of 'the democrats of Lancashire and Yorkshire', and found himself excusing the meagre attendance. The importance of Halifax was pointedly illustrated by the absence of mass turn-outs and familiar speakers from the town. Jones immediately reversed his comparative neglect of Halifax and announced a new fund to support the *People's Paper*, which was to be organised from Halifax by an executive representing the core of the town's Chartist leadership. Policy emphasis changed too. Jones no longer concentrated on the Mass Movement and the trades but on political aims, often related directly to Halifax. In early September he singled out the Crossleys, 'the modern millocracy', for attack, once more urging their working-class townsmen to have nothing to do with the Dissenting radicals, these

> Liberals of the Whig-Manchester School – they once called themselves Chartists and voted for the Chartist candidate . . . they are likewise very charitable, being large subscribers to the various Dissenting Chapels – giving the Dissenting parson a thousandth part of what they make out of their working men – and accordingly the Dissenting parsons cry them to the skies.[62]

In Halifax meetings were urged to agitate during a period of trade depression and against government policy in embarking on 'a treasonable war' in the Crimea. In mid-September a second Blackstone Edge Camp was organised with the Halifax Chartists in a leading role. They drove Jones up into the Pennines in a carriage-and-four with the Chartist flag flying. A good crowd started proceedings with a Chartist hymn and heard John Snowden of Halifax stress that 'political power is the only means whereby a man can secure himself a position in Society where he could be free from want, and the fear of want.'[63] Early in October Adam Beaumont, Halifax Chartist secretary, restated Chartism's identity with the old crafts. Taking Jones's theme of the ruthlessness of the Manchester radicals Beaumont related this to the cumulative misery caused by the current mechanisation of wool-combing:

> An entire handicraft has been superseded in West Yorkshire by mechanical intervention; and what is the result? They are men with the instinct of preservation like other men, . . . they seek employment in every direction . . . the employer takes advantage of their necessity and pays them wages considerably less than ordinary rates . . . reducing the wages of the old and experienced hands . . . Shall this state of things continue? Forbid it ye whose hearts have thrice this sixteen years made tyrants tremble and oppressors fear the hour of retribution . . .[64]

Halifax Chartism was more firmly than ever committed to its original themes and lines of development and by the end of 1854 its rhetoric had become predominantly retrospective. Rushton's funeral (in July 1853) had been the last great Chartist occasion in Halifax which combined pride in past strengths with a forward momentum into expanded fields of struggle. Jones's social programme and Mass Movement had been practical expressions of this momentum. Halifax Chartism opted out of this expansion at that critical point for current and future developments in the British labour movement, the question of the relationship between the political wing or party and the organised trade unions. The absence of union organisation or surviving traditions in either the old crafts or the 'new' industries in Halifax robbed Chartism there of a whole dimension of potential growth. Jones's Mass Movement received only limited and very short-lived success, mainly in Lancashire, but the absence of support from the West Riding and Halifax in particular, areas chosen by Jones as being exceptionally strong power bases, was a crucial factor in stultifying potential industrial/political developments.

On this deliberately narrowed basis Halifax Chartism continued into its final years of separate existence 1855-8. This period was characterised by spasmodic but lively, retrospectively orientated activity in increasing isolation from other areas. Activity was centred on individual events. For example on Good Friday 1855 a Chartist tea-party was held to commemorate the famous Skircoat Green meeting of 1848, however the contrast with the estimated 80,000 crowd in 1848 was stark.[65] A few veterans were still active, such as Isaac Clissett and John Snowden, but during 1855 decline was apparent. A Blackstone Edge Camp was abandoned for lack of support and funds for a Chartist missionary could not be found.[66]

Two events proved the highlights of activity in 1856 and each was the last of its kind – the last of the lively Chartist street processions through Halifax, and the last Chartist 'revival' directly linked to past events, in this case the Newport Rising of 1839. The procession was a counter to the official celebrations of the end of the Crimean War and proclaimed the Chartist retort to the empty middle-class slogans of peace, retrenchment and reform – 'Peace and Plenty! of what? Poverty and want!' The Chartist message, their band and their sheep (a fat specimen labelled 'For the drones, the aristocracy, and all who live by other people's labour', and a lean carcass 'For the better paid operatives and low government officials') failed to compete with the official entertainments.[67] It was the determination of Halifax Chartists to give John

Frost, transported leader of the Newport Rising, a home-coming reminiscent of those for O'Connor and Jones that provided the *raison d'être* of Chartist activity throughout the rest of 1856 and early 1857. In July 1856 the Halifax men managed to organise the first joint Lancashire and Yorkshire meeting for over two years, representing twelve centres.[68] A Frost Testimonial Fund was set up. Its chief officers (Harrison Holt, treasurer, and Thomas Wood, secretary) were from Halifax. Optimistic plans for a local Chartist library and hall were put forward. West Riding links were built up again and eight towns sent delegates to the Dewsbury meeting in November. A county levy of one penny per month was set up to finance Chartist lecturers (including John Snowden) and a Chartist newsagent established.[69] This showed the impressive resilience of local activists rather than a reactivation of mass support. In February 1857 a county delegate meeting voted to discontinue the levy, and by May the Frost Testimonial Fund had failed to meet its targets. Its treasurer, Holt, was left financially and administratively overburdened by its collapse.[70]

By 1856 Halifax Chartism was thrown back on its hard-core activists, struggling to build up the movement from very low levels of activity. The organisational network based on NCA membership and personal links throughout the district had ebbed away since 1853 as had that large, amorphous body of support which showed its anonymous but collective identity with Chartism on occasions like Rushton's funeral. The failures of 1856 were followed by an unprecedented exodus from the local Chartist leadership. In May 1857 Adam Beaumont, throughout the eighteen-fifties an office-holder and one-time secretary of the Halifax Chartists, emigrated to America.[71] During the autumn another executive member, Isaac Crowther, moved to Newcastle-on-Tyne as a newsagent. In October Alexander Patterson of Ripponden, Halifax and former West Riding secretary defected, taking the county records and minutes with him. After this Harrison Holt, second only to Thomas Wood as a Halifax Chartist activist, disappeared from their meetings, and was never wooed back, despite the pleas of a county delegate meeting. All these men had weathered repeated frustration of their hopes for Chartism. What really broke the continuity of Halifax Chartism, and now became current, was the issue of alliance with the limited reform programme of the middle-class Liberals.

As early as 1855 Halifax Chartists had been aware of the pressures to join middle-class reformers, but categorically rejected this 'transfer of power from the aristocracy to the moneyocracy' as represented by the then newly formed Administrative Reform Association.[72] Instead they still hoped to find new sources of support which involved for the first time an appreciable break from their wholly political stance. Thomas Wood, who had previously rejected links with the trades, now urged that 'something to practically illustrate the benefits to be obtained from the possession of political power must be attempted before the people can be aroused from their present apathy.'

That something was retail co-operation to be kept 'entirely in the hands of the staunchest democrats . . . so as not to lose sight of political power as the leverage whereby people can socially emancipate themselves.'[73] This move was significant as a change of direction for the Chartists rather than as a real solution. Co-operation was already firmly established and was not to be suddenly moulded into an ancillary wing of a political organisation. With this alternative course blocked the option of political alliance presented itself with renewed force.

In October 1856 the Halifax Chartist committee was 'desirous of making the day of Mr. Frost's visit to Halifax, a day of general reconciliation between all the reformers in this town', but reconciliation was defined in their own terms – the six points of the Charter.[74] In May 1857 the West Riding delegates again considered the middle-class reform movement. Any reform bill they decided must be framed 'so that we can join it – but we shall, in *this* district, agitate for nothing less than the Charter.'[75] It was at this stage that clear divisions emerged. It was now a question of whether to accept some measure of reform as a step on the way to the Charter and an end in itself at a time when lack of mass interest in the Charter had become crushingly clear. The thoughts of a seasoned and prominent Halifax Chartist are clear from Alexander Stradling's reply to Ernest Jones's continued labelling of the reform movement as middle-class.

> If it is to be conducted by them, the people are to blame, for they form the great majority, and if they are disposed to sleep and let the world go on as it will, the responsibility rests on them . . . I am a Chartist . . . I think there are but two ways by which we are to get power – the one is by moral persuasion, and the other is by physical force. If the former way is best then we ought to work with the party that has power. From them it must come in the end. If I understand what the object of the middle classes is, I am convinced that it is worthy of our co-operation, although it does not ask for as much as I could like. If the Tories even were to offer Household Suffrage,

protected by the Ballot, I would work with them as freely as any
other party, – for I do not care how reform comes so long as it comes
at all.[76]

Stradling could not know how accurate his then outlandish fantasy
of Tory reform was to be. His dilemma was a real and present one.
Chartism had reached a stage when in Halifax and nationally a decision
was being forced upon its adherents. Ernest Jones brought the issue to
a head in April when he proposed a national reform conference in
London to which middle-class figures would be invited. As soon as the
conference issue arose Halifax withdrew from its central role in West
Riding Chartism. National conference delegates elected at Bradford and
Halifax did not attend the meetings. Some Halifax Chartists left, some
fixedly adhered to the full Charter or nothing, others saw the way forward in compromise. The town submitted no delegate to the conference
until late October and then refused to do so through the delegate body
in Bradford.[77] The meeting which eventually elected a local delegate
consisted of a 'few friends', a handful of familiar names like Joseph
Binns, the new secretary, Benjamin Wilson, and John Snowden, the
elected delegate. It was these men who ten years later could be seen to
epitomise the passage of Chartism, in its surviving institutional sense,
into popular Liberalism.

The Chartist Conference finally took place in February 1858. It
included representatives of the trades, invited into Chartist councils for
the first time since 1853, and on the fourth day middle-class figures,
including Francis Crossley of Halifax. Of forty-one Chartist delegates
only nine represented Lancashire and Yorkshire. Already the new reform
movement was tied to the metropolitan scene and parliamentary pressure groups. Ernest Jones dominated the conference and was elected sole
executive of the Chartist Movement. On reform, seconded by John
Snowden, he stipulated a minimum platform of manhood suffrage and
no property qualifications for MPs.[78] From this emerged the Political
Reform Union. The composition of its managing committee summed
up the new alliance with three Chartists, three trade unionists, and six
middle-class men.[79] Thereafter there was a bewildering proliferation of
suffrage and ballot associations in London and nationally. The mainstream of the new reform movement became identified with John
Bright, MP for Rochdale, and his proposed reform bill, the main points
of which were household suffrage in the boroughs, a £10 suffrage in the
counties, the redistribution of 125 seats in favour of the industrial

towns, and the ballot.[80] The scene had shifted from the Charter, which had been the touchstone of working-class reformers for over twenty years. Halifax Chartists clung to a form of independence longer than almost any other provincial centre. After the 1853 conference they lost most of their stalwarts. This last-ditch position brought back a few old figures, notably George Webber, who had proposed the Lancashire and Yorkshire republic in 1848, but had not taken a leading part in late Chartism. He represented the small minority who still stood unambiguously for the whole Charter and reappeared in the mid-1850s representing an exactly opposite political development to John Snowden and his kind. In 1858 their efforts were in vain.

Snowden summed up the situation in a well-known letter in reply to an appeal for funds by Ernest Jones in October 1859:

> I am sorry to inform you that there is no Chartist organisation in Halifax nor in any of the numerous villages surrounding it . . . Many of those that were once active Chartists have emigrated. And others, though residing here as usual have become so thoroughly disgusted at the indifference and utter inattention of the multitude to their best wishes that they too are resolved to make no more sacrifices in a public cause.

Moved by Jones's 'foolish integrity and zeal' in seeking an extension of the franchise he and other ex-Chartists held a private collection for Jones, but with 'the ardent wish that you will in future look to your own personal interest and work for yourself regardless of the multitude.'[81]

III

It would be wrong to conclude an account of Halifax Chartism without briefly considering the nature of its leadership, which was vital to its character between 1847 and 1858, and which carried the movement after 1853. Given the enormous appeal of 'outside' leaders like O'Connor and Jones, it was the local leaders who gave Halifax Chartism continuity and consistency. They were drawn from two main elements – the traditional textile craftsmen and the small shopkeepers and workshop manufacturers. Post-1847 Chartism contained both groups with strong elements of continuity from the earlier period, and in several individual cases a direct translation from the role of independent craftsman to independent tradesman, often servicing the Chartist movement and the working-class community. Joseph Foreman advocated the example of the French revolution in 1848. He subsequently turned to local co-operative enterprises and became one of the first co-op shop-keepers of the new Halifax Society in 1851. He became a director of this and the Mechanics Institute. He set up as a bookseller and in the late 1860s and 1870s was an active radical and National Education Leaguer. Bill Cockcroft was involved in Halifax Chartism from its earliest days and was a handloom weaver. In 1847 Wilson regarded him as leader of the 'physical forceists' in Skircoat. Cockcroft remained a Chartist throughout the 1850s and continued to hold local office until c. 1855. He became a secondhand bookseller. Isaac Clisset was also a leading activist during 1847–8 and continued to play a major role until 1856. He earned his living by bill-sticking for radical meetings and for other, paying, customers. Joshua Nicholl was the landlord of the local temperance hotel, which provided a chief Chartist meeting place. Isaac Crowther became a newsagent. Such employments provided relative independence and continued personal and written links with political ideas and working-class people.

Chartism always drew on the support of small tradesmen. For example one of the best-known original Halifax Chartists was 'Radical Bob' Wilkinson, a shoemaker. The shoemaker's shop in Skircoat was a recognised radical meeting place where newspapers were read by groups. The same concern with disseminating the political message continued into the late Chartist period and it was Wilkinson whom Latimer, first editor of Halifax's new Liberal paper, the *Halifax Courier* (1853), found took the keenest interest in this possible new platform, along with a 'Chartist Bookseller' (Cockcroft), and a 'Chartist billsticker' (Clisset).[82] The importance of the small tradesman is also clear from the composition of the leadership of Halifax Chartism in its final years which is shown below.

The sections of this leadership group had much in common with each other. The ties of the craftworkers with the tradesmen were stronger than those of the craftsmen with the factory proletariat, or the small tradesman with the industrial middle class. Their values of independence and self-determination were the backbone of Halifax Chartism, and they, not millworkers, trade unionists or middle-class politicians, dominated it. No major change in this balance occurred until about 1855. It was at this stage that Halifax Chartism had firmly rejected any trade-orientated development, but had found its old, contracted bases of support insufficient to sustain further growth. As it turned tentatively towards the idea of sinking its identity with other groups, so it shed the old hands. Those who persisted doggedly to the end in 1858 were predominantly the younger working men (for example, Snowden, Wilson and Stradling), and the tradesmen. Yet the latter were *not* identified with pressures for middle-class alliance. Indeed Adam Beaumont and Harrison Holt, with Thomas Wood the most active leaders of the years 1854-8, both stood firm on the cause of manhood suffrage (they were themselves already electors) and abandoned Chartism only on Ernest Jones's wooing the reform movements.

The ten most active Chartist leaders in Halifax between 1852 and 1858 were[83]

1	Thomas Wood	?
2	Harrison Holt	Grocer, cloth presser
3	Adam Beaumont	Currier, mill-strap manufacturer
4	Isaac Crowther	Newsagent
5	John Snowden	Wool-comber (to 1856), Chartist lecturer, dyer
6	Plinny Barrett	General dealer and carpet-shoe manufacturer
7	James Spencer	Shopkeeper
8	William Cockcroft	Weaver, second-hand bookseller
9	Joseph Binns	Hatter
10	Alexander Stradling	Weaver

IV

What were the legacies of Halifax Chartism? They were strong in terms of both men and ideas. The leaders of working-class politics in the town continued to be drawn from Chartists for almost twenty years after the formal demise of the movement. The seldom-faltering belief in political means and priorities within the local working-class movement persisted, heavily influenced by the traditions and mythology of the Chartist years. The ideas and policies of Chartism continued to be independently articulated after 1858, later putting considerable pressure on 'established' Liberalism, and later still rediscovered in Labourism.[84]

The legacies are apparent in Halifax popular politics after 1858. Parliamentary elections between 1859–74 always showed Halifax to be politically lively by national standards. However the exhaustion of Chartism and the national shift to a trade union identified labour movement and a Leeds and London orientated political reform movement were reflected in the fact that 1859–65 saw the heyday of co-operation in Halifax, whilst popular politics were quiescent. The resurgence of political interest came with the Reform campaign which culminated in the 1867 Reform Act. The Chartist legacy was most clearly seen in the Reform campaign and in the parliamentary election of 1868, the first with the new, extended electorate.

Events in many ways mirrored the state of Halifax politics in 1847 with Liberalism again split into two wings represented by the two MPs, the familiar Edward Akroyd (Whig, Anglican and National Reform Unionist) and James Stansfeld (nationally known radical, successor to the mantle of Francis Crossley and leading Reform Leaguer). The former Chartists also split two ways. John Snowden was with the NRU and Akroyd. In the years since 1858 he had become 'the statutory working man' of the party Liberals.[85] George Webber, on the other hand, was branch secretary of the Reform League and still refusing in 1866 to dismiss possible violent struggle.[86]

The election of 1868 carried this split to its conclusion. The radicalism of Stansfeld, hobbled by his dependence on the Liberal party machine in Halifax, was unacceptable to working-class reformers and numbers of radical middle-class activists. There was the same enthusiasm to implement a new measure of democracy which had triggered action in 1832 and 1848. (In 1868 the electorate rose from 1900 to 9442.) A working man's candidate was adopted in opposition to Stansfeld and Akroyd, with no Tory standing. The candidate, after an attempt to secure Ernest Jones who stood for Manchester instead, was E. O. Greening – Co-operator, autodidact from a family of small manufacturers, a Dissenter, advocate of temperance and Reform Leaguer. After a lively, tough-fought campaign Greening lost (Stansfeld 6278; Akroyd 5141; Greening 2802) but frightened the party Liberals. The campaign clearly showed Chartist influences, firstly in the issues – the ballot, annual Parliaments, redistribution of seats, abolition of entail and primogeniture for example; secondly in the people involved – of the ten main Chartist leaders of the 1850s, five reappeared as supporters of Greening, whose meetings were held at Nicholls Temperance Hotel, whilst one, Snowden, supported Akroyd and Stansfeld and was branded 'a ten shillings a week lad', as a former Akroyd pensioner,[87] (of the remaining four Chartists two had left Halifax in 1857 and two were not active); and thirdly in the areas from which Greening received his principal support – the townships like Ovenden, Skircoat and Southowram.

The aftermath of the election was also akin to that in 1847. Moves were made to heal the breach in Liberalism, which in many other areas seemed already to have subsumed the energies of working-class and popular elements. True to Halifax form the radicals refused to compromise and set up the Liberal Electoral Association as a rival to the official Liberal Registration Association. For four years the popular challenge of 1868 was carried on through lobbying and agitation until the shock loss of the adjoining parliamentary constituency (West Riding north) to a Tory candidate in the 1872 by-election so scared the Liberals that a rushed marriage between the two Halifax organisations was arranged. The circumstances of the party Liberals forced them into accepting the sort of specific programme for the new Halifax Liberal Association which they had rejected in 1868:

First, perfect religious equality; second, the adoption of a national system of education which shall provide that in schools wholly or partially supported from public funds no distinctive creeds shall be taught; third the assimilation of the occupation franchise in the counties to what exists in the boroughs; fourth an equitable apportionment of parliamentary representation to population. and fifth, the ballot.[88]

The partnership was an uneasy one. At the grand inaugural Edward Akroyd and the guest of honour, Gladstone's nephew Lord Frederick Cavendish, were heckled and there were interventions from the floor on republicanism and the bastardy laws.[89] Only a new 'democracy', the first School Board elections of January 1874, finally brought anything like harmony to the sections of Halifax Liberalism with an unsectarian 'working man', John Snowden, heading the poll.

The general election of 1874, which followed immediately, cemented this united 'popular' Liberalism which finally overtook any overt, independent working-class political activity in the Chartist tradition. The election of John Crossley, brother of the late Francis, symbolised this.[90] He represented one way in which the Liberals had disarmed popular opposition, in providing a booming industrial base in Halifax, in being seen to make strategic concessions politically, in lavish and enlightened philanthropy of public parks, housing, orphanages, schools and churches, and in financially bolstering the Liberal party and Liberal press. In a climate of such pervasive influence we are left with only faint echoes of Chartism – George Webber's complaint that the Gladstonian Liberalism of Irish Disestablishment is a complete irrelevance to the true interests of the working man;[91] and John Snowden's rhetorical cadences now preaching the benefits of Free Trade with all the fervour of a convert.[92]

The political passage of Chartism into popular Liberalism was never an easy, passive, untroubled or complete process in Halifax. The political dialogue remained two-way until 1874. Paradoxically the very rigour of the debate meant that the resulting union had greater depth than in many other areas, where, although popular Liberalism and popular Toryism manifested themselves earlier and with apparent ease, the marginality of formal politics to working-class concerns meant that the merging of political fortunes was of less significance.[93]

The evidence from Halifax offers a vivid picture of late Chartism of its perhaps surprisingly long independent survival, and of a continuing development of ideas, as for example in Jones's programme of 1852. It also shows the limits that development reached when the movement failed to attract the new industrial work-forces and to relate to changes in the labour movement, particularly in the trade unions. The fragmentation and loss of direction among working-class movements in the mid-century, and their absorption into middle-class politics, has been the subject of intense historical debate.[94] Numerous causes for this change have been suggested. The Halifax case is interesting in that several of the major suggested causes do not seem to apply here. For example the effects of a more stable second phase of industrialisation were slow to make themselves felt in the area. It was the continuing upheavals of mechanisation that gave further life to Chartism in the 1850s, although the relative prosperity of a new generation in the mills began to make itself felt in a narrowing long-term base for Chartism. More strikingly absent in the Halifax equation seem to be the new labour aristocrats of the mid-century, on whom some historians place so much emphasis as agents of growing accommodation with the middle classes. Artisans were vital in the Halifax working-class movement, but they were the traditional textile handworkers and small crafts and tradesmen, and they were the most militant of all. Even in the late 1860s new labour aristocrats were not prominent in local affairs, nor were the new model unionists so emphasised by historians of the institutional and metropolitan labour movement. In a similar way consideration of the effects of large-scale middle-class philanthropy and the associated gospel of self-help frequently leads one back to the indigenous working-class values of independence and self-determination so strong in the Halifax Chartist tradition. Some of these factors were particularly marked in the Halifax experience but it would be a mistake not to consider their relevance to the mid-century labour movement elsewhere. During the 1850s and 1860s the working-class movement lost general direction and is characterised by increasingly localised responses to differing conditions and a breakdown of wider links. Late Chartism in Halifax demonstrates this slow, often painful, process at work.

NOTES

1. All references to Halifax apply to the town and its surrounding area unless specifically stated otherwise.

2. By late 1841 there were twelve local Chartist associations in the area, linked as a district. They had an estimated 500–600 paid-up members. (G. R. Dalby, 'The Chartist Movement in Halifax and District', in *Transactions of Halifax Antiquarian Society* (1956)). A fuller account of early Chartism in Halifax will be found in K. Tiller, *Working Class Attitudes and Organisation in Three Industrial Towns 1850–75* (Univ. of Birmingham Ph.D. thesis, 1975). See also Dalby, 'Chartist Movement in Halifax', and Benjamin Wilson, *Struggles of an old Chartist* (Halifax, 1887).

3. PRO BT 41/474 (I owe this reference to Mrs D. Thompson).

4. Halifax Chartism provides a practical demonstration of what Eileen Yeo has called 'an alternative society', in S. Pollard and J. Salt (eds), *Robert Owen, Prophet of the Poor* (1971) pp. 103–8.

5. See for example the comparative studies of Halifax, Wigan and Kidderminster in Tiller, *Working Class Attitudes*. In Kidderminster craft trade unionism was the dominant focus of local working-class activity, whilst in Wigan the important features were the non-institutionalised, confrontational violence of the main work-force of miners, and ethnic feeling related to a large local population of Irish.

6. Daniel Defoe, *A Tour through the Whole Island of Great Britain* (1971 edn) pp. 490–9.

7. *Northern Star* (*NS*) 24 July 1847 lists 19 constituencies. R. G. Gammage, *History of the Chartist Movement 1837–1854* (1894) pp. 283–4 lists 24 constituencies contested by candidates who 'came forward on Chartist principles'.

8. *NS* 4 August 1846.

9. John Saville, *Ernest Jones, Chartist* (1952).

10. For example his letter on becoming a Chartist delegate in *NS* 9 June 1846.

11. At a meeting on 24 January 1847; (quoted in D. and E. Thompson, 'Halifax as a Chartist Centre', unpublished MSS in possession of the authors).

12. This closely mirrored party developments in the adjoining county con-

stituency. See F. M. L. Thompson, 'Whigs and Liberals in the West Riding 1830–60', *English Historical Review* (1959).

13. Wilson, *Struggles of an old Chartist.*

14. Obituary of Henry Edwards, in *Halifax Guardian* 24 April 1886.

15. So heated that Jonathan Akroyd, the millowner, collapsed and died whilst chairing a noisy pro-Wood meeting. This, and the siege of their Bowling Dyke Mill during the Plug Plot in 1842, strengthened the drift of his son and political heir, Edward Akroyd, to the conservative Whig Constitutionalism of which he became the leader in Halifax, an ever-present figure in local politics.

16. *NS* 3 July 1847.

17. *Halifax Guardian* 31 July 1847.

18. *Pollbook* in Halifax Reference Library.

19. See analysis in J. R. Vincent, *Pollbooks* (1966) pp. 106–9.

20. *NS* 14 August 1847.

21. Ibid.

22. Ibid., 8 January 1848.

23. Gammage, *History of the Chartist Movement*, p. 325.

24. Ibid, p. 328.

25. *Halifax Courier* 16 and 23 November 1901.

26. *Halifax Reformer* 24 May 1848.

27. J. J. Mulroy (ed.), *The Story of the Town that Bred Us* (Halifax, 1948) p. 17.

28. For example, *Halifax Guardian* 17 June 1848.

29. Ibid, 3 June 1848; Gammage, *History of the Chartist Movement*, p. 333.

30. Resolution at the county meeting reported in *NS* 22 July 1848.

31. John James, *History of the Worsted Manufacture in England* (1857) p. 506, wrote 'were a spinner or manufacturer of modern times to point out two years of consecutive good trade, he would undoubtedly select these two, (1849, 1850) . . . where the workman, along with the boon of cheap provisions enjoyed high wages . . .'

32. Wilson, *Struggles of an old Chartist*, p. 15.

33. See G. J. Holyoake, *Co-operation in Halifax, and some other institutions around it* (1866); Wilson, *Struggles of an old Chartist*, p. 15; M. Blatchford, *History of the Halifax Industrial Society Ltd* (1901). Halifax co-operation was heavily involved with producing goods, e.g. unadulterated and cheap flour, and not just with retailing. This emphasis faded in the late eighteen-sixties.

34. Wilson, *Struggles of an old Chartist*, p. 15.

35. Gammage, *History of the Chartist Movement*, p. 354.

36. *Notes to the People* 3 January 1852.

37. Ibid., vol. 1, no. 2 (1851).

38. Ibid., vol. 2 (1852) pp. 584–8; Gammage, *History of the Chartist Movement*, p. 382.

39. *NS* 10 August 1852.

40. Gammage, *History of the Chartist Movement*, pp. 369–72.

41. Saville, *Ernest Jones*, p. 25.

42. Until his death in 1853.

43. The national emphasis had now shifted to the activity of trade union rather than political leaders, with the result that William Newton of the ASE's

stand at Tower Hamlets has been called 'the first working class candidacy' (F. E. Gillespie, *Labour and Politics in England, 1850-67* (1927) ch. 3).

44.   *People's Paper*, 26 June 1852.

45.   Ibid., 17 July 1852.

46.   Wilson, *Struggles of an old Chartist*, p. 20.

47.   The engineering of this alliance and the abrupt rupture of the Wood-Edwards links is described in two Tory satirical pamphlets issued during the election – *The Halifax Election A Whig Melodrama, in Three Acts* (Leeds 1852), and a *Report of the Principal Speeches and Songs at the Great Whig-Radical Banquet*, February 3 1853. Akroyd, presiding at this banquet, likens the alliance to the Aberdeen coalition (p. 4) – 'it comprises all shades of religion and politics. Churchmen, Chapelmen, and Papists – Whigs, Radicals and Chartists – (a voice 'No Chartists') – Monarchists, Republicans and Levellers. Can anything be more liberal, more beautiful?'

48.   *People's Paper* 24 July 1852.

49.   Ibid., 17 July 1852.

50.   *Pollbook* in Halifax Reference Library.

51.   *People's Paper* 14, 21 August 1852.

52.   Ibid., 25 September 1852.

53.   Ibid., 23 October 1852.

54.   Ibid., 6 November 1852.

55.   Ibid., 13 November 1852.

56.   Ibid., 2 July 1853.

57.   Ibid., 20 August 1853.

58.   See Ben Turner, *Heavy Woollen District Textile Workers Union* (1917) p. 103; Todmorden Weavers' Association, *50 years of Progress 1880-1930*.

59.   *People's Paper*, 5 November 1853 (it was of 200 weavers at Queenshead).

60.   Ibid., 18 February 1854.

61.   Ibid., 10 June 1854.

62.   Ibid., 16 September 1854.

63.   Ibid.

64.   Ibid., 7 October 1854.

65.   Ibid., 14 April 1855.

66.   Ibid., 23 June, 7 July 1855.

67.   Ibid., 7 June 1856.

68.   Ibid., 27 July 1856. The centres were Halifax, Todmorden, Midgeley, Bradford, Leeds, Manchester, Bolton, Royton, Oldham, Ripponden Small Lees and Burnley.

69.   Ibid., 15 November, 20 December 1856.

70.   Ibid., 14 February, 30 May 1857.

71.   Ibid., 30 May 1857.

72.   Ibid., 26 May 1855.

73.   Ibid.

74.   Ibid., 4 October 1856.

75.   Ibid., 2 May 1857.

76.   Ibid.

77.   Ibid., 24 October 1857.

78.   Ibid., 13 February 1858.

79. Ibid., 20, 27 February 1858.

80. Gillespie, *Labour and Politics*, p. 147.

81. John Snowden to Ernest Jones, 16 October 1859 (Letter in Chetham's Library, Manchester).

82. Letter from J. Latimer to F. R. Spark, 16 December 1886, quoted in F. R. Spark, *Memories of My Life* (1886).

83. Degree of activity is based on Chartist offices held locally, for the West Riding and nationally, speeches made, letters to the press, etc. These and other biographical details are drawn from the Chartist and local press directories, pollbooks, 1851 Census enumerators' returns etc.

84. J. Lister: *Early History of the ILP in Halifax* (typescript in Halifax Reference Library).

85. See *Report of National Reform Conference at London, 20th and 21st May 1862* (London, 1862), when Snowden stated that working men in Halifax no longer desire manhood suffrage. In 1866 he was one of four working men in a national NRU lobby to Lord Russell and was willing to accept a £6 household franchise (*Halifax Courier* 6 September 1884).

86. *Halifax Courier* 7 April 1866.

87. *Halifax Guardian* 7 November 1868.

88. *Proposed Rules for Halifax Liberal Association*, in Newspaper Cuttings (Political) Box SH. / JN46, Halifax Reference Library.

89. *Halifax Courier* 28 September 1872.

90. Ibid., 31 January 1874; T. Turner: *Halifax Newscuttings Collection*, vol. 4.

91. *Halifax Courier* 19 October 1868.

92. Ibid., 16 April 1870.

93. This was the case in both Kidderminster and Wigan, where political action had never been, and did not become in the 1860s and 1870s a major form of working-class expression.

94. A useful bibliography of the large number of books and articles relating to this debate appears in R. Gray: *The Aristocracy of Labour in Nineteenth-century Britain c 1850–1914* (1981).

10. Some Practices and Problems of Chartist Democracy

EILEEN YEO

THE Chartists will always be important in the history of the struggle for democracy. But historians have tended to shrink what the Chartists meant by democracy to the six points of the Charter. Even if it was revolutionary at the time to challenge property as the basis of political rights and to extend citizenship to (male) humanity none the less the call for a representative Parliament, largely elected by, composed of and annually accountable to working men was only a part of Chartist democracy.[1] In this chapter I will explore some practices of self-government within the Chartist Movement, partly as a way of recapturing the larger Chartist project, but also to bring out the relationship between class situation and organisational possibility in the Chartist period. To create a real democratic practice, the Chartists had to manoeuvre consciously within enormous constraints. This chapter will explore not only the changing and enlarging scope of Chartist democratic ambition, but also Chartist attempts to deal with the scarcity of time and money in working-class life and their attempts to grapple with the State and the law. Once the Chartists are seen as practical democrats and movement builders who tried to work within formidable difficulties, some of the clichés of existing historiography begin to crumple. The endless twists and turns in Chartist strategy and organisation become less easy to chalk up to Chartist ineptitude, to insufficient class consciousness or to incessant bickering among leaders.[2] A different logic to Chartist chronology begins to emerge.

There are many other possible ways to explore what the Chartists meant by democracy – at least as many ways as there were contested areas of social life where the Chartists were practising their own version of government as against alternatives posed by other groups. Eventually I hope to produce a more rounded analysis not only of Chartist democracy but also of the ubiquitous class conflict over democracy in the first half of the nineteenth century. Here I will not try to trace Chartist attempts to enter and to democratise the constitutional forms of national politics, like the county or public meeting, like the franchise or Parliament. The resistance to such 'intrusions' helped to fix and expose the limits of ruling-class definitions of representative government before 1850. Even within the Chartist Movement such issues exposed deep class rifts: middle-class groupings continually baulked at giving up all property qualifications and allowing too-frequent elections and repeatedly held the line at household suffrage and triennial Parliaments. Nor will I focus on the active part that Chartists played in struggles over local government in their areas – over the potential of the vestry for direct democracy, over the centralisation of the new Poor Law and over the acceptability of the Municipal Corporations Act as a blueprint for local democracy. Rather it is to some practices and problems of democracy in the Chartist Movement itself that I will turn.

CHARTIST AMBITION

The main strategy of the Chartist Movement was to mobilise vast numbers of the working classes (and their friends) and become the irresistible movement of the People which no government could withstand: as O'Connor put it, 'exert your power as a great and united people and then, like Sampson shorn of his locks, they would lose their strength, and no longer possess the power to enslave you'. Influenced by the success of the Catholic Emancipation movement and the 1832 parliamentary reform agitation, the dominant Chartist strategy was 'open, intimidating constitutionalism' on a huge scale, which involved massive petitions, public meetings, appearances as non-electors at the official hustings and even in 1839 a General Convention of the Industrious Classes, a people's parliament elected by universal suffrage.[3] There were groups in the movement, however, which were deeply suspicious of large demonstrations, seeing them only as happy hunting grounds for demagogic leaders in search of passive followers: the London Working Men's Association (LWMA) in the words of William Lovett, resolved instead 'to manage their own affairs, and *dispense with leadership of every description*'. There was a real misapprehension here because Lovett could never see that 'northern' Chartism also relied on the routine meetings of smaller local associations. Indeed however much they disagreed on the means and misunderstood each other's practice, all working-class sections of Chartism were concerned to make the movement 'as democratic in its workings as the principles of it are democratic in their nature.'[4] In many ways those pursuing the constitutional strategy had the more difficult task. While the LWMA was ready to limit its constituency to 'the *intelligent* and *useful* portion of the working classes in town and country', the constitutional strategy wanted to recruit numbers unlimited. But how could a meaningful controlling role be given to working people who had little spare time when they were in work or too much spare time but no spare money when they were out of work?

The problems were compounded as the Chartists enlarged their activities. When their 1839 constitutional campaign began to meet with stiffening government resistance from May onwards, climaxing in mid-July with Parliament's rejection of the National Petition, the Chartists tried to increase the pressure by putting their ulterior measures into operation. To some extent, these measures were a package of familiar political tactics which had been used or mooted many times before.[5] But taken together and placed in working-class hands, they posed a new challenge: they showed an awareness of and willingness to dramatise the working-class role in the production of the social life of the nation. The tendency of ulterior measures was to undermine the hostile institutions of State and society by withdrawing working-class energies from them. The Chartists wanted to deprive the State of a significant part of its revenue (by abstaining from taxed articles) and challenge its monopoly over legitimate force: not only did Chartists argue the constitutional and biblical right of free-born Englishmen to bear arms but after the Birmingham Bull Ring episode in which the Metropolitan Police were imported to help break up Chartist meetings, the Chartists in several places formed 'committees of public safety' to defend the people against any further unconstitutional uses of force by the authorities.[6] By means of exclusive dealing the Chartists aimed to withhold working-class consuming power and by a run on the banks to ensure that working-class money, particularly the aggregate savings of trade unions and friendly societies, prohibited by law from carrying on banking themselves, would not finance hostile institutions: reportedly a number of Sheffield societies managed to withdraw some £7000 between them.[7] The Chartists realised that a withdrawal of labour was their most potent weapon, but decided against a month-long general strike when a canvas of the localities suggested that the people were unready to sustain such action and its consequences which would, they felt, include a massive show of government force.

Neither the constitutional campaign nor the ulterior measures delivered a quick Charter. As 12 August, the first day of the National Holiday, drew near and then passed, and as mass arrests began in earnest, relations between Chartists and their opponents were strained to the breaking point. These opponents, who now included almost the whole of the local bourgeoisie and gentry as well as the government, seemed intent upon enclosing the constitution and civil society for the benefit of the rich alone. Instead of suspending ulterior measures as ineffective, the Chartists knuckled down to operate them in the longer term, not only as a tactic of confrontation but also as a means of building an independent social nucleus in and against the existing social order. In the autumn of 1839 Chartist local groups extended the practice of collective self-provision at the same time that many were secretly arming: self-provision was seen as a test of serious political intent. Robert Lowery in Newcastle insisted, 'the man that will not go to the length of the street to spend his money in the shop of a friend or a store the profits of which he may be sure, will never walk ten miles with the musket on his shoulder to fight for freedom'.[8] Exclusive dealing further developed in many places into Chartist co-operative stores, while abstention from excisable articles often became Chartist teetotalism and led to the adoption of a new kind of festivity, the tea-party, soirée and ball. The logic of collective self-help extended in other directions. Religion had been hotly contested territory in 1839: this was no marginal area, for religion stood guard not only over moral legitimacy but also over conceptions of human potential. From May onwards, but particularly after the three-day holiday, many local groups began what O'Connor scornfully called 'an exclusive dealing in religion: a kind of spiritual co-operative store' by absorbing non-sectarian Christian preaching and worship into their weekly routine.[9] Following the direction of this argument into the period after the activity and repression of 1842, the national land plan and the Land and Labour bank do not seem a total departure from what had come before and cannot be written off as O'Connor's personal hobbyhorses. In some ways they were the most extended development of the principle of Chartist self-provision, promising not only escape from the wage contract but also total independence from all the subordinating relationships of capitalist social life.

The strategy of self-provision was to be an integral strand in Chartism for the rest of its life as a mass movement. With the thrust towards taking the whole of social life into their own hands, the Chartists were raising questions of self-government in a very wide-ranging way. Democracy was not only a matter of the formal government of the local association or of the wider movement although the discussion here will be largely confined to these areas. The question of how to organise and manage activities appeared everywhere: in recreation, education, distribution, religion and in settlements on the land. The problems of building a practical democracy for potential members who were poor and could relate to the movement only in an intermittent way were further compounded by the growing range of Chartist activities and the expanding social territory for self-government.

THE PROBLEM OF INCLUSIVENESS

The majority Chartist Movement wanted to recruit numbers unlimited and create an internal democracy. Recent research has shown that numbers unlimited included women.[10] Their specific presence in the movement was shaped both by the fact that Chartism was relevant to their experience and feelings and also that it did not propose a feminist reconstruction of social life, as did some Owenite socialists. In their public addresses Chartist women presented themselves mainly in a multi-faceted family role – as the primary tenders of the family, as contributors to the family wage and as political auxiliaries who demanded the vote for their male kinfolk in a bid to help the family as a whole. 'We have been told', wrote the Female Political Union of Newcastle upon Tyne,

> that the province of woman is her home, and that the field of politics should be left to men; this we deny; the nature of things renders it impossible .... Is it not true that the interests of our fathers, husbands, and brothers ought to be ours? If they are oppressed and impoverished, do we not share those evils with them?[11]

Chartism spoke directly to their family concerns. By absorbing the earlier Ten Hours and Anti-Poor Law campaigns, Chartism continued to resist two deeply felt threats: the power of capitalists to replace male with female and child labour and State power to destroy the family in the new workhouse where wives would be separated from husbands and children from their parents. Chartism also offered ways for women to be active in their family role. Besides the familiar politics of demonstrations and processions, for which women produced the elaborate banners, exclusive dealing placed critical importance on women as the family shoppers while soirées and schools called upon their skills as cooks and teachers. There is evidence that Chartists deliberately tried to accommodate family life as local activity elaborated: from autumn 1839 the tea-party, soirée and ball became the dominant form of festivity, replacing the public-house dinner, and was urged, in the words of Bronterre O'Brien, because it was 'less expensive, interferes less with working hours and above all, because working men may more conveniently take their wives and sisters'.[12]

Women did hold office in the movement but only in segregated women's groupings, on the pattern already established in local female friendly societies.[13] They did not seem to hold office either in the mixed local Chartist associations or on regional and national bodies which would have required travelling away from home: nor did they become paid itinerant lecturers as did some socialist women. None the less activity in the movement did stretch the roles of both women and men in some ways: some women insisted that a commitment to equality meant that they too must eventually have political rights, while some men spoke 'on the duty of the men stopping at home on Tuesday evenings in order to give their wives and sweethearts the privilege of attending the female meeting'.[14] For many Chartist women it would seem that stretching their role was not so much their project as their problem. Already stretched on the rack by capitalist employers and Poor Law guardians, they grasped the chance to reconstitute in the movement, if only for a few hours, what they felt was proper family life.

To recruit men and women unlimited was an immensely difficult task which required making the Chartist Movement as financially and as culturally accessible as possible. The movement never had a chance of becoming totally accessible so long as material deprivation persisted, but how creatively did the Chartists move in the room left for manoeuvre? The 'constitutional' strategy provided ways of relating to the movement which were intermittent and did not involve payment: there was no charge for signing a petition or for taking part in periodic processions and public meetings (although 1*s.* tickets were sold for a perch near the platform). But maintaining the more continuous local associations, which were always an integral part of the movement, cost money, and cost more money as the localities began to provide a wider range of activities. There was both awareness and worry that such expansion, in the words of George White, citing the socialist experience of running halls and the Chartist experience of running co-operatives, 'might lead to the establishment of a sort of aristocracy in our ranks or take the attention of our most active men from the great question of the Charter'.[15] The problem was resolved and re-resolved in a typically Chartist way, not by jettisoning attempts at collective self-provision but by trying to find the most accessible forms for them.

White expressed the dilemma about exclusion and diversion in 1843 when the movement was about to add a land scheme to its constitution. His solution was not to oppose the land plan but to ask for restrictions which would make 'the performance of political duty a qualification for the enjoyment of the Land Fund'. He also urged that the movement provide subsidies to allow poorer members access to the land so that a branch could elect for settlement a person who was 'a good and useful Chartist but could not afford to pay to the Land Fund'. Far from reinforcing social divisions,

> It would create a brotherly feeling throughout the whole society, and enable those whose trades are not yet crushed by the abuse of capital and machinery, to hold out a helping hand to their more unfortunate brethren, besides enabling them to protect those who were persecuted, or driven from their employment through the advocacy of Chartism.

The Chartist co-operative stores, although criticised by White, were often aware of the same dangers. The Sunderland Chartists, having found the socialist co-ops too exclusive and having failed to bring about a change of rules, set up their own store which tried to avoid 'making another middle class of the present and from the better paid portion of the working class at the expense of the poor class'.[16] They halved the socialist price of shares and made it possible to pay up shares through shopping. Chartist charges tended to be lower than those of other movements.

Lower charges were not the whole story. Like other working-class movements, Chartism tended to use organisational forms which were multipurpose, culturally accessible and which provided a packed experience at low cost.[17] The class meeting system, for example, had many uses. Adapting and often democratising Methodist practice, the Chartists recurrently organised themselves into classes, often of ten people, who met together weekly and elected a leader from among themselves to liaise with the next tier of local organisation.[18] Class meetings were very useful in times of repression and became widespread from June 1839: they could be held fairly invisibly in people's houses and yet, by means of the leaders acting as two-way couriers, they could still generate simultaneous action, 'without having public meetings'.[19] Classes were useful for collecting money and were built into the first constitution of the National Charter Association (NCA) in a situation where 'they had so much difficulty in getting money that without the class system . . . they would not get it for any purpose whatever'.[20] The class was a highly participatory and supportive kind of grouping which was already associated in many working people's experience with politics, with education and with the legitimacy of true religion. Radical Methodists had used their classes to study Paine during the French Revolution: mutual improvement societies, used by many adult working people to educate themselves, often resembled classes: earlier movements from the London Corresponding Society in the early 1790s to the National Union of the Working Classes in the early 1830s had used large classes as organisational divisions and as reading groups. Thus it was quite natural for the Sunderland Chartists, for example, to use their class meetings also as reading groups to consider 'works by which human nature may be elevated by the consciousness of its dignity' and hasten the time when 'each man is fit to be his own leader'.[21] The *consciousness* of human dignity was not a peripheral matter to most Chartists. Except from some middle-class sections of the movement, there were constant efforts to inculcate a vision that working people were not subordinate and in need of outside leadership, but that they were the really productive classes, not only capable of producing commodities and services, but also capable collectively of producing their politics and indeed the whole of their social lives. The class meeting system was an effective way of opening up the social roles, like teacher and preacher, which had custody over people's conceptions of their own potential.

Yet in a world of differing and sometimes conflicting cultural styles, the expansion of cultural activity could become another source of division. O'Connor warned that some types of knowledge, teetotal and Church Chartism could alienate people from the movement. Most localities, however, welcomed such activity if it was located within the NCA and not established as a rival base outside. There was an effort to create a kind of cultural pluralism and to make the NCA into a house of many cultural mansions. Chartists not only used friendly society halls, which were often licensed and catered as easily for drinking as for temperance functions, but also tried to lease or to build their own. In 1846 a delegate Convention recommended meeting in halls rather than pubs as a way to transcend 'sectional feelings' and to pull together dispersed local groups. But delegates were aware that, given their scant resources, if they chose to go for halls, other important areas of work would slide. The Sheffield delegate echoed the Marylebone experience of being forced 'either to give up their Hall or cease to supply the Executive'.[22] Thus ironically even the arrangements calculated to make the movement more inclusive could be undermined, at any moment, by poverty.

THE PROBLEM OF INTERNAL DEMOCRACY

The more the Chartist Movement succeeded in being inclusive the more difficult became the task of finding adequate forms of democratic control. Poverty and casuality were like enormous roadblocks standing in the way of self-government for how did you ensure control to people who were unequal in material condition and often very poor, who sometimes had little or irregular time to spare, who had unlimited time if unemployed but no money to subscribe. The usual form of local Chartist association indicated some attempt to grapple with this range of problems. The local association was the organisational bedrock of Chartism, often predating and outlasting attempts to build regional federations or national structures, always resurfacing as soon as a period of repression lifted although sometimes in camouflaged form. The practice of these local associations needs highlighting not least because it has been obscured by historians concentrating too narrowly on occasional platform meetings and on charismatic leaders. Most of these associations did not govern themselves like early trade unions and friendly societies, which held frequent general meetings of the members to transact all the business and, when delegation was necessary, rotated offices around the membership, punishing the defaulters with a stiff fine.[23] Rather the Chartists, like the socialists, democratised and developed other features of the age-old parish system of local government with its quarterly general meeting of the vestry.

No matter how many weekly meetings the Chartists held, they tended to make a quarterly general meeting the governing body of the local association, giving it the final authority to lay down policy and elect not only officers but also an executive committee to carry out the day to day business.[24] Calling the whole membership together every three months, rather than more frequently for government by general meeting alone, was more appropriate for working people who could not make a very regular commitment of time to the movement. Also dispensing with rotation of offices was probably an adjustment to the inequality of situation among Chartists themselves. Office-holding in a political movement could be an impossible burden for those whose employment was precarious, either because they were very subordinate to employers (there were continual stories of people being harassed simply for bringing the *Northern Star* to work) or because they needed nearly every available hour to overwork for a subsistence. It was often people with a certain measure of independence, publicans or shopkeepers or skilled artisans with some power in their jobs, who could more easily undertake local office. However, this point must not be exaggerated: it was a mark both of Chartism's accessibility and of the commitment of individual Chartists, that people whose depressed work situations made it difficult for them to serve (like labourers in Northampton, weavers in Barnsley, stockingers in Leicester and wool-combers near Bradford) still took on office as local councillors in the National Charter Association.[25]

Since authority was to be delegated to officers and a committee, and not everybody was to hold office, keeping the officers under the control of the ordinary members was a main preoccupation in Chartism and other working-class movements. Short terms of office and frequent elections were a main way of ensuring accountability. If the Charter demand was for annual Parliaments, within the movement the tenure of local office before the period of the NCA was usually shorter and often quarterly. In 1839 the Brighton Radical Reform and Patriotic Association, for example, had a Managing Committee of ten to twelve which included a secretary and treasurer. These two officers came up for election each quarter (or re-election is probably the better word as Messrs Morling and Flowers held the posts on this basis for years); likewise three committee places came up for election every three months.[26] The chairman was elected at each public meeting, a common practice which opened at least one office to members who could not serve in a more continuous way.

So important was the practice of frequent local elections that it persisted even after the formation of the NCA in 1840, whose rules stipulated an annual process whereby local officers would be nominated locally but appointed by the National Executive to evade the prohibition of the Seditious Meetings Act against self-governing branches. None the less some groups like the Bradford Charter Association, Wapping district, constituted itself part of the NCA but also enshrined local practice by adopting 'numerous bye-laws for the government of the association' and then electing officers for the new quarter. Even after the NCA rules were changes in 1841 to take on board the objection that it was not only autonomous branches which were illegal but also any branches at all, the practice of quarterly elections still continued in some localities (and probably in more than would dare publicise the fact). Leeds reported that 'a new council was elected for the ensuing three months' and Carlisle Chartists forced their reluctant local Council to submit to quarterly elections.[27]

With the reorganisation of 1840 a more critical problem of accountability arose about paid personnel on regional and national level. It was widely agreed that the movement would need to pay wages if working men were to be able to serve: Feargus O'Connor made the point with respect to the National Executive (General Secretary, Treasurer, plus five in a General Executive Committee):

> If you have an unpaid Executive, you must have a purely middle class Executive, because you cannot get working men to live without wages and the very moment you elected working men as your officers, that moment every door is closed against them, and at once they are marked, and if in work are dismissed.[28]

But equally there was a fear that paid officers, once removed from a common work and living situation, might lose touch with their constituents and become 'irresponsible'. So the task became to find ways of controlling salaried officials from below.

From their experience of the 1839 General Convention, many Chartists took the lesson that it was less important to have a para-parliament than to channel scarce resources into organising the localities. One of the most influential voices in the discussion about national organisation in 1840, Robert Lowery, insisted that:

> a Convention sitting in London or any town is worse than useless.

What we want is men deputed to agitate and combine our party together. If a district can pay a man to sit in a Convention, it can pay him to agitate, and he will do the cause ten times as much good; and unless he is fit for an agitator; he is of no use. We are not in the position of a party having legal power, merely requiring heads to plan; we require hands to execute.[29]

The NCA put great emphasis on such organisers. Significantly it was the district delegate meetings (called County or Riding Councils in 1840 but then District Councils) which were given the power to hire, pay and control their own missionaries (called district lecturers from 1843): the National Executive could use the general fund for missionary work only to open up new areas. Some of the district bodies, including the dynamic south Lancashire and West Riding of Yorkshire delegate meetings, had come into Chartism from earlier movements like the Ten Hours and Anti-Poor Law campaigns, and had already built up much local experience and credibility. The district delegate body seemed to satisfy the demand for local control and was also the only local grouping capable of raising enough money to finance missionary work. The desire for local control had been partly responsible for blocking the 1839 Convention's half-hearted attempts at missionary work. The Convention delegates had been paid directly by their constituents who resisted paying for activity which did not directly benefit them: Peter Bussey was generously financed by his West Riding constituency, but they flatly refused to pay for a missionary trip to Scotland, although they reconsidered when he threatened to resign.[30] In the NCA missionaries were hired for a short term only, which enabled the districts to keep them in close check and to dispense with them when funds were short. The North and East Riding of Yorkshire District replaced their lecturers each month like clockwork, including some of the most brilliant figures in the movement like Jonathan Bairstow and John West: but in March 1842 the double burden of debts and the deepening depression forced the decision to give up the paid lecturer for a time.[31]

Despite all the arrangements to ensure local control, there was still the fear that paid missionaries might enclose and professionalise an important area of political work, making it the province only of a paid élite. To offset this possibility, debating societies and lecturing classes were formed which aimed, at a delegate meeting as Thornton put it, 'to place Chartism on a proper basis by making every man his own lecturer, and thus prevent it from being a mere system of lectureship'.[32]

Some large areas like south Lancashire and London (for at least four years) even managed a significant part of the missionary work without paid lecturers by organising themselves on the Methodist model and publishing monthly lecturer's plans (equivalent to circuit preaching plans, telling who would speak where and when). In a further parallel development south Lancashire started monthly lecturers' meetings, equivalent to preachers' meetings, where they hammered out the agreed line and necessary facts that lecturers should have at their disposal.

The problems about accountability and finance appeared most sharply in relation to the National Executive. The first two versions of the NCA rules laid down that the Executive was to be directly elected each year by all of the members of the association, from a list of nominees submitted by the County or Riding Secretaries. The Executive were to pay their own salaries when in session (£2 a week for the General Secretary, £1 10s. for the Treasurer and five other Committee members) and to finance their organisational work from a general fund, at first one-half of the subscriptions collected locally, then in a recognition of financial reality from 1841 onwards, one-quarter of the subscriptions. The Executive were also entitled to compensation 'by being employed as missionaries during any recess that may happen while they continue in their official capacity, or in such other way as may be most convenient for the Association, the question of compensation to be determined by the County or Riding Councils'.[33] By the end of 1842, however, the worst kinds of fears about paying office-holders seemed to have come true: a situation which had been smouldering privately for some time finally burst into print with accusations from London and Leicester activists and from the editor of the *Northern Star*, Revd Hill, that the Executive was guilty of inefficiency bordering upon fraud. The charges were specifically that the balance sheets were sloppy and uninformative, that expenses were suspiciously inflated and that the Executive was paying itself salaries outside the period of its sitting and even paying an ordinary member, Dr McDouall, an extra ten shillings 'fully one third more than he was entitled to'.

Whether the charges were fair or unfair, the episode was traumatic. So much so that when the next delegate convention met in September 1843 it created a new body to keep control of the Executive, despite real concern that the added expense might prove too great a burden.[34] It decided unanimously to establish a short Annual Delegate Convention to act as a legislature to the Executive which could 'only be of use to execute the commands and measures of the legislative body'. After a more divided discussion, it was decided to give the Convention the power to elect the Executive (from nominations made by the localities): although some delegates were reluctant to take this power away from the membership at large, W. P. Roberts retorted, 'it was very well to talk about responsibility, and making the Executive responsible to the whole people – he knew that responsibility so minutely divided amounted to something like no responsibility at all'. To ensure responsibility, Chartists clung even more tenaciously to the idea of accountable delegacy, making widespread use of mandating and insisting on a report-back of conduct from delegates. So for example Hobson, now the editor of the *Northern Star*, wanted to vote in favour of the Convention electing the Executive 'but he was tied down by his [Leeds] constituents to vote against it, he must therefore do so': one of the West Riding delegates, Dewhurst, intimated that his constituents would not obey a decision against direct elections but promised that when he reported back 'he would do his utmost to carry out the views of the majority (of the Convention) . . . he would not be a good Chartist unless he did'.

While the Convention machinery seemed well-calculated for its task, the Executive never worked properly because it was permanently starved of funds. Constituencies tended to look to their own needs first and the Executive continually complained that 'the irregularity of many localities in transmitting their quota of the Executive fund has tended materially to cripple our exertions'.[35] Even when the movement was expanding most vigorously at the end of 1841, when over 282 local groups were enrolled in the NCA, all kinds of special devices like levies and soirées had to be used to collect for the Executive. Other suggestions for funding were made but, however financially sound, in terms of democratic control they appeared more tenuous. One was that the Executive be paid out of the profits of some Chartist enterprise, particularly a newspaper. O'Connor several times suggested using the *Northern Star* in this way and a key feature of his 1840 proposal for a form of national organisation was a squad of twenty elected delegate/lecturers financed from the profits of a new national daily paper to be called the 'Morning Star'.[36] His proposal was politely ignored, probably because of the fear that under the scheme officers would become responsible to a newspaper and to him rather than to a duly constituted body of the People (although O'Connor had suggested a district Committee of Review to adjudicate complaints).

O'Connor was a problem this way but not such a demagogic 'blight of democracy' as Lovett and most subsequent historians have imagined.

Certainly O'Connor had immense personal magnetism (which he clearly enjoyed), electric oratory, indefatigable energy and, not least, an independent income. Recent research is showing not only that his role as gentleman leader and platform orator was an established part of the 'constitutional' strategy, but also that he used his charisma and the platform (including his national platform in the *Northern Star*) in a new way to help build an inclusive, national, working-class movement with democratic structures.[37] Thus he was a great defender of the 1839 Convention and kept calling for another to assemble: he was also fierce in his condemnation of splinter tendencies in the NCA or rival new moves from outside. But his behaviour was still contradictory. Even while he was warmly supporting accountable structures, he was often living beyond effective control and sometimes even undercutting what he was trying to build. He tended to see the people at large as his constituency and tribunal rather than feel accountable to a particular group of electors or body of delegates. Even though he was a delegate in 1839, he sometimes used the *Northern Star* rather than the Convention to launch critical initiatives, like his proposal to commute the month of general strike into a three-day holiday. He did not run for office in the NCA until 1843, claiming that he did not want to be accused of 'dictation'. However, after the crisis over the Executive, he stood under the new Rules 'to do something towards establishing confidence and union', using his stature to reinforce democratic structures. The trouble was that, by then, he had already fired Revd Hill from the *Northern Star* over their differences in the Executive dispute and had also alienated some other activists who were both democrats and firm supporters of the NCA.

Poverty was a more powerful corrosive eating away at all the democratic structures of the movement. The accountable district lecturers who were to stimulate local activity often could not be afforded and, in some years, the Executive, which was to co-ordinate the national movement, could not be properly paid. To try to make ends meet, the Executive even took money from the enterprising makers of Pinder's bootblack, the Chartist Beverage and the Chartist Pills, who all gave a small part of their profits and advertised in the *Northern Star* to this effect to drum up Chartist trade. For some years, the financial problem was 'solved' most unsatisfactorily by having identical Executive Committees in the National Charter Association and the Chartist Co-operative Land Company, latterly the National Land Company. The Land Company sat on large amounts of money and could pay but some

NCA Chartists did not feel that they were getting the best service through this arrangement.[38] Even the Annual Delegate Convention, introduced to guide and check the Executive, was never at full strength: localities could send messages of solidarity but could not always afford to send a delegate.

THE PROBLEM OF NATIONAL ORGANISATION AND THE LAW

As if the internal problems of democracy coupled with poverty were not enough, there were also heavy legal constraints on a movement which became a large public presence. It is true that the government did not take extraordinary powers, like suspending Habeas Corpus, during the Chartist period, as had been the pattern between 1795 and 1820:[39] the State dealt with the Chartists quite satisfactorily by means of executive order, statute law and judicial due process. When the law was considered too weak, it was simply changed; so in 1848 the 'Gagging Act' was passed which made seditious utterance not just a crime carrying a penalty of two years' imprisonment but a transportable offence. Even without this change the law was treacherous enough. The heart of the Corresponding Societies Act of 1799 (39 Geo. III, c.79) had been transplanted into the Seditious Meetings Act of 1817 (57 Geo. III, c.19), making it virtually impossible for the Chartists to embody their democratic ambitions in organisational form and still remain within the law.

The Chartists were acutely sensitive to the discrepancy between constitutionality and legality (when the law was made by corrupt factions) but none the less they wanted not only to be impeccably constitutional (in their extended definition of constitutional) but also if possible to remain legal as well. In part this was an attempt to muster all moral authority on their side. Revd William Hill, in a *Northern Star* editorial, argued that

the next best thing to being right yourself is to put your enemy completely in the wrong. . . . We have ever been most anxious that the operations of the people should be conducted peacefully and legally: knowing that if their moral strength was well marshalled, and their numbers well organised, they were invincible and irresistable: - able to carry any measure of a wholesome and sanatory tendency, without violating any of those forms and appearances of law with which the harpies have fenced around the carcase of corruption, in the hope of feasting undisturbedly thereon.[40]

Also, more simply, legal circumspection was a way to prevent arrests. This was an urgent consideration after the arrest of nearly 500 Chartists between January 1839 and June 1840, resulting in over 250 prison sentences and 6 death sentences which were commuted at the last moment to life transportation. The Chartists were nervous about unnecessarily risking this kind of sacrifice again. The prison ordeal resulted for many in permanently broken health and for a few, like Clayton and Holberry, in death. Although gladly undertaken, the support of the prisoners and their families, who often had only what the movement could give between them and the workhouse, was also a burden, consuming scarce money and energy and thereby restricting other activity. Every delegate convention from July 1840 onward spent a large part of its time discussing the prisoners' situation. Even if the relief effort kept the movement going through the doldrums and even if the release of prisoners occasioned a resurgence of local energy, it was thought better, if possible, to avoid having victims. Not only legality but also legal recognition and protection became an urgent issue particularly in the land plan phase when the movement found itself sitting on large amounts of money paid in as share capital.

But the law heavily circumscribed the form a national movement could take. The Seditious Meetings Act, section XXV, stipulated that

every Society or Club that shall elect, appoint, nominate or employ any Committee, Delegate or Delegates, Representative or Representatives, Missionary or Missionaries, to meet, confer or communicate with any other Society or Club, or with any Committee, Delegate or Delegates, Representative or Representatives, Missionary or Missionaries, of such other Society or Club, or to induce or persuade any Person or Persons to become Members thereof, shall be deemed and taken to be unlawful Combinations and Confederacies.

Section XXVII then added that

every Society that shall be composed of different Divisions or Branches, or of different Parts acting in any manner separately or distinct from each other, or of which any Part shall have any separate or distinct President, Secretary, Treasurer, Delegate or other Officer elected or appointed by or for such Part, or to act as an Officer for such Part, shall be deemed and taken to be unlawful Combinations and Confederacies.

It was also made illegal for societies, their members or officers to correspond with each other or for individuals to correspond with societies or their officers. Radical movements felt they had successfully overcome this last provision by establishing their own newspapers, like the *Northern Star*, which made it possible to have communication without entering technically into correspondence.[41] Other sections of the Act were less easy to get around. The law was essentially saying that local self-governing groups could exist separately but were not allowed to federate in any way and that a national movement could exist legally but only without separate branches or divisions. What was illegal was just what the Chartists wanted – a national movement which still allowed for a large measure of local autonomy and control. The penalty for contravening the act was seven years' transportation. The only groups exempted from the legislation were the Freemasons, other societies which had the approval of two or more magistrates and confirmation from quarter sessions, religious and charitable societies, and after 1846 friendly societies approved and registered by the State.

A centralised organisation was the only legal form a national movement could take during the long period which embraced the dominance of landed capital and then the steady political ascendance of industrial and finance capital from 1832 onwards. It is worth noting that while working-class movements tried to find a way through the thorny legal maze, the middle-class movements which were most analogous in the period did not even try. The predominantly working-class socialists registered as a Protestant society of 'Rational Religionists' (thus getting exemption from the Seditious Meetings Act) and also as a friendly society to protect their community funds.[42] The affiliated orders of friendly societies, like the Odd Fellows and Foresters, after years of being refused registration by Tidd Pratt on the grounds that they were national movements with branches, helped bring about about a change in the Seditious Meeting Act from which, ironically, they did not even benefit. Until the 1850 Friendly Societies Act, they still could not register as affiliated orders but only lodge by lodge and the cost was prohibitive: while they were unregistered, even after 1846, they were still liable to be deemed unlawful combinations!

By contrast, the middle-class controlled Birmingham Political

Union, which was obsessed with legality in its 1829–32 campaign for extending the franchise, simply opted for a highly authoritarian local organisation: all effective power was in the hands of a political council, composed of members who could pay their own expenses and were thus safely middle-class: the closest thing to divisions were the unofficial, largely working-class 'sections' which met in various public houses in the town. Until the Chartist period there was no real federation with groups elsewhere: the Union simply bought a large amount of space in the London and provincial press and issued resolutions and directives as though they were already in command.[43] The Anti-Corn Law League, the national movement *par excellence* of the industrial and urban middle classes, which pressurised Parliament during some of the years of the Chartist campaign, was more cavalier about local control. The League was governed by a non-elected council open to all who had donated £50 or more, and effectively run by such members who lived near Manchester. The lecturers who spread the gospel of free trade to other localities were paid by and directly controlled by this centre: occasional delegate meetings were called but more as a show of strength than as decision-making bodies. The evidence seems to point towards the hypothesis that only working-class movements were committed enough to 'vigilant popular control' to brave the hurdles of the law.

The persistent search for an adequate form of national organisation which was both democratic and legal underlay the continual twists and turns, chops and changes in Chartist organisation. Even in the earliest period, legality was a preoccupation, not least because it was the Birmingham Political Union which took the initiative in launching the Convention and Petition strategy. A Convention was widely recognised to be legal (even by the Home Secretary) to the extent that it was a petitioning body: the election of delegates was also supposed to be legal if carried out at public, county hustings (rather than at private meetings of local Chartist associations).[44] Obviously the Convention strategy was attractive to other areas of the movement because it also carried other layers of meaning and potential. The Chartists argued that they were the true constitutionalists and often created parallel but democratised versions of existing political bodies both to dramatise this claim and expose the nature of the official institutions: the House of Commons 'was the mock, the self-elected, the Whig and Tory Parliament', while the Convention was 'the real, the universal-suffrage, the People's Parliament'.[45] Beyond this, a National Convention, which had existed in radical thought from the period of the French Revolution at least, was often seen as the body which would sit during a period of national crisis, particularly during a general strike, and restructure the whole of the State. After the middle-class delegates had nearly all resigned, and once the Commons had rejected the Petition and ulterior measures had come into operation, the idea of the Convention as the legitimate ruling body of the State and preview of the really reformed Parliament came unambiguously to the fore: William Barnett of Macclesfield declared, as the national holiday drew near, 'that I owe the British Government no allegiance but what I am obliged to give it. I declare, that I will obey the Convention; nor death nor hell shall prevent me from being obedient to them. They are my Government. I had a hand in chusing them.'[46]

Historians have tended to scold the Convention for being a pusillanimous general, unable to lead at critical points, always looking back to the constituencies and asking for orders.[47] Interestingly, at the point where Chartists were again trying to build an adequate national movement in the spring of 1840, they criticised the Convention less for being a weak central body than for inhibiting local agitation and organisation. 'A Convention' again to use the words of Lowery, 'sitting in London or any town is worse than useless. What we need is men deputed to agitate and combine our party together.' Nearly all the rival schemes of national organisation submitted to the *Northern Star* at this time rejected a Convention sitting continuously as a para-parliament. It was not until 1843, that a *short* Annual Delegate Convention was installed as a fixed part of the NCA constitution to put a check on the Executive. In the interim, short Conventions were held for specific purposes, for example, to revise the NCA rules or to supervise petitions both for the prisoners and for the Charter.[48]

The rules of the National Charter Association were hammered out and formally adopted by a national delegate conference in Manchester on 20 July 1840.[49] Both in the way that it came into being and its constitution, the NCA bore a closer family resemblance to the practice of other working-class movements (whether schismatic Methodism, trade unionism, socialism or the friendly societies) than to the earlier Convention. The subcommittee charged with drafting the constitution was instructed to use the best parts of each proposal and incorporate the best from existing practice. The result was a complex array of interlocking tiers of organisation which allowed a great deal of scope for active participation and control by local members. At the grass roots, there were to be Methodist-type classes of ten – this an incorporation of existing practice in many areas, particularly Scotland which had been reorganised along these lines in August 1839 and the Newcastle Northern Political Union which adopted this structure in April 1840.[50] Each class was to choose a leader who was to bring subscriptions and report progress to the monthly general ward meeting (the wards to be the divisions created by the 1835 Municipal Corporations Act). The local executive body was to be a Town Council of nine which was to meet weekly. Here then, as William Farish the Carlisle handloom weaver wrote in 1880, 'was the scheme, properly laid down and well worked out, which is at present called the "caucus", and for the honour of the inception of which, after fifty years, big men have lately been contending'.[51] Indeed the Leeds Chartists put the new structure to work and achieved some stunning victories in vestry and borough council elections. The next tier of organisation actually anticipated governmental structures: there was the County or Riding Council, whose composition and frequency of meetings was left vague, but which amounted to a formalisation of already-existing district delegate meetings. Finally the general government of the NCA was to be vested in a General Executive Committee which was annually elected by a ballot of the whole membership and was to be paid while sitting and receive missionary work when in recess.

What was supposed to rescue this structure from illegality, although it apparently teemed with divisions, was that all local officers, from class leaders to County Councillors were to be locally nominated (not elected) and then formally appointed by the National Executive. Not surprisingly this structure still did not satisfy some influential Chartists like William Lovett, who was just out of gaol, but not yet discredited by his attempt to found a rival New Move. After so many Chartists had gone to prison questions of legality, once raised, could not be ignored. In February 1841 another national delegate conference met, and with NCA rules and the statutes governing association side by side, tried to hammer out a more unexceptionable constitution.[52] The most significant change was to eliminate all mention of local subdivisions, absorb all councils into a General Council and make all officers into officers of the General Council. The new camouflage behind which to hide local self-government was that once a year each locality was to submit a slate of nominees for the General Council (really the people it wanted for local officers) and then every member of the NCA would vote for every nominee, an exercise which amounted to endorsing the local slates. Only the General Executive Committee was chosen by competitive national election. The more the rules were brought into conformity with the law the less satisfactory they became: the 1841 plan was seen as distinctly inferior to the 1840 plan and Chartists were urged to 'make up, by their practical and individual exertion, for every discrepancy in active operation, which might otherwise have existed between the two plans': they were also sharply warned against talking carelessly about what they were doing.[53]

The year 1842 was a critical one. The NCA kept growing while the economic situation became bleaker all over the country. Another, more massive Petition for the Charter was produced and then failed in May. In August a general strike actually did take place, affecting fifteen counties in England and Wales and eight in Scotland, with activity most intense in south Lancashire, the midlands Potteries (chapters five and six above) and in West Yorkshire: local Chartists were prominently involved and the strike had clear political overtones. Not only strike action but also, in the Potteries, clashes with troops and large-scale rioting provoked the heaviest repression of the whole of the Chartist period: transportations alone numbered some two hundred. And if external pressures were not enough, towards the end of the year came the accusations that the Executive was mishandling Chartist funds. The movement nearly buckled under these multiple blows.

In a salvage attempt in December, Thomas Cooper of Leicester (one of the recent victims) proposed a constitution which would curb the Executive: but by the time the next delegate convention actually met in early September 1843, a very different plan had emerged.[54] A National Charter Association for Mutual Benefit was now proposed which aimed to kill several birds with one stone. By enrolling under the Friendly Society Acts, the movement aimed to end the doubts about legality for good and at the same time to put itself in a position to be able to prosecute officers for fraud and thus inspire more confidence (without state licensing, associations had no existence in the eyes of the courts). More than this, the worst economic depression of the century coupled with the bitterness of class struggle gave tremendous impetus to strategies for collective working-class self-provision. If exclusive dealing had developed after the failure of the 1839 Petition, and had continued to grow during the 1842 period of 'political excitement', the 1842 disasters resulted in a further extension of the principle into the areas of employment and subsistence: the second object of the NCA for Mutual Benefit was 'to provide for the unemployed, and means of support for those who are desirous to locate upon the land'. The Chartists were not alone in pursuing this path; besides the socialists, there was also a trade union push in the same period towards self-employment and using the land for this purpose.[55]

Modelling their organisation closely on that of the socialists, which had been registered in 1839, the Chartists were buoyant about being able openly to have classes, local branches (explicitly called 'branches' and governed by a board of seven, three of whom would come up for election each quarter), District Councils (composed of branch delegates and elected quarterly) an Annual Convention and a General Executive. In the best spirits, the Chartists went off to enrol with Tidd Pratt the Registrar. Early in October Pratt refused to certify and, shortly after, was induced to give his reasons in writing. He began by insisting that the 'object and means' of the NCA were 'not within the provisions' of the Friendly Society Acts and then called attention to 39 Geo. III, c. 79 and 57 Geo. III, c. 19 which provided 'that every society except of a religious or *charitable* NATURE only which shall be composed of different divisions or branches ... shall be deemed and taken for an unlawful combination and confederacy'.[56] Here was the classic double-bind situation indeed. The Chartists tried to escape the clutches of the Seditious Meetings Act by enrolling as a friendly society, but were prevented from enrolling on the grounds that they fell foul of the Seditious Meetings Act! The ensuing eight years were marked by a relentless tussle with the law, its makers and administrators, which revealed the impossible situation in which working-class associations found themselves. The more successful they were in their own terms at being large-scale, vigorous, democratic movements, the more they were at odds with the existing law and the more debarred from its protection.

After Pratt's opinion was confirmed by their own legal adviser, the Chartists marked time by operating only the 'legal' parts of the plan until the next scheduled Delegate Convention in April 1844 when it was decided to separate the political movement from the land scheme (which was left in limbo).[57] The NCA once more absorbed the local and district councils into a huge General Council, but kept the short Annual Delegate Convention and an Executive reduced in number to five who would appoint the General Council from local nominees. Formal separation was to be the pattern, with the NCA holding separate Conventions from the land plan after April 1845: none the less the same people served on both Executives and the situation was more fudged in the localities.[58]

So attractive was the land scheme proving, that the Convention of April 1845 declared for a Chartist Land Co-operative Society, whose rules were first formulated by a working party and then revised and approved at a Convention in December 1845, where discussion was conducted on a very high level.[59] However, it was clear that the law was enforcing unwanted deformations. There was no longer a formal way to make membership in the land scheme contingent on political commitment (as White had urged and as the 1843 plan allowed by making the Land Fund only a part of and only open to members of the NCA). There was also no longer a way to locate poor comrades on the land if they were not paid-up shareholders. None the less the delegates still tried to tackle the issue of how to make shareholding accessible and the related questions of how to prevent the relatively more affluent members from having too much weight and reaping too many of the rewards of the plan. Two very working-class devices were again used. Shares were made fairly cheap (£2 10s. and later £1 6s.) and payable in small weekly instalments (minimum 3d.) and a 'ballot' was used to select who would get the homesteads: the names of all paid-up shareholders in a section were placed into a hat, when an estate became available, and the names drawn would get farms, thus distributing the chances of success more broadly than a 'first pay first served' scheme (called the priority system). The first working-class organisation to make this daring move, the Chartists also set up a Land and Labour Bank. The idea was to attract deposits from the working-class public and use a proportion of this money to mortgage the Chartist estates so as to give the Land Society more cash in hand with which to purchase more land more quickly: the land itself would be the security for the banking operation.

More than ever (as moved by Joshua Hobson, editor of the *Northern Star*, and seconded by O'Connor), it was 'highly essential . . . that the rules should be enrolled under the Benefit and Building Societies' Acts inasmuch as such course will alone give security to the members and limit the responsibility of all concerned to the extent of the society's operations.' The Directors were instructed to seek enrolment and, if the name proved a barrier, it was agreed by a majority of one, to let the Directors change the name to the National Co-operative Land Society.

So early in January 1846 the Chartists went again about registering. Once more Tidd Pratt refused to certify, again saying that some of the rules were illegal under the Corresponding Societies and Seditious Meetings Acts and also that choice of homesteaders by ballot contravened the Lottery Acts. Further discussions disclosed that Pratt was interpreting the Friendly Societies Acts in an even more narrow way than before because of Justice Wightman's opinion in a recent appeal case that the clause enabling societies to be formed 'for any other purpose which is not illegal' had to be read *ejusdem generis* that is, for any other purpose of the same kind as those already enumerated by the act.[60] The Chartists now joined with other groups to push for an amendment to broaden the scope of the acts: T. S. Duncombe, MP, proposed that the contested words be changed to 'for any legal purpose whatsoever'. A new Act, 9 and 10 Vict., c. 27 was passed in 1846 but had the diametrically opposite effect to what had been intended by the working-class lobby. As before, purposes for which a society could be enrolled under the Act were enumerated as, firstly, life insurance and burial expenses, secondly, relief of members and families in sickness etc. and any other natural state whose probability 'may be calculated by average', thirdly, insuring for loss of property, fourthly, 'the frugal investment of the savings of members for better enabling them to purchase food, firing, clothes or other necessaries, or the tools or implements of their trade or calling, or to provide for the education of their children etc.' Then the sting in the tail,

> Fifthly, for any other purpose which shall be certified to be legal in England or Ireland by Her Majesty's Attorney or Solicitor-general . . . and which shall be allowed by one of Her Majesty's principal Secretaries of State, as a purpose to which the power and facilities of the said Acts ought to be extended.

Not only was it the Attorney-General's office which was to decide upon legality, but also the legal adviser on these matters, barrister Edward Lawes, made the narrowest possible construction of the law: 'I think that the provision in that Act with respect to societies established "for any other purpose, which shall be certified to be legal", etc. applies only to societies established for some purpose *ejusdem generis* with those specifically enumerated.' The Attorney-General refused to supply a certificate of legality to the Chartists in July 1846: Lawes' main objections were that the ballot was illegal under the Lottery Acts and that the bank was a trading speculation outside the terms of legitimate Friendly Society activity.[61]

What was clearly emerging was that the door to legal protection under the Friendly Society Acts was still being firmly shut against national movements with branches which were too numerous (and therefore could not afford to pay the fees for enrolling each lodge individually), against any self-employing society which wanted to sell its products outside its own membership (co-ops trading with their members could slip in through the frugal investment clause, but a group of London builders who wanted to erect houses and then sell them on the open market was excluded), against any society which distributed things among its members by continuous raffle, ballot or lottery (as already-mentioned a popular way of attracting working-class involvement) and against any activity which smacked of banking because the Friendly Society Acts laid down that money could only be invested in Government securities, in mortgages on land (not in purchase of land) and in licensed savings banks, thus insuring that working-class money could only be used to finance the State or more conventional capitalist enterprise!

With members and funds increasing and with pressure mounting from the localities to enrol promptly if the land scheme was to maintain grass-roots confidence, the Directors redrew the rules and got provisional registration under the Joint Stock Companies Act in October 1846.[62] Unfortunately this was tantamount to jumping from the frying pan into the fire. However carefully drawn to prevent any more spectacular capitalist frauds like the South Sea Bubble, the Act was completely inappropriate to a company based on *mass* shareholding among poor people. There was no equality before this epitome of enabling capitalist law. Registration under the act involved a stamp tax which had to be paid on every fifteen folios of signatures attached to the deed. Most companies might need only a handful of signatories for complete registration, which required, in the first instance, the signatures of at least one-quarter of the shareholders owning one-quarter of the maximum value of the share issue with the rest of the shareholders signing later in due course. In August 1847, when the Chartists got approval for the wording of their draft deed they had 43,847 shareholders, which meant that 7566 people representing a holding of £33,000 of the total £130,000 had to sign the deed before complete registration could be secured: all members would have to sign in due course afterwards. Not only that, but the Act contemplated no open-ended issue of shares, as did the Chartists, and in August 1847 the Land Company announced that it would take no more members after 1 January 1848 in order to comply with the Act: in the period of grace between August and January 'as many members joined . . . as had joined in the two previous years'. G. W. Chinery, the solicitor handling the registration for the Chartists, estimated that the stamp tax alone would come to £3 15s. for every

100 names and beyond that there were the legal expenses involved for example, in seeking out and attesting signatures all over the country (and in France and Belgium). In stamps alone the first stage of complete registration would cost over £800 and, by February 1848, the legal expenses had already come to more than £2400. Moreover penalties had been piling up for non-compliance with the requirements of the Act. For example, particulars about the proposed capital of the company and the number and amount of shares was supposed to be returned 'within one month after such particulars had been ascertained and determined' – easy enough with a small number of shareholders. But Chinery had spent six or seven weeks travelling around England and then several weeks in Manchester and in London between September 1847 and February 1848 to get the fraction of signatures now on the deed: and he now needed two more months for alphabetising the names, a requirement the assistant registrar was approached about several times, but refused to waive. Asked how much more money would be needed to effect total permanent registration of the company exclusive of stamps, Chinery said 'I mentioned that sum of £3000, but I said I was afraid to name the sum; I think it would be much more than that.' Asked the question 'that would be ultimately a very large proportion of the capital of the company?' he replied 'It would . . . . to a company of capitalists it would be a mere bagatelle, but to us it is a ruinous sum.' As Captain Pechell concluded 'It is your success which has created the difficulty? – It is.'[63]

Blocked by the financial penalties being levied on their success, the Chartists suspended their attempts to register under the Companies Act and returned to trying to amend the Friendly Societies Act. In February 1848 O'Connor proposed an amendment to extend it to cover societies formed

> for the purpose of purchasing land in the United Kingdom of Great Britain and Ireland, and of erecting on such land dwellings to be allotted to members of the society, together with certain portions of such land for agricultural purposes, and of raising a fund for the advancement of money to or for the benefit of such allottees on taking possession of their allotments and of creating a fund for the objects aforesaid etc.

It was at this point that the House of Commons set up a Select Committee to inquire into the National Land Company. The legal boffins who gave evidence were inflexible: Francis Whitmarsh, Registrar for Joint Stock Companies, could not appreciate that the Land Company with its unprecedented number of shareholders had special problems, while Lawes and Pratt were unwilling to stretch their minds to admit that this new-fangled working-class creation ðould ever be considered legal unless specifically indemnified by a private Act of Parliament. The proposed amendment to the Friendly Society Acts would not, they insisted, cover the National Land Company because the choice of homesteaders by lottery, even if relegated to by-laws was still illegal while the banking operation was illegal under both the Acts relating to friendly societies and to banks. The Joint Stock Bank Act allowed more than six persons to engage in banking with letters patent which could be granted only if the capital was not less than £100,000 divided into shares of not less than £100 each – not exactly a recipe for working-class banking![64] Even though O'Connor argued that the bank was technically in his name alone, several witnesses insisted that the bank was an integral part of the Land Company.

The final Report of the Committee followed the line taken by the civil servants and thereby blocked all realistic exits for the Chartists. Dated 1 August 1848, it confirmed that O'Connor's amendment would not cover the National Land Company which 'as at present constituted, is an illegal scheme, and will not fulfil the expectations held out by the Directors to the Shareholders'. However it left 'open to the parties concerned to propose to parliament any new measure':[65] but a private act which had no certain chance of success was an impossibly expensive proposition. In a last search for a way out, O'Connor turned to the Court of Queen's Bench and obtained in 1849 a writ of mandamus ordering Pratt to register the Company, which he refused to do. When a year later the case came up for argument, the verdict went against the Chartists. At this point the Directors finally gave up and petitioned the Commons for a bill to dissolve the Company: it became law in August 1851.

The Chartist search, over ten long years, for an adequate and legal form of national organisation reveals what a potent shaping and ultimately deforming influence the State was, whether it was showing an iron fist, as custodian of public order suppressing Chartist militancy, or wearing a velvet glove, as framer of legislation giving legitimacy and protection to selected forms of working-class association. The land scheme collapsed, exhausted by its attempts to clear the hurdles of the law and debilitated by internal difficulties. This casualty coming so soon after the rejection of the third National Petition, which dealt a body blow to the whole 'constitutional' strategy, it could be argued that a political era had come to an end. Historians talk of a watershed even within Chartism, pointing both to the decline in mass politics and the appearance of a more overtly social or socialist programme. But given the developing strategy of exclusive dealing within Chartism, it is difficult to drive a wedge cleanly between the social and the political. The famous Convention of 1851 passed resolutions on a range of issues which were already comprehended in collective self-provision (although some of the actual positions, like nationalisation of the land, were new national policy), while new demands for 'the right of Co-operative Societies to registration and enrolment' and a State Credit Fund for 'advancing money to bodies of working men desirous of associating together for industrial purposes'[66] grew quite naturally out of the Chartist registration saga and the complementary thrust towards workers' self-employment during the 1840s. Indeed it could be argued that Chartism, more dramatically than any other movement, took the risks and made the case for the more enabling labour legislation that was won in the mid-century.[67]

Historians also often argue that after 1848 divisions within the working-class were more important than divisions between the classes for shaping the forms of working-class action. For a number of reasons, the labour aristocracy were able to consolidate their position and develop their characteristic institutions, like co-operatives. However, it is important to stress that co-operation was not a new departure and indeed had been, in a variety of forms, an integral strand of Chartist activity since the autumn of 1839. It did not signify a real change of direction that many of the founders of mid-century co-operatives were Chartists, and not noticeably affluent Chartists at that, like the majority of the Rochdale pioneers who were also flannel-weavers recently defeated in a strike. But it opens up the more interesting question for mid-century investigation about whether the Chartist attempt persisted to find forms for collective self-provision which were not exclusive: it is interesting, for example, that the Great Horton Co-operative Society, started by Chartist wool-combers, allowed its members to buy on credit for the first twenty-five years of its life.[68]

The actual practice of democracy in the Chartist Movement calls into question the textbook conclusion that the Chartist demands have all been met, except the one for annual Parliaments (rather important since it was to insure the accountability of Parliament to people). The six points of the Charter, however revolutionary in their time, were not all that the Chartists meant by self-government. In the course of their struggles, their ambitions for self-management began to extend over many areas of social life and the issue of collective control was raised in a comprehensive way. The majority Chartist Movement aimed to include as many working people as possible within its range of activities, knowing full well the difficulty of the task, given the material inequalities and cultural divisions existing within the working class. On the whole, the Chartists did not 'falsely' solve their problems by constricting their ambitions, by restricting their constituency or by relying on finance from outside the working class. Instead they tried continually, and of course managed only partially, to keep the movement accessible and even to encourage a situation where 'brotherly feeling' would begin to dissolve some of the divisions from outside. The very way in which the Chartists tried to govern their movement disclosed a blueprint for collective control which involved much more than periodic voting for Parliament. Aware of the need for an effective national movement but jealous of the right of local members to control their political lives, the Chartists tried to satisfy both of these incompatible requirements in a continual and vigilant way. They turned to federation and accountable delegacy, where our twentieth-century habit has been to sacrifice local control to centralisation. It is interesting to speculate upon how parliamentary democracy might have been different had it been won by the Chartists and erected on a foundation of vigorous local self-activity. As it was, their efforts broke against huge resistances, like poverty and the State, not of their own making. None the less, the Chartists tried to construct a real democratic practice which was relevant to the hard material situation of working people but which still used and enlarged their capacities as political producers who could declare:

we have no rich men leading or driving us but, in
the true democratic spirit, manage our own affairs.[69]

NOTES

1. In 1855 Marx thought the suffrage demand revolutionary in Britain 'The Association for Administrative Reform (People's Charter)', in Marx and Engels, *Articles on Britain* (Moscow, 1975) p. 234. Nearly all the secondary literature focuses on suffrage democracy: however, D. Jones, *Chartism and the Chartists* (1975) explores Chartist organisation and the financial constraints on Chartist action; also Behagg's chapter 2 above.

2. The first historian of Chartism, R. G. Gammage, set the style for stressing rivalries between leaders, *History of the Chartist Movement* (1854; 2nd edn, 1894; reprint 1976); for inefficiency, e.g. K. Judge, 'Early Chartist Organisation and the Convention of 1839', *International Review of Social History*, XX (1975); for insufficient class consciousness, e.g. T. Rothstein, *From Chartism to Labourism* (1929) p. 92; for working-class movements needing to manoeuvre creatively within huge constraints, see S. Yeo, 'Some Problems in Realising a General Working-Class Strategy in Twentieth-century Britain' (unpublished paper read to the BSA 1977, in author's possession).

3. *Northern Star* (*NS*) 17 August 1839, p. 5; for the constitutional strategy, see J. A. Epstein, 'Feargus O'Connor and the English Working-Class Radical Movement, 1832–41' (Univ. of Birmingham, Ph.D. thesis, 1977) and Belchem's chapter 8 above.

4. *NS* 16 May 1840, p. 6; LWMA – *NS* 24 February 1838, p. 4, *Address and Rules of the London Working Men's Association for Benefiting Politically, Socially and Morally the Useful Classes* [1836] p. 6. Usually seen as the archetypal democrat, Lovett's practice was not always above reproach: he manipulated the election of London delegates to the Convention in 1838 (see Bennett's chapter 3 above) and suggested another gerrymander in 1842 to ensure a Sturgeite presence at the second Complete Suffrage Union Conference.

5. Exclusive dealing, i.e. trading only with people sympathetic to your cause, was a standard political tactic of the period and an important way for non-electors to influence voting: N. Gash, *Politics in the Age of Peel* (1953) p. 175; J. Foster, *Class Struggle and the Industrial Revolution* (1974) pp. 52 ff, for Oldham. Tax refusal was practised in the 1832 parliamentary reform agitation and a run on the banks and on gold proposed: I. Prothero, 'William Benbow and the Concept of the "General Strike"', *Past & Present*, no. 63 (1974), which also analyses changing ideas of and plans for a general strike in the early 1830s. In 1838 Thomas Attwood revived the project of a political strike of the productive classes, working and middle, against a corrupt State (during which masters would continue to pay wages!): C. Flick, *The Birmingham Political Union and the Movements for Reform in Britain* (Hamden, Conn.; Folkestone, Kent, 1978) p. 158, p. 82 for earlier tactics.

6. *Northern Liberator* 13 July, 3 August 1839, p. 7; *NS* 20 July 1839, p. 5; 20 October 1838, p. 4 for use of popular texts, Luke.XXII.36 and Lamentations. IV.9, on banners to assert the biblical right to arm: for the constitutional right, see Epstein, 'O'Connor', p. 216.

7. *NS* 14 September 1839, p. 4; 3 August 1839, p. 4 for worry about a partial strike.

8. Ibid., 5 October 1839, p. 1.

9. Ibid., 3 April 1841, p.7; for religion see my 'Christianity and Chartist Struggle 1838–42', *Past & Present*, no. 91 (1981).

10. Especially D. Thompson, 'Women and Nineteenth-century Radical Politics: a Lost Dimension', in J. Mitchell and A. Oakley (eds), *The Rights and Wrongs of Women* (Harmondsworth, 1976); B. Taylor, 'The Feminist Theory and Practice of the Owenite Socialist Movement in Britain 1820–1845' (Univ. of Sussex Ph.D. thesis, 1981).

11. *NS* 9 February 1839, p. 6; 2 February 1839, p. 3 for Ashton women and

3 August 1839, p. 6 for Bristol. D. Thompson, 'Women', pp. 125–7 for participation in family and community roles.

12. *NS* 14 August 1841, p. 4; p. 1 for Leeds.

13. D. Thompson, 'Women', pp. 115 ff. for earlier traditions of female organisation; for segregated women's groups continuing into the NCA period: *NS* 14 November 1840, p. 1 for Oldham female classes, 1841–2 *passim* for local women's groups in the petitioning effort, 8 July 1843, p. 7 for all-female slate of candidates from Nottingham. The role of women in the land plan needs work to track developments after 1843.

14. *NS* 2 February 1839, p. 3; 3 April 1841, p. 8.

15. Ibid., 2 September 1843, p. 4.

16. *Northern Liberator*, 21 September 1839, p. 5; *NS* 1 February 1840; see *NS* 17 October, p. 1, 21 November 1840, p. 1 for the Bradford co-op halving the price of shares as 'an inducement to the working classes to join their ranks'; also Epstein's chapter 7 above for Chartist charges.

17. For the tendency of working-class movements and popular culture more generally to provide a packed experience at low cost, see E. and S. Yeo (eds), *Popular Culture and Class Conflict 1590–1914* (Brighton, 1981) ch. 10; in ch. 6 I explore the multipurpose nature of the soirée more fully.

18. R. F. Wearmouth, *Methodism and the Working-Class Movements of England 1800–1850* (1937) pp. 144 ff. for Chartist classes; for Wesleyan and Primitive-Methodist classes, R. Currie, *Methodism Divided* (1968), pt I and Revd H. B. Kendall, *The Origin and History of the Primitive Methodist Church*, 2 vols (n.d.) I, p. 31.

19. *NS* 17 August 1839, p. 6. Class meetings could develop into insurrectionary cells, as in Sheffield: see depositions reprinted in D. Thompson (ed.), *The Early Chartists* (1971) pp. 264 ff.

20. *NS* 25 July 1840, p. 1, also for Leach's feeling that classes were more suited to rural areas than to Manchester.

21. Ibid., 22 August 1840, p. 1. For previous use of classes, S. Bamford, *Early Days* (1849, reprint 1967) p. 43; J. F. C. Harrison, *Learning and Living 1790–1960* (1961) pp. 49–51; E. P. Thompson, *The Making of the English Working Class* (1963) pp. 152–5; W. Lovett, *Life and Struggles* (1876) p. 68; *New Moral World*, 14 April 1838, p. 195, for details of socialist practice.

22. *NS* 15 August 1846, p. 5; 17 October 1840, p. 1 for Norwich using a chapel on weekdays and a pub on Saturday; 3 April 1841, p. 7 for O'Connor's critique and p. 4 for Revd Hill's defence of cultural activity within the NCA.

23. For friendly societies and trade unions, P. H. J. H. Gosden, *The Friendly Societies in England 1815–75* (Manchester, 1961) pp. 7, 18; S. and B. Webb, *Industrial Democracy* (1902) pt I, ch. I and *English Local Government from the Revolution to the Municipal Corporations Act: The Parish and the County* (1924), for the vestry system.

24. There were exceptions: Dumfries and Maxwellton WMA was governed by weekly general meeting and had a secretary and treasurer elected quarterly; Jones, *Chartism and the Chartists*, p. 77; before the NCA was formed, Leeds insisted that one-half of the committee be re-elected each month: *NS* 2 May 1840, p. 8.

25. Ibid., 30 April 1842, p. 2: 'Members and Contributions of the Chartist Association of Great Horton, 1842–1866', Bradford Central Library Archives,

D.B. 4, case 1, no. 1. For threats of dismissal for bringing *NS* to work: *NS* 3 March 1838, p. 4, 6 July 1839, p. 7.

26. T. Kemnitz, 'Chartism in Brighton' (Univ. of Sussex Ph.D. thesis, 1969) p. 123; *NS* 10 October 1840, p. 6.

27. Ibid., 14 August 1841, p. 1 for Leeds; 2, 16 April 1842, pp. 7, 2 for Carlisle, 8 August 1840, p. 6, 5 September 1846, p. 8 for Bradford.

28. Ibid., 4 February 1843, p. 1; 8 July 1843, p. 4 for Hill's agreement.

29. Ibid., 2 May 1840, p. 6.

30. A. J. Peacock, *Bradford Chartism 1838–1840* (York, 1969) p. 21: Judge, 'Early Chartist Organisation', pp. 377, 381 overlooks the demand for local control in his critique of the Convention's missionary work, an omission not made by a *NS* editorial, 19 December 1840, p. 5.

31. Ibid., 2 April 1842, p. 8; A. J. Peacock, 'Chartism in York' (typescript in his possession).

32. *NS* 28 August 1841, p. 1; London: *NS* 21 August 1841, p. 4, 14 September 1844, p. 1; South Lancs: *NS* 30 May 1840, p. 4, 17, 24 July 1841, pp. 6, 3; a Lecturers' plan is reproduced in Jones, *Chartism and the Chartists*, p. 105.

33. 1840 and 1841 Plans under 'Remuneration of Officers' and 'Compensation', see *NS* 1 August 1840, p. 1, 27 February 1841, p. 1.

34. For criticism of the Executive, see ibid., 19, 26 November 1842, pp. 4, 5: 9 September 1843, p. 1 for discussion of an Annual Convention. Webbs, *Industrial Democracy*, p. 37, on a legislature as an adequate check.

35. *NS* 17 May 1845, p. 4; 18 December 1841, p. 1 for Worcester special levy; by contrast, Belper suspended its missionary to make payments to the E.C., ibid., 8 January 1842, p. 1; 27 November 1841, p. 1 for the number of local groups. Competing financial claims at this time included expenses for Convention delegates and local prisoners' aid, also necessitating special levies, e.g. ibid., 2 October, 6 November 1841, pp. 1, 5 for Sheffield and Stafford.

36. Ibid., 18 July 1840, p. 6; Hull and Newcastle 'Proposals for a national movement built around a national press', 23 May, p. 8, 6 June 1840, p. 2; Burnley and Bilston on using newspaper sales to finance local activity, *NS* 3 October 1846, p. 8; 1 January 1842, p. 2.

37. Epstein, 'O'Connor', pp. 414–6, 320–1 and *passim*; also his 'Feargus O'Connor and the *Northern Star*', *International Review of Social History*, XXI (1976) and John Belchem, 'Radicalism as a "Platform" Agitation in the Periods 1816–21 and 1848–51: with special reference to the Leadership of Henry Hunt and Feargus O'Connor' (Univ. of Sussex, Ph.D. thesis, 1974). For O'Connor on a Convention, see *NS* 23 November 1839, p. 3 and on standing for the NCA Executive, ibid., 16 September 1843, p. 6. For his defence of the Executive, ibid., 4 February 1843, p. 1 and p. 5 for Hill's reply. For his sacking of Hill in sadness more than anger see ibid., 12 August 1843, p. 4.

38. For criticism and expression of confidence, ibid., 27 December 1845, p. 1.

39. Historians like Judge, 'Early Chartist Organisation', p. 396 and L. Radzinowicz, 'New Departures in Maintaining Public Order in the Face of Chartist Disturbances', *Cambridge Law Journal* (1960), note the change and tend to argue that Chartist fear of the authorities was misplaced; they also underestimate such concern as a factor shaping Chartist organisation.

40. *NS* 6 March 1841, p. 4. For numbers of Chartist victims, see *A Return from each Gaol . . . in the United Kingdom . . . of every Person Confined for Charges of . . . Seditious or Blasphemous Libel, or for Uttering Seditious Words, or for Attending any Seditious Meetings, or for Conspiring to Cause such Meetings to be Held, or for any Offence of a Political Nature, 1 January 1839 to 1 June 1840,* (PP) Parliamentary Papers 1840, XXXVIII, pp. 691–750. Other charges included riot and high treason.

41. *NS* 18 July 1840, p. 4.

42. See my 'Robert Owen and Radical Culture' in S. Pollard and J. Salt (eds), *Robert Owen Prophet of the Poor* (London, 1971) p. 102, n. 60 for socialists registering their halls as places of worship also to avoid the interruption of Sunday meetings under still operative provisions of the Six Acts. Hill urged Chartists to go and do likewise: *NS* 6 March 1841, 26 August 1843, p. 4. Gosden, *Friendly Societies*, pp. 181, 187–8 for the legal situation of friendly societies.

43. Flick, *Birmingham Political Union*, pp. 29, 38, 42–6; N. McCord, *The Anti-Corn Law League, 1838–1846* (1958) ch. VII: the League had a large paid secretariat in Manchester as well as district offices with paid staff: see pp. 43, 103–6 for stage-managed conferences.

44. Legality: Epstein, 'O'Connor', pp. 272, 366 n. 46; throughout the life of the movement the same adamant advice was given about delegate elections, 'ALL DELEGATES MUST BE ELECTED AT PUBLIC MEETINGS, CALLED BY PLACARD FOR THE PURPOSE . . . . Delegates from private bodies, clubs or societies, of a political character, are illegal. Every man must be delegated from a public meeting of the inhabitants of the town or place from whence he is sent.' *NS* 20 March 1841, p. 4; 20 April 1844, p. 6.

45. *Bolton Free Press*, 20 April 1839, p. 3; see Prothero, 'William Benbow' for earlier conceptions of a Convention, also T. M. Parssinen, 'Association, Convention, Anti-Parliament in British Radical Politics, 1771–1848, *English Historical Review*, LXXXVIII (1973).

46. *NS* 3 August 1839; Epstein, 'O'Connor', ch. IV for the development of the Convention.

47. Ibid., pp. 315 ff and Judge, 'Early Chartist Organisation', pp. 371, 392 ff. among others.

48. In an editorial, *NS* 18 July 1840, p. 4, Hill argued that a delegate convention could legally meet to draw up a constitution and bring a society into being until 'the moment the society is formed'. This may be one reason why trade unions resisted national delegate assemblies except for very restricted purposes like altering their constitutions: Webbs, *Industrial Democracy*, p. 18 ff.

49. *NS* 25 July 1840, pp. 1, 5, for deliberations, 1 August, p. 1, for the agreed plan.

50. Ibid., 24 August, p. 2, 31 August 1839, p. 3; 18 April 1840, p. 8.

51. W. Farish, *The Autobiography of William Farish. The Struggles of a Hand-Loom Weaver* [Carlisle, 1889] p. 35; in Tulliehouse (Carlisle) Public Library; for municipal politicking, *NS* 19 September 1840, p. 1; J. F. C. Harrison, 'Chartism in Leeds', in A. Briggs (ed.), *Chartist Studies* (1959), pp. 86–91.

52. *NS* 27 February 1841, p. 1 for discussions. Lovett's own proposed National Association of the United Kingdom for the Political and Social Improve-

ment of the People, had national officers, a large General Board (really an annual delegate Convention meeting for a fortnight), and local councils only in the form of elected committees of management of the district halls which were a central feature of the plan. W. Lovett and J. Collins, *Chartism a New Organization of the People* (1840; reprint Leicester, 1969) pp. 27 ff.

53. *NS* 13 March 1841, p. 4.

54. Ibid., 9 September 1843, p. 1 for delegate conference, 16 September, p. 6 for proposed Rules, 15 July, pp. 7–8 for an epitome of the movement's prolonged discussion in the form of letters from around the country. For Cooper's plan proposing an Annual Convention and a peripatetic Executive, Gammage, *History of the Chartist Movement* (1894 edn) p. 244.

55. I. Prothero, 'London Chartism and the Trades', *Economic History Review*, 2nd ser., XXIV (1971) 215 ff. explores this issue showing how land schemes were not mere backward-looking nostalgia but served very real material needs of trade unionists; also his 'Chartism in London', *Past & Present*, no. 44 (1969) 98 ff. For developments outside London, see *NS* 8 July 1843, p. 5, for the Bradford Woolcomber's Joint Stock Land Company and J. West, *History of the Chartist Movement* (1920) pp. 200 ff. The National Association of United Trades (1845 ff.) and its sister-organisation which was committed to promoting collective self-employment and co-operative production were really Chartist bodies.

56. *NS* 14 October 1843, p. 4.

57. Ibid., 4 November 1843, p. 5 for the opinion of Bodkin the legal adviser: in ibid., and in 7 October 1843, pp. 1, 5, the Executive announced it would not establish branches and cautioned that 'locality must be substituted for the word branch': it insisted that all Councillors could be only nominated by a locality but must be appointed by the Executive. *NS* 27 April 1844 for the revised constitution.

58. In established Chartist localities, an NCA often had a sister land company group meeting on the same premises, although some land companies existed on their own: e.g. in January 1848 six South London NCAs had related land companies but in Bermondsey there was an independent land society: C. Wickenden, 'The Chartist Movement in South London and the Agitation of 1848' (Univ. of Sussex Chartism Special Subject Dissertation, 1979) p. 8; Prothero, 'Chartism in London', p. 98.

59. *NS* 13 December 1845, pp. 1, 8: 20 December p. 1, for the scheme.

60. *Select Committee on the National Land Company*, PP (Reports from Committees) 1847–8, XIX, evid. of Tidd Pratt, 3286–9. I have reconstructed the ensuing chronological account mainly from evidence to this enquiry and from *NS* coverage; J. MacAskill, 'The Chartist Land Plan', in Briggs, *Chartist Studies*, pp. 309–13, for a useful account which underplays the financial constraint.

61. *S.C. . . . Land Company*, evid. of E. Lawes, 2849, 2870; evid. of G. W. Chinery, solicitor acting for the Chartists over registration and managing clerk to W. P. Roberts, 208.

62. Ibid., evid. of Chinery, 155; *NS* 3 October 1846, p. 8.

63. Ibid., 167–81, 247, 252, 270–9: evid. of Richard Whitmarsh, 113.

64. Ibid., evid. of Lawes, 2876–80, 3020; Pratt, 3241–52, 3334–8.

65. Ibid., 'Sixth Report'.

66. Gammage, *History of the Chartist Movement*, pp. 371–2 for the resolutions.

67. Arguably the Chartist Land Company, as the first mass-shareholding company, actually took the risks for the Limited Liability Act from which capitalists then benefited. The Christian socialist influence in starting the move towards Ltd has been highlighted by J. Saville, 'Sleeping Partnership and Limited Liability, 1850–6', *Economic History Review*, 2nd ser., VIII (1955).

68. West, *History of the Chartist Movement*, pp. 200–1: H. Hodgson, *Fifty Years of Co-operation in Great Horton and District* (Manchester, 1909) p. 101. For a firm statement about co-operatives as the organisations of the labour aristocracy, see Foster, *Class Struggle*, pp. 220–2.

69. *NS* 22 December 1838, p. 8.

Notes on Contributors

GARETH STEDMAN JONES is Fellow of Kings College, Cambridge.

CLIVE BEHAGG is Lecturer in History at the West Sussex Institute of Higher Education.

JENNIFER BENNETT is a school teacher.

DOROTHY THOMPSON is Lecturer in Modern History at the University of Birmingham.

ROBERT SYKES is a teacher of history and sociology at Mellow Lane School, Hillingdon.

ROBERT FYSON is Senior Lecturer in History at North Staffordshire Polytechnic.

JAMES EPSTEIN is visiting assistant Professor of British History at Duke University, North Carolina, USA.

JOHN BELCHEM is Lecturer in Modern History at the University of Liverpool.

KATE TILLER is Tutor in Local Studies at the University of Oxford.

EILEEN YEO is Lecturer in History at the University of Sussex.

Index